# Henrico County Virginia Deeds

## 1750-1774

*Virginia Lee Hutcheson Davis
and Gary Murdock Williams*

HERITAGE BOOKS
2007

# HERITAGE BOOKS
*AN IMPRINT OF HERITAGE BOOKS, INC.*

### Books, CDs, and more—Worldwide

For our listing of thousands of titles see our website at
www.HeritageBooks.com

Published 2007 by
HERITAGE BOOKS, INC.
Publishing Division
65 East Main Street
Westminster, Maryland 21157-5026

Copyright © 1997 Virginia Lee Hutcheson Davis
and Gary Murdock Williams

All rights reserved. No part of this book may be reproduced or transmitted in any form or by any means, electronic or mechanical, including photocopying, recording or by any information storage and retrieval system without written permission from the author, except for the inclusion of brief quotations in a review.

International Standard Book Number: 978-0-7884-4378-X

# HENRICO COUNTY DEEDS, 1750-1774

Abstracted by Gary Murdock Williams
Edited by Virginia Lee Hutcheson Davis

Dr. Benjamin B. Weisiger, III (1924-1995) made an enduring contribution to the study of colonial Henrico County records with his meticulous abstracts and indices of county wills, 1677-1781, and deeds, 1677-1750. To help fill the void in the colonial land records of Henrico County, this compiler now undertakes to provide abstracts of such additional records by providing extracts of the deeds recorded in Henrico County Wills & Deeds, 1750-1767 and Henrico County Deed Book, 1767-1774. It is hoped that this work will be a suitable tribute and memorial to Dr. Weisiger. If these abstracts enhance our knowledge of those early citizens of Henrico County and the land they knew, this undertaking will have accomplished its purpose.

Editor's note: Names have been transcribed as written in the original documents. In some instances the spelling varies within a single document, in others it is known that the spelling is not the modern accepted spelling. No attempt has been made to note the variances, or correct the obvious deviations from current spellings. It is with a great appreciation that I have been able to publish the work of Gary Williams. Mr. Williams is an historian and a meticulous researcher, he lives at "Chester", 10447 Newville Road, Waverly, VA 23890.

It is also with a great deal of admiration for his dedication in his meticulous abstraction all 1577 pages of these two Henrico County Deed Books. His work spans the issues of *Tidewater Virginia Families: A Magazine of History and Genealogy,* from the November issue of 1999 (Volume 8, Number 3, beginning on page 159) through the November issue of 2003 (see end of abstractions for reference for appearance in each issue of the publication). The information contained in these deeds is now available to thousands of researchers, providing not only the dates and locations of land ownership, but the relationships and associations of the residents of the County of Henrico for a period of twenty-five years. It is a major contribution to the preservation of our Virginia heritage, in a county which provided the early home of many of our ancestors. We are indeed indebted to Gary Williams for this contribution, and we offer him our deep gratitude.

Virginia Lee Hutcheson Davis, Editor/Publisher *Tidewater Virginia Families*

Copyright © 2006 TIDEWATER VIRGINIA FAMILIES
Virginia Lee Hutcheson Davis

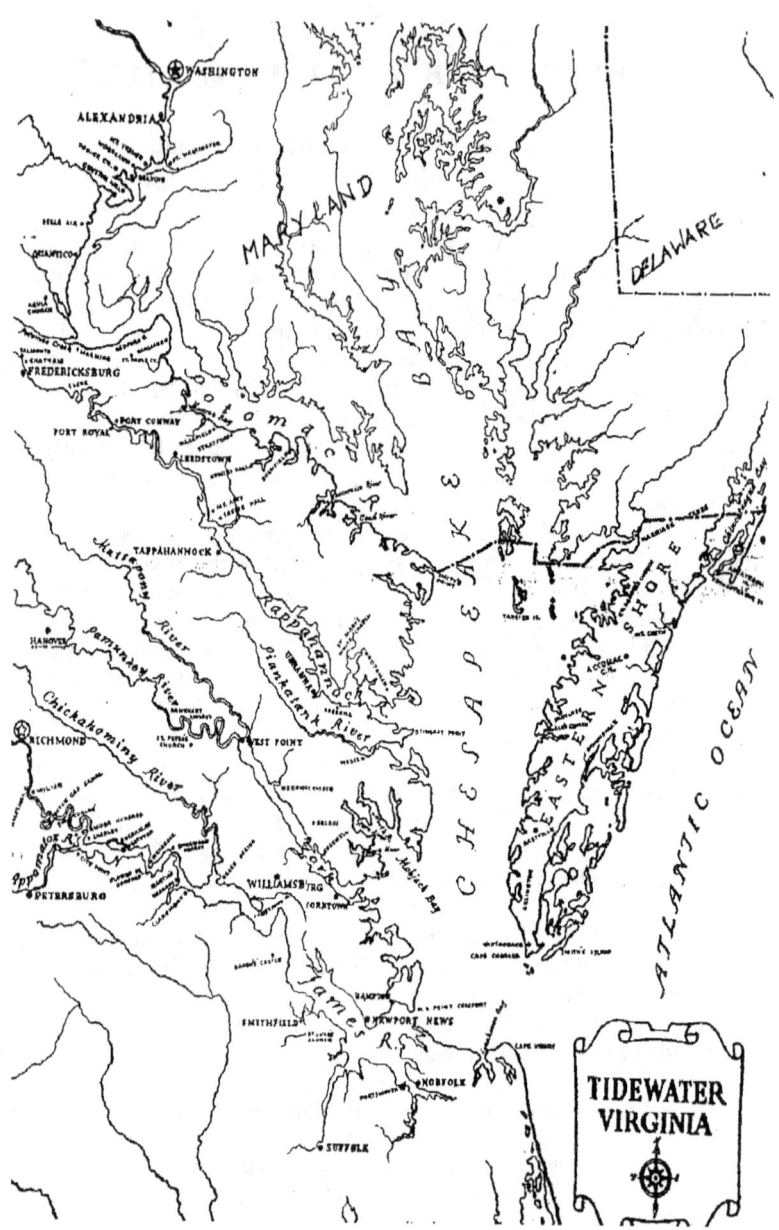

# HENRICO COUNTY DEED BOOK, 1750-1767

p.1  25 March 1750 Stephen Pankey to Joseph Parsons, both of Henrico County, for 90 pounds, 125 acres on the south side of Chickahominy Swamp, bounded by Matthew Hobson (formerly Edmund Patrick), John Owen, Thomas Owen and by Turner's Run, being the same land Pankey purchased of Peter Patrick.
Wit: Charles Woodson, Matthew Woodson, Joseph Parsons, Junr., Matthew (his X mark) Hobson
Signed: Stephen (his mark) Pankey
Recorded 1st Mon. April 1750 ** [see Note at end of text]


p.5  13 November 1749 John Robertson, schoolmaster, & Amey Robertson, his wife, of Henrico County, to Thomas Cocks, for 10 pounds, 50 acres, being all of that tract formerly granted by William Spraggins unto his daughter Amey, "the then wife of the sd. John Robertson," by deed of 20 April 1740.
Wit: James Cocks, Daniel Price, Junr., William Price
Signed: John Robertson, Amey (her + mark) Robertson
Recorded 1st Mon. April 1750


p.6  31 March 1750 Elizabeth Matthews to son, Anthony Matthews, and to the heirs of his body lawfully begotten "after my decease," for love, goodwill and affection, four Negroes: Fanny, Judy, Sarah & Tom, "together with all the rest of my estate whether real or personal." Three Negroes only excepted: Dirk, Sue & Will, "which I reserve for to be at my disposal."
Wit: Julius Allen, William Garthright, Joseph (his + mark) Childers
Signed: Elizabeth (her + mark) Matthews
Recorded 1st Mon. April 1750


p.7  7 November 1749 John Leeson of Henrico County to William Ross of Prince George County, for 50 pounds, 150 acres on Gilley's Creek and on the Southern Branch, bounded by Isaac Breeding, Joseph Lewis, Micael Jones & William Spraggins, "it being all of that tract the said Leeson now lives on."
Wit: Joseph Lewis, Richard Williamson, Alexander Robson
Signed: John Leeson                    Recorded 1st Mon. April 1750


p.10  4 June 1750 Daniel Fitchpatrick to Joseph Mitchell, both of Henrico County, for 40 pounds to James Crafford, 196 acres on the south side of the Northern Run and on the Rocky Branch, beginning at a branch on Patman's line, thence to Col. John Brown's line, thence to Watson's line, thence to Cattail Branch and down branch, thence along line between Grinstead and said Mitchell to a branch began

at Patman's line.  No witnesses
Signed: Daniel Fitchpatrick
Recorded 1st Mon. in June 1750


p.11  4 June 1750 Daniel Fitchpatrick to John Grinstead, both of Henrico County, for 20 pounds, 197 acres on the southside of the Northern Branch, beginning at a branch concluded as a dividing line between Mitchell and Grinstead and where William Patman's line crosses said branch, thence down Patman's line, John Williamson's line, Watson's line to a branch.  No witnesses
Signed: Daniel Fitchpatrick
Recorded 1st Mon. in June 1750


p.12  3 March 1749 Power of Attorney from Thomas Yuille of Darleith; John Murdock & James Donald, merchants in Glasgow; Robert Donald, merchant in Greenock; & Andrew Giles, shipmaster therefor; and for George Murdock, merchant of Glasgow; to Thomas Yuille, Jr., Charles Turnbull, Alexander Makie & James Donald, merchants in Virginia, "to appear before all and any Court or Courts in Virginia...to represent before the General Court at the instance of David Bell, merchant of Virginia, and several other patrons against us," etc.
Acknowledged before Robert Christie, magistrate of Glasgow, and witnessed by William Miller and John Hyndman.
Signed; Thomas Yuille, John Murdock, James Donald, Robert Donald and Andrew Giles; on motion of John Wayles ordered to be recorded.
Recorded 1st Mon. in June 1750 at a Court held at Varina


p.14  4 June 1750 John Williamson to Thomas Conway, both of Henrico County, for 27 pounds, 10 shillings, 25 acres on the north side of the brook adjoining said Conway.
Wit: Nathaniel Bacon, Julius Allen, William Patman
Signed: John Williamson                    Recorded 1st Mon. in June 1750


p.15  26 May 1750 Thomas Finton to George Chambers, both of Henrico County, for 15 pounds, 97 acres whereon the said Thomas Finton now lives, adjoining the said George Chambers' own land whereon he now lives (metes & bounds description).
Wit: William Street, William Lawless, Anthony Street
Signed: Thomas Finton
Recorded 1st Mon. in June 1750


p.16  17 November 1749 Power of Attorney from John Martin, "late of Virginia but now in Dublin", to Col. Lewis Burwell, John Martin, Esq. & Samuel Martin, to

collect debts & in his name to prosecute for the same.
Wit: John Holliday, William Bragg
Signed: John Martin                             Recorded 1st Mon. in June 1750

p.16 undated account against the county filed by William Kennon, Jr.
Dr. for tobacco sold Col. Randolph, Julius Allen, John Cobbs and Even Owen, for insolvents amounting to 1515 pounds of tobacco — 111 pounds 19 shillings 6 pence.
Cr. for collection 1500 pounds of tobacco I was to collect by order of the court for the county — 112 pounds 17 shillings 3 pence.
Recorded 1st Mon. in June 1750

p.18  13 February 1749 Power of Attorney from Patrick Bogle for himself and his father, John Bogle; Richard Oswald for himself and his brother, Alexander Oswald; & Matthew Bogle and Alexander Morson factor for the heirs & executors of Mr. John Bard, deceased; all merchants of the City of Glasgow, North Britian, to William Sellor, merchant of Glasgow, & Andrew Spraile, merchant of Norfolk in the Colony of Virginia in America, both or either of them to recover from Duncan Graham, Thomas Atkinson & Robert Scott, all merchants of Virginia, formerly factors for the said John, Patrick and Matthew Bogle; Richard & Alexander Oswald; & the heirs of the deceased John Bard, to collect debts in Virginia and Maryland.
Signed: Patrick Bogle, Richard Oswald, Matthew Bogle, Alexander Morson
Recorded 1st Mon. in June 1750

p.19  19 December 1749 Power of Attorney from John Mills, Esq., of Twyford in the County of Southampton & Matthew Mills, Esq., of Soho Square in the County of Middlesex to Beverley Randolph & Walter Charles of Virginia, as joint attorneys and then to the survivor, to enter into lands in Hanover County and elsewhere in Virginia to receive rents, issues and profits & to occupy the same for best advantage for said constituents & to appoint servants and overseers & to recruit the necessary slaves, cattle and implements, etc.
Wit: Robert Robinson, Andrew Watkins, Thomas Dixon
Signed: John Mills, Matthew Mills                Recorded 1st Mon. in June 1750

p.21  7 May 1750 Joseph Childres to Julius Allen, both of Henrico County, for 23 pounds, 40 acres on the south side of the Chickahominy River, beginning at a corner white oak at the head of Robin's Spring Branch, thence to Bull's Branch, thence to the foot of Deep Bottom, thence to dividing line between said Allen and Childres; being land said Childres purchased of Robert Childres, son of Robert Childres, deceased.

Wit: Charles Woodson, Samuel (his S mark) Gaithright, William Farris, Miles Garthright
Signed: Joseph (his I mark) Childres    Recorded 1st Mon. in July 1750

p.22 7 May 1750 Miles Gathright to Julius Allen, both of Henrico County, for 3 pounds, one acre and a half on the south side of the Chickahominy River and on the east side of Bool's (Bowles's) Branch, joining the said branch against the parcel of land Allen purchased of Joseph Childress.
Wit: Charles Woodson, Samuel (his S mark) Garthright, William Farris, Joseph (his I mark) Childress
Signed: Miles Garthright    Recorded 1st Mon. in July 1750

p.22 15 January 1749 Power of Attorney from Gabriel Griffith, of White Haven, County of Cumberland, merchant, to David Meade of Virginia, merchant, to recover from legal representatives of William Copeland, merchant, late of Virginia, deceased, and from Richard Cocke & Benjamin Cocke of Virginia, executors of James Johnson, merchant, late of James River in Virginia, deceased, all sums and money due to me for goods sold & delivered to said Copeland and Johnson in their lifetimes.
Wit: John Knaile, William Bunn
Signed: Gab Griffith    Recorded 1st Mon. in July 1750

p.24 1 October 1750 Samuel Pincham of Amelia County to Alexander Padason of Henrico County, for 20 pounds, 100 acres on Deep Run, adj. Sincock, Thomas Baughn, Thomas Alley & Cottrell's Deep Run; being the same piece of land said Pincham bought of Thomas Cottrell.
Wit: Robert Gordin, Godfry Piles
Signed: Saml. (his P mark) Pincham
Jane, wife of Samuel Pincham, relinquished her right of dower
Recorded 1st Mon. in October 1750

p.25 29 September 1750 George Dabney of King William County & William Dabney of Hanover County to Darcey Southall of Amelia County, for 151 pounds, 417 acres where James Young formerly lived, transferred to William Mouat, mariner, by indenture dated 24 June 1746, and transferred by Alexander McKenzey & Charles Stuart, merchants, attorneys for William Mouat, to the said Dabneys, by indenture dated 25 April 1749.
Wit: John White, Samuel Clarke, Robert Templeton, Barrett White
Signed: George Dabney, William Dabney
Recorded 1st Mon. in October 1750
Subsequently recorded 4 October 1756: Upon commission directed to John Henry

and James Littlepage, Anne Dabney, wife of George Dabney, and Anne Dabney, wife of William Dabney, were examined for the relinquishment of their dower, both being "too sickly to travel to the Court."

p.26  1 July 1750 William Allen, taylor & Elizabeth Allen, his wife, to James Conway, all of Henrico County, for 12 pounds, 50 acres, being the same tract said James Conway sold to James Young.
Wit: Christopher John Thomas, Richard Cottrell, Ann (her  M  mark) Buxton
Signed: William Allen, Elizabeth Allen
Recorded 1st Mon. in October 1750

p.28  31 July 1750 James Conaway & Ann Conaway, his wife, of Henrico County, to William Buxton, of Westover Parish, Charles City County, for 23 pounds, 100 acres on both sides of the Eastern Branch, being the tract of land John Walters gave James Conaway & Ann Conaway, his wife, by a deed of gift.
Wit: Christopher John Thomas, Richard Cottrell, Ann (her  X  mark) Buxton
Signed: James (his  C  mark) Conaway, Ann (her X mark) Conaway
Recorded 1st Mon. in October 1750

p.31  3 April 1750 Articles of Agreement between Jane Randolph, widow to Richard Randolph, Gentleman, her son, in which she agrees to convey in lawful writing to the said Richard Randolph, when required to do so, all of her right, title & interest in land and plantation known as Curles, except the dwelling house, kitchens, dairies, meat house & smoke house & slaves: Betty, Cate, Joan, Phillis, Jenney, Sukey, Nelly, Rhodah, Hannibal, Boumshire, Jamy & George, devised to her by the will of her husband, Richard Randolph, late of Curles, which she reserves to her own use, but that Boumshire, the tailor, shall make all the clothes for all the Negroes belonging to the said Richard Randolph.
Wit: Richard Bland, Robert Pleasants, John Lancaster
Signed: Jane Randolph, Richard Randolph
Recorded 1st Mon. in October 1750

p.32  5 November 1750 John Smith of Henrico County to Pierce Griffing of St. Anne's Parish, Essex County, for 25 pounds, 200 acres on the Long and Hungry Branch of the Chickahominy Swamp, adj. John Staples, Capt. John Watson and William Turner; being part of a greater tract granted by patent to Obadiah Smith, father of the said John Smith & said 200 acres whereon said Obadiah Smith formerly had a quarter (metes & bounds description).          No witnesses
Signed: John Smith
Mary, wife of John Smith, relinquished her dower
Recorded 1st Mon. in November 1750

p.33  5 November 1750 John Smith to Theophil Favour, both of Henrico County, for 50 pounds, 200 acres on the Long and Hungry Branch of the Chickahominy Swamp, adj. John Staples, Pleasants, Capt. John Ellis & Robert Childers; being part of a greater tract patented by Obidiah Smith, father of the said John Smith, and on which 200 acres the said Obidiah Smith formerly had a quarter (metes & bounds description).
No witnesses                                            Signed: John Smith
Mary, wife of John Smith, relinquished her dower
Recorded 1st Mon. in November 1750

p.34  30 August 1750 John Whealer of Henrico County to David Jennings, "for many kindnesses and services done unto me by David Jennings & George Jennings", 50 acres at the upper end of the tract whereon I now live, adj. Robert Morris (metes & bounds description).
Wit: Pierce Griffing, Theophil Favour, John (his B mark) Blackbrurn
Signed: John (his W mark) Whealor     Recorded 1st Mon. in November 1750

p.35  5 November 1750 Deed of gift from John Smith to Drury Wood, both of Henrico County, for natural love and affection, 30 acres adj. said John Smith and Joseph Pleasants.
Wit: Nathaniel Vandewall, William Leavons, Ann (her AF mark) Feild
Signed: John Smith
Mary, wife of John Smith, relinquished her dower
Recorded 1st Mon. in November 1750

p.36  1 October 1750 George Chambers, shewmaker, to William Harding, both of Henrico County, for 70 pounds, 200 acres on Harding's Branch, being a branch of Tokahe (Tuckahoe) Creek, adj. said Harding, Chambers, William Street, Thomas Finton & Peter's Branch; being "that parcel I now live on".
Wit: Christopher John Thomas, Rena Laforce, William Lawless, James Hughs
Signed: George Chambers            Recorded 1st Mon. in November 1750
Elizabeth, wife of George Chambers, relinquished her dower at Henrico County Court on 1st Mon. in September 1753.

p.37  1 October 1750 George Chambers, shewmaker, to William Lawless, both of Henrico County, for 30 pounds, 100 acres, being part of land that William Street now lives on, beginning at the mouth of a little branch that runs between George Chambers and where William Street now lives, then up branch to the head and thence a straight course to Peter's Branch, thence to Harding's Branch, thence to beginning.
Wit: Christopher John Thomas, Rene Laforce, James Hughs, William Harding

Signed: George Chambers
Recorded 1st Mon. in November 1750
Elizabeth, wife of George Chambers, relinquished her dower at Henrico County Court 1st Mon. in September 1753.

p.38  29 October 1750 Jacob Robertson of Henrico County to Agge Willis, for 35 pounds, 100 acres on the branches of Deep Run, part of land granted by patent to Jacob Robertson & that part whereon he now lives; adj. Old House Branch, John Lancaster & John Williamson.
Wit: John Williamson, Jr., Charles Ballow, Daniel Porce, Jr.
Signed: Jacob (his I mark) Robertson
Recorded 1st Mon. in November 1750

p. 41  20 November 1750 Deed of gift from Thomas Jennett/Genett, of Henrico County, for love, good will and affection to my children, to son-in-law, Story Hall, & daughter, Elizabeth Hall, 50 acres, being all that tract whereon I now live; to son, Robert Genett, one feather bed & furniture; and to son, Thomas Genett, one feather bed & furniture and one bay horse; all conveyances "after my decease".
Wit: John Ellis, William Street, William (his W mark) Willis
Signed: Thomas (his X mark) Genett
Recorded 1st Mon. in December 1750

p.43  6 April 1750 Marriage contract among John Pleasants of Henrico County, of the first part; Mary Woodson of Chesterfield County, of the second part; and Henry Turrill & David Turrill of Caroline County, Wyke Hunnicutt of Prince George County and John Pleasants, son of Thomas Pleasants, all of the third part, in consideration of a marriage between the first two parties, " by the permission of Almighty God", 200 acres and dwelling house at the mouth of Four Mile Creek in Henrico County, being part of a larger tract said John Pleasants purchased of Robert Blaws, 100 acres of which was purchased by said Blaws' father of one James Batte, 50 acres purchased by said Robert Blaws of one Robert Sharp, and 50 acres, the residue, purchased of said Robert Blaws of James Cocke; 600 acres in Cumberland County purchased by said John Pleasants of David Lyles; this property to belong to the said John Pleasants for life and then at his decease to Mary, his intended wife, under specific circumstances herein set forth.
Wit: Tarleton Woodson, Charles Woodson, Thomas Chedle, Jacob Woodson, Tarleton Pleasants, Susanna Pleasants, Rodorick (his X mark) Evans
Signed: John Pleasants, Mary Woodson, Henry Turrell, Wyke Hunnicutt, John Pleasants, Jr.
Recorded 1st Mon. in December 1750

p.44  4 February 1750 James Woodfin to Thomas Robinson, Jr., both of Henrico County, for 45 pounds, 245 acres on branches of Four Mile Creek, being all of the said Woodfin's land that lies on north or upper side of the Eastern Run of Four Mile Creek; beginning at the mouth of the Clay Branch on said Eastern Run, thence up the Eastern Run to the mouth of the Great Branch, etc.
Wit: Charles Woodson, James Hatcher, Joseph Woodson
Signed: James Woodfin                    Recorded 1st Mon. in February 1750/51

p.45  4 February 1750 Richard East to Philip Mayo, both of Henrico County, for 10 pounds, 30 acres between the lands of Edward Prior, Thomas Conaway, Robert Williams and the Deep Run.
No witnesses                             Signed: Richard East
Elizabeth, wife of Richard East, relinquished her dower
Recorded 1st Mon. in February 1750/51 at a court held at Varina

p.46  4 February 1750 John Williamson to John White, both of Henrico County, for 6 pounds, being all of his right & title to 100 acres which he had in possession by the last will and testament of James Gowing, deceased, "who bargained with James Young for the same in a Publick manner for the payment of sundry debts, which said Young transferred to said John White."
 No Witnesses                            Signed: John Williamson
Recorded 1st Mon. in February 1750/51

p.47  27 November 1750 William Spraggins of Lunenburg County to David Binns of Henrico County, for 40 pounds, 273 acres, beginning at a corner pine of William Cockes & Stephen Woods; adj. Michel Jones, Gillee's Creek, John Robinson & Capt. Cocke.
Wit: William Spragen, Ann Baze, Glora Spragen, John Leeson
Signed; William Spragen                  Recorded 1st Mon. in March 1750/51
Martha, wife of William Spragen, relinquished her dower at Henrico County Court on 1st Mon. in December 1750/51

p.48  1 March 1751 William Lawless to Gervas Burdett, both of Henrico County, for 25 pounds, 100 acres on Harding's Branch, a branch of Tuckahoe Creek, being the same parcel on which said Lawless formerly dwelt; adj. Hardwick, Evan Shewmaker's Spring Branch & Leonard Henley (metes & bounds description).
Wit: George Chambers, William Harding, Thomas (his T mark) Williams
Signed: Wm Lawless
Sarah, wife of William Lawless, relinquished her dower
Recorded 1st Mon. in March 1750/51

p.49 4 March 1750 Thomas Robinson to Bernard Ege, both of Henrico County, for 30 pounds, 100 acres on Gilley's Creek, adj. George Robinson, Ellinor Williams & Mary Franklin; being same land conveyed to the said Thomas Robinson from his father, Thomas Robinson.
Wit: Charles Woodson, James Woodson, Thomas Cocke
Signed: Thomas (his R mark) Robinson
Mary, wife of Thomas Robinson, relinquished her dower
Recorded 1st Mon. in March 1750/51

p.50 4 February 1750 Charles Ballow to William Randolph, both of Henrico County, for 107 pounds, 140 acres adj. land of the said Randolph at the World's End, John Giles & Abram Bayley.
Wit: Bowler Cocke, Jr., Nathaniel Wilkinson, John Ellis
Signed: Chas. Ballow          Recorded 1st Mon. in March 1750/51

p.51 10 February 1750 David Holt of Henrico County to Jacob Bugg of Chesterfield County, for 200 pounds, 200 acres lying near the Falls of the James River and on the said river, beginning at a beach at the mouth of the Deep Bottom (metes and bounds description).
Wit: Philemon Frayser, James Hatcher, William Totty
Signed: David Holt
Mabel, wife of David Holt, relinquished her dower
Recorded 1st Mon. in March 1750/51

p.53 19 March 1751 Gregory Matthews/Mathis to Anthony Matthews/ Mathis, both of Henrico County, for 16 pounds, 125 acres on the south side of the Chickahominy Swamp, it being a certain tract devised to the said Gregory Mathis by his father in his last will and testament.
Wit: David Burton, James Allen, Isham Allen
Signed: Gregory Matthews          Recorded 1st Mon. in May 1751

p.54 22 August 1750 Duncan Graham of Hanover County to Richard Weir of Henrico County, for 245 pounds, two lots in a Town called Richmond, together with all the buildings, lying below Shockoe Creek.
Wit: Thomas Atchison, Cary Heslet Happer, William Seller
Signed: Dun. Graham          Recorded 1st Mon. in May 1751

p.56 2 June 1750 Abraham Bailey to Joseph Bailey, his son, both of Henrico County, for 10 shillings, 125 acres, being part of a tract granted to Thomas Farrar by patent dated 24 October 1701; beginning at a corner gum standing on Cornelius Creek, thence adj. Benjamin Burton, Jr., Richard Ren, John & Richard Cox & Lizbe

Turpin.  No witnesses
Signed: Abraham Bailey
Recorded 1st Mon. in June 1751


p.57  3 June 1751 John Gunn to Robert Cook, both of Henrico County, for 45 pounds, 150 acres lying between the lands of the said John Gunn, Nathaniel Vanderwall and the said Robert Cook.  No witnesses
Signed: John Gunn
Recorded 1st Mon. in June 1751


p.57  8 June 1751 Robert Cook to Thomas Frankling, both of Henrico County, for 15 pounds, 50 acres between the lands of the said Robert Cook, Nathaniel Vanderwall, John Gunn & Brazieh Branch.  No witnesses
Signed: Robert (his  R  mark) Cook
Ann, wife of Robert Cook, relinquished her dower
Recorded 1st Mon. in June 1751


p.59  3 June 1751 Bond of John Williamson as an inspector at Shockoe Warehouse, with Philip Mayo and William Lewis being his sureties for 500 pounds sterling. No witnesses
Signed: John Williamson, Philip Mayo, William Lewis
Recorded 1st Mon. in June 1751


p.60 through p.83  49 deeds all dated 5 August 1751 and executed by Peter Randolph, Esq. of Chatsworth, Henrico County, for half-acre lots in a Town called "Westham" "lately laid off in the County of Henrico", for 5 pounds 7 shillings 6 pence per lot, 10 pounds 15 shillings for two lots and 16 pounds 2 shillings 6 pence for three lots; the grantees and the lots conveyed:

| | | |
|---|---|---|
| p.60 | Francis Steger of Richmond in Henrico County | Lot 79 |
| p.60 | John Woodson of Cumberland County | Lot 2 |
| p.61 | Povall Carter of Henrico County | Lots 119,120 & 130 |
| p.61 | John Nicholas, Gent. of Albemarle County | Lots 23 & 60 |
| p.61 | William Stith, Gent. of Henrico County | Lot 77 |
| p.62 | Aaron Higginbothem of Albemarle County [page repeated] | Lot 72 |
| p.62 | Moses Higginbottom of Albemarle County | Lot 75 |
| | George Nicholas, Gent. of Cumberland County | Lot 81 |
| p.63 | Abraham Cowley, Jr. of Richmond in Henrico | Lot 99 |
| p.63 | Samuel Duval of Henrico County | Lot 54 |
| p.64 | Silas Letcher of Henrico County | Lot 26 |

| | | |
|---|---|---|
| p.64 | John Payne of Goochland County | Lot 50 |
| p.65 | James Parker | Lot 3 |
| p.65 | Valentine Wood, Gent. of Goochland County | Lot 52 |
| p.66 | Peter Jefferson, Gent. of Albemarle County for 21 pounds 10 shillings, four lots | Lots 57, 107, 108 & 151 |
| p.66 | Joshua Fry, Gent. of Albemarle County | Lots 117, 118 & 83 |
| p.67 | Matthew Jordan of Albemarle County | Lot 15 |
| p.67 | John Harvie of Albemarle County | Lot 27 |
| p.68 | Andrew Johnson | Lot 28 |
| p.68 | Charles Ellis of Henrico County for 16 pounds 2 shillings 6 pence, | Lots 4 & 152 |
| p.69 | John Hood, Gent. of Prince George County | Lots 68 & 153 |
| p.69 | Carter Braxton, Gent. of King & Queen County for 15 pounds 1 shilling, five lots | Lots 105, 106, 154, 155 & 156 |
| p.70 | John Woodson of Goochland County | Lot 5 |
| p.70 | Thomas McDaniel of Albemarle County | Lot 1 |
| p.71 | Paul Micheaue of Cumberland County | Lot 90 |
| p.71 | Andrew Anderson of Essex County for 21 pounds 10 shillings four lots | Lots 16, 44, 94 & 98 |
| p.72 | Philip Mayo, Gent. of Henrico County | Lot 70 |
| p.72 | Lunsford Lomax, Gent. of Caroline County | Lots 56 & 57 |
| p.73 | Richard Weir of Richmond in Henrico | Lot 69 |
| p.73 | John Chiswell, Gent. of Hanover County | Lots 13 & 62 |
| p.74 | Robert Craig of Hanover County | Lot 78 |
| p.74 | Thomas Atkison of Richmond in Henrico | Lot 84 |
| p.75 | Benjamin Harris of Cumberland County | Lot 38 |
| p.75 | Tucker Woodson of Cumberland County | Lot 37 |
| p.76 | Archibald Ritchie | Lots 39 & 40 |
| p.76 | Francis James, Gent. of Cumberland County | Lot 34 |
| p.77 | Richard Randolph, Gent. of Curles, Henrico | Lot 10 |
| p.77 | John Bolling, Gent. of Chesterfield County | Lots 49 & 95 |
| p.78 | Thomas Topling of Albemarle County | Lot 43 |
| p.78 | William Bogle | Lot 42 |
| p.79 | James Gray | Lots 15 & 25 |
| p.79 | Samuel Gleadon of Richmond in Henrico | Lot 97 |
| p.80 | Walter King of James City County | Lot 96 |
| p.80 | Samuel Spencer of Albemarle County | Lots 53 & 73 |
| p.81 | John Fleming, Gent. of Cumberland County [Note: The above deed inadvertently identifies the town as Randolph, rather than Westham] | Lot 20 |
| p.81 | William Meggenson of Albemarle County | Lots 74 & 93 |

p.82 Langston Bacon of Henrico County     Lots 109 & 110
p.82 John Hunter of Albemarle County     Lot 35
p.83 Howard Cash     Lot 29
No witnesses
Signed: Peter Randolph
Recorded 1st Mon. in August 1751

p.83 29 June 1751 Samuel Bugg to Richard Whitlock, both of Henrico County, for 30 pounds, 75 acres, beginning at Bottom's corner white oak on the north side of his spring branch; adj. Whitlock, Bottom and Francis Wilkinson.
No witnesses     Signed: Samuel Bugg
Sarah, wife of Samuel Bugg, relinquished her dower
Recorded 1st Mon. in August 1751

p.84 5 August 1751 Bond of Richard Randolph as Sheriff of Henrico County, with Philip Mayo and Richard Bland being his sureties for 1,000 pounds sterling under a commission from Hon. Lewis Burwell, Esq., President of this Colony.
No witnesses
Signed: Richard Randolph, Philip Mayo, Richard Bland
Recorded 1st Mon. in August 1751

p.85 8 April 1751 Power of Attorney from John Hanbury & Capel Hanbury, London merchants, to Peter Randolph & William Randolph, Esq. of James River in the Colony of Virginia, to Ask, demand, levy, sue for, etc. in the Colony of Virginia.     Wit: William Walker, W. Eccleston
Signed: J. Hanbury, Capel Hanbury
Recorded 1st Mon. in September 1751

p.86 2 September 1751 Julius Allen to Isham Allen, both of Henrico County, for brotherly love & affection and for better maintenance of the said Isham Allen, 200 acres on the southside of the Chickahominy Swamp, adj. Valentine Freeman, deceased; Richard Williamson and Littleberry Allen.
Wit: Joseph Lewis, John Harwood, William Garthright
Signed: Julius Allen
Recorded 1st Mon. in September 1751

p.87 2 September 1751 Julius Allen to Littleberry Allen, both of Henrico County, for brotherly love and affection and for the better maintenance of the said Littleberry Allen, 80 acres with appurtenances on the southside of the Chickahominy Swamp, adj. Thomas Elmore, Martin Martin & Anthony Matthews.
Wit: Joseph Lewis, John Harwood, William Garthright
Signed: Julius Allen

Recorded 1st Mon. in September 1751

p.88 1 April 1751 John Kersey of Lunenburg County to William North of Henrico County, for 20 pounds, 100 acres adj. William North, Randolph, John Williams & Old House Branch; being the land James Brownen now live on.
Wit: John Williamson, Jr., Robert Sharpe, Benjamin Burton, Jr.
Signed: John Kersey
Recorded: 1st Mon. in September 1751

p.89 23 July 1751 Nicholas Hobson of Lunenburg County to William Hobson of Henrico County, for 150 pounds, 370 acres on Bailey's Run, adj. John Hobson, Joseph Hobson, James Hatcher, Samuel Garthright, Col. Richard Randolph, William Taylor, deceased, John Fussell & John Jordan.
Wit: Samuel Garthright, Joseph Goode, Samuel Hobson
Signed: Nicholas Hopson
Aggy, wife of Nicholas Hobson, relinquished her dower.
Recorded 1st Mon. in November 1751

p.90 19 October 1751 James Cocke, Gent., of Henrico County, to William Randolph, being in the Commission of the Peace for the said County, for 5 pounds, one-half acre lot in the Town of Richmond, being Lot 22 on the plan of the said Town, for the use of the said County of Henrico, to the said William Randolph and his successors so long as they agree to have a Courthouse on the said lot, but if at any time hereafter the said Courthouse for the use of the said County shall be removed to some other lot or part of the County, then the said lot with the appurtenances shall revert and be the property of the said James Cocke and his heirs forever.
Wit: Philip Mayo, Samuel Gleadome, William Lewis, A. Cowley
Signed: James Cocke
A dedimus for the relinquishment of the dower of Sarah, wife of James Cocke, was taken on 27 November 1751 by Samuel Gleadome and William Lewis, commissioner, and recorded the 1st Mon. in December 1751 on p.92.
Recorded 1st Mon. in November 1751

p.91 11 April 1751 Ware Rochell, of Chesterfield County, to Richard Rochell of Henrico County, for 20 pounds, 1200 acres on Peter's Branch
Wit: Francis West, John Forsie, Jr., Abraham Cowley, Jr.
Signed: Ware Rochell          Recorded 1st Mon. in November 1751

p.92 4 November 1751 Bond for Thomas Ellis as an inspector at Shockoe Warehouse, with Samuel Gleadone, his surety, for 500 pounds.

Signed: Thomas Ellis, Samuel Gleadone
Recorded 1st Mon. in November 1751

p.93 2 December 1751 William Whitlow of St. James Parish, Goochland County, to Richard Whitlow, for the natural love & affection and for the better maintenance & livelyhood of the said Richard Whitlow, the plantation said William Whitlow moved from, known as the Reeds, with 150 acres adjoining, on the southside of Cornelius Creek adj. John Whitlow.
Wit: Henry Thomson, Hannah Letcher, Giles Lecher.
Signed: John Whitlowe
Recorded 1st Mon. in December 1751

p.95 27 November 1751 John Jones to Benjamin Jones, his son, both of Henrico County, for love, goodwil & affection, 75 acres with appurtenances adj. Richard Cottrell.
Wit: William (his M mark) Jones, Edmond Alley
Signed: John (his I mark) Jones
Recorded 1st Mon. in December 1751

p.95 23 November 1751 John Jones to Samuel Jones, his son, both of Henrico County, for 10 pounds, 125 acres on Plum Tree Branch, adj. John Williamson, Ralph Umphries, John Price, William Jones.
Wit: Charles Ellis, Richard Gording, Edmond Alley
Signed: John ( his I mark) Jones
Recorded 1st Mon. in December 1751

p.97 7 October 1751 John Freeman of Henrico County to John Price of Goochland County, for 60 pounds, 258 acres adj. Col. William Randolph, David Staples, Scraping Branch, Hall Branch and Fish Branch.
Wit: Richard Holland, William Harding, William Allen, Agnes Allen, William Willis.
Signed: John Freeman, Abigail Freeman
Recorded 1st Mon. in December 1751

p.98 2 December 1751 William Garthright of Varina Parish, Henrico County, to Thomas Rogers of Westover Parish, Charles City County, for 55 pounds, 185 acres and appurtenances, bounded as in the patent mentions for 165 acres, taken up by Ephraim Garthright, father of the said William Garthright, by patent bearing date 1700, and 20 acres bought of John Warriner by the said Ephraim Garthright; my father's buring place excepted.
Wit: Julius Allen, Samuel Garthright, Jr., Ephraim Garthright

Signed: William Garthright
Ann, wife of William Garthright, relinquished her dower.
Recorded 1st Mon. in December 1751

p.99  2 December 1751 William Matthews to Samuel Garthright, Jr., both of Henrico County, for 30 pounds, 125 acres near Chickahominy River adj. Joseph Childers and Miles Garthright; being the land left the said Matthew by his father, Thomas Matthews, deceased.
Wit: William Garthright, Ephraim Garthright, Jacob (his ✚ mark) Webb
Signed: William Matthews
Recorded 1st Mon. in December 1751

pp.102-106  7 January 1752 Polls for the Election of Two Burgesses from Henrico County on said date.

For Col. William Randolph: 244 (votes)

| | | | | |
|---|---|---|---|---|
| 1. | Benjamin Harrison | | 14. | Jacob Smith |
| 2. | Geo. Sherrer | | 15. | Theo. Favor |
| 3. | Jacob Eggy | | 16. | Theo. Carter |
| 4. | Peter Randolph | | 17. | Edward Osborne |
| 5. | Archibald Cary | | 18. | Alexr. Long |
| 6. | William Byrd | | 19. | Charles Ellis |
| 7. | Garrard Ellyson | | 20. | Robert Pleasants |
| 8. | Wm. Stith | | 21. | Ben Hopson |
| 9. | Richd. Rochell | | 22. | Nich. Sherrer |
| 10. | Abram Cowley | | 23. | Wm. Lewis |
| 11. | Wm. Buxton | | 24. | David Burton |
| 12. | Wm. Turner | | 25. | John Bransford |
| 13. | John Ford | | 26. | Geo. Sherrer |
| 27. | Jas. Woodfin | | 66. | Thomas Holmes |
| 28. | John Orange | | 67. | Richd. Renyard |
| 29. | Bremillion Holloway | | 68. | Geo. Adams |
| 30. | Wm. Burton | | 69. | Langston Bacon |
| 31. | Miles Garthright | | 70. | Wm. Mills |
| 32. | Story Hall | | 71. | Humphry Smith |
| 33. | John Mosbey | | 72. | Francis Wagstaff |
| 34. | Henry Ellis | | 73. | Alexr. Patterson |
| 35. | Lusby Turpin | | 74. | Foliett Powers |
| 36. | Gerret Burdet | | 75. | Edward Prior |
| 37. | Hutchings Burton | | 76. | Nath. Bridgewater |
| 38. | Henry Wooddie | | 77. | Peirce Griffin |

| | | | |
|---|---|---|---|
| 39. | John Price | 78. | Robt. Webb |
| 40. | Thomas Jordan | 79. | Sam Allen |
| 41. | John Redford, Junr. | 80. | John Clarke |
| 42. | Francis West | 81. | Robt. Weatherley |
| 43. | John Childers | 82. | John Harwood |
| 44. | Thomas Robenson | 83. | John Smith |
| 45. | Isham Allen | 84. | Thomas Robinson |
| 46. | Jacob Burton | 85. | Rowland Blackborn |
| 47. | Ben Burton, Junr. | 86. | Thos. Binford |
| 48. | Daniel Price | 87. | John Jordan |
| 49. | David Atkinson | 88. | Hays Whitloe, Sr. |
| 50. | John Dupree | 89. | James Whitloe, Sr. |
| 51. | Richd. Weir | 90. | James Whitloe, Jr. |
| 52. | Thomas Atchison | 91. | Hen Whitloe |
| 53. | William Giles | 92. | Valentine Ball |
| 54. | David Staples | 93. | Geo. Baker |
| 55. | William Barker | 94. | Jos. Hopkins |
| 56. | John Grinstone | 95. | John Hopson |
| 57. | John Royster | 96. | John Oakley |
| 58. | Martin Burton | 97. | Thos. Pass |
| 59. | John Price | 98. | David Jennings |
| 60. | Jos. Lewis | 99. | Ben. Childers, Senr. |
| 61. | Geo. Poke | 100. | Jos. Freeman |
| 62. | Edward Enroughty | 101. | Robt. Sharpe, Junr. |
| 63. | Wm. Allen | 102. | Thos. Robinson, Junr. |
| 64. | John Hales | 103. | Richd. Loving |
| 65. | John Bolling | 104. | John Staples |
| 105. | Elisha Millar | 144. | John White |
| 106. | Richd. Whitloe | 145. | Isaac Sharpe |
| 107. | John Bryant | 146. | Nat. Bacon |
| 108. | John Warrinner | 147. | Henry Stokes |
| 109. | John White, Junr. | 148. | John Jude |
| 110. | James Briton | 149. | Robt. Childers |
| 111. | Micael Jones | 150. | Wm. Kelley |
| 112. | Thos. Bowls | 151. | Edward Goode, Junr. |
| 113. | Wm. Snead | 152. | John Stewart |
| 114. | Robt. Maddox | 153. | Sam Ligon |
| 115. | John Pleasants, P. | 154. | Benjamin Porter |
| 116. | Amos Hix | 155. | John Gunn |
| 117. | Ben Burton, Senr. | 156. | John Povall |
| 118. | Joseph Ellis | 157. | Robt. Sharpe |

| | | | |
|---|---|---|---|
| 119. | Robt. Morris | 158. | Joseph Atkins |
| 120. | Thomas Owen | 159. | Sam Bugg |
| 121. | John Lipscombe | 160. | John Alley |
| 122. | Jos. Mitchell | 161. | Francis Peirce |
| 123. | Jas. Allen | 162. | Ephraim Garthright |
| 124. | John Lancaster | 163. | Nt. Vandewall |
| 125. | Thos. Bethill | 164. | Chas. Floyd |
| 126. | Richd. East | 165. | James Jones |
| 127. | Wm. Edwards | 166. | John Garthright |
| 128. | Richd. Whitloe | 167. | John Law |
| 129. | Wm. Whitloe, Senr. | 168. | John Williamson, Senr. |
| 130. | Wm. Whitloe, Junr. | 169. | Thos. Alley |
| 131. | John Cornell | 170. | James Hatcher |
| 132. | Nich. Giles | 171. | Robt. Bullington |
| 133. | John Cocke | 172. | Thomas Perkins |
| 134. | Wm. Briton | 173. | Alxr. Robinson |
| 135. | Ben. Clarke | 174. | Antho. Matthews |
| 136. | Wm. North | 175. | James Austin |
| 137. | Dan. Price | 176. | Amos Liptrot |
| 138. | Wm. Sharpe | 177. | Frans. Stegar |
| 139. | John Lacy | 178. | Thos. Cardwell |
| 140. | David Breeding | 179. | Thos. Bottom |
| 141. | John Middleton | 180. | Jos. Hopson |
| 142. | Robt. Williamson | 181. | Ben. Goode, Sen. |
| 143. | Wm. Bridgewater | 182. | Thos. Jolley |
| 183. | Robt. Williams | 222. | Wm. Ellis |
| 184. | Jacob Bugg | 223. | Richd. Cottrell |
| 185. | Nicho. Mealer | 224. | John Ellis |
| 186. | Wm. Hopson | 225. | Wm. Bacon |
| 187. | Wm. Parker | 226. | Wm. Bottom |
| 188. | Jos. Bailey | 227. | Thos. Alley, Sr. |
| 189. | Jos. Woodson | 228. | Thos. Wood |
| 190. | Wm. Peirce | 229. | John Owen |
| 191. | John Frazer | 230. | Wm. Lawless |
| 192. | John West | 231. | Matt Hopson |
| 193. | Robt. Gordan | 232. | John Brackett |
| 194. | Sam Gordan | 233. | John Bottom |
| 195. | Francis Franklin | 234. | John Giles, Sr. |
| 196. | John Alday, junr. | 235. | John Williams |
| 197. | Walter Leigh | 236. | Julius Allen |
| 198. | Robt. Cocke | 237. | Wm. Ross |

| | | | |
|---|---|---|---|
| 199. | Thos. Branch | 238. | John Pleasants, B. |
| 200. | Sam. Jones | 239. | Edward East |
| 201. | Isaac Winstone | 240. | Drury Wood |
| 202. | Daniel Warriner | 241. | Thos. Matthews |
| 203. | Milener Redford | 242. | Phil. Freizure |
| 204. | David Binns | 243. | Darry Southall |
| 205. | Hutchings Burton | 244. | John Bullington |
| 206. | John Whitloe | | |
| 207. | Chas. Amos | For Bowler Cocke, 162 | |
| 208. | Thos. Bates | 1. | Benjamin Harrison |
| 209. | Jos. Jas. Whiteman | 2. | Geo. Sherrer |
| 210. | John Wms. | 3. | Jacob Eggy |
| 211. | Evan Shoemaker | 4. | Peter Randolph |
| 212. | Thos. Jenell | 5. | Archibald Cary |
| 213. | Saml. Garthright | 6. | William Byrd |
| 214. | Matt. Bridgeman | 7. | Garrard Ellyson |
| 215. | Thos. Goode | 8. | Wm. Stith |
| 216. | Wm. Freizure | 9. | Richd. Rochell |
| 217. | Saml. Garthright | 10. | Abram Cowley |
| 218. | Sam Duvall | 11. | Thos. Merritt |
| 219. | Wm. Ferris, Junr. | 12. | Theo. Carter |
| 220. | Wm. Clarke | 13. | Edward Osborne |
| 221. | Wm. Shields | 14. | Alex. Long |
| 15. | Charles Ellis | 54. | John Jordan |
| 16. | Robt. Pleasants | 55. | Hays Whitloe, Sr. |
| 17. | Ben. Hopson | 56. | Richard Truman, Sr. |
| 18. | Nicholas Sherrer | 57. | James Whitlow, Sr. |
| 19. | John Bransford | 58. | James Whitloe, Jr. |
| 20. | Geo. Sherrer | 59. | Henry Whitloe |
| 21. | Jas. Woodfin | 60. | Thos. Thorpe |
| 22. | Wm. Burton | 61. | George Baker |
| 23. | Henry Ellis | 62. | Joseph Hopkins |
| 24. | Lusby Turpin | 63. | John Hopson |
| 25. | Sam Leggy | 64. | John Oakley |
| 26. | Thomas Jordan | 65. | Ben. Childers |
| 27. | John Redford, Junr. | 66. | John Eals |
| 28. | John Childers | 67. | Elisha Millar |
| 29. | Thos. Robinson | 68. | Richard Whitloe |
| 30. | Isham Allen | 69. | John Bryant |
| 31. | Jacob Burton | 70. | John Warrinner |
| 32. | Ben Burton, Junr. | 71. | Robt. Mattox |

| | | | |
|---|---|---|---|
| 33. | Richd. Weir | 72. | John Pleasants, P. |
| 34. | Thos. Atcheson | 73. | Ben Burton, Sr. |
| 35. | Wm. Ferris | 74. | Joseph Ellis |
| 36. | John Royster | 75. | Thos. Owen |
| 37. | Geo. Poke | 76. | James Allen |
| 38. | Edward Henroughty | 77. | Thomas Bethill |
| 39. | John Hales | 78. | Joseph Childers |
| 40. | John Bolling | 79. | John Cocke |
| 41. | Thomas Joines | 80. | Daniel Price |
| 42. | Richd. Renyard | 81. | William Sharpe |
| 43. | George Adams | 82. | Mat. Herbert |
| 44. | Langston Bacon | 83. | David Breeding |
| 45. | Wm. Mills | 84. | John Middleton |
| 46. | Humphry Smith | 85. | Isaac Sharpe |
| 47. | Benjamin Jones | 86. | Nat. Bacon |
| 48. | Francis Wagstaff | 87. | Hen Stokes |
| 49. | Folliott Powers | 88. | John Jude |
| 50. | Sam Allen | 89. | Edward Goode, Junr. |
| 51. | John Harwood | 90. | John Stewart |
| 52. | Thomas Robinson | 91. | Ben Porter |
| 53. | Thomas Binford | 92. | John Povall |
| 93. | Robt. Sharpe | 132. | John Williams |
| 94. | Jos. Adkins | 133. | Saml. Garthright |
| 95. | Sam Bugg | 134. | Matt Bridgeigian |
| 96. | John Alday | 135. | Thomas Goode |
| 97. | Frans. Peirce | 136. | Wm. Fraser |
| 98. | Ephraim Garthright | 137. | Saml. Garthright |
| 99. | Nat. Vandewall | 138. | Sam Duvall |
| 100. | Chas. Floyd | 139. | Wm. Ferris, Jr. |
| 101. | John Garthright | 140. | Wm. Shields |
| 102. | John Williamson | 141. | Wm. Ellis |
| 103. | Jam. Hatcher | 142. | Richard Cottrell |
| 104. | Robt. Bullington | 143. | John Ellis |
| 105. | Thos. Perkins | 144. | Wm. Bacon |
| 106. | Antho. Matthews | 145. | William Bottom |
| 107. | James Austin | 146. | Thos. Alley, Sr. |
| 108. | Amos Liptrott | 147. | Richd. Truman, Jr. |
| 109. | Thos. Cardwell | 148. | Thos. Wood |
| 110. | Thos. Bottom | 149. | John Owen |
| 111. | Jos. Hopson | 150. | Matt Hopson |
| 112. | Ben Goode, Senr. | 151. | John Brackell |

| | | | | |
|---|---|---|---|---|
| 113. | Thos. Jolley | | 152. | John Bottom |
| 114. | Jacob Bugg | | 153. | John Williams |
| 115. | Nichs. Melar | | 154. | Julius Allen |
| 116. | Wm. Hopson | | 155. | Wm. Ross |
| 117. | Wm. Parker | | 156. | John Pleasants, B. |
| 118. | Joseph Bailey | | 157. | Edward East |
| 119. | Joseph Woodson | | 158. | Drury Wood |
| 120. | Wm. Peirce | | 159. | Thos. Matthews |
| 121. | John Freizur | | 160. | Phil. Freizure |
| 122. | John West | | 161. | Darey Southall |
| 123. | Francis Frankland | | 162. | John Bullington |
| 124. | John Allday, Jr. | | | |
| 125. | Wat. Leigh | | For William Harding, 102: | |
| 126. | Robt. Cooke | | 1. | William Buxton |
| 127. | Thos. Branch | | 2. | Thomas Merritt |
| 128. | Isaac Winston | | 3. | William Turner |
| 129. | Dan. Warrinner | | 4. | John Ford |
| 130. | Miliner Redford | | 5. | Jacob Smith |
| 131. | John Whitloe | | 6. | Thomas Favour |
| | | | | |
| 7. | William Lewis | | 46. | David Jennings |
| 8. | David Burton | | 47. | Joseph Trueman |
| 9. | John Orange | | 48. | Robert Sharpe, Jr. |
| 10. | Bremillion Holloway | | 49. | Thomas Robinson, Jr. |
| 11. | Miles Garthright | | 50. | John Eals |
| 12. | Story Hall | | 51. | Richard Loving |
| 13. | John Mosbey | | 52. | John Staples |
| 14. | Sam Liggy | | 53. | John White, Jr. |
| 15. | Gerret Burdet | | 54. | James Britain |
| 16. | Hutchin Burton | | 55. | Micael Jones |
| 17. | Henry Woddie | | 56. | Thomas Bowls |
| 18. | John Price | | 57. | William Snead |
| 19. | Francis West | | 58. | Amos Hix |
| 20. | Daniel Price | | 59. | Robert Morris |
| 21. | David Adkinson | | 60. | John Lipscombe |
| 22. | John Dupree | | 61. | Joseph Mitchell |
| 23. | William Giles | | 62. | John Lancaster |
| 24. | William Ferris | | 63. | Richard East |
| 25. | David Staples | | 64. | William Edwards |
| 26. | William Barker | | 65. | Joseph Childers |
| 27. | John Grinstone | | 66. | Richard Whitloe |

| | | | |
|---|---|---|---|
| 28. | Martin Burton | 67. | William Whitloe |
| 29. | John Price | 68. | William Whitloe, Jr. |
| 30. | Joseph Lewis | 69. | John Cornett |
| 31. | William Allin | 70. | Nicholas Giles |
| 32. | Benjamin Jones | 71. | William Briton |
| 33. | Alexander Patterson | 72. | Ben Clarke |
| 34. | Edward Prior | 73. | William North |
| 35. | Na. Bridgewater | 74. | John Lacey |
| 36. | Peirce Griffin | 75. | Matt Herbert |
| 37. | Robert Webb | 76. | Richard Williamson |
| 38. | John Clarke | 77. | William Bridgewater |
| 39. | Robert Weatherley | 78. | John White |
| 40. | John Smith | 79. | Robert Childers |
| 41. | Rouland Blackbourn | 80. | William Kelley |
| 42. | Richard Trumand, Sr. | 81. | Sam Ligon |
| 43. | Thomas Thorpe | 82. | John Gunn |
| 44. | Valentine Ball | 83. | James Jones |
| 45. | Thomas Pass | 84. | John Law |
| 85. | Thomas Alley | 94. | Charles Amos |
| 86. | Alexander Robinson | 95. | Thomas Bates |
| 87. | Francis Steagar | 96. | Joseph Tan Whitewan |
| 88. | Robert Williams | 97. | Evan Shoemaker |
| 89. | Robert Gordan | 98. | Thomas Jennett |
| 90. | Sam Gordon | 99. | William Clarke |
| 91. | Samuel Jones | 100. | Richard Truman, Jr. |
| 92. | David Binns | 101. | William Lawless |
| 93. | Hutching Burton | 102. | John Giles, Sr. |

Sworn to as a true copy of the Poll taken at an Election for Henrico County January 7, 1751/2 by Nathaniel Wilkinson, one of the under Sheriffs of the said county, before John Povall on 20 January 1752.
Date of record not indicated by Bowler Cocke, Jr., Clerk of Henrico County Court.

p.107 23 December 1751 Theophil Favour to John Ford, both of Henrico County, for 25 pounds, 142 acres, being the same land whereon said Theophil Favour now lives; adj. Thomas Griffin, John Ellis and Robert Childers
Wit: John (his  +  mark) Cornett, Francis (his  +  mark) Cornett,
Sam (his ✚ mark) Ford, John (his  +  mark) Mosby
Signed: Theophil Favour, Elizabeth (her  E  mark) Favour
Recorded 1st Mon. in June 1752

p.108  6 January 1751 Joseph Childers to Benjamin Hobson, both of Henrico County, for 33 pounds 10 shillings, 285 acres on the south side of White Oak Swamp (metes and bounds description).
Wit: Julius Allen, Samuel Garthright and Shadrack (his S mark) Martin
Signed: Joseph (his I mark) Childers
Elizabeth, wife of Joseph Childers, relinquished her dower.
Recorded 1st Mon. in June 1752

p.110  11 August 1751 Theophil Favour of Henrico County to Thomas Griffin of Essex County, for 20 pounds, 100 acres on the Long and Hungry Branch, being part of a tract of 400 acres where on said Favour now lives and which he bought of John Smith; adj. Pierce Griffin, John Staples and John Ellis (metes and bounds description).
Wit: Pierce Griffing, Georg (his ✚ mark) Gining, William (his ✚ mark) Ginnins
Signed: Theophill Favour, Elizabeth Faver
Elizabeth, wife of Theophil Favour, relinquished her dower.
Recorded 1st Mon. in June 1752

p.114  29 February 1752 Owen Martin of Albemarle County to John Carter of Henrico County, for 55 pounds, 214 acres on Chickahominy Swamp, White Oak Swamp and Round Hill Branch, adj. John Cocke, Thomas Watkins and George Adams.
Wit: George Adams, Theodorick Carter, Marke Clarke
Signed: Owen (his O mark) Martin
Recorded 1st Mon. in June 1752; further proven on 1st Mon. in July 1752

p.115  6 May 1752 Folliott Power of St. Peter's Parish, New Kent County, to Bowler Cocke, Jr., of Henrico County, for 160 pounds, two Negro men, Jack and Davey.
Wit: Nathaniel Wilkinson, John Gomer, John Bransford
Signed: Foliett Power                    Recorded 1st Mon. in June 1752

p.115  23 May 1752 Foliott Power to Matthew Cole, both of New Kent County, for 18 pounds 4 shillings 3 pence, 200 acres granted by patent to Erasmus Oakley 1 October 1747 for 340 acres of the south branch of White Oak Swamp.
Wit: William Street, William Ellis, Benoni Boatwright
Signed: Foliott Power
Anne, wife of said Power, relinquished her dower.
Recorded 1st Mon. in June 1752

p.116  29 May 1752 Joseph and Jane Freeman to Richard Holland, all of Henrico

County, for 200 pounds, 372 acres on Tuckahoe Creek, being tract whereon said Joseph and Jane Freeman now live; adj. Randolph, George Freeman and William Harding.
Wit: John Ellis, Amos Hix, William Street, William Harding
Signed: Joseph Freeman, Jeane (her I mark) Freeman
Recorded 1st Mon. in June 1752

p.118  1 May 1752 Richard Holland of Henrico County to William Hughes of Hanover County, for 200 pounds, 950 acres on the south side of Chickahominy Swamp, adj. Robert Morris, Robert Webb, John Wheler, John Puryear and land said Holland purchased of James Meredith and lines of land devised to said Holland by his father Michael Holland, late of Henrico County.
Wit: Elisha Meredith, Joseph Freeman, James Gunn
Signed: Richard Holland
Sarah, wife of said Holland, relinquished her dower.
Recorded 1st Mon. in June 1752

p.119  1 June 1752 William Bacon and Mary Bacon, his wife, of Henrico County, to David Whitlock of Hanover County, for 20 pounds, 254 acres in Bacon's patent of 5 September 1749.
Wit: Nathaniel Bacon, T. Wilkinson, William Hughes
Signed; William Bacon, Mary Bacon
Recorded 1st Mon. in June 1752

p.120  29 May 1752 Joseph Freeman and Jane Freeman, his mother, to William Harding, all of Henrico County, for 12 pounds, 24 acres on Tuckahoe Creek, being part of tract whereon Joseph and Jane Freeman now live on; adj. Harding's land he bought of Joseph White, formerly Hatcher's.
Wit: Richard Holland, William Street, John Ellis, Amos Hix
Signed: Joseph Freeman, Jeane (her I mark) Freeman

p.121  29 May 1752 Joseph Tanner Whiteman of Goochland County to William Harding of Henrico County for 20 pounds, 70 acres on Tuckahoe Creek near the mouth of the Deep Run, being the land and plantation called Griffin's; adj. Col. Randolph and Joseph Freeman.
Wit: Richard Holland, William Street, John Ellis, Amos Hix, Joseph Freeman
Signed: Joseph Tanner (his I mark) Whiteman
Recorded 1st Mon. in June 1752

p.122  7 October 1751 William Prier of Albemarle County to William Harding of Henrico County, for 5 pounds, 208 acres (also described as 280 acres), being part

of a greater tract of land granted to William Laffoon by patent and is the upper part of said tract; bounded upon the branches of Drinking Hole and the head branches of the Chickahominy and adj. Evan Shoemaker, Benjamin Johnson, John Martin and Simond Ligon
Wit: Christopher John Thomas, James Conaway, William Lawless, Jesse Ellis
Signed: William Pryor
Recorded 1st Mon. in June 1752; further proved 1st Mon. in Oct. 1752

p.122  4 December 1751 Richard Caudle and Mary, his wife, of Brunswick County to William Harding of Henrico County, for 5 pounds, 208 acres being part of a greater tract of land granted to William Laffoon by patent; adj. the land William Pryor sold to William Harding out of the same patent.
Wit: Christopher John Thomas, William Allen, Robert Williams,
James (his X mark) Conaway
Signed: Richard Caudle, Mary (her Q mark) Caudle
Recorded 1st Mon. in June 1752

p.124  4 April 1752 Joseph Woodson to John Woodson, his grandson, an infant, eldest son and heir of his son, Joseph Woodson, deceased, in consideration of a Negro boy, Dick, valued at £30, received of my son Joseph Woodson, deceased, in his lifetime, for 100 acres on the upper side of Four Mile Creek, being all of the remaining tract whereon I now dwell that I did not convey to my son Joseph during his lifetime, but reserving a life estate in said residue.
Wit: John Pleasants, Jr., and Thomas Pleasants, both Quakers, who acknowledged by affirmation rather than oath; Henry Sharp
Signed: Joseph Woodson, Senr.              Recorded 1st Mon. in June 1752

p.124  1 June 1752 Benjamin Burton, Jr., to John Parker, both of Henrico County, for £15, 198 acres on the Deep Run; adj. John Goode, Benjamin Burton, Sr. and James Whitlow.
Wit: none                                    Signed: Benja. Burton, Junr.
Anne, wife of said Burton, relinquished her dower.
Recorded 1st Mon. in June 1752

p.126  8 May 1752 John Spear of Albemarle County to Robert Spear, Jr., of Henrico County, his brother, for good will and natural affection, all right, title and interest in land which was my father's, Robert Spear, Sr., being 212 acres on the south side of the Chickahominy which he purchased of the Mortons.

Wit: Julius Allen, Miles Garthright, William Gathwrit, Ann Garthwright
Signed: John Spears                          Recorded 1st Mon. in June 1752

p.126  27 January 1752 Samuel Bugg to Thomas Watkins, Jr., both of Henrico County, for £200, 773 acres on the south side of the Chickahominy Swamp and on both sides of the Cabin Branch; adj. Richard Whitlock, Francis Wilkinson, Francis Wagstaff, Thomas Bates and Gerard Ellyson.
Wit: Charles Woodson, Mark Clarke, Gearrard Ellyson
Signed: Samuel Bugg, Sarah, wife of said Bugg, relinquished her dower.
Recorded 1st Mon. in June 1752

p.127  6 January 1752 Samuel Bugg to Thomas Bates, both of Henrico County, for one bay gelding, 30 acres at the fork of the Miery Branch; adj. Wagstaff and Ellyson.               Wit: Anselm Bugg, John Borum, Elizabeth Bates
Signed: Samuel Bugg, Sarah, wife of said Bugg, relinquished her dower.
Recorded 1st Mon. in June 1752

p.128  8 March 1752 Richard Randolph (Gent.) to James Linsey, both of Henrico County, for £36, 266⅔ acres on the north side of the James River; adj. Samuel Garthwright, Jr., William Hobson and William Taylor, deceased.
Wit: Hutonio Morosini, Samuel Daniel, John Halling
Signed: Richard Randolph
Recorded 1st Mon. in June 1752; further proved 1st Mon. in Sept. 1752

p.129  21 February 1752 Power of Attorney of John Rockett, mariner, to Richard Rockett of Henrico, to recover of Abraham Cowley of Henrico County debts owing.
Wit: Benjamin Burton, Jacob Burton, Drury Wood
Signed: Jno. Rockett
Recorded 1st Mon. in June 1752

p.130  1 June 1752 Thomas Bates, planter, to Henry Sharp, Gent., both of Henrico County, for £30, 70 acres on Four Mile Creek, bounded on the south by Four Mile Creek Mill, on the west by Henry Sharp and on the north and east by John Bates, son of Thomas, which he purchased of William Sharp.
Wit: none                          Signed: Thomas (his T mark) Bates
Recorded 1st Mon. in June 1752

p.131  26 December 1751 John Pleasants, son & heir of Thomas Pleasants, of Henrico County, deceased; Mary Pleasants and Jane Pleasants, daughters of the said Thomas; and John Pleasants, Robert Pleasants, John Crew and Robert Ellyson, surviving trustees appointed under the will of said Thomas Pleasants, deceased

(James Lead, David Johnson, David and Henry Terril and John Cheadle, the other trustees named in will dated 19 November 1743 being now deceased), all parties in the consideration for the better and more easie and amicable settlement of a dispute regarding the estates of Sarah and Elizabeth Pleasants, deceased, sisters of the aforesaid John, Mary and Jane Pleasants; the dispute being whether the estates of the said Sarah and Elizabeth, who died under age, should be vested in their brother John, as the heir-at-law of their father, Thomas Pleasants, or should be vested in their surviving sisters, Mary and Jane. The settlement of the matter was referred to Benjamin Waller, attorney in Williamsburg. By his will, the said Thomas Pleasants devised to his said four daughters several slaves (Moll and four of her children, Bess, Billey, Jane and Jo; a mulatto girl, Nan; Jacob, son of Grace; Jacob and Peter, sons of Jane; Sam, son of Judith) and land in Nansemond and Norfolk counties, all said property to be divided upon their marriage or arrival at 21 years of age. Pursuant to agreement, this aforesaid legacy is hereby vested entirely among the said John, Mary and Jane Pleasants, for which their other siblings, Thomas Pleasants, Robert Pleasants and Benjamin Jordan (apparently a half-brother) on 8 April 1752 each received of John, Mary and Jane Pleasants the sum of 8 pounds 6 shillings and 8 pence of the divided estate of their deceased sisters or half-sister. This part of the agreement was witnessed by Elizabeth Poythress, Jane Poythress and James Bates.
Wit: James Hatcher, Robert Pleasants, John Pleasants, Jr., John Webster
Signed: John Pleasants, Jr., Mary Pleasants, Jr., Jane Pleasants,
John Pleasants, Robert Pleasants, John Crew and Robert Ellyson
Recorded 1st Mon. in June 1752

p.132  1 June 1752 Richard Whitlowe to William Randolph of Wilton, both of Henrico County, for 15 pounds, 100 acres, being the land on which the said Richard Whitlowe formerly lived and joyneth the said William Randolph's back land.
Wit: none　　　　　　　　　　Signed: Richard (his ✚ mark) Whitlowe
Recorded 1st Mon. in June 1752

p.133  15 February 1752 Capt. John Rockett, mariner, to William Ellis, both of Henrico County, for 36 pounds, 240 acres on Peter's Branch and Booth's Branch, branches of Tuckahoe Creek, being part of 1200 acres which was entered by Mr. Baldwin Rockett, deceased, in his lifetime and since then surveyed and patented by his sons, whom he left under age when he died; adj. Col. John Ellis, William Ellis, Joseph Ellis and Col. Richard Randolph (metes and bounds description).
Wit: William Street, John Ellis, Henry Ellis
Signed: Jno. Rockett　　　　　　　Recorded 1st Mon. in June 1752

p.134  1 June 1752 William Ellis to John Ellis (Gent.), both of Henrico County, for

12 pounds, 80 acres on Booth's Branch of Tuckahoe Creek, being part of 240 acres which said William Ellis bought of John Rockett; adj. Col. Richard Randolph and John Ellis (metes and bounds description).
Wit: Christopher John Thomas, William Street, Henry Ellis
Signed: Wm. Ellis                    Recorded 1st Mon. in June 1752

135  1 June 1752 William Ellis to Joseph Ellis, both of Henrico County, for 8 pounds, 60 acres on Peter's Branch of Tuckahoe Creek, being part of 240 acres which said William Ellis bought of John Rockett, adj. Joseph Ellis (metes and bounds description).
Wit: Christopher John Thomas, William Street, Henry Ellis
Signed: Wm. Ellis                    Recorded 1st Mon. in June 1752

p.139-150  23 deeds all dated 5 December 1751 and executed by Peter Randolph, Esq., of Chatsworth, Henrico County, for half-acre lots in the town of Westham in said county, in consideration of 5 pounds 7 shillings and 6 pence per lot; the grantees and lots conveyed:

| | | |
|---|---|---|
| p.139 | John Miller | Lot 22 |
| p.139 | Isham Richardson | Lot 41 |
| p.140 | Harding Burley of Henrico County, for 10 pounds 15 shillings | 2 lots |
| p.140 | William Cabell of Albemarle County, for 32 pounds 5 shillings | 6 lots: Lots 6, 18, 31, 51, 87 & 100 |
| p.141 | Charles Bond of Albemarle County | Lot 8 |
| p.141 | Andrew Christian of Albemarle County | Lot 61 |
| p.142 | John Hinson of Albemarle County | Lot 82 |
| p.142 | Robert Hughes of Cumberland County | Lot 24 |
| p.143 | Edward Pyechamberlayne (sic) of New Kent County | Lot 55 |
| p.143 | Gideon Marr of Albemarle County | Lot 19 |
| p.144 | Stephen Hughes of Cumberland County | Lot 71 |
| p.144 | Samuel Jordan of Albemarle County | Lot 89 |
| p.145 | Samuel Glover | Lot 64 |
| p.145 | Robert Davis of Albemarle County | Lot 30 |
| p.146 | Samuel Burk | Lot 33 |
| p.146 | John Cannon of Albemarle County | Lot 65 |
| p.147 | Nathaniel Dandridge of King William County | Lot 7 |
| p.147 | James Christian of Albemarle County | Lot 14 |
| p.148 | Philip Morris of Albemarle County | Lot 48 |
| p.148 | Allen Howard of Albemarle County | Lot 86 |
| p.149 | Thomas Cottrell | Lot 58 |
| p.149 | James Shelton, Gent., of Hanover County | Lot 21 |
| p.150 | John Robards of Goochland County | Lot 11 |

Recorded 1st Mon. in July 1752

p.150  2 December 1751 Joseph Pleasants to William Sharp, blacksmith, both of Henrico County, for 150 pounds, 125 acres to be laid off between the lines of Edward Goode, John Pleasants of Baileys, Four Mile Creek, the line of the land belonging to Four Mile Creek Mill of Thomas Bates & a new line to be made to include said 125 acres.
Wit: Charles Woodson, Joseph Woodson, Samuel Garthwright, Junr., Isaac (his S mark) Sharp
Signed: Joseph Pleasants
Elizabeth, wife of Joseph Pleasants, relinquished her dower
Recorded 1st Mon. in July 1752

p.152  3 July 1752 Thomas Watkins the elder of Southam Parish, Cumberland County, to Benjamin Jordan of Henrico County, for 150 pounds, 250 acres on the north side of White Oak Swamp which said Watkins acquired from Thomas Pleasants, late of this county, deceased, by deed of lease dated 1 August 1719 and by deed of livery and seizin dated 5 May 1729.
Wit: Gearrard Ellyson, Henry Watkins, Thos. Watkins
Signed: Thomas Watkins
Recorded 1st Mon. in July 1752

p.153  6 July 1752 Joseph Mitchell of Henrico County to James Eubank of Caroline County, for 22 pounds, 150 acres, being part of a tract of 393 acres belonging to said Joseph Mitchell and whereon he is now living (metes and bounds description).
Wit: none                                                                   Signed: Joseph Mitchell
Mary, wife of Joseph Mitchell, relinquished her dower
Recorded 1st Mon. in July 1752

p.154  6 July 1752 Pelham Moore of New Kent County to Charles Floyd of Charles City County, for 25 pounds, 50 acres on the Secretary's Mill Pond, adj. land formerly belonging to William Irby, the land of Peter Burton and said Charles Floyd.
Wit: none                                                                   Signed Pelham Moore
Recorded 1st Mon. in July 1752

p.155  31 January 1752 Power of attorney from Daniel Stephenson of Whitehaven, Cumberland County, Kingdom of England, to my Trusty and well beloved Friend, Israel Younghusband, merchant of Whitehaven aforesaid, to recover from John Pleasants, Anselm Bailey, James Jordan Scott, Josiah Jordan, James Coupland,

Thomas Pretlow, Beverley Randolph, Charles Thomas and William Binford, all of Virginia, merchants, sums of money, goods, wares and merchandise owing me.
Wit: James Atkinson, Hugh Codam, Joseph Fisher
Signed: Danl. Stephenson
Recorded 1st Mon. in July 1752

p.156  15 February 1752 Israel Younghusband, of Whitehaven, etc. to Isaac Younghusband, his brother, also of Whitehaven, mariner, and to Roger Atkinson of Virginia, as substitute attorneys for me on behalf of Daniel Stephenson, to recover from said Virginia merchants indebted to said Stephenson.
Wit: James Atkinson, Hugh Codam, Joseph Fisher
Signed: Israel Younghusband           Recorded 1st Mon. in July 1752

p.157-161 devoted to wills [previously published by Dr. Benjamin Weisiger].

p.162  3 August 1752 Samuel Coke and John Coke, son and father, to Samuel Duvall, with the consent of said father and the Henrico County Court, an apprenticeship of seven years from said date to the said Duvall, to learn the occupation of a house carpenter and joyner, during which time the said Samuel Coke shant frequent ordinaries, nor horse racing, or cock fighting and shant play at cards, dice, billards and any other unlawful games without his master's consent and said Coke shant contract matrimony, commit adultery or fornication; he is to be provided with sufficient meat, drink, washing and lodging.
Wit: John Wmson, John Williamson, Jun., Benj. Burton, Junr.
Signed: Samuel Coke, Jno. Coke, Samuel Duvall
Recorded 1st Mon. in September 1752

p.163  15 September 1752 John Caudle and Ann, his wife, of Brunswick County, to William Harding of Henrico County, for 5 pounds, 209 acres, the remaining part of 628 acres patented in William Lafoon's name; joining Watson, Holland and my own line.
Wit: Richard Holland, Joseph Matthews, Robert (his + mark) Webb, Jr., Robert Burton, Jr., John (his + mark) Lankestar
Signed: John Caudle, Ann (her + mark) Caudle
Recorded 1st Mon. in September 1752

p.164 2 April 1752 Joseph Hopkins of Richmond Town, Henrico County, and Peter How, merchant, of Whitehaven, Kingdom of Great Britain, merchant, to John Williamson, of Henrico County, for 79 pounds and 20 shillings, three lots in the Town of Richmond, identified on the plan of the town as Lots G, H and I, cites that by indenture of 8 July 1745 said Hopkins mortgaged to Thomas Dawson and

Charles Thomas, factors and agents for said How, the said lots, which secured debts then due to the said How and also due to Nathaniel Vandewall; said How has appointed Matthew Branch of Chesterfield County to act as his attorney to acknowledge satisfaction of the debt. Wit: none
Signed: Joseph Hopkins, Matt. Branch, Jr., Nath. Vandawall
Mary, wife of Joseph Hopkins, relinquished her dower
Recorded 1st in September 1752

p.165 2 April 1752 Joseph Hopkins of Richmond Town, Henrico County, and Peter How, merchant, of Whitehaven, Kingdom of Great Britain to Andrew Castlin of the Town of Richmond, for 7 pounds, Lot 71, shown on the plan of the Town of Richmond, which was mortgaged under the same indenture of 8 July 1745, cited in previous deed, with same individuals joining as parties to release said lot.
Wit: none
Signed: Joseph Hopkins, Matt. Branch, Jr., Nathl. Vandewall
Mary, wife of Joseph Hopkins, relinquished her dower
Recorded 1st Mon. in September 1752

p.167 2 April 1752 Joseph Hopkins of Richmond Town, Henrico County, and Peter Haw, merchant, of Whitehaven, Kingdom of Great Britain, to Loudwick Worrack of the Town of Richmond, for 48 pounds, Lot 49 and ½ of Lot 36 shown on the plan of the Town of Richmond, which was mortgaged under the same indenture of 8 July 1745 previously referenced with same individuals joining as parties to release said parcels. Wit: none
Signed: Joseph Hopkins, Matt. Branch, Jr., Nathl. Vandewall
Mary, wife of Joseph Hopkins, relinquished her dower
Recorded 1st Mon. in September 1752

p.168 2 October William Tyree of Hanover County to Edmund Borum, also of Hanover County, for 28 pounds 1 shilling and 6 pence, 200 acres on the north side of Ufnam Branch, a great branch of the Chickahominy Swamp; adj. John Williamson, John Lankford and Robert Sharp (metes and bounds description); said land was conveyed by Henry Stoakes to David Tyree by deed of 1 August 1747 and by last will and testament of David Tyree to William Tyree, his son and heir.
Wit: none                                          Signed: William Tyree
Recorded 1st. Mon. in October 1752

p.171 3 August 1752 David Whitlock of St. Paul's Parish, Hanover County, to William Tyree of said parish and county, for 8 pounds and 10 shillings, 113 acres on a branch of Chickahominy Swamp; adj. Pleasants, Holloway, Watson and Whitlock; being ¼ part of 454 acres purchased of William Bacon, 250 being

granted to said Bacon by patent of 5 September 1749 and 200 acres being granted to John Watson on 26 June 1731.
Wit: Wm Smith, Edward Curd, Joseph Lewis
Signed: David Whitlock                                  Recorded 1st Mon. in October 1752

p.173  3 August 1752 David Whitlock of St. Paul's Parish, Hanover County, to James Tyree of said parish and county, for 8 pounds and 10 shillings, 113 acres on a branch of Chickahominy Swamp; adj. Lacy Holloway and William Tyree; being ¼ part of 454 acres cited in previous deed.
Wit: Wm Smith, Edward Curd, Joseph Lewis
Signed: David Whitlock                                  Recorded 1st Mon. in October 1752

p.174  16 September Nathaniel Bridgwater to son, Nathaniel Bridgwater, Jr., of Henrico County, in consideration of love, goodwill and affection, 133 acres on John's Branch, being the land whereon Nathaniel Bridgwater, Jr., now lives; adj. Daniel Price and Wm. Bridgwater; life estate in said tract reserved by Nathaniel Bridgwater and his wife, Elizabeth.
Wit: John Conway, Samuel Allen, Elizabeth (her C mark) Conway
Signed: Nathaniel (his N mark) Bridgwater
Recorded 1st Mon. in October 1752

p.176  15 July 1752 James Woodfin to John Williamson, both of Henrico County, for 20 pounds, 115 acres on Horsepen Branch, adj. John Price, John Lankford, Benjamin Clark and Hon. William Byrd, Esq. (metes and bounds description)
Wit: John Williamson, Junr., Wm. Kelley, Robert Williamson
Signed: James Woodfin
Recorded 1st Mon. in October 1752

p.178  15 July 1752 James Woodfin, Executor of William Warburton; late of Henrico County, to George Kelley, of said county, for 30 pounds, 50 acres on west side of Ufnam Branch, adj. John Wootten, William Killey and Ben Clarke; same land sold to Warburton by John Lankford by deed on 1 October 1748.
Wit: John Williamson, Junr., Robert Williamson, William Killey
Signed: James Woodfin
Recorded 1st Mon. in October 1752

p.179  22 September 1752 Report returned by Jacob Ashurst, Surveyor of Henrico County, defining the prison bounds by metes and bounds, pursuant to an order of 6 July 1752. Survey reveals boundaries to include 9.7 acres on the northeast side of a lot recently purchased by Mr. Duvall on the Main Street, takeing in Cowley's dwelling house and part of his Garden, also including Stegare's and the present

Courthouse, as well as the old Courthouse, the prison and the Saddler's Shop, and crossing the brickyard and running along the side of Ware's Garden pales.
Recorded 1st Mon. in November 1752

p.180  6 November 1752 David Staples and Christian, his wife, of Henrico County, to Robert Anderson of St. Martin's Parish, Hanover County, for 9 pounds, 200 acres on Beel's path, adj. Laffoon and adj. 200 acres sold to John Thompson; granted to the said David Staples by patent of 15 September 1752.
Wit: Henry Ellis, Samuel Gording, Hutchins Burton
Signed: David Staples, Christian Staples
Recorded 1st Mon. in November 1752

p.182  6 November 1752 Jacob Smith to Drury Wood, both of Henrico County, for 35 pounds, 100 acres adj. Mr. Byrd, Cannon, William Smith and his own lines.
Wit: none                                                            Signed: Jacob Smith
Anne, wife of Jacob Smith, relinquished her dower
Recorded 1st Mon. in November 1752

p.184  6 November 1752 deed of gift from John Goode of Henrico County to daughter, Susannah Clarke, wife of John Clarke, 100 acres for her natural life, being bounded by the Deep Run and the Great Meadow of Four Mile Creek; adj. James Whitlow and crossing Darby's Branch to the Deep Run and being the land whereon said John and Susannah Clarke now dwell; land to pass to grandson, Edward Clarke, son of the said John and Susannah Clarke.
Wit: none                                       Signed: John (his J mark) Goode
Recorded 1st Mon. in November 1752

p.184  6 November 1752 Samuel Garthright, Junr. to Julius Allen, both of Henrico County, for 34 pounds, 125 acres near Chickahominy Swamp, joining Joseph Childers and Miles Garthright; being the land purchased of William Matthews.
Wit: William Garthright, William Farris
Signed: Samuel Garthright
Recorded 1st Mon. in November 1752

p.185  18 June 1752 John Robinson of Lunenburg County to John Robinson, Jr., of Henrico County, his son, in consideration of natural love and affection and for the better maintenance and livelihood of the said John Robinson, Jr., all the lands which I hold in Henrico County: 130 acres whereon said John Robinson, Jr., now lives and 106 acres being on White Oak Swamp.
Wit: John Williamson, Jr., Richard Williamson, Robert Williamson
Signed: John (his 2 mark) Robertson

Recorded 1st Mon. in November 1752

p.187  30 November 1752 Thomas Atcheson, merchant, to John Orr, taylor, both of Henrico County, for 31 pounds 5 shillings, one-fourth of an acre in the Town of Richmond, Henrico County, being ½ of Lot 35 on the plan of said town and being the NW side of said lot.
Wit: Ch. Chalmers, Geddes Winston
Signed: Tho: Atchison
Recorded 1st Mon. in December 1752

p.187  4 December 1752 William Harding to John Robinson, Jr., both of Henrico County for 30 pounds, 50 acres on the Main Road a little below Deep Run and being the same parcel of land William Allin bought of John Robinson, Sr., father of the said John Robinson, Jr., and which said Allin conveyed to said Harding.
Wit: none                                              Signed: Wm. Harding
Recorded 1st Mon. in December 1752

p.188  4 December 1752 John Robinson to Alexander Robinson, both of Henrico County, for 35 pounds, 75 acres on the branches of Gillies Creek, being the parcel given to Jacob Robinson, by the last will and testament of John Robinson dated 5 December 1720, together with all right and title said John Robinson might now or hereafter claim to the tract of land given in the aforesaid will.
Wit: none                                              Signed: John Roberson
Ann, wife of John Robinson, released her dower
Recorded; 1st Mon. in December 1752

p.189  2 December 1752 Duncan Graham, merchant, of Hanover County to Mr. James Dennistonne, Michael Herries & Co. of Glasgow, merchants, for 245 pounds, two lots, each containing one-half acre, in Town of Richmond below Shockoe Creek in Henrico County, being Lots 31 and 44 on the plan of the said town.
Wit: Phil Watson, Abraham Cowley, Jr., James Lyle, Henry Timberlake
Signed: Dun. Graham              Recorded 1st Mon. in December 1752

p.190  4 December 1752 John Williamson to John Williamson, Jr., both of Henrico county, for 200 pounds, 600 acres, beginning at a corner pine of Henry Stokes standing in the fork of Trumpet Branch.
Wit: John (his ✚ mark) Mosby, Samuel (his S mark) Allin, Jr.,
Robert Williamson
Signed: John Williamson
Judith, wife of John Williamson, relinquished her dower

Recorded 1st Mon. in December 1752

p.191   4 December 1752   John Williamson to Samuel Allin, both of Henrico County, for 64 pounds and 14 shillings, 161 acres, on the NS of the brook, beginning at a corner pine on Henry Stokes' line and adj. Sharp (metes and bounds description).
Wit: John (his ✚ mark) Mosby, John Williamson, Jr., Robert Williamson
Signed: John Williamson
Judith, wife of John Williamson, relinquished her dower
Recorded 1st Mon. in December 1752

p.192   John Spears and James Spears, both of Albemarle County, brothers, to William Garthright of Henrico County, for 50 pounds, 200 acres on the SS of the Chickahominy River in the fork of a branch called Bore Swamp; adj. Robert Spears and Jacob Faris and the said William Garthright, adj. land formerly called William Mayes, and also adj. Richard Truman and Clopton; being land willed to his sons by Robert Spears and which Spears purchased of William Owl.
Wit: Julius Allin, Robert Spears, Matthew (his J mark) Johnson
Signed: John Spears, James Spears       Recorded 1st Mon. in December 1752

p.194   6 November 1752 William Harding to Martin Martin, both of Henrico County, for 30 pounds, 150 acres near Chickahominy River, adj. Thomas Elmore, Valentine Freeman, deceased, Anthony Matthews and Littleberry Allin; part of land belonging to Thomas Harding, deceased, father of said William Harding.
Wit: none                                       Signed: Wm. Harding
Recorded 1st Mon. in December 1752

p.195   1 January 1753 William Giles of Amelia County to Nicholas Giles of Henrico County, for 15 pounds, 150 acres being the land John Giles now lives on, adj. Thomas Moseley, Cary and Redford, Giles Branch and the road to Redford's Ferry.
Wit: Thomas Moseley, William Frayser, John Worsham
Signed: Willm Giles,  Ann, wife of William Giles, relinquished her dower
Recorded 1st Mon. in January 1753

p.196 1 January 1753 John Orange of Henrico County to John Douglas of Henrico County, for 3 pounds, 10 acres at John Watkins and John Lane's corner white oak at the ES of the Main road and crossing the said road; also adj. Henry Stokes, Capt. Watson, deceased and John Law.
Wit: William Miller, Rowland (his R mark) Blackburn
Signed: John (his f mark) Orange

Judith, wife of John Orange, relinquished her dower
Recorded 1st Mon. in January 1753

p. 198  20 November 1752 Power of attorney from Joseph Farrell of the City of Bristol, merchant, surviving partner with and executor under the will of his uncle, Joseph Farrell, deceased, of the same city to William Randolph of James River in the colony of Virginia, to settle with and to receive debts owing from Samuel Gleadon, Robert Stobs, and Col. John Henry, merchants of Virginia.
Wit: George Adderby, Benjamin King;  acknowledged before John Clements, mayor of Bristol.
Signed: Jos Ferell                           Recorded 5 February 1753

p.200  26 January 1753, Williamsburg, commission of Thomas Adams, Gent. as Clerk of Henrico County, from Thomas Nelson, Esq. Deputy Secretary, under authority of William Adair, Esq., Secretary of the Colony
Signed: Thos. Nelson                         Recorded 5 February 1753

p.200  Temperance Ballow, wife of Charles Ballow, relinquished her dower in land conveyed by her husband by deed recorded 1st Mon. in March 1750 to William Randolph, Gent.
Recorded 5 February 1753

p.200  3 February 1753 Edward Cooper, Esq., of the City of Bristol, to Richard Weir, merchant of Henrico County, for 355 pounds, a lot in the Town of Richmond, being Lot 18 on plan of said town.
Wit: Philip Rootes, Jr., Phil Watson, Henry Timberland
Signed: Edward Cooper by Philip Rootes, Gent., of King and Queen County, by a power of attorney dated 12 March 1749 under the seal of the Majoralty of the City of Bristol.                           Recorded 1st Mon. in February 1753

p.202  3 February 1753 Richard Weir of Henrico County to Philip Rootes, Gent., of King and Queen County, for 355 pounds, a lot in the Town of Richmond, being Lot 18 on plan of said town.
Wit: Philip Rootes, Jr., Phil Watson, Henry Timberlake
Signed: Richard Weir                         Recorded 5 February 1753

p.203  12 March 1749 Power of attorney from Edward Cooper, Esq., of the City of Bristol, to Major Philip Rootes of York River, Colony of Virginia, to contract for the sale of a lot in the Town of Richmond in the said Colony, which was conveyed to the said Edward Cooper by indenture dated 17 August (1748) from William Hopkins of Hanover County in said Colony, in order to be discharged from a bond

of indebtedness to the said Cooper in the amount of 537 pounds sterling.
Wit: Rowles Scudmore and Thomas Stokes of the City of Bristol on 30 April 1750 before Thomas Curtis, Mayor of said City
Signed: Ed Cooper                                          Recorded 5 February 1753

p.205  19 January 1753 report of Charles Woodson, Jno. Pleasants, Jr. and Henry Sharp, subscribers (commissioners), pursuant to the order of the Henrico County Court of January 1753 to assign the dower of Anne Enroughty, widow and relict of Edward Enroughty, deceased, being her third part of all lands and tenements her said husband possessed at the time of his death: beginning at a white oak in the line of Henry Sharp, thence a straight line to a corner red oak in Four Mile Creek, thence up the same to the bridge, thence down the Main Road to Henry Sharp's line, thence along his line to the beginning.
Recorded 5 February 1753

p.205  23 June 1751 Deed of Mortgage from Robert Weatherby of Goochland County to Hon. Peter Randolph, Esq., of Henrico County, to secure 38 pounds to be paid on or before 1 October next, collateral being all his Houses and Lots in the Town of Richmond.
Wit: Nicholas Scherrer, George Sherrer, James Lyle
Signed: Robert Withearle                                   Recorded 5 February 1753

p.206  31 January 1753 Report of Gearrard Ellyson, Francis Wagstaff and John Cocke, subscribers (commissioners), pursuant to the order of Henrico County Court of December 1752 to settle the estate of George Barker, deceased, and to assign the widow's dower. Met with the executors of the said George Barker, deceased, and after deducting charges against said estate, assigned to Rebecca Barker, widow, 24 pounds 17 shillings and 8 pence, being her one-third part of the personal estate of 75 pounds 8 shillings and 6 pence, and also assigned her third share in her deceased husband's land and plantation.
Recorded 5 February 1753

p.207  5 March 1753 Henry Cox of Chesterfield County to Joseph Bayley of Henrico County, for 25 pounds, 50 acres given to the said Henry Cox by his deceased father, Richard Cox, except half an acres where the said Richard Cox and his wife and son's children of my brother John Cox are buried; bounds are mentioned in the will of Richard Cox, land being bounded by John and Richard Cox, running down to the Holly Spring.
Wit: none                                                  Signed: Henry Cox
Recorded 5 March 1753

P.207 18 January 1753 John Monrow of Prince William County to Bowler Cocke, Jr., of Bremo, Henrico County, for 100 pounds, one Negro man named Toney.
Wit: Charles Carter, Nathaniel Wilkinson, H. Byrd
Signed: John Monroe
Recorded 5 March 1753

p.208 22 November 1752 Power of attorney from Gabriel Mathie, merchant, of Grenock, County of Renfrew, North Britain, lawful father of Alexander Mathie, deceased, later assistant storekeeper with Mr. James Stark, merchant, of Appomattox [River], Colony of Virginia, to the said James Starke, to ask, levy, demand and recover debts owing to said deceased son in the Colony of Virginia.
Wit: James Dunlop, John McKenzey, James Barnhill
Signed: Gabriel Mathie, before James Butcher, a baliff of Grenock
Recorded 5 March 1753

p.209 6 August 1752 William Sharp, blacksmith, to John Pleasants, merchant, son of Thomas Pleasants, deceased, both of Henrico County, for 150 pounds, 125 acres on Four Mile Creek; being bounded on the south by the said creek, on the west by the lands of Four Mile Creek Mill and the lands of Thomas Bates, on the east by the lands of John Pleasants and Edward Goode and on the west by Joseph Pleasants, and being the land said Sharp bought of the said Joseph Pleasants, bearing date the second of this Instant [2 December 1751].
Wit: Richard Coward, Robert Pleasants, Jr., George Robertson, John Fussell, William (his + mark) Focitt, Henry Watkins and James (his ✚ mark) Lipshott
Signed: William (his W mark) Sharp
Susanna, wife of William Sharp, relinquished her dower
Recorded 5 March 1753

p.211 14 February 1753 George Adams to John Pleasants of Baileys, both of Henrico County, for 15 pounds and 10 shillings, 100 acres adj. Benjamin Jordan, Walter Leigh, Richard Moore, Thomas Watkins and John Carter.
Wit: Henry Watkins, David Gill, Nathaniel Wilkinson
Signed: George Adams                         Recorded 5 March 1753

p.212 5 December 1752 John Cole of Lunenburg County to Archibald Cary of Chesterfield County, for 25 pounds, 25 acres, being the tract contiguous to and commonly know as Cary's Ferry and being on the James River adj. the lines of William Randolph, Gent.
Wit: Ben Watkins, Seth Ward, Thomas Yuille
Signed: John (his I mark) Cole                Recorded 5 March 1753

p.213  5 March 1753 Brazure Cocke, Gent., late of Henrico County to Charles Turnbull, merchant of Petersburg, Dinwiddie County, for 210 pounds, 628 acres, being the tract granted to Thomas Cocke, lately deceased, by patent of 24 October 1701.
Wit: none                                          Signed: Breazare Cocke
Recorded 5 March 1753


p.214  19 February 1753 Deed of Mortgage from William Shields to John Pleasants & Son, all of Henrico County, for 15 pounds 12 shillings and 11 pence to be paid by 1 March 1754, collateral being 50 acres, the plantation whereon said William Shields now dwellest, adj. John Middleton and John Brackett.
Wit: Robert Elan, John Webster, Thomas Stoors
Signed: William Shiels
Received 5 March 1753 and, for further proof, recorded 2 April 1753


p.215  2 April 1753 Stephen Wood of Goochland County to John Wood of Henrico County, for 25 pounds, 100 acres that I bought of William Spraggings, adj. David Brodne (?), William Fleming Cocke and Thomas Cocke.
Wit: James Gunn, John Forsie, David Burton
Signed: Stephen Wood
Ann, wife of Stephen Wood, relinquished her dower
Recorded 2 April 1753


p.216  6 November 1752 Deed of Mortgage from Samuel Gleadowe, Gent. to Isaac Winston, both of Henrico County, for 200 pounds to be paid Winston within four years from date, collateral being Gleadowe's right, title and interest in slaves, viz.: Cesar, Pharoah, Tom, Primus, Samuel, John, Harry & Billey, men slaves; Aggy, Phebe, Charlotte, Sarah & Lucy, women slaves; and Sarah and Nimrod, children of Aggy; one chaise & harness for two horses; five beds and furniture; two chests with drawers; two desks; one clock. two looking glasses; and two horses.
Wit: W. Battersby, Richard Rockett, Daniel Vandewall
Signed: Sam Gleadowe                               Recorded 2 April 1753


p.217  2 April 1753 Apprenticeship Bond between Henry Timberlake, son of Richard Timberlake of Henrico County, and Philip Watson and Philip Rootes, Junr., to be trained in the science or trade which they now use until said Henry shall arrive at the age of 21 years.
Wit: none                                          Signed: Henry Timberlake
Recorded 2 April 1753


p.218  same Apprenticeship Bond dated 2 April 1753 as preceding

Signed: Philip Watson, Philip Rootes, Junr.   Recorded 2 April 1753

p.219  2 April 1753 Apprenticeship Bond between John Forsie, joyner, and Thomas Dean, orphan, to be apprenticed to Forsie until he arrives at 21 years of age, to be trained in the full art and mystery of a shop joyner.
Wit: Robert Burton, James Gunn
Signed: John Forsie, Thomas (his  M  mark) Dean   Recorded 2 April 1753

p.219  20 December 1752 Andrew Castlin to Ann Skinner, for 9 pounds, lot of ½ acre in Town of Richmond, and being Lot 71 on the plan of the town.
Wit: Benj. Burton, Junr., Philip Rootes, Junior
Signed: Andrew Castlin   Recorded 2 April 1753

p.220  2 April 1753 William Smith and Mary, his wife, of Cumberland County, to Jacob Smith of Henrico County, for 40 pounds, 400 acres on the south side of the Chickahominy Swamp, adj. Robert Morris, William Turner and Pierce Griffin; being the tract of land formerly belonging to Thomas Conner.
Wit: William Smith, Barrett White, John White
Signed: William Smith, Mary Smith
Recorded 2 April 1753

p.221  2 April 1753 Apprenticeship bond from James Cheek to Elisha Miller, saddler, both of Henrico County, to learn Miller's trade or mystery for the term of three and one half years ensuing.
Wit: Langston Bacon, Thomas Owen
Signed: James (his  ✚  mark) Cheek   Recorded 2 April 1753

p.223  29 November 1752 Power of attorney from George Sterlin, merchant of Glasgow, to James Lyle, merchant in Richmond, Virginia, to ask, demand, sue for, recover and receive from Robert Lyon sometime barber in Greenock and now wigmaker in Williamsburg, Virginia and James Crawford, sometimes weaver in Glasgow and now merchant in Norfolk, Virginia.
Wit: Patrick Telfer, James Clarke
Signed: George Sterling, certified by John Brown, Esq., provost of the city
  of Glasgow
Recorded 2 April 1753

p.224  17 January 1753 William Randolph, Gent., of Henrico County, to William Byrd of Westover, Charles City County for 2,500 pounds, 5,000 acres known as Westham, being the entire tract lately purchased by the said William Randolph of his brother, Hon. Peter Randolph, Esq., to whom the same was devised by his later

father, the Hon. William Randolph, and his brother, Beverley Randolph, deceased; but agreement for Randolph's slaves to be suffered to continue on the within lands until 20 October next ensuing to finish their crop.
Wit: Peyton Randolph, Charles Carter, Bowler Cocke, Jr., John Wayles
Signed: William Randolph                            Recorded 3 April 1753

p.225   27 March 1753 Mary Allin of Henrico County, for love, goodwill and affection, and upon her decease, to son, James Allin, the land and plantation whereon I now live and which I bought of John Shoemaker, containing 100 acres, also one feather bed, iron pot and one cow and calf; to daughter, Elizabeth, one feather bed and furniture, flat pewter dish, two deep pewter plates, one gold ring and one pewter basin; and to daughter, Mary, two cows and calves, one large deep dish, three deep pweter plates, one small iron pot and one gold ring.
Wit: William Street, Jane Street, Joseph Street
Signed: Mary (her  T  mark) Allin                    No date of record

p.226   25 September 1752 Robert Sharp of Henrico County to James Brewer of Hanover County, for 40 pounds current money of Virginia and 1,000 pounds of tobacco, 130 acres lying on the main Uphram Brook, adj. William Tyree and William Kelley.
Wit: William Sharp, Williamson [?] Snead, Joseph Bailey
Signed: Robert (his  R  mark) Sharp
Susanna, wife of Robert Sharp, relinquished her dower
Recorded 7 May 1753

p.227   7 March 1753 John Robertson, son of Isaac Robertson of Chesterfield County, to Matthew Bridgeman, for 8 pounds, a tract given to me by my deceased grandfather, John Robertson, by his last will and testament dated 5 December 1720, and bounded as in the said will is mentioned.
Wit: Richard Hooper, William Bridgeman
Signed: John (his  R  mark) Robertson                Recorded 7 May 1753

p.228  25 April 1753 Alexander Robinson, Sr., to Alexander Robinson, Jr., for love and effects that I bear, the tract of land which my father left me, adj. my sons John Robinson and Thomas Robinson.
Wit: Edmund Brewer, John Rice
Signed: Alexander (his  +  mark) Robertson           Recorded 7 May 1753

p.229  24 May 1753 William Cannon of Amelia County to Drury Wood of Henrico County, for 30 pounds, 100 acres, 50 acres of which are described by patent bearing date of 17 August 1725 to John Cannon, adj. Obidiah Smith, Col. Byrd and Gilley;

and the other 50 acres adj. the above, adj. William Byrd, Esq., Samuel Duvall, Nathaniel Vanderwall, Jacob Smith and Drury Wood.
Wit; Dasey Southall, Stephen Wood, Isaac Johnson
Signed: William Cannon                                    Recorded 7 May 1753

p.230  4 June 1753 Archibald Cary of Chesterfield County to William Randolph of Henrico County, for 53 pounds and 15 shillings, 25 acres adj. the said William Randolph whereon he now lives and is land whereon said Cary formerly kept a ferry.
Wit: none                                                 Signed: Archibd. Cary
Recorded 3 June 1753

p.231  4 June 1753 Power of attorney from James Cocke of Henrico County to Thomas Cocke and James Cocke of Goochland County, trusty and loving friends, to recover debts.
Wit: John Pleasants, William Ellis
Signed: James Cooke                                       Recorded 3 June 1753

p.232  4 June 1753 William North to John North, both of Henrico County, for 35 pounds, 100 acres on a branch of the Deep Run called the Old House Branch, which said William North bought of John Kenny.
Wit: Christopher John Thomas, Rene Laforce, Robt. Gooding
Signed: William North
Mary, wife of William North, relinquished her dower
Recorded 3 June 1753

p.233  10 June 1753 Deed of Mortgage from Richard Holland of Henrico County to Robert Donald of Hanover County, merchant, for 5 shillings, Negroes Jenny, Sarah, Nead, Phillis, Leddis and Hannah, to secure payment of a bill of exchange this day drawn by said Holland on Mr. Leighton Ward of Bristol, merchant, for 200 pounds sterling with lawful interest thereon to be paid at or upon 1 April next.
Wit: Hard. Burnley, William Harding
Signed: Richd. Holland                                    Recorded 3 June 1753

p.236  2 June 1753 William Buxton to Nicholas Conaway, both of Henrico County, for 50 pounds, 100 acres, being the tract William Buxton bought of James Connaway.
Wit: Christopher John Thomas, Charles Cottrell, John North, John Lankester
Signed: William Buxton                                    Recorded 2 July 1753

p.237  16 June 1753 Edward Watkins of Cumberland County to Edward Curd,

William Smith, Samuel Morris, Turner Richardson, Joshua Morris, John White, Aaron Truhart, Michel Jones, John Oakly, Alexander Robinson, Richard Williamson, Obadiah Smith, Jacob Smith, Henry Stoakes, Nathaniel Bacon, John Owen, Julius Allin, Martin Burton, John Warrinner, Richard Truman, John Price and Dudly Brook, all of Henrico County, for 20 shillings, one acre or thereabout, being part of the tract my son, Thomas Watkins, now lives on.
Wit: Matthew Taylor, Samuel Bellamy, Thomas Watkins, John Watkins, Mark Taylor
Signed: Edward (his ✚ mark) Watkins                    Recorded 2 July 1753

p.238   2 July 1753 Nicholas Connaway to William Buxton, both of Henrico County, for 100 pounds, 100 acres, being the tract which John Walters gave James Connaway and Ann, his wife by deed of gift.
Wit: Christopher John Thomas, Charles Cottrell, John North
Signed: Nicolas (his N mark) Connaway
Agnes, wife of Nicholas Connaway, relinquished her dower
Recorded 2 July 1753

p.239  (blank) 1746 John Patterson of Dale Parish, Henrico County, to Ralph Jackson and Joseph Jackson, sons-in-law, for careful maintenance while I live with a decent burial Christianlike, all my lands to be equally divided, Ralph Jackson to have the plantation with the appurtenances and personal estate thereon, except my Great Bible and great brass kettle and one young cow; Bible to Ralph and kettle to Joseph; sealed by the gift and delivery of a key to the new house to said Ralph and Joseph Jackson.
Wit: George Cogbill, Elkanah Anderson, Francis (his I mark) Histole
Signed: John (his II mark) Pattison
Recorded 1st Mon. in January 1746; further proved 2 July 1753

p.240 (no date) Philemon Frayser to William Frayser, both of Henrico County, for 12 pounds, 50 acres on the north side of the Main Road and on the upper side of Four Mile Creek, beginning at mouth of the Miery Run, thence along William Frayser's old line to Joseph Adkinson's line to the Main Road, thence down the road to Sandy Bottom, thence down the Miery Run.
Wit: John Williams, Edward Enroughty, Henry Watkins
Signed: Philemon Frayser
Mary, wife of Philemon Frayer, relinquished her dower
Recorded 2 July 1753

p.241  5 June 1753 Apprenticeship bond from Zachariah White, son of John White of Lunenburg County, to Richard Green of Henrico County, to be apprenticed to

42

learn the art, trade and mystery of a house joyner and to serve six years from 9 March next ensuing.
Wit: Samuel Duvall, Wood Jones
Signed: Zachariah White, Richard Green, John White
Recorded 2 July 1753; (same instrument re-recorded on page 242).

p.243  5 June 1753 Apprenticeship Bond from William White, son of John White of Lunenburg County to Jonathan Ray of Henrico County, to be apprenticed to learn the art, trade and mystery of a house joyner and to serve six years from this date.
Wit: Samuel Duvall, Wood Jones
Signed: William White, Jonathan Ray, John White
Recorded 2 July 1753; same instrument re-recorded on page 244

p.245  2 July 1753 Martin Martin and Barbary, his wife, to James Allin, all of Henrico County, for 65 pounds, 200 acres on the southside of Hughes Branch, adj. Valentine Freeman, Thomas Elmore, Littleberry Allin and Anthony Matthews.
Wit: John Roberson, William Warrinner
Signed: Martain Martain
Barbary, wife of Martin Martin, relinquished her dower
Recorded 2 July 1753

p.247  1 July 1753 John Roberson, Jr., to Martin Martin, both of Henrico County, for 40 pounds, 106 acres on the south side of White Oak Swamp, being one-fifth part of a tract taken up by Thomas East, Sr., Robert Woodson, Sr., John Woodson, William Parker and Robert Clarke, which said one-fifth was given by Thomas East to his daughter, Navel, grandmother to the said John Robinson, Sr., by deed bearing date 1690.
Wit: Ephraim Garthright, William Warrinner, James Allin
Signed: John Roberson, Jr.
Ann, wife of John Roberson, Jr., relinquished her dower
Recorded 2 July 1753

p.248  2 July 1753 Edmund Borum to Richard Hynes of Henrico County, for 50 pounds, a parcel on Upram Brook adj. John Williamson and John Lankford (metes and bounds description).
Wit: none                                         Signed: Edmund Borum
Recorded 2 July 1753

p.249  2 July 1753 Michael Jones, and Ann, his wife, of Henrico County, to John Barnes of James City County, for 10 pounds, 92 acres on Gilley's Creek, adj. John

Fason, John Watson's old survey to the said Michael Jones bearing date 1 June 1750.
Wit: James Cocke, Joseph Lewis, Robert Spears
Signed: Michael Jones, Anne (her ✚ mark) Jones
Recorded 2 July 1753

p.251  5 August 1753 Thomas Cardwell of Henrico County to Robert Yaxley, bricklayer, for 12 pounds, a lot in the Town of Richmond below Shockoe Creek containing near half an acre, being Lot Q on the plan of the town.
Wit: Dasby Southall, John Branch
Signed: Thos. Cardwell

p.254  7 July 1753 William Harding, merchant of Henrico County, to Philemon Williams, planter, for 20 pounds, 200 acres adj. David Staples (metes and bounds description).
Wit: Richard Loving, Thomas Harding, John (his I mark) Lankaster
Signed: Wm. Harding                                    Recorded 6 August 1753

p.255  24 August 1753 John Pleasants, Jr., to George Adams, both of Henrico County, for 15 pounds 18 shillings 2 pence half penny, 100 acres, being the same land said Adams made a deed of bargain and sale to said Pleasants for 15 pounds 10 shillings debt, and being all the land the said Adams is possessed within the county of Henrico.
Wit: Henry Watkins, John Carter, John (his S mark) Warrinner,
  John (his O mark) Toms
Signed: Jno. Pleasants, Jr.                          Recorded 3 September 1753

p.257  25 August 1753 George Adams to John Carter, both of Henrico County, for 15 pounds, 50 acres near Chickahominy Swamp, adj. said Carter, an old field called Willises and Benjamin Jordan.
Wit: Jno. Pleasants, Jr., Henry Watkins, John Warrinner,
  John (his [blank] mark) Tombs
Signed: George Adams                                 Recorded 3 September 1753

p.258  1 September 1753 John Shoemaker of Henrico County to Godfrey Piles of Amelia County, for 22 pounds, 10 shillings, 110 acres on Deep Run, being part of tract of 192 acres granted to said Shoemaker by patent and is part of tract said Godfrey Piles formerly lived on.
Wit: David Staples, Richard Cottrell, Thomas Harding, William Buxton
Signed: John Shewmaker                               Recorded 3 September 1753

[pages 259-266 estate records]

p.266  1 October 1753 Harding Burnley of Hanover County to John Martin of the Kingdom of Ireland, for 5 pounds, 7 shillings and 6 pence, Lot 66 in the Town of Westham. Wit: none
Signed: Hard. Burnley     Recorded 1 October 1753

p.267  1 October 1753 Harding Burley of Hanover County to John Martin of the Kingdom of Ireland, for 5 pounds, 7 shillings and 6 pence, Lot 17 in the Town of Westham. Wit: none
Signed: Hard. Burnley     Recorded 1 October 1753

p.267  1 October 1753 William Edwards of Henrico County to John Harwood, carpenter, for 50 pounds, 100 acres adj. Nathaniel Vandewall, John Harwood & Edward Curd, which land was formerly conveyed to said William Edwards by Henry Brazeab by deed of gift dated 21 June 1720.
Wit: Wm. Dinquid, Milner Redford, Thomas Williams
Signed: William (his W mark) Edwards
Elizabeth, wife of William Edwards, relinquished her dower
Recorded 1 October 1753

p.269  1 October 1753 John Shewmaker of Henrico County to Major Bowler Cocke, Junr., and Samuel Duvall, church wardens of Henrico Parish, for 100 pounds of tobacco, an acre of land on which the church of Deep run is built and now standing, forever.
Wit: none     Signed: John Shewmaker
Ann, wife of John Shewmaker, relinquished her dower
Recorded 1 October 1753

p.270  1 October 1753 John Shewmaker to John Pimble, both of Henrico County, for 10 pounds, 100 acres, less & except the acre whereon the chappell house stands, adj. one Foard and Thomas Alley on one side and the Main Road on the other side.
Wit: H. Wilkinson, Leonard Henley, Nathaniel Wilkinson
Signed: John Shewmaker
Anne, wife of John Shewmaker, relinquished her dower
Recorded 1 October 1753

p.271  4 August 1753 Charles Ellis and Susanna Ellis, his wife, to William Ellis, all of Henrico County, for 100 pounds, 100 acres on Tuckahoe Creek, being the parcel of land whereon the said Charles Ellis now lives and which was left to him by his

father, John Ellis, in his last will and testament, and now being in the possession of the said William Ellis; adj. William Ellis, Joseph Ellis, Peter Brown, Col. Richard Randolph and Tuckahoe Creek.
Wit: Wm. Street, John Ellis, Joseph Ellis, Abraham (his A mark) North
Signed: Charles Ellis, Susanna Ellis
Recorded 1 October 1753

[pages 274-276 estate records]

p.277  1 October 1753 John Oakley to Philip Mayo, both of Henrico County, for 18 pounds, 123 acres near the head of White Oak Swamp, being part of a tract of 532 granted to Thomas Oakley by patent of 30 August 1744; adj. Isaac Breeding, New Kent Road and Stegar's line (metes and bounds description).
Wit: none                                                              Signed: John Oakley
Elizabeth, wife of John Oakley, relinquished her dower
Recorded 1 October 1753

p.279  25 April 1753 William Acrill of Charles City County to Thomas Adams of Henrico County, for 155 pounds, 184 acres at a place called Pirtranoquy, the land known by the name of Locust Neck.
Wit: W. Byrd, John Pettit, John Wayles, Richard Adams, George Webb, Junr.
Signed: William Acrill
Received 3 June 1753 and recorded 1 October 1753 upon further proof

p.280  5 March 1753 a release from John Pleasants, Jr. to John Oakley for a mortgage of 40 pounds on 26 August 1751, for a slave Phillip.
Wit: Thomas Wild, William Smith, Dudley Brooke
Signed: Jno. Pleasants, Junr.                          Recorded 5 March 1753

p. 281  7 January 1754 Nathaniel Bridgwater to son, William Bridgwater, both of Henrico County, for love, good will and affection, 133 acres whereon said William Bridgwater now lives, on south side of Uphram Brook, adj. William Snead, William Sims and Johnnathan Bridgwater.
Wit: William Kelley, Johnnathan Bridgwater, William Snead
Signed: Nathaniel (his NB mark) Bridgwater

p.282  7 January 1754 Nathaniel Bridgwater to son, Johnnathan Bridgwater, both of Henrico County, for love, good will and affection, 133 acres whereon said Johnnathan Bridgwater now lives, on main Uphram Brook and Parker's Horsepen Branch, adj. William Kelley, William Sims and William Bridgwater.
Wit: William Kelley, William Bridgwater

Signed: Nathaniel (his NB mark) Bridgwater
Recorded 7 January 1754

p.283  7 January 1754 John Law to John Cornet, both of Henrico County, for 15 pounds, 39 acres adj. Matthew Hobson, William Owen, and John Owen.
Wit: none                                         Signed: John (his  I  mark) Law
Sarah, wife of John Law, relinquished her dower
Recorded 7 January 1754

p.284  3 December 1753 Thomas Wood of Henrico County to Jacob Ege of the Town of Richmond in same county, for 10 pounds, 4 acres on Shockoe Creek, being part of the tract whereon said Thomas Wood now lives, adj. Col. Bird (metes and bounds description).
Wit: William Street, Joseph Pleasants, Nicholas Scherrer
Signed: Thomas (his  T  mark) Wood
Martha, wife of Thomas Wood, relinquished her dower
Recorded 7 January 1754

p.286  10 July 1753 Evan Shoemaker to Samuel Gleadowe, both of Henrico County, for 6 pounds, 15 shillings and 4 pence, 100 acres including the plantation I now live on on Tuckahoe (Creek), adj. Benjamin Johnson and Gervas Burdett.
Wit: Abraham Cowley, Loudwick Worrock, Giles Letcher
Signed: Evan (his  E  mark) Shoemaker
Recorded 4 February 1754

p.287  10 July 1753 Gervas Burdett to Samuel Gleadowe, for 20 pounds, 17 shillings and 6 pence, 103 acres ye land I now live on lying on Tuckahoe (Creek), which was purchased of William Lawless.
Wit: Abraham Cowley, Loudwick Worrock, Giles Letcher
Signed: Gervas Burdett                            Recorded 4 February 1754

p.288  1 February 1754 John Pleasants, son of Thomas, to David Gill, both of Henrico County, for 16 pounds, a tract of land bounded as shown in deed of record for the same from Jane Scott to said John Pleasants.
Wit: Henry Watkins, John Bell, Edward (his ✚ mark) Matthews
Signed: Jno. Pleasants, Junr.                     Recorded 4 February 1754

p.289 9 January 1754 James Meredith of Cumberland County and Southam Parish to Richard Holland of Henrico County, for 36 pounds and 15 shillings, 250 acres on Meredith's Branch, joining Robert Webb, Thomas Bowles and the plantation said Holland sold to William Hughes.

Wit: Tucker Woodson, John Mouldon, James (his ✚ mark) Dunn
Signed: Jas. Meredith                               Recorded 4 February 1754

p.290  30 October 1753 William Buxton of Henrico County to Charles Cotterall of Cumberland County, for 26 pounds, 120 acres, being the tract of land which John Walters gave James Connaway and Ann, his wife, by deed of gift.
Wit: Christopher John Thomas, Robert Burton, Nowell Burton, Benjamin Clarke, John (his I mark) Lankaster, Richard Cotterall
Signed: William Buxton
Jane, wife of William Buxton, relinquished her dower
Recorded 4 February 1754

p.291  4 February 1754 Edward Goode, the elder, to John Pleasants, (Junr.), son of Thomas Pleasants, both of Henrico County, for 60 pounds, that tract on the branches of Four Mile Creek known by the name of Hackney; one moiety of which was purchased of John Matthews by deed dated 3 November 1716 and the other moiety purchased of Henry Matthews by deed dated 9 August 1729, said lands were devised to said John and Henry Matthews by their father, Edward Matthews by his last will and testament dated 26 August 1706.
Wit: none                                           Signed: Edward Goode
Recorded 4 February 1754

p.294  30 January 1754 Francis Redford to Robert Pleasants, both of Henrico County, for 107 pounds and 10 shilings, 225 acres being at a place called Gravely Hill and being the land given him by his late father, John Redford, deceased; bounded by the land of the said Robert Pleasants, Kingsland Road, the run called the Little Round, John Bolling and Abraham Childers.
Wit: William Clark, Thomas Royster, John (his J mark) Jordan, Thomas Storrs, John Williams
Signed: Frans: Redford                              Recorded 4 February 1754

p.296  4 March 1754 William Britton to Isaac Winston, Junr. both of Henrico County, for 150 pounds on the south side of the Chickahominy Swamp, adj. said Winston and Robert Moseby.
Wit: Robert Yaxley, William Sharp, William Allin
Signed: William (his W mark) Britton
Elizabeth, wife of William Britton, relinquished her dower
Recorded 4 March 1754

p.297  20 November 1753 Charles Ellis of Henrico County to Colonel John Martin of the City of Dublin, Kingdom of Ireland, for 50 pounds, two lots in the Town of

Westham, each containing one-half acre, being Lots 4 and 152.
Wit: Philip Rootes, Junior, Alexander McCaul, James Lyles; also Benjamin Harrison and William Ellis to the receipt of 50 pounds by the said Ellis.
Signed: Charles Ellis                                              Recorded 4 March 1754

p.298  2 October 1753 Deed of Mortgage from Giles Letcher of Henrico County to Richard Oswald & Co. of London, merchants, for 200 pounds, 19 shillings and 8 pence to be paid within 30 months next ensuing, collateral being Sue, a Negro wench; Silvia, a Negro girl; Jack, a Negro boy; seven feather beds and furniture; three horses and one mare; one desk; one chest of drawers and two tables.
Wit: Charles Chalmers, Thomas Skinner, Thomas Atchison
Signed: Giles Letcher
Recorded 7 January 1754; further proved on 4 April 1754

p.300  30 August 1753 William Linch, and Mary, his wife, of Halifax County, to John Pleasants, Junr., of Henrico County, for 10 pounds, all their right, title and interest as heirs-at-law of John Matthews in a tract of land devised under the will of Edward Matthews of Henrico County dated 26 August 1706 to his sons, John and Henry Matthews; said John Matthews died without issue; Mary, wife of William Linch and Sarah, wife of William Hargess of Albemarle County, were the daughters of Edward Matthews the younger, a son and heir of the testator.
Wit: Henry Watkins, Henry Sharp, Thomas Matthews, Mary Sharp, Marthew (Martha) (her ✚ mark) Matthews
Signed: William Linch (his ⚔ mark), Mary (her | mark) Linch
Recorded 4 February 1754

p.301  28 December 1753 William Hargess, and Sarah, his wife, of Albemarle County, to John Pleasants, Junr., of Henrico County, for 9 pounds, all their right, title and interest as heirs-at-law of John Matthews, in a tract of land devised under the will of Edward Matthews of Henrico County dated 26 August 1706 to his sons, John and Henry Matthews; said John Matthews died without issue; Mary, wife of William Linch and Sarah, wife of William Hargess of Albemarle County, were the daughters of Edward Matthews the younger, a son and heir of the testator.
Wit: John Williams, Thomas Matthews, John Jordan, Amos Liptrol
Signed: William (his W mark) Hargess, Sarah (her V mark) Hargess
Recorded 4 February 1754

p.304  Dedimus [writ to examine witness] of 13 August 1753 to Richard Booker, Thomas Tabb and Samuel Terry, Gentlemen [Justices] of Amelia County, for Mildred, wife of William Cannon of Amelia County. so sickly that she cannot travel to court. Deed of 4 May 1753 from William Cannon to Drury Wood of

Henrico cited. Said Mildred Cannon relinquished her right to dower in reference to said deed.
Signed: Saml. Terry, Thomas Tabb
Recorded 4 March 1754


p.305  1 April 1754 John Lipscomb, and Judith, his wife, of Henrico County, to William Sims of Lunenburg County, for 50 pounds, 200 acres, it being the one part of the land whereon said John Lipscomb now liveth; adj. Jonathan and William Bridgwater, Col. Byrd, William Sims and Jordan's Branch.
Wit: none                                                                    Signed: Jno. Lipscomb
Recorded 1 April 1754


p.306  1 April 1754 David Staples, and Christian, his wife, to John Thompson, all of Henrico County, for 12 pounds, 200 acres adj. Michael Goings, Thomas Bowlses, Robert Anderson and Laffoon, and adj. tract known as Beeals.
Wit: Leonard Henley, Charles Ellis, William Ford
Signed: David Staples, Chrisn. Staples
Recorded 1 April 1754


p.307 Elizabeth Tyree, wife of William Tyree, relinquished her right to dower upon examination by the Court, to land conveyed to Edmond Borum.
Recorded 1 April 1754


p.307 Mortgage of 4 January 1754 from Richard Holland and Sarah, his wife, to Andrew Cockran and James Donald of Glasgow, Scotland, merchants, to secure indebtedness of 235 pounds, 18 shillings and 8 pence, collateral being 372 acres on Tuckahoe Creek acquired by deed of 9 May 1752 from Joseph and Jane Freeman; 250 acres on Meredith's Branch, adj. Robert Webb, Thomas Boles and the land lately sold to William Hughes, acquired by deed of 9 January 1752 from James Meredith of Cumberland County; and three Negro slaves: Robin, Harry and Daniel.
Wit: Robert Donald, David Hudson, George Hudson, Elis Hardson, Alexander Boyd
Signed: Richard Holland, Sarah Holland
Recorded 1 April 1754


p.311 25 January 1754 Richard East to William Buxton, both of Henrico County, for 30 pounds, 100 acres on the east side of Deep Run, adj. Edward Pryer, Drinking Hole Branch, Thomas Pass, John Lacey, Robert Childers and John White.
Wit: Thomas (his T mark) Pass, Nicholas (his N mark) Conaway,
Walter (his M mark) Crew, Richard Cotteral
Signed: Richard East

Elizabeth, wife of Richard East, relinquished her dower
Recorded 1st Mon. in April 1754

p.313 4 May 1754 Francis Wagstaff of Henrico County to Isaac White of Lancaster County (and upper precinct of Christ Church Parish), for 200 pounds, 300 acres adj. Francis Watkins, Thomas Watkins, Thomas Bates, Gerrard Ellyson, Richard Moore and Robert Faris.
Wit: Elizabeth (her ✚ mark) Baker, Agness (her O mark) Moore, Marke Clarke
Signed: Francis Wagstaff           Recorded 4 May 1754

p.314 6 May 1754 William Smith to Drury Wood, both of Henrico County, for 38 pounds, 150 acres adj. Kennon's Branch on the Brook Road, Jacob Smith, John Smith, Meadow Road and Drury Wood.
Wit: none           Signed: William Smith
Mary, wife of William Smith, relinquished her dower
Recorded 6 May 1754

p.316 6 May 1754 Drury Wood to Samuel DuVal, both of Henrico County, for 25 pounds, 110 acres on Cannon's Branch adj. the Honorable William Byrd and Nathaniel Vandevall (metes and bounds description).
Wit: none           Signed: Drury Wood
Susanna, wife of Drury Wood, relinquished her dower
Recorded 6 May 1754

p.317 6 May 1754 Jacob Burton to Lizbit Tirpin (male), for 90 pounds, 200 acres adj. Abraham Bailey, said Tirpin, John Cox, Cole's Run, John Ellis and Miery Run.
Wit: none           Signed: Jacob Burton
Recorded 6 May 1754

p.318 18 October 1753 John Hanbury, London merchant, to Col. Richard Randolph of James River, Colony of Virginia, Esq., one of the executors of his father, Richard Randolph, deceased, for 25 shillings and for divers other good causes, the assignment of a mortgage and all interest in collateral thereunder. The estate of the elder Randolph assumed the liability of a debt incurred by an indenture of mortgage of 19 November 1748 between John Randolph, Gent., formerly of Bruton Parish, York County, Virginia, but then of Middle Temple, London, and said John Hanbury, in which said John Randolph was to pay 1200 pounds by the first of June next ensuing but he defaulted in the terms of payment, collateral being a tract of land in James City County, Virginia, by name of Porter's, and which came into said Randolph's possession by will of his father, the late Sir John Randolph of Virginia.
Wit: William Tudman of the Parish of St. Edmund, by deposition taken before the

Lord Mayer of London, Sir Crisp Gascoyne
Signed: John Hanbury                                    Recorded 6 May 1754

p.321  2 April 1754 William Allin, and Agness, his wife, of Henrico County to John Norton of Cumberland County, for 50 pounds, 100 acres, being the tract Jacob Robertson sold to Agnes Willis by deed of record.
Wit: Christopher John Thomas, William North, Thomas North, Price Willis, William Willis, Anthony North
Signed: William Allen, Agness (her A mark) Allen
Recorded 6 May 1754

p.322  6 May 1754 William Lewis of Henrico County to Charles Lewis, son, for natural love and affection and for better maintenance and livelihood, tract on the south side of the Chickahominy Swamp which I purchased of Luke Smith; life estate reserved for said William Lewis and Mary, his wife.
Wit: none                                               Signed: William Lewis
Recorded 6 May 1754

p.322  8 December 1753 William Harding to Stephen Spurlock, both of Henrico County, for 8 pounds, 60 acres on Pounces road, adj. Philemon Williams, Evan Shewmaker, Benjamin Johnson and Richard Levin's path.
Wit: Christopher John Thomas, Benjamin Johnson,
James (his C mark) Conaway, John (his I mark) Decree
Signed: William Harding                                 Recorded 6 May 1754

p.325  3 June 1754 Pouncy Anderson and Henry Martin, executors of Michael Holland, deceased to John Lankaster, Jr., of Henrico County, for 20 pounds and divers other good causes, 200 acres adj. John White (metes and bounds description).
Wit: William Harding, John Ellis, Christopher John Thomas
Signed: Pouncey Anderson, Henry Martin
Recorded 3 June 1754

p.326  3 June 1754 Jacob Bugg of Chesterfield County to Isaac Younghusband, mariner, for 205 pounds, 200 acres on the James River about 3½ miles below the Falls and at the mouth of Deep Bottom (metes and bounds description).
Wit: Matthew Woodson, Geddes Winston
Signed: Jacob Bugg                                      Recorded 3 June 1754

p.327  31 April 1754 Pouncy Anderson and Henry Martin, executors of Michael Holland, deceased, to Robert Allin of Henrico County, for 34 pounds and 125

shillings, 346 acres on the northern branch of Upram Brook, which was patented by said decedent and directed to be sold pursuant to his last will and testament (metes and bounds description). Wit: none
Signed: Pouncey Anderson, Henry Martin
Recorded 4 June 1754

p.328  11 May 1754 John Ellis, Gent. to William Randolph, Gent., both of Henrico County, for 110 pounds, 217 acres on the north side of the James River, adj. John Stewart, Benjamin Burton & William Randolph.
Wit: Richard Pringle, John Britton, Robert Gibson
Signed: John Ellis                                         Recorded 4 June 1754

p.329  3 June 1754 Isaac Winston, Jr., & Mary Ann Winston, his wife, to Thomas Wilkinson, all of Henrico County, for 322 pounds and 10 shillings, 287 acres on the southside of the Chickahominy Swamp, touching Miery Run and along the main run of the Chickahominy Swamp, and purchased by said Winston of Lyddal Bacon (metes and bounds description). Wit: none
Signed: Isaac Winston, Jr., Mary Ann Winston
Recorded 4 June 1754

p.332  4 June 1754 John Roberson, Jr., blacksmith, of Henrico County, to William Stone, planter of New Kent County, for 130 acres adj. Alexander Robertson, David Bins & James Cocke, being all the land given my father, John Roberson, Senr. by deed from my grandfather. (metes and bounds description).
Wit: none                                        Signed: John Roberson, Junr.
Anne, wife of John Roberson, Jr., relinquished her dower
Recorded 4 June 1754

p.333  4 June 1754 Langston Bacon to Benjamin Burton, Jr., both of Henrico County for 5 pounds and 6 shillings, Lot 109 on the plan of Westham, being a half-acre.
Wit: John Williamson, Jr., John Woodson, Joseph Hopkins
Signed: Langston Bacon                              Recorded: 4 June 1754

p.334  4 June 1754 Langston Bacon to Merry Carter (male), both of Henrico County, for 4 pounds and 6 shillings, Lot 110 on the plan of Westham, being a half-acre.
Wit: John Williamson, Jr., John Woodson, Joseph Hopkins
Signed: Langston Bacon                               Recorded 4 June 1754

p.335  4 June 1754 John Woodson of Goochland County to Merry Carter of

Henrico County, for 5 pounds, 7 shillings and 6 pence, Lot 5 on the plan of Westham, being a half-acre.
Wit: none  Signed: John Woodson
Recorded 4 June 1754

[pages 336 to 349 probate records]

p.350  22 June 1754 Thomas Pass to Thomas Miller, both of Henrico County, for 12 pounds 100 acres on a branch of the Deep Run called the Drinking Hole Branch, part of a greater tract granted by patent to Thomas Conway, adj. Edward Pryor, Christopher John Thomas and John Larey.
Wit: Nicholas Scherrer, Jacob Powers, Jacob Ege
Signed: Thomas (his  P  mark) Pass
Lucy, wife of Thomas Pass, relinquished her dower.
Recorded 1 July 1754

p.352  16 February 1754 Power of Attorney from John Houlder of Eagle Street in the Parish of St. George the Martyr in the County of Middlesex, hackney coachman, to Anderson Stith, Gent., of Charles City County on James River in his majesty's plantation of Virginia, attorney-at-law, to ask, demand, sue for and recover of and from William Hall, late of London, surgeon, but now residing in the said Island, several sums of money herein described.
Wit: Edward Randolph, Gent., J. Pettit
Signed: John Houlder  Recorded 1 July 1754

p.353  16 May 1754 John Oakley & Elizabeth, his wife to Jacob Vallentine of King William County, for 72 pounds, 400 acres on the Falls road, adj. Phillip Mayo, Francis Stego, Alexander Robinson, William Rose and Isaac Breeding, part of patent granted to Thomas Oakley on 30 August 1744.
Wit: Joseph Lewis, Nicholas Vallentine, Michael Jones
Signed: John Oakley, Elizabeth (her  X  mark) Oakley
Recorded 1 July 1754

p.354  8 June 1754 William Hambleton of Cumberland County to John Moseby of Henrico County, for 25 pounds, two tracts of land: 171 acres by patent dated 20 October 1704, and 80 acres by patent dated 7 March 1731.
Wit: Daniel Price, Robert Williamson, John Williamson, Jr.
Signed: William Hambleton  Recorded 2 September 1754

p.355  5 August 1754 Michael Jones of Henrico County to William Nance of St. Peter's Parish, James City County, for 6 pounds, 93 acres adj. Lewis, Breeding and

Watson. Wit: David Vaughan, William Stone
Signed; Michael Jones
Anne, wife of Michael Jones, relinquished her dower.
Recorded 5 August 1754

p.357  5 June 1751 William Byrd of Westover, Charles City County, to Nicholas Scherer of Richmond, Henrico County, for 35 pounds and 13 shillings, 11 acres on the east side of Schoces [Shockoe] Creek at corner of land laid off for the Town of Richmond (metes and bounds description); also two lots in the Town or Richmond, being Lot 51 and Lot 52 on the plan of said town.
Wit: Jacob Bugg, Olive Branch, John Howlett
Signed: W. Byrd                                    Recorded 5 August 1754

p.360  6 October 1754 John Pleasants, Junr., of Henrico County, to Jacob Vallentine of King William County, for 5 shillings, an assignment of a mortgage executed by John Oakley in his lifetime to the said John Pleasants, Junr., conveying 336 acres on the branches of Gilley's Creek, which mortgage is hereby assigned to the said Jacob Vallentine.
Wit: none                                    Signed: Jno. Pleasants, Jr
Recorded 7 October 1754

p.361  19 March 1754 Povall Carter of Henrico County to John Payne of Goochland County, for 2 pounds and 3 shillings, Lot 130 on the plan of the Town of Westham.
Wit: Benjamin Burton, Junr., Richard Pleasants, John Payne, Junr.
Signed: Povall (his PC mark) Carter
Recorded 7 October 1754

p.362  5 October 1754 Robert Allen to Richard Allen, his son, of Henrico County, for 60 pounds, 100 acres on the northern branch of the Brook (metes and bounds description), part of a tract of 246 acres granted by patent unto Michael Holland; and also a Negro man named Will Allen, in whom a life estate is reserved.
Wit: William Street, John Mosely, Rowland Blackburn
Signed: Robt. Allen                          Recorded 7 October 1754

p.363  31 October 1754 William Smith and Elizabeth, his wife, of Cumberland County, to William Finncy, for Negroes Will, Tom, Day and Isabell and ⅔ of the value of a Negro wench Temp and a Negro girl Hannah being delivered to us, all right, title and interest in the Negroes mentioned in a bill of complaint exhibited against the said William and Elizabeth Smith in Henrico County.
Wit: Abner Bates, John Gibbs

Signed: William Smith, Elizabeth Smith
Recorded 4 November 1754

p.364  1 November 1754 Robert Morris to William Morriss, both of Henrico County, for good causes and considerations (his mother to have a maintenance for her lifetime) and after my decease, two parcels of land: 110 acres adj. Robert Hobbs and Michael Holland and 375 acres adj. Michael Holland; and Negro fellow named Newport.
Wit: Robert (his R mark) Webb, Senr., Robert (his X mark) Webb, Junr.
Signed: Robert (his X mark) Morriss
Recorded 4 November 1754

p.364  Margaret Bugg, wife of Jacob Bugg, relinquished her dower in open court in the land her husband conveyed to Isaac Younghusband.
Recorded November Court 1754

p.365  Undated confirmation of marriage between Joseph Parsons, son of Joseph Parsons of Henrico County, and Mary Woodson, daughter of Stephen Woodson, of Henrico County.  Cites that couple on 5 April 1747 at a public meeting near White Oak Swamp at the [Quaker] Meeting House did declare themselves to be husband and wife.
Wit: Stephen Woodson, Agnes Woodson, Mary Woodson, Tarleton Woodson, Jr., Elizabeth Woodson, Mary Pleasants, Judith Woodson, Jemima Bell
Signed: Joseph Parsons, Mary Parsons
Recorded 4 November 1754

p.367  25 November 1754 Deed of Gift from John Gunn to James Gunn, his son, both of Henrico County, for natural love and affection and for better maintenance & livelihood, 250 acres, being half of a tract whereon I now live and the parcel whereon James Snowton now lives.                                   Wit: none
Signed: John Gun                                   Recorded 2 December 1754

p.369  Col. Richard  Randolph Gent., to Miles Garthright, both of Henrico County, for 85 pounds, 433 acres on the southside of the Chickahominy River, joining the lands of Julius Allin on said river and Joseph Childers and William Garthright, being the parcel left him by his father, Col. Richard Randolph, deceased.
Wit: William Duguids, Alexander Robertson, Samuel (his ✚ mark) Garthright
Signed: Richard Randolph                          Recorded 5 February 1755

p.370  10 September 1754 David Atkins, planter, to William Atkins, his son, both of Henrico County, 100 acres on the Hungary Swamp, adj. John Moseby, John

Watson and Thomas Meritt.
Wit: Pierce Griffing, Thomas Merritt
Signed: David (his ✚ mark) Atkins, Magdelin (her ✚ mark) Atkins
Recorded 2 December 1754

p.371  7 January 1755 Deed of Gift from Thomas Conaway to James Conaway, his son, for life, and to Thomas Conaway, his grandson, for remainder, for love, good will and affection, 68 acres adj. John Shoemaker, Watson, Rorkett (sic) and Alley.
Wit: none                    Signed: Thomas (his X mark) Conaway
Recorded 6 January 1755

p.372  5 January 1755 Deed of Gift from Matthew Bridgman of Chesterfield County to his son, Hezekiah Bridgman, of Henrico County, for 3 pounds, 50 acres on the New Kent Road, adj. John Harwood, James Cocke and William Stone.
Wit: none                    Signed: Matthew Bridgman
Recorded 6 January 1754

p.373  2 December 1754 Richard Randolph, Gent., to Phillip Watson, merchant, for 59 pounds, 2 shillings and 6 pence, two half-acre lots in the town of Richmond, being Lot 4 on plan of the said town, which was conveyed by the late William Byrd, Esq., deceased, by deed of 1 June 1740 to Richard Randolph, deceased, father of the said Richard Randolph, and the lot adjoining thereto.
Wit: none                    Signed: Richard Randolph
Recorded 2 December 1754

p.374  6 December 1754 Deed of Gift from John Staples, planter, and Anne, his wife, to John Staples, Jr., his son, both of Henrico County, 50 acres on the south side of the Hungary Swamp, adj. William Patman and Thomas Pleasants.
Wit: Pierce Griffin, William Atkins, William Gainings [?]
Signed: John (his I mark) Staples, Anne (her A mark) Staples
Recorded 2 December 1754

p.376  30 November 1754 David Binns to his sons, David Binns, Joseph Binns, Dionishous Binns, Peter Binns and Christopher Binns, for natural love and affection, 1) to David Binns, 55 acres, the upper end of my land, adj. William Stone, Captain James Cock, Thomas Cocke and John Woodsodown; 2) to Joseph Binns, 55 acres adj. his brother, David and the land called Thomas Robinson; 3) to Dionishous Binns, 55 acres adj. lands given his brothers, David and Joseph, adj. William Fleming Cocke; 4) to Peter Binns, 55 acres, being the plantation whereon I new live, adj. land given to Dionishous Binns, William Fleming Cocke, Michael Jones, John Barrow and Gilley's Creek; and 5) to Christopher Binns, 55 acres on the

south side of Gilley's Creek, adj. William Rose, John Barnes and the land given to Peter Binns.
Wit; Joseph Lewes, John Barnes, William Barnes
Signed: David Binns
Recorded 2 December 1754

p.377  2 December 1754 Isham Allin of Henrico County, to his daughter, Susanna Williamson Allin, for love and natural affection and for her better maintenance and livelihood, a Negro girl named Phyllis and her increase and twenty pounds.
Wit: Joseph Lewes, Daniel Price, Michael Jones
Signed: Isum (his I mark) Allen
Recorded 2 December 1754

p.378  29 November 1754 John Bryan to James Gaddy of Henrico County, for 12 pounds, Lot 10, being a half-acre lot on the plan of the Town of Richmond.
Wit: none                                            Signed: John Bryan
Obedience, wife of John Bryan, relinquished her dower.
Recorded 3 February 1755

p.379  2 December 1754 Thomas Alley, Sr., to son, Edmund Alley, for love, good will and affection, 200 acres on Stony Run, adj. William Ellis and said Thomas Alley.
Wit: Samuel Alley, David Alley, Jr.
Signed: Thomas (his A mark) Alley
Recorded 2 December 1754

p.382  1 February 1755 William Ford to Samuel Ford, both of Henrico County, for 10 pounds, 100 acres adj. John Moseby, James Britton, said Samuel Ford and David Ford.
Wit: John Cornett, William Jennings, Richard Allen
Signed: William (his W mark) Ford               Recorded 3 February 1755

p.383  3 February 1755 John Williamson to Phillip Watson of the Town of Richmond, both of Henrico County, for 20 pounds. one patrimonial tract of land containing 106 acres granted by patent unto William Warbourton and by deed from James Woodfin, executor of said Warbourton, transferred to the said John Williamson.
Wit: none                                   Signed: John Williamson Judith,
wife of John Williamson, relinquished her dower.
Recorded 3 February 1755

p.383  3 February 1755 John Lipscomb, planter, to Phillip Watson, merchant of the Town of Richmond, both of Henrico County, for 40 pounds, 200 acres, whereon the said John Lipscomb now lives, being one moiety of 400 acres granted by patent to John Pure and by him conveyed by deed to said John Lipscomb, adj. Hon. William Byrd, Esq., John Williamson, the Elder, Jonathan Bridgewater and William Sims.
Wit: none                                            Signed: John Lipscomb
Recorded 3 February 1755

p.385  2 December 1754 Deed of Gift from Joseph Pleasants to his son, Joseph Pleasants, Jr., both of Henrico County, for love and affection, tract left my brother, Robert Pleasants, by my father, Joseph Pleasants, by his last will and testament, being 200 acres.
Wit: Wishier Redford, Noel Burton, John Price
Signed: Joseph Pleasants                    Recorded 2 December 1754

p.386  3 February 1755 David Staples of Henrico County to William Ford of Hanover County, for 10 pounds, 50 acres, being part of the land whereon said David Staples now lives, adj. Thomas Alley, Henry Allen and the orphans of George Freeman, deceased.
Wit: Robert Burton, Richard Holland, Henry Ellis
Signed; David Staples                          Recorded 3 February 1755

p.387  2 December 1754 James Cocke to Richard Randolph, Gent., both of Henrico County, for 190 pounds, 150 acres known as Curles, which was formerly the inheritance of William Garris, and by him sold to Abraham Childers and by said Childers sold to John Pleasants, grandfather to the said James Cocke.
Wit: William Ginguid [?], Alexander Robertson, Samuel Garthright
Signed: James Cocke                            Recorded 3 February 1755

p.388  31 January 1755 Nicholas Scherer to Mary O'Bryan, both of the Town of Richmond, Henrico County, for 12 pounds, one half-acre lot on the plan of the Town of Richmond, being Lot 52.        Wit: Jacob Ege, George Scherer
Signed: Nicholas Scherer                       Recorded 3 February 1755

p.390  2 December 1755 Benjamin Burton to Jacob Burton of Henrico County, for 100 pounds, 200 acres on Cornelius Creek, adj. John West and John Whitlow.
Wit: John Williamson, Jr., John Redford, Jr., Benjamin Burton, Jr.
Signed: Benjamin (his ✚ mark) Burton
Recorded 3 February 1755

p.391  5 June 1754 William Byrd of Charles City County to Jacob Ege of Henrico

County, for 7 pounds, one half-acre lot in the town of Richmond, being Lot 50 on the plan of said town.
Wit: Abraham Cowley, Thomas Adams, Robert Goode
Signed: W. Byrd                                              Recorded 2 December 1755

p.392  28 November 1754 Edward Enroughty to George Williamson, both of Henrico County, for 27 pounds, 50 acres on Four Mile Creek, bounded as by Deed of Gift for the said land from Edward Enroughty, father of the party.
Wit: John Pleasants, Jr., John Bell, John Enroughty, John Williams
Signed: Edward Enroughty
Edy, wife of Edward Enroughty, relinquished her dower.
Recorded 2 December 1754

p.393  [–] December 1754 James Britton of Henrico County to his son, Samuel Britton, for 100 pounds, 100 acres adj. William Ford, James Britton (where he now lives) and James Cornett.
Wit: John Williamson, Henry Burrus, Daniel Price
Signed: James (his IB mark) Britton                    Recorded 2 December 1754

p.394  3 February 1755 Ralph Hunt of Henrico County to Benjamin Bowles of the Parish of St. Paul's, Hanover County, for 50 pounds, 180½ acres on a branch called Deep Bottom, being land conveyed to the said Ralph Hunt by Stephen Gunter (metes and bounds description).
Wit: none                                                Signed: Ralph Hunt
Recorded 3 February 1755

p.396  Dower assigned for Elizabeth Allen by order of 6 June 1751, being her share of the estate of Cuthburt Williamson, deceased: four Negroes: Sam, Bob, Temp and Jane; seven head of cattle, three horses and twenty pounds cast. The other part to three orphans: 1) Susanna Williamson, three Negroes: Joe, Lucy and Patt; 2) Mary Prior, three Negroes: Jack, Sarah and Chloe; and 3) Cuthburt Williamson, two Negroes: Moll and Matilda; thirteen head of cattle, three mares and parcel of household goods.
Signed: Philip Mayo, William Lewes
Recorded 2 December 1754

p.397  3 March 1755 Henry Woody to William Henley, both of Henrico County, for 30 pounds, 175 acres adj. Benjamin Johnson, Leonard Henley and John Martin, being the land said Woody now lives on and part of 400 acres that John Martin obtained a patent for.
Wit: none                                    Signed: Henry (his H mark) Woody

Webby, wife of Henry Woody, relinquished her dower.
Recorded 3 March 1755

p.399  6 May 1754 Deed of Mortgage from Richard Holland, Gent., of Henrico County, to Andrew Corbin, James Donald & Co., merchants of Glasgow, for 200 pounds, slaves Patt, Terry, York, Caesar and Margaret, four beds and furniture, twenty head of cattle, one horse branded with two hearts, one sorrel mare, and all the rest of the stock.
Wit: Rachel Gwin, Frances Wager, Samuel East, James Donald, George Mutton, William Johnson, Charles Waddill and James Eaddy
Signed; Richd. Holland					Recorded 3 March 1755

p.400  26 March 1754 Christopher John Thomas to William Harding, both of Henrico County for 60 pounds, 100 acres, the tract John Walters gave him by will.
Wit: William Wills, William Cabell, Alexander McCaul, Nathanial Wilkinson
Signed: Christopher John Thomas
Recorded 4 November 1754

p.401  4 April 1755 Isaac Winston, Jr., to Robert Moseby, Jr., both of Henrico County, for 31 pounds, 11¾ acres, adj. Parson and Moseby, part of a larger tract conveyed by deed to William Britton by Tarleton Woodson, one of the executors of John Woodson, Gent., deceased, and by the said William Britton to the said Isaac Winston (metes and bounds description).
Wit: none					Signed: Isaac Winston, Jun.

p.403  7 April 1755 James Graham of Hampton in Virginia, merchant, acting on a power of attorney dated 6 January 1749 from Richard Oswald, Robert Scott and John Mill of London, merchants, to James Lyle, merchant, of Henrico County, to ask, sue for and recover debts new due and outstanding at a store in Richmond where Thomas Atkinson has been kept as their factor or deputy.
Wit: none					Signed: James Graham
Recorded 7 April 1755

p.405  29 March 1755 Thomas Bottom and Rebecca Bottom, his wife, to John Bottom, for 25 pounds, 50 acres adj. said John Bottom, Walsey Clopton and Richard Whitlock.
Wit: Thomas Watkins, John Middleton, John Binford
Signed; Thomas Bottom, Rebecca Bottom
Recorded 7 April 1755

p.407  3 March Robert Allen of Henrico County to his son, Joseph Allen, for 50

pounds, 200 acres, being part of the land said Robert Allen bought of Michael Holland, adj. John Moseby, John Ford, Richard Allen; and also a Negro woman named Philis.
Wit: none  Signed: Robert Allen
Recorded 7 April 1755

p.410 26 October 1748 Bond of James Cocke of Henrico County to Martha Cocke, for 1,000 pounds, the condition being that the principal will keep unmolested use during her natural life all of the slaves, goods and chattels left her by the last will and testament of his father, the late James Powell Cocke.
Wit: John Povall, Hays (his H mark) Whitlow, William Whitlow
Signed: James Cocke  Recorded 2 June 1755

p.411 2 June 1755 Apprenticeship Bond of Samuel Welden, ward to Edward Maynard of Henrico County, with the consent of Rhoderick Easely guardian of the said Samuel Welden, who is to be trained in the mystery of a tanner for a period of four years from date hereof.  Wit: none
Signed: Samuel Welden, Edward Maynard, Rhoderick Easely
Recorded 2 June 1755

p.412 2 April 1755 George Wilkinson, the Elder of New Kent County, to his son, Thomas Wilkinson of Henrico County, for natural love and affection and for 5 shillings, all that patrimonial tract of land containing 200 acres on Meredith's Branch, a branch of the Chickahominy Swamp.
Wit: George Wilkinson, Jr., Geddis Winston, Foard Wilkinson, William Wilkinson
Signed: George Wilkinson  Recorded 2 June 1755

p.413 2 June 1755 Jacob Burton to Lisbit Turpin, both of Henrico County, for 100 pounds, 200 acres on the south side of Cornelius Creek, adj, John Whitlow and John Wood and bounded by Bridge Branch.
Wit: none  Signed: Jacob Burton
Recorded 2 June 1755

p.414 9 September 1747 William Knott of Nansemond County to George Frith of said county, for 40 pounds, two Negro slaves, a Negro woman Fanny and a small boy named Tark, son of the said Fanny.
Wit: Tarleton Woodson, Charles Woodson, Jacob Woodson, William Nohnes [Nolms?], William (his X mark) Perrot
Signed: William Knott  Recorded 2 June 1755

p.415  9 September 1747 George Frith of Nansemond County to Charles Woodson of Henrico County, for 42 pounds and 10 shillings, two Negro slaves, Fanny and son Tark.
Wit: Tarleton Woodson, Jacob Woodson, William Nohnes,
  William (his X mark) Perrot
Signed: George Frith                                    Recorded 2 June 1755

p.415  2 June 1755 David Breeding and Rachell Breeding, his wife, of Henrico County, to Jonathan Williams, for 15 pounds, 50 acres, adj. Col. William Randolph, Darby Roughty, Ben Scott, David Giles and Iduzo Whitlowe, being part of the land Breeding purchased of Henry Whitlowe.
Wit: Thomas Robinson, Anthony Matthews, John White, Thomas Frankling
Signed: David Breeding, Rachell (her X mark) Breeding
Recorded 2 June 1755

p.417  11 March 1755 Philemon Frayser to William Frayser, both of Henrico County, for 25 pounds and 10 shillings, 100 acres adj. John Frayser, George Williamson and other lands of said William Frayser.
Wit: Robert Atkins, George Robinson, Ben Boulders
Signed: Philemon Frayser
Mary, wife of Philemon Frayser, relinquished her dower.
Recorded 2 June 1755

p.420  7 July 1755 William Bottom to Thomas Bottom, both of Henrico County, for 12 pounds, 100 acres at Ferris' path near Ephraim Garthright's path and near Boor's [Boar's] Swamp; being part of the tract said William Bottom purchased of Gerrard Ellyson.
Wit: Thomas Watkins, Jacob Bugg
Signed: William Bottom                                  Recorded 7 July 1755

p.421  7 July 1755 Robert Cooke to Abraham Cowley, both of Henrico County, for 20 pounds, 16½ acres lying between the lands of William Byrd, Esq., and John New.
Wit: George Scherer, William Orr, Alexander (his X mark) Long
Signed: Robert (his I mark) Cooke
Recorded 7 July 1755

p.422  7 July 1755 Deed of Mortgage from Ralph Hunt of Henrico County to George Norvell of Hanover County, for 13 pounds, 18 shillings and 8 pence, one Negro woman named Sue, to be paid on the first of January next ensuing.
Wit: none                                               Signed: Ralph Hunt

Recorded 7 July 1755

p.423 7 July 1755 Michael Jones to Nicholas Valentine and his wife (unnamed) for their natural lives and then to their son, James Valentine, for 10 pounds, 100 acres at the head of Gilley's Creek, adj. William Nance, [----] Watson and Joseph Lewis; being part of the patent granted to Michael Jones.
Wit: none  Signed: Michael Jones
Anna, wife of Michael Jones, relinquished her dower.
Recorded 7 July 1755

p.424 4 January 1755 Capt. James Cocke, Gent. to Samuel DuVal, Gent., both of Henrico County, for 110 pounds, 110 acres on the branches of Shark's Creek (commonly called `Bacon's Quarter Branch') on the east side of Cannon's Branch and on the west side of Johnson's Branch; adj. to Luke Smith (now Samuel DuVal), John Gunn, Thomas Wood and Mr. Byrd; being part of the tract Thomas Wood bought of William Randolph and by the said Wood sold to John Phelps and by the said Phelps sold to the said James Cocke (metes and bounds description).
Wit: John Williamson, William Dinguid, Daniel Price, Robert Yaxley,
 Jesse (his I mark) Flowers
Signed: James Cocke
Sarah, wife of James Cocke, relinquished her dower.
Recorded 4 August 1755

p.426 [-----] 1755 John Redford, Sr., to his son, John Redford, Jr., both of Henrico County, for love and natural affection and for 5 shillings, 125 acres on Roundabout Swamp and on the main road that goes from Branch's Ferry to Four Mile Creek Mill.  Wit: none
Signed: John Redford  Recorded 7 July 1755

p.427 10 June 1755 Gerrard Ellyson to William Bottom, both of Henrico County, for 33 pounds, 275 acres bounded as by a patent granted to the said Gerrard Ellison dated 22 September 1739.
Wit: Charles Woodson, Humphrey (his S mark) Smith, James Lindsey
Signed: Gerrard Ellison
Sarah, wife of Gerrard Ellison, relinquished her dower.
Recorded 7 July 1755

p.428 23 May 1755 Power of Attorney from Richard and Alexander Oswald, James Dennistoune, John Stevenson, Michael Herrids and Alexander Walker, merchants of Glasgow [William Sellar, not in the caption and not signing is also mentioned in the text of the instrument] to James Lyle, of Richmond in Henrico County,

merchant, to ask, demand, levy and sue for debts from all persons in the colony of Virginia as well as Maryland or elsewhere upon the continent of America.
Wit: George Baird, Ebenezer Munro
Signed: James Dennistoune, Michael Herrids, John Stevenson, Alexander Walker, Richard Oswald, Alexander Oswald (acknowledged before the Honorable John Brown, Esq., provost of the City of Glasgow)
Recorded 1 September 1755

p.435  6 October 1755 Nathaniel Bacon and John Williamson, Jr., executors of Langston Bacon, deceased; and Susannah Bacon, widow and relict of John Bacon, deceased; and Sarah Bacon, widow of said Langston Bacon, deceased; to Nathaniel Wilkinson of the Town of Richmond in Henrico County, for 287 pounds, 287 acres on the Chickahominy Swamp, being the tract whereon the said Langson Bacon, deceased, lately dwelt, and directed to be sold pursuant to his will.
Wit: none                      Signed: Natl. Bacon, John Williamson, Jr., Susannah (her S  mark) Bacon, Sarah Bacon
Recorded 6 October 1755

p.436  23 April 1755 Benjamin Burton, planter, to William Randolph, Esq., Gent., both of Henrico County, for 15 pounds, 50 acres bounded by Cole's Run and by the lines of the land said Randolph bought of Lizby Turpin and being all of the land that said Burton owns on the north side of said run.
Wit: John (his ✚ mark) Whitlow, Richard Pringle, William Harwood
Signed: Benjamin (his B  mark) Burton
Recorded 6 October 1755

p.438  6 October 1755 Philemon Childers to Nicholas Childers, both of Henrico County, for 5 pounds, 104 acres whereon his plantation now is and part of 204 acres granted to Thomas Bates by patent dated 20 May 1742.
Wit: James Alley, Robert Gording, Philemon Williams
Signed: Philemon (his I  mark) Childers
Recorded 3 November 1755

p.438  3 November 1755 Peter Burton of Amelia County to Charles Floyd of Charles City County, for 25 pounds, 50 acres on Turkey Island Creek, adj. John Povall and Charles Floyd; being part of the land given by John Cooke to his daugher, Elizabeth.
Wit: none                      Signed: Peter (his ✚ mark) Burton
Recorded 3 November 1755

p.439  6 October 1755 John Williams, and Mary, his wife to Leonard Henly, all of

Henrico County, for 10 pounds, 100 acres adj. Col. Peter Randolph, Esq., John Alldays and Sampson's Slash.
Wit: Edward Curd, Lizby Turpin
Signed: John Williams, Mary (her ✚ mark) Williams
Recorded 6 October 1755


p.441  12 December 1754 William Parker to John Pleasants, son of Thomas Pleasants, both of Henrico County, for 50 pistoles [a Spanish coin], one-half part of a 61-acres parcel with a water grist mill now out of repair by overflowing of water, on Four Mile Creek, being the land and mill devised by John Pleasants, first of the name in this colony, unto his son, Joseph in joint partnership with John, his other son, which part was sold to John Redford, the Elder by Thomas Pleasants, father of the party to this deed.
Wit: John (his J mark) Jordan, John Williams, John Fussill,
Edward (his O mark) Matthews                    Signed: William Parker
Recorded 1 December 1755

p.442  1 December 1755 Richard Randolph, Gent., to George Scherer, Jr., for 35 pounds, one half-acre lot in the Town of Richmond, being Lot 5 on plan of said town; conveyed by the late William Byrd, Esq., by deed of 25 August 1742 unto Richard Randolph, deceased, father of the said Richard Randolph.
Wit: none                                       Signed: Richard Randolph
Recorded 1 December 1755

p.443  3 November 1755 Robert Williams to John Millar, both of Henrico County, for 21 pounds and 10 shillings, 70 acres on the north side of Deep Run between the lands of William Buxton, John White, Thomas Conaway, John Shewmaker and Major Mayo.
Wit: Drury Brazeal, William Buxton, Martin (his ✚ mark) Burton
Signed: Robert Williams, Mary, wife of Robert Williams, relinquished her dower.
Recorded 1 December 1755

p.444  1 December 1755 Edward Goode of Henrico County, to Robert Goode, son of my nephew Benjamin Goode, for the true love I bear, 150 acres being one dividend of land on the Deep Run of Four Mile Creek, at the fork of a branch called Ben Childers' Cornfield Branch and to the head thereof; adj. Benjamin Burton.
Wit: none                                       Signed: Edward Goode
Recorded 1 December 1755

p.447  9 July 1755 Deed of Mortgage from Francis Redford to John and Milner

Redford, all of Henrico County, for 250 pounds, collateral being 130 acres purchased by the said Francis Redford of Philemon Perkins; and seven Negro slaves: Daniel, Pompey, Toney, Dinah, Sarah, Matt and Little Grace; for 120 pounds 8 shillings and one penny and ¼ and costs of judgment obtained in the County Court of Prince George due William Kennon on or before 10 August nest ensuing; and also to indemnify said John Redford by reason of a writ served on said Francis Redford for ten pounds damage by Anderson Stith, likewise for 16 pounds, 2 shillings and interest which said Francis borrowed of his brother, William Redford, deceased, whereof the said John Redford is one of the executors.
Wit: Francis Redford, Jr., John Cox, John Redford, Jr.
Signed; Francis Redford                          Recorded 2 February 1756

p.448  1 December 1755 Thomas Bates and Annis, his wife, of Henrico County, to William Davis, ditcher, of King William County, for 12 pounds, 30 acres on Miery Branch, adj. Wagstaff and Ellyson.
Wit: Thomas Watkins, Jr., William (his  +  mark) Clarke, Thomas Watkins, Sr.
Signed: Thomas (his  T  mark) Bates, Anis (her  I  mark) Bates
Recorded 2 March 1756

p.449  1 January 1756 Nicholas Amos of Henrico County, to his son, William Amos, for love and affection that I bear, and reserving a life estate, 100 acres on the branches of Tuckahoe Creek, adj. Col. Richard Randolph, Richard Holland, George Freeman and Thomas Ellis and which was purchased from John Cox and Alice, his wife.
Wit: Charles Woodson, Agness Woodson, Daniel Warrinner
Signed: Nicholas (his  N  mark) Amos
Recorded 2 March 1756

p.449  1 March 1756 Julius Allin to Elizabeth Dorton, both of Henrico County, for 20 pounds, 100 acres on the Great Branch, adj. lands of John Watson, Matthew Johnson, Valentine Freeman, deceased, and Isham Allin.
Wit: none                                         Signed: Julius Allin
Mary, wife of Julius Allin, relinquished her dower.
Recorded 2 March 1756

p.450  15 December 1755 William Harding to John Jude, both of Henrico County, for 50 pounds, 100 acres, part in Henrico County and part in Goochland County, on both sides of Tuckahoe Creek; being part of the tract of Thomas Harding, deceased, including a mill; adj. Ware and said Jude.
Wit: Giles Letcher, Richard Holland, William (his  A  mark) Barker
Signed: Wm. Harding

Sarah, wife of William Harding, relinquished her dower in open court on 5 July 1756. Recorded 2 March 1756

p.452  15 January 1756 Richard Randolph, Gent., to John Eales, both of Henrico County, for 30 pounds, 200 acres on the west side of the Deep Run, adj. William Ellis (formerly Edward Rorriss) and John Simcock, deceased.
Wit: Ryland Randolph, Stephen (his S mark) Childers, Robert Harding, Jr.
Signed: Richard Randolph Recorded 2 March 1756

p.452  31 October 1755 Robert Cooke to John Williamson, Jr., both of Henrico County, for 30 pounds, 100 acres purchased of John Gunn, between the lands of said John Gunn, Nathaniel Vanderwall, Thomas Franklin and the said Robert Cooke.
Wit: William Bacon, Robert Williamson, Sam Williamson
Signed: Robert (his R mark) Cooke Recorded 2 March 1756

p.454  31 October 1755 Robert Cooke of Henrico County to John Williamson, Jr., for 50 pounds, 217 acres adj., John Gunn, Dasey Southall, Nathaniel Vanderwall and Henry Brazell's branch.
Wit: William Bacon, Robert Williamson, Sam Williamson
Signed: Robert (his R mark) Cooke
Recorded 2 March 1756

p.455  24 January 1756 Deed of Mortgage from Benjamin Burton, Jr., to Philip Watson, merchant of Shockoe, for 78 pounds, 10 shillings, 11 pence and 3 farthings with lawful interest thereon from the date hereof; four Negro fellows, viz., Prince, Toby, Mingo and Harry.
Wit: William Harrison Signed: Benjamin Burton, Junr.
Recorded 2 May 1756

p.455  [-----] September 1755 William Frogmorton to his son, Robert Frogmorton, both of Henrico County, for love and affection, 50 acres on Four Mile Creek, being one-half of the tract whereon the said William now dwelleth, including the houses and plantation.
Wit: Henry (his X mark) Sharp, John Enroughty, Robert Sharp,
Edward (his X mark) Mathis (Matthews)
Signed: Wm. Frogmorton Recorded 3 May 1756

p.456  15 May 1756 William Lewis of Henrico County, to sons, Joseph and Charles Lewis, for natural love and affection and for their better maintenance and livelihood, nine Negro slaves: to son, Joseph Lewis, three slaves: man, Jack;

woman, Frank; boy, George; said slaves to continue in my possession for life, to son, Charles Lewis, six slaves: man, Isaac; woman, Hannah; boy, York; girl, Fib; boy, Jacob; girl, Jude.
Wit: Daniel Price, Abraham Cowley, William Flemming Cocke
Signed: William Lewis                                    Recorded 5 July 1756

p.457  5 July 1756 William Roan and Lucy, his wife, of Amelia County, to John Nance of New Kent County, for 60 pounds, 150 acres on Gilley's Creek, adj. Joseph Lewis, John Barnes and Christopher Bins.
Wit: Michael Jones, Richard Williamson
Signed: William Roane
[No signature or acknowledgment for release of dower indicated for Lucy Roane].
Recorded 5 July 1756

p.458 [-----] 1756 Benjamin Clarke of Henrico County to son, John Clarke, for love, good will and affection, 140 acres on the south side of Upknam (sic) Brook, adj. Valentine Ball, Gording, Thomas Lowit and said Benjamin Clarke.
Wit: none                                    Signed: Benjamin Clarke
Recorded 6 September 1756

p.459  6 September 1756 Richard Randolph, Gent., to Samuel Gathwrite, both of Henrico County, for 41 pounds, 510 acres, beginning at John Gathwright's upper corner on White Oak Swamp and along his line to the western branch of Deep Run; adj. said Samuel Gathwight, James Lindsay and Samuel Gathwright, Jr.
Wit: none                                    Signed: Richard Randolph
Recorded 6 September 1756

p.460  23 August 1756 James Hibdon to David Binns, both of Henrico County, for 6 pounds, 56 acres on Gilley's Creek, adj. Robertson and Spraggins; by patent (metes and bounds description).
Wit: Joseph Lewis, Christopher Binns, David Binns
Signed: James Hibdon                          Recorded 6 September 1756

p.461  6 September 1756 William Mouat, Administrator of Samuel Gleadowe, deceased, to John Orr of Henrico County, for 19 pounds, 103 acres on Tuckahoe Creek, which land Jervas Burdett formerly bought of William Lawless and afterwards sold to said Samuel Gleadowe by deed dated 20 July 1753. Wit: none
Signed: William Mourat by William Dinguid, attorney for said Mourat.
Recorded 6 September 1756

p.462  3 April 1756 John Price of Goochland County to Samuel Shephard of

Henrico County, for 100 pounds, 258 acres on the branches of Deep Run (Flat Branch and Scraping Branch) and part of a greater tract granted by patent unto George Freeman and by the said Freeman given to his son, John Freeman, who by his last will and testament sold the land to John Price.
(metes and bounds description)
Wit: William Street, William (his  X  mark) Willis,
Susannah (her  X  mark) Willis
Signed: John (his  I  mark) Price             Recorded 3 April 1756

p.464  21 October 1756 John Alday to Cox Whitlowe, both of Henrico County, for 25 pounds, 200 acres on the south side of Tom Fields Creek, part of a tract of 400 acres granted to the said John Alday by patent dated 5 March 1747; adj. Matthew Harburt, Mayo and Baley.
Wit: James (his  +  mark) White, Josiah (his  I  mark) Alday, John Stewart
Signed: James (his  J  mark) Alday
Recorded 21 October 1756

p.465  4 August 1756 Thomas Wood to Samuel Duvall, both of Henrico County, for 2 pounds and 18 shillings, four acres on the east side of Johnson's Branch, adj. Samuel Duvall, being the line of the land he bought of James Cocke.
Wit: Daniel Lloyd, John Kelley, James Wilkins, William Low
Signed: Thomas (his  X  mark) Wood
Martha, wife of Thomas Wood, relinquished her dower.
Recorded 1 November 1756

p.466  7 August 1756 Deed of Gift from Thomas Wood to his son, John Wood, both of Henrico County, for natural love and affection and for the better maintenance, livelihood and performance, 100 acres adj. John Gunn, Jacob Egge, Samuel Duvall (being the land he bought of James Cocke) and Johnson's Branch.
Wit: Samuel Duvall, Daniel Lloyd, John Kelley, James Wilkins
Signed: Thomas (his  T  mark) Wood
Martha, wife of Thomas Wood, relinquished her dower
Recorded 1 November 1756

p.467  1 November 1756 Deed of Gift from Thomas Wood to his son, William Wood, both of Henrico County, for natural love and affection..., 100 acres adj. John Gunn, Hon. William Byrd, Esq., Abraham Cowley, John New, Dasey Southall and Bonner's Spring Branch.
Wit: Benjamin Clarke, Thomas Owen, Samuel Duvall, John McNemara, James Wilkins
Signed: Thomas (his  T  mark) Wood

Martha, wife of Thomas Wood, relinquished her dower
Recorded 1 November 1756

p.467   30 October 1756 Benjamin Cannon, planter, to Jeremiah Cannon, both of Cumberland County, for 20 pounds, 100 acres on the south side of Deep Run, being the same 100 acres given by deed of gift from John Walters; adj. James Connaway.
Wit: Charles John Thomas, Sarah (her X mark) Connaway,
Susannah (her X mark) Lacy
Signed: Benjamin (his B mark) Cannon
Susannah, wife of Benjamin Cannon, relinquished her dower.
Recorded 1 November 1756

p.468   1 November 1756 Jeremiah Cannon, planter, of Cumberland County, to Richard Cottrell, planter, of Henrico County, for 20 pounds, 100 acres on the south side of Deep Run, which John Walters gave by deed of gift to Benjamin Cannon (metes and bounds description).
Wit: Christopher John Thomas, Sarah (her X mark) Connaway,
Susannah (her X mark) Lacy
Signed: Jeremiah Cannon
Susannah, wife of Jeremiah Cannon, relinquished her dower.
Recorded 1 November 1756

p.469   1 November 1756 Joseph Matthews of Cumberland County, to Anthony Matthews of Henrico County, for 32 pounds, 125 acres adj. the upper part of a tract that William Matthews sold Samuel Gathwright and being the said tract given to Joseph Matthews by his father.
Wit: James Cocke, Richard Cottrell, Miles Gathwrite
Signed: Joseph Matthews                                         Recorded 1 November 1756

p.470   1 September 1756 Deed of Mortgage from James Cocke to John Pleasants, Sr., both of Henrico County, for payment of 284 pounds, 9 shillings and 8 pence, to be paid with lawful interest on or before 1 December 1760; collateral being three tracts of 1,428 acres: 1) 540 acres near the Chickahominy Swamp whereon he now lives; 2) 400 acres in Cumberland County on Jones' Creek; and 3) "Franklin's," a tract of 480 acres in Henrico County.
Wit: John Pleasants, Jr., John Jude, Thomas Watkins, John Stewart, Thomas Storrs
Signed: James Cocke                                             Recorded 1 November 1756

p.471   22 November 1756 John Elmore of Lunenburg County to Isham Allen of Henrico County, for 15 pounds, 137 ½ acres on the south side of the Chickahominy River, being a part of the land devised to the said John Elmore by the will of his

grandmother, Rebeckah Elmore.
Wit: Lydall Bacon, Thomas Thorp, Watson Patman, John Blackwell, Julius Allen
Signed: John Elmore                                        Recorded 6 December 1756

p.473   10 November 1756 John Elmore of Cumberland Parish, Lunenburg County, to Thomas Elmore of Henrico County, for 25 pounds, 137 acres on the south side of the Chickahominy Swamp, being a tract devised to Elizabeth Elmore by the will of her mother, Rebeckah Elmore and to John Elmore, her grandson, in case of her dying without issue; adj. Edmund Allin, deceased, James Allin, Valentine Freeman, deceased, Joseph Watson, deceased, and by the Chickahominy Swamp.
Wit: Charles Woodson, Robert Spears, Samuel Gathright, Junr.,
Samuel (his S mark) Gathwright
Signed: John Elmore                                        Recorded 6 December 1756

p.474   6 December 1756 William Battersby to Andrew Castlen, for 7 pounds, 10 shillings and 6 pence, 50 acres adj. Alexander Robinson, William Duiguid, John Harwood and Samuel Ligon.
Wit: John Orr, George Donald, Drury Wood
Signed: W. Battersby                                     Recorded 3 January 1757

p.475   4 November 1756 Deed of Gift from Thomas Gennett to son-in-law, Story Hall, and daughter, Elizabeth Hall, for love, good will and affection, the grantor relinquishes his life estate previously reserved in 50 acres lying on a branch of Deep Run called Stony Run.
Wit: Nathaniel Dennis, Alexander (his A mark) Patterson, Aaron (his A mark) Freeman                              Signed: Thomas (his X mark) Genett
Recorded 3 January 1757

p.476   6 November 1756 Story Hall and Elizabeth Hall, his wife, to William Street, all of Henrico County, for 25 pounds, 50 acres, as noted in preceding deed, bounded on the southeast by James Alley's line (formerly Thomas Alley), on the northwest by William Ellis's line and on the northeast by Stony Run.
Wit: Nathaniel Dennis, Alexander (his A mark) Patterson, Aaron (his A mark) Freeman
Signed: Story Hall, Elizabeth (her X mark) Hall
Recorded 3 January 1757

p.477   7 July 1756 Robert Cooke to Alexander McCaul, both of Henrico County, for 14 pounds and 8 shillings, 26 acres, being the land and plantation whereon Robert Cooke now lives and being part of a tract patented by the said Cooke by patent dated 5 June 1746.

Wit: Dasey Southall, James Ingram, George Donald
Signed: Robert (his R mark) Cooke
Recorded 3 January 1757 and further proven on 4 April 1757

p.478 24 December 1767 The Honorable William Byrd, Esq., to Philip Watson, merchant, for annual rent to be paid in the amount of 58 pounds and 17 shillings from 10 December last past for the term of eleven years, the lease of a brick tenement upon Shockoe Hill with the outbuildings, offices and appurtenances thereunto belonging, with 128 acres contiguous thereto (metes and bounds description).
Wit: Richard Randolph, Thomas Adams, J. Wayles
Signed: W. Byrd                              Recorded 7 January 1757

p.479 24 January 1757 Deed of Lease for William Eppes, Gent., of the Province of Massachusetts Bay, to Richard Eppes, Gent., of Chesterfield County, for 5 shillings and paying one grain of Indian corn at the end of one year, 608 acres known as Longfield and 300 acres adjoining known as Huddes. being the lands devised to the said William Eppes by his brother, Francis Eppes, deceased; from the 24th day of this instant for the full term of one year.
Wit: John Wayles, LeRoy Griffin, John Hylton, Benjamin Harris, Nathaniel Wilkinson, Tabitha Wayles, Eliza Hylton.
Signed: Wm. Eppes
Recorded 7 February 1757 and further proven on 4 April 1757

p.480 25 January 1757 William Eppes, Gent., of the Province of Massachusetts Bay, to Richard Eppes, Gent., of Chesterfield County, for 1,000 pounds, 608 acres known as Longfield and 300 acres adjoining known as Huddes, now in possession of the said Richard Eppes by virtue of previously recorded lease.
Wit: John Wayles, LeRoy Griffin, John Hylton, Benjamin Harris, Nathaniel Wilkinson, Tabitha Wayles, Eliza Hylton.
Signed: Wm. Eppes
Recorded 7 February 1757 and further proven on 4 April 1757

p.481 19 June 1756 Deed of Mortgage from Robert Scott of Henrico County to John Pleasants and Robert Pleasants, his son, for payment of 15 pounds, 9 shillings and 6 pence, and lawful interest, to be paid before 19 June next ensuing, 100 acres, being the tract whereon said Robert Scott now dwelleth, bounded on the east by Francis Redford, on the south by Abraham Childers, on the west by Hayes Whitlow, on the north by John Frazier and David Gill.
Wit: Thomas Pleasants, William Gathright, Thomas Perkins, Thomas Storrs
Signed: Robert (his R mark) Scott             Recorded 7 March 1757

p.482  3 February 1757 Deed of Release from George Norvell to Ralph Hunt, which released Deed of Mortgage dated 7 July 1755, for 13 pounds, 18 shillings and 8 pence, the collateral being one Negro woman, Sue; paid by John Pierce, Gent., of Hanover County for the use of Ralph Hunt.
Wit: Thomas Wilkinson, Nathaniel Wilkinson
Signed: George Norvell                                    Recorded 7 February 1757

p.482  7 September 1756 The Hon. William Byrd. Esq., of Charles City County, to Richard Crouch, blacksmith, of Henrico County, for 21 pounds and 10 shillings, one-half acre lot adj. the south east end of Richmond Town and on the south side of Sorrel Bottom adj. the Main Road.
Wit: Philip Watson, John Woodson, Robert Goode
Signed: Wm. Byrd                                          Recorded 7 February 1757

p.483  7 September 1756 The Hon. Wm. Byrd, Esq., of Westover, Charles City County, to John Woodson of Henrico County, for the annual rent of 20 pounds, the lease of Shockoe Ordinary, with the old storage house and all other houses thereunto belonging, from 25 December next.
Wit: Philip Watson, Robert Goode
Signed: W. Byrd, John Woodson
Recorded 7 February 1757

p.485  17 September 1756 Power of Attorney from Samuel Martin of Dublin, Ireland, to Richard Sqr. Taylor, merchant of Virginia, to ask, demand and receive all debts due and owing to the said Martin and his ward, his ward being George Barclay, which guardianship was granted by the Court of King & Queen County on the York River in Virginia.
Wit: Daniel Carver, Robert Jones, clerk to Benjamin Johnson and Richard Thwates, notaries public, Percevall Hunt, Lord Mayor of Dublin, Kingdom of Ireland
Signed: Saml. Martin                                      Recorded 8 March 1757

p.486  31 December 1756 Mary Martin, relict of George Martin, late of New Kent County, to her daughters, Mary Martin, Glais Martin, Judith Martin and Frances Martin, for natural affection I bear to my four children, one Negro man named Bristol, and stock and sundry household goods to be equally divided.
Wit: Charles Woodson, William Sharp, Isaac Sharp, George Richardson
Signed: Mary (her X mark) Martin                          Recorded 8 March 1757

p.487  7 March 1757 John Cox of Goochland County to William Randolph of Henrico County, for 60 pounds, 145 acres adj. lands of said Randolph.
Wit: none                                                 Signed: John Cox

Recorded 7 March 1757

p.487 3 January 1757 William Sharp to Robert Pleasants, both of Henrico County, for 103 pounds and 15 shillings, 100 acres adj. said Robert Pleasants, John Pleasants and John Sharp near the Roundabout Swamp and whereon the said Sharp now dwelleth.
Wit: Thomas Storrs, William (his X mark) Foster, Frederick Childers
Signed: William (his X mark) Sharp                Recorded 7 March 1757

p.488 27 August 1756 Deed of Mortgage from Abraham Childers and Henry Childers of Henrico county, to John Pleasants and Robert Pleasants, his son, merchants, for the payment of 100 pounds, with lawful interest, on or before 27 August 1763, collateral being 50 acres on the place called Roundabout adj.
Henry Sharp, Milner Redford and said John Pleasants and is the place whereon the said Abraham and Henry Childers now dwelleth; also 77 acres lying near the Gravelly Hill patented in the name of Abraham Childers, adj. Joseph Woodson, Francis Woodson, Robert Scott and the said Robert Pleasants.
Wit: Sarah (her X mark) Redford, Milner Redford, Ann Childers
Signed: Abraham Childers, Henry (his X mark) Childers
Recorded 7 March 1757

p.490 24 December 1756 Deed of Lease from the Hon. Wm. Byrd, Esq., to Philip Watson, merchant, a brick tenement and outbuildings on Shockoe Hill, together with 128 acres adjoining (metes and bounds) [see deed recorded 7 January 1757 on p.478]; repossession of premises will ensue if rent goes unpaid for two months.
Wit: none                                       Signed: Phil. Watson
Recorded 7 March 1757

p.491 30 November 1756 Deed of Mortgage from Joseph Childers to John Pleasants & Son, merchants, for the loan of 37 pounds and 4 shillings to be paid by 25 June 1758, collateral being 160 acres, being all my land and plantation whereon I now live.
Wit: Nathaniel Wilkinson, Samuel Childers, Samuel (his S mark) Childers, Jr.
Signed: Joseph (his I mark) Childers
Recorded 4 April 1757

p.492 7 March 1757 Richard Randolph, Gent., to James Lindsey, both of Henrico County, for 22 pounds, 100 acres between the branches of Four Mile Creek and White Oak Swamp, adj. said Lindsay, Samuel Garthright and William Hudson.
Wit: Nicholas Giles, Henry Sharp, Samuel Hobson
Signed: Richard Randolph                        Recorded 4 April 1757

p.493  13 August 1757 John Williamson, Sr., Gent., to William Jones, both of Henrico County, for 22 pounds, 125 acres on the branches of Deep Run, adj. said William Jones' land where he now lives and adj. land formerly owned by Jacob Roberson; on Plumtree Branch and on the south side of the Main Road . (metes and bounds description).
Wit: Leonard Henly, John Jude, Benjamin Clarke
Signed: John Williamson                                    Recorded 6 June 1757

p.494  10 February 1757 Deed of Mortgage from David Burton to Robert Goode, for the faithful performance of the will of Gilly Marrin upon the decedent's children coming of age and receiving their proper part of the estate. Robert Goode was surety of Mary Marrin, executrix of the will of her late husband, Gilley Marrin, deceased, who has intermarried with David Burton and who with her husband has been ordered by Henrico County Court to deliver to said Goode sufficient counter security. The collateral being seven Negroes: three men (Caesar, Will and Archer) and three women (Cloe, Amy and Betty) and a child (Edy), to be Goode's property until Marrin's will has been settled.
Wit: Philip Mayo, Isaac Younghusband
Signed: David Burton                                       Recorded 6 June 1757

p.495  13 October 1756 Orson Martin of Albemarle County to John Carter of Henrico County, for 55 pounds, 214 acres on the north side of White Oak Swamp at the mouth of Round Hill Branch of Chickahominy Swamp; adj. said John Carter and Orson Martin, Benjamin Jordan and John Cock.
Wit: Thomas Watkins, George Adams, Thomas Watkins, Jr., John Hales
Signed: Orson (his O mark) Martin                          Recorded 6 June 1757

p.496  6 June 1757 Eleanor Ford and John Ford, her husband, to Martin Martin, all of Henrico County, for 80 pounds, 100 acres on the north side of a branch called the Western Run, adj. Col. Peter Randolph, John Williams, William Porter, deceased, John Bracket, William Porter, Jr., deceased (being in possession of John Martin and Hannah Porter and Thomas Jolly) and the run of Western Run.
Wit: none                                   Signed: Eleanor Ford, John Ford
Recorded 6 June 1757

p.497 [—] June 1757 Deed of Gift from Nicholas Valentine of Henrico County to his son, James Valentine, for natural love and affection and also for son's "maintaining...and providing necessaries for his mother during her natural life, one horse and mare, four head of cattle, 15 head of hogs, two beds and furniture and all remainder of furniture.
Wit: W. Battersby, Benjamin Burton, Jr.

Signed: Nicholas Valentine                    Recorded 6 June 1757

p.497  25 June 1757 Power of Attorney from Gervas Elam of Richmond in Henrico County, being shortly for leaving this colony, to his brother, Joseph Elam, also of Richmond, to receive sums of money due and owing,
Wit: Charles Mackie, George Donald
Signed: Gervas Elam                           Recorded 4 July 1757

p.498  29 November 1756  Hon. William Byrd, Esq., to Samuel Duval, both of Henrico County, for 21 pounds, two lots in the Town of Richmond, each containing one half acre, laid off in the year 1742, being Lots 41 and 42 on the plan of the said Town.
Wit: Archibald Cary, Thomas Adams, Peter Randolph
Signed: W. Byrd     Recorded 7 March 1757 and further proven on 4 July 1757

p.499  2 July 1757 Deed of Gift from Thomas Connaway of Henrico County to his son, John Connaway, for love, good will and affection, 100 acres, being part of a tract of 268 acres; adj. John Shoemaker, Richard East and Holland.
Wit: William Kelley, Jonathan Bridgwater, Martha (her M mark) Kelley
Signed: Thomas (his T mark) Connaway
Recorded 4 July 1757

p.500  25 May 1757 Isham East of Lunenburg County to Thomas Jolly, for one Negro boy, Isaac, valued at 45 pounds, who was originally the right of Mary, the wife of the said Thomas Jolly; a Negro girl slave named Aggy, now in possession of the said Thomas Jolly, and one Negro child, Will, son of the said Aggy.
Wit: Charles Woodson, John Fussel, Benjamin (his B mark) Porter, James Lindsay
Signed: Isham East                            Recorded 4 July 1757

p.500  4 July 1757 Deed of Gift from Robert Sharp of Henrico County to his son, William Sharp, for love and good will and affection, 50 acres, adj. Maj. Adams and John Britton.                                                   Wit: none
Signed: Robert Sharpe                         Recorded 4 July 1757

p.501  4 July 1757 Deed of Gift from Robert Sharp of Henrico County to his son, Robert Sharp, Jr., for love and good will and affection, 100 acres, adj. Maj. Adams.
Wit: none                                     Signed: Robert Sharpe
Recorded 4 July 1757

p.502  30 July 1757 Joseph Lewis to William Barnes, both of Henrico County, in consideration of him thereunto moving and 20 pounds, 100 acres on Gilley's Creek,

adj. said Lewis and said Barnes.
Wit: Daniel Price, Jr., James Brittain, Dasey Southall
Signed: Joseph Lewis                    Recorded 1 August 1757

p.503  4 April 1757 Francis George Steger of Cumberland County, planter, to Jacob Valentine, of King William County, planter, in exchange for a tract of 85 acres in Henrico County, 70 acres on the southern branch of Gilley's Creek in Henrico County, granted to said Steger by patent dated 13 June 1755 and adj. John Oakley, Isaac Breeding, and Robertson (metes and bounds description).
Wit: William Battersby, James Vaughan, William Yarbrough
Signed: Francis George (his F mark) Steger, Jacob Valentine
Recorded [1] August 1757

p.504  4 April 1757 Jacob Valentine of King William County, planter, to Francis George Steger of Cumberland County, planter, in exchange for a tract of 70 acres in Henrico County, 85 acres in Henrico County adj. said Valentine, Alexander Robertson, Philip Mayo and part of the land said Jacob Valentine purchased of John Oakly.
Wit: William Battersby, James Vaughan, William Yarbrough
Signed: Jacob Valentine, Francis George (his F mark) Steger
Recorded 1 August 1757

p.505  12 June 1757 Deed of Gift from Derby Enroughty of Henrico County to his three grandsons, William, Derby and Nathan Whitlowe, for the natural affection I have and bear unto my daughter, Sarah Whitlowe, about 200 acres, adj. their father, William Whitlowe and David Breeden, Jonathan Williams and William Childress; 95 acres to Derby Whitlowe, being the land I live on; to Nathan Whitlowe the upper part of the tract; and to William Whitlowe, Jr., the middle part of the tract.
Wit: John Whitle, Richard Whitle, William Whitle
Signed: Derby Enroughty                 Recorded [1] August 1757

p.506  1 July 1757 Thomas Connaway to Nicholas Connaway, both of Henrico County, for 5 pounds, 50 acres adj. James Connaway, Holland, and Rocketts (metes and bounds description); granted to Thomas Connaway by patent.
Wit: Nathaniel Bridgwater, Agness (her X mark) Bridgwater, John Conway
Signed: Thomas (his T mark) Conway
Recorded 1 August 1757

p.507  1 August 1757 Deed of Gift from Dorsie Southall of Henrico County to his son, Turner Southall, for natural love and affection and for his better maintenance and livelihood, 100 acres adj. Maj. John Cole and Henry Brazeal's Swamp.

Wit: none Signed: Dasey Southall
Recorded (1) August 1757

p.508  30 July 1757 Deed of Gift from David Binns of Henrico County to his son, Joseph Binns, for natural love and affection and for his better maintenance and livelihood, 56 acres on the north side of Gilley's Creek; adj. Dioneshus Binns, Peter Binns, and Robertson, being the land said Binns purchased of James Hibton.
Wit: Joseph Lewis, Daniel Price, Jr., Dasey Southall
Signed: David Binns          Recorded [1] August 1757

p.509  1 August 1757 Deed of Gift from Nicholas Mealer to his son, Peter Mealer, 100 acres on the west side of Canaloses [Creek?] and adj. Abraham Bailey and Philip Mayo.
Wit: William Boull and William Bullington
Signed: Nicholas Mealer          Recorded [1] August 1757

p.509  16 April 1757 Power of Attorney from Arthur Robertson of the City of Glasgow, North Britain, merchant, and his son, Thomas Robertson, and for William and John Robertson, also his sons, to Robert Gilchrist, of Caroline County, merchant, to recover debts from Alexander Wodrow and John Neilson, Virginia merchants.
Wit: William Clarke, Alexander Ferrie, John Scott
Signed: Arthur Robertson, Thos. Robertson          Recorded 1 August 1757

p.510  1 August 1757 Deed of Gift from Benjamin Goode of Henrico County to his son, John Goode, for love, good will and affection and for 5 shillings, 50 acres, bounded by the land and plantation whereon I now live and Four Mile Creek.
Wit: none          Signed: Benjamin (his B mark) Goode
Recorded 3 October 1757

p.510  [—] 1757 Nicholas Mealer of Henrico County, to his daughter, Elizabeth Bullington, and her husband, William Bullington, for life and then to their male heir, and for want of such heir to descend to their eldest daughter, Mary Bullington, 100 acres on Caterpillar Branch.          Wit: none
Signed: Nicholas Mealer          Recorded 3 October 1757

p 511  2 October 1753 William Edwards, planter, to Drury Brazeil, planter, both of Henrico County, for 100 pounds, 200 acres on the north branch of Gilley's Creek, being part of the land given by Henry Brazeil, Sr., in his Deed of Gift dated 2 October 1720 (metes and bounds description).
Wit: Benjamin Burton, Jr., John Bryan, William Dinguid

Signed: William (his W mark) Edwards
Recorded 3 October 1757, having been continued for further proof from 4 February 1754

p.512  5 September 1757 Deed of Gift from Abraham Bailey of Henrico County to his son, Peter Bailey, for love, good will and affection and five shillings, 200 acres, adj. [--?--] Herbert, Peter Randolph, Henry Cox and John Alday (metes and bounds description).
Wit: Henry Sharp, William Redford, Abraham (her X mark) Childers
Signed: Abraham Bailey                              Recorded 3 October 1757

p.513  5 September 1757 Deed of Gift from Abraham Bailey of Henrico County to his son, Henry Bailey, for love, good will and affection and five shillings, 200 acres, adj. Peter Bailey and Alday (not a metes and bounds description).
Wit: James Lindsey, Thomas Childrey, and Henry Sharp
Signed: Abraham Bailey                              Recorded 3 October 1757

p.513  1 October 1757 Evan Shoemaker and Judith, his wife, to Benjamin Johnson, Jr., and Elizabeth, his wife, for 3 pounds and 5 shillings, 123 acres adj. Benjamin Johnson, Hardwick and Burdit.
Wit: Leonard Henley, Leonard Henley, Jr., Molly Henley
Signed: Evan (his I mark) Shewmaker, Judith (her M mark) Shewmaker
Recorded 3 October 1757

p.514  4 July 1757 William Harlowe of Albemarle County to Nathan Dunaway of Hanover County, for 4 pounds, 50 acres, being part of a patent of 400 acres granted to Thomas Farrar, deceased; adj. John Harlowe and David Bowles and Farrar's Branch.
Wit: John Harlowe, Jr., George Lucas, Edmund (his A mark) Humphrey
Signed: William Harlow                              Recorded 3 October 1757

p.515  5 September 1757 John Lankister to his son, Nathaniel Lankister, both of Henrico County, for 50 pounds, 180 acres on the south side of Deep Run, adj. John North, Richard Cottrell, John Eales and William Jones (metes and bounds description).
Wit: Christopher John Thomas, John Lankister, Francis (his X mark) Lankister
Signed: John (his I mark) Lankester                 Recorded 3 October 1757

p.516  20 November 1757 Deed of Mortgage from Richard Rockett of Henrico County to Robert Tucker of the Borough of Norfolk, in Norfolk County, merchant, for the payment of 316 pounds, 3 shillings and a penny on or before 20 April 1758,

the collateral being 480 acres on Peters Branch, 240 acres of which were purchased of his brother Ware Rockett by deed dated 11 April 1751; and 240 acres of which were devised by the will of Baldwin Rockett, deceased father of the said Richard Rockett; also six Negro slaves: Jammy, Hannah, Sue, Lett, Caesar and Peter; also three feather beds, one black walnut desk, one black walnut chest of drawers, six black walnut chairs with leather bottoms, two black walnut tables and six maps–one of the whole world, one of America, one of Europe, one of Asia, one of Africa and one of Great Britain.
Wit: none                                        Signed: Richd. Rockett
Recorded 5 December 1757

p.517  5 October 1757 Marriage Contract by and between Robert Mosby, Sr., of Henrico County and Agness Pulliam of Hanover County, upon the penal sum of 500 pounds, the said Mosby agrees to lend to the said Pulliam two Negroes, Grace and Peter, one feather bed, five head of cattle, six sheep, ten hogs and the liberty of my small room during her natural life, and the said Agness not to lay any right, title or claim to any more of the said Mosby's estate.
Wit: Charles Snead, James Norvell, John Pulliam
Signed: Robt. Mosby, Agness (her  X  mark) Pulliam
Recorded 7 November 1757

p.517  7 November 1757 James Geddy to George Donald, both of Henrico County, for 60 pounds, Lot 101 on the plan of the Town of Richmond.
Wit: none                                        Signed: James Geddy
Elizabeth, wife of James Geddy, relinquished her dower
Recorded 7 November 1757

p.518  3 March 1757 Benjamin Hubbard, merchant, to Elisha Miller, planter, of Henrico County, for 54 pounds, two Negro girls, Abigail and Frank, and their future increase.                          Wit: Thomas Adams, Thomas Wilkinson
Signed: Benja. Hubbard                        Recorded 7 November 1757

p.519  10 October 1757 Robert Mosby, the Elder, to his son, Robert Mosby, both of Henrico County, for natural love and affection, 560 acres, being the tract whereon I now live; said Mosby reserves life estate in same.
Wit: Nathaniel Wilkinson, Nathaniel Bacon, Thomas (his  T  mark) Gadbury
Signed: Robt. Mosby                              Recorded 7 November 1757

p.520  28 November 1757 John Clarke to his son, Peter Clarke, for 20 pounds, 50 acres, part of the tract I now live upon, joining Edward Pryor.
Wit: Ann (her  ♯  mark) Clarke, Thomas Eales, John Eales, Jr.,

Christopher John Thomas
Signed: John (his ╫ mark) Clark
Recorded 5 December 1757

p.521  3 December 1757 James Whitlowe to his son, Francis Whitlowe, for natural love and affection and for his better advancement in the world, 100 acres on my back line.
Wit: none  Signed: James (his ╪ mark) Whitlowe
Recorded 5 December 1757

p.521  28 November 1757 John Eales to John Eales, Jr., for 40 pounds, 100 acres on Deep Run; adj. Edward Pryer, Christopher John Thomas, and Richard Cottrell.
Wit: John (his X mark) Clarke, Sarah (her X mark) Clarke, Christopher John Thomas, Thomas Eales
Signed: John Eales  Recorded 5 December 1757

p.522  7 November 1757 Richard Holland and Sarah, his wife, of Henrico County, and Robert Donald of Hanover County, factor and agent for Andrew Cockson, James Donald & Co. of Glasgow, Scotland, merchants, to Benjamin DuVal of Henrico County, for 160 pounds, 372 acres on Hall's Branch, adj. Randolph, William Harding and Tuckahoe Creek; cites indenture of mortgage dated 14 January 1754, from Holland to Cockson & Donald in which the premises were the collateral and which land was acquired by Holland from Joseph and Jane Freeman by deed dated 29 May 1752, and also a chancery proceeding brought by William Harding against the said Richard Holland, in which the court decreed the sale of the premises to satisfy Harding's judgment against Holland.
Wit: Thomas Ellis, Henry Ellis, Thomas Alley, Junr.
Signed: Richard Holland, Sarah Holland, Robert Donald
Recorded 7 November 1757 and further proven on 5 December 1757

p.523  3 December 1757 Thomas Jordan of Henrico County to his son, Thomas Jordan, for true love and natural affection, 75 acres adj. George Cox, Edward Osborne, Thomas Perkins, the late William Randolph of Tuckahoe and the late John Bolling; which he purchased of Henry Jordan.
Wit: John Redford, Josiah Bullington, David Gill
Signed: Thomas (his X mark) Jordan  Recorded 6 March 1758

p.523 (no date) Luzby Turpin to Abraham Bayly, both of Henrico County, for 40 pounds, 47 acres between the lands of Bayly, Randolph and Turpin and part of a tract sold to the said Turpin by Jacob Burton.
Wit: Mark Clarke, Jr., Robert Adkines, Abraham (his X mark) Childers

Signed: Luzby Turpin
Sarah, wife of Luzby Turpin, relinquished her dower
Recorded 6 March 1758

p.524  7 March 1758 William Parker to John Whitlaw, both of Henrico County, for 30 pounds, 200 acres on Cornelius Creek, adj. Randolph and on the Great Branch and on the South Branch.
Wit: none                                                           Signed: William Parker
Ruth, wife of William Parker, relinquished her dower
Recorded 6 March 1768

p.525  6 March 1758 David Gill of Edgecomb County, North Carolina, to Mark Clarke, of Henrico County, for 18 pounds, 90 acres on Roundabout Swamp, adj. Randolph, Jonathan Williams, Elizabeth Scott, Joseph Atkins, John Fraser, Robert Scott and Hays Whitlow.
Wit: none                                                           Signed: David Gill,
Mary, wife of David Gill, relinquished her dower
Recorded 6 March 1758.

p.526  15 August 1757 Deed of Mortgage from Benjamin Childers, Sr., to John and Robert Pleasants, all of Henrico County, for the loan of 40 pounds with interest to be paid on or before 30 July 1761, collateral being 100 acres on which Childers now dwelleth, adj. James Woodfin, Thomas Mathews and William Taylor, also seven head of cattle and three feather beds.
Wit: William Lamby, William Irby, Thomas Storrs, John Brackett, Morris (his M mark) Hamblett, Saml. Pleasants, Thomas Pleasants, Robert Pleasants, Jr.
Signed: Benjamin (his B mark) Childers
Recorded 6 March 1758

p.527  4 March 1758 Elizabeth Dorton to her son, John Dorton, both of Henrico County, for 5 pounds per annum, 50 acres on the south side of the Chickahominy River, in the fork of the Great Branch, adj. John Wilson and Matthew Johnson; being part of the land said Elizabeth Dorton purchased of Julius Allen.
Wit: George Clopton, William Boselt, William Garthright
Signed: Elizabeth (her E mark) Dorton
Recorded 6 March 1758

p.528  23 January 1758 Milner Redford, planter and millright, to John Pleasants (of Baylies Creek), both of Henrico County, for 70 pounds, one-half part of a tract of 61 acres on both sides of Four Mile Creek and one-half part of a water grist mill standing thereon "now in repair"; bounded as by a former deed from Thomas and

Joseph Pleasants to John Redford, father of the said Milner Redford, and James Powell Cocke for the same land.
Wit: Lewis Hancock, William Clopton, John Redford, Jr.
Signed: Milner Redford    Sarah, wife of Milner Redford, relinquished her dower
Recorded 6 March 1758

p.529  6 March 1753 Stephen Pankey of Chesterfield County to William Brittan, Jr., of Henrico County, for 5 pounds, 77 acres adj. John Watson, John Bowe, Crafford, Patman and Patrick.
(metes and bounds description).
Wit: none                              Signed: Stephen (his S mark) Pankey
Recorded 6 March 1758

p.530  1 August 1758 Roland Blackburn to John Ellis, Gent., both of Henrico County, for 3 pounds and 10 shillings, 7 acres on the Deep Run; adj. the mill now belonging partly to the said John Ellis and partly to David Staples (metes and bounds description).
Wit: William Street, Henry Ellis, Nicholas (his N mark) Amos
Signed: Roland (his RB mark) Blackburn
Recorded 1 May 1758

p.531  20 March 1758 John Mosbey and Lucy, his wife, to Francis Cornett, all of Henrico County, for 15 pounds, 30 acres adj. said Mosbey, Capt. John Watson and William Ford.
Wit: Nathaniel Bacon, John Bryan
Signed: John (his I mark) Mosbey [wife did not sign]
Recorded 1 May 1758

p.532  17 December 1757 John Lacy of Henrico County to Charles Cottrell of Cumberland County, for 10 pounds, 100 acres on the Eastern Branch of the Deep Run, being part of the same tract wherepm saod John Lacy now lives.
(metes and bounds description).
Wit: William Street, John (his ✝ mark) Lankester, Richard Cottrell
Signed: John Lacy                              Recorded 1 May 1758

p.533  28 November 1757 John Eales of Henrico County to Thomas Eales, for 30 pounds, 200 acres on the north side of the Deep Run, adj. lines of Edward Rives and John Sincocks.
Wit: John Clarke, Sarah Clarke, Christopher John Thomas, John Eales, Junr.
Signed: John Eales                              Recorded 1 May 1758

p.534 3 December 1757 Thomas Alley, Sr., to David Hall, both of Henrico County, for 7 pounds, 50 acres on the Deep Runn, being part of the land whereon the said Thomas Alley now lives and on a branch called Stony Run; adj. Alexander Patterson, John Blackburn, David Staples and said Thomas Alley (metes and bounds description.
Wit: William Street, Edmund Alley, John Eales, Jr.
Signed: Thomas (his A mark) Alley                                  Recorded 1 May 1758

p.535 1 May 1758 William Harding of St. James Parish Northam, Goochland County, to John Jude of Henrico Count, for 100 pounds (10 shillings per acre), a tract adj. said John Jude, Henry Ware and Thomas Fenton and the former line of George Chambers, including all the land of Thomas Harding Patten not heretofore made mention of.
Wit: Leonard Henley, William (his X mark) Barker, Giles Letcher, George Henderson
Signed: William Harding                                  Recorded 1 May 1758

p.536 1 August 1756 (1757) Philemon Childers, Sr., to John Pleasants & Son, merchants, all of Henrico County, for 11 pounds, 100 acres, being one-half part of the land which said Philemon Childers bought of Thomas Bates; adj. Capt. John Williamson.
Wit: Joseph Lewis, William Lewis, Nathaniel Bacon, Robert Gording
Signed: Philemon (his | mark) Childers
Recorded 5 December 1757

p.537 7 March 1758 Deed of Mortgage from William Harding of Goochland County to John Wayles of Charles City County, for payment of two sums of money: 27 pounds, 19 shillings and 9 pence current money; and 33 pounds, 4 shillings and 9 pence sterling, plus interest on a Protested Bill of Exchange, to be paid within twelve months; collateral being 218 acres on the branches of Tuckahoe Creek, being the same tract Harding purchased of George Chambers and the plantation Richard Holland now dwelleth on.
Wit: Robert Hughes, George Henderson, Thomas Farrar, Jr.,
Signed: William Harding                                  Recorded 5 June 1758

p.538 5 June 1758 John Williams, Jr., to Leonard Henley, both of Henrico County, for 30 pounds, 100 acres at the mouth of Sampson's Slash, adj. the Hon. Col. Peter Randolph.
Wit: Robert Shapard, William Ellis, William Rountree
Signed: John (his W mark) Williams                                  Recorded 5 June 1758

p.539  8 December 1757 Thomas Matthews to his brother, Edward Matthews, both of Henrico County, for love and good will and to fulfill the last will and testament of his father, Thomas Matthews, deceased, and 20 shillings, 50 acres, being the moiety of the tract where the said Thomas Matthews now dwells and to be laid off on the south part of the said tract — the dividing line to begin at the spring now commonly used.
Wit: Charles Woodson, William Hatcher, James Lindsey
Signed: Thomas Mattis                                           Recorded 5 June 1758

p.540  5 June 1758 John West to Isham West, both of Henrico County, for 10 pounds and 1 shilling, 50 acres on the branches of Cornelius Creek whereon the said John West now lives; adj. the land of the last John Whitlow, deceased.
Wit: William (his X mark) Berns, John Robertson, William Robertson
Signed: John Weast
Sarah, wife of John West, relinquished her dower.
Recorded 5 June 1758

p.541  7 August 1758 Matthew Harbord to his son, John Harbord, for natural love and affection and for his better advancment in the world, 50 acres adj. Abraham Bailey, John Alday and Isaac Younghusband.
Wit: none                                        Signed: Matthew Harbord
Recorded 7 August 1758

p.542  7 August 1758 Philip Watson to George Donald, both of Henrico County, for 26 pounds, 17 shillings and 6 pence, Lot 4 on the plan of the Town of Richmond, beng the back lot of the brick store in the said town.
Wit: A. Stith, Nathaniel Bacon
Signed: Phil. Watson                                           Recorded 7 August 1758

p.543  18 January 1758 Hickason Cox of Chesterfield County to William Randolph of Henrico County, for 50 pounds,  105 acres adj. said Randolph, Turpin and Bailey, and which was given to the said Cox by the will of his grandfather, Richard Cox.                    Wit: John Armour, John Ker, Richard West
Signed: Hickason (his  X  mark) Cox
Recorded 7 August 1758

p.544  5 May 1758 John Williams to John Martin, both of Henrico County, for 25 pounds, 180 acres in the fork of White Oak Swamp, being one-half part of a patent granted to the said John Williams and to be laid off by two of the neighbors whom the said Martin shall choose to make a division line.
Wit: Mark Clark, Jr., Thomas (his        mark) Robinson, Jr., Edward Parker

Signed: John Williams                          Recorded 4 September 1758

p.545  23 September 1758 William Stone of Henrico County to John Robinson the Elder, of Lunenburg County, for 5 shillings, all of his right and title to 130 acres adj. Alexander Robinson, David Binns and James Cocke.
Wit: John Pride, Junr., George Colebrooke
Signed: William Stone                        Recorded 2 October 1758

p.546  6 November 1758 Thomas Merrit to Matthew Hobson, both of Henrico County, for 11 pounds, 85 acres on the Long and Hungry Branch and bounded as specified in a deed from Thomas Baughan to the said Thomas Merrit.
Wit: John Crosse, William (his *M* mark) Jones, Nathaniel Wilkinson
Signed: Thomas Merrit
Eleanor, wife of Thomas Merrit, relinquished her dower.
Recorded 6 November 1758

p.547  8 January 1758 Apprenticeship Contract between Emanuel Johnson, son of Robert Johnson of Henrico County, to George Robertson, carpenter, also of Henrico County, for the said Emanuel Johnson to be apprenticed for six years next ensuing in the trade of a carpenter, to be given a full suit of clothing and also a set of carpenter's tools; said apprentice to behave himself as a good and faithful apprentice ought.
Wit: James Woodfin, George Clarke, William (his X mark) Robertson
Signed: George Robertson, Emanuel Johnson
Recorded 6 November 1758

p.547  6 November 1758 William Morris to James Britton, Jr., both of Henrico County, for 12 pounds, 112 acres adj. Robert Webb and Michael Holland (metes and bounds description).
Wit: John Crosse, James Ball, Samuel Brittain
Signed: Wm. Morris                        Recorded 6 November 1758

p.549  6 November 1758 Michael Jones, and Ann, his wife, of Henrico County, to John Weaver of St. Peter's Parish, New Kent County, for 58 pounds, 100 acres on Gilley's Creek, adj. William Fleming Cocke, David Binns and John Barnes, excepting a Burying place where one of my children is Interred. (metes and bounds description).
Wit: William Garthright, John Perkins, Nathaniel Wilkinson
Signed: Michael Jones, Ann (her X mark) Jones
Recorded 6 November 1758

p.550  18 September 1758 Peter Gottie, and Sally, his wife, to Francis George Stegar, all of Cumberland County, for 50 pounds, seven lots in the Town of Richmond, being the same lots devised by the last will and testament of Samuel Shiffely to his daughter Sally, being lots 59, 60, 73, 74 and a lot that I bought of Adam Earnest (No. 61) and two lots called C and D as by said Schiffely's will may more fully and at large appear.
Wit: William Diuguid, George Scherer, Thomas Hales Stegge
Signed: Petrus Gottie, Sarah Gottie             Recorded 6 November 1758

p.552  27 March 1758 Thomas Owen of Henrico County to Samuel DuVal, for 15 pounds, 496 acres granted by patent dated 1744, adj. John Sheppherd, Robert Webb, Robert Morris, Wheeler, Holland and Royall (metes and bounds description).
Wit: John Bryan, Groves Harding, James (his I B mark) Briton, Benjamin Duval
Signed: Thomas Owen             Recorded 6 November 1758

p.555  3 April 1758 Michael Harfield to Waldegrave Clopton, both of St. Peter's Parish, New Kent County, for 259 pounds, 952 acres at the mouth of the Boar Swamp and thence up the swamp to Harden's Branch, adj. Richard Truman and down the Road from Bottom's Bridge to the Falls of the James River to Thomas Bottom and thence to the Chickahominy Swamp and along said swamp to Boar Swamp.
Wit: Julius Allin, John Bryan, Joseph Brown, Edmond Alley
Signed: Michl. Harfield             Recorded 6 November 1758

p.558  3 July 1758 William Harding of Goochland County to William Henly of Henrico County, for 5 pounds, 50 acres in the upper end of Henrico County and being part of a larger tract which said Harding bought of the heirs of William Laffoon, deceased, and adj. the tract said Henly bought of Henry Woodey (metes and bounds description).
Wit: Julius Allin, George Adams, Benjamin Clarke
Signed: William Harding             Recorded 4 December 1758

p.559  1 December 1758 Deed of Mortgage from John West, planter, to John Pleasants, merchant, both of Henrico County, to cause to be paid 100 pounds with lawful interest before the expiration of twelve months, collateral being three Negroes: Frank, Esther and Jamey and their increase.
Wit: Samuel Garthright, Jr., John White
Signed: John West             Recorded 4 December 1758

p.561  30 October 1758 John West, son and heir of John West, late of Henrico

County, to my mother, Mary West, for 63 pounds and 10 shillings, two Negro men slaves: Peter and Dick, being the property of my father, John West, deceased.
Wit: Charles Woodson, Francis Redford, Richard (his X mark) Whitloe
Signed: John West                                                Recorded 1 January 1759

p.561 1 January 1759 Deed of Mortgage from John Bryant of Henrico County to the Reverend Miles Selden, Clerk, for 5 shillings, for securing to the said Miles Selden all manner of court charges, troubles or damages that may anyways happen or arise to the said Miles Selden by reason of his suretyship to Samuel DuVal, High Sheriff of Henrico County, for the said John Bryant's faithful execution of the office of Deputy Sheriff, collateral being four lots lying in the Town of Richmond whereon the said John Bryant now dwelleth, and slaves: Phyllis, a woman; Iris, a girl and Cuffy, a boy, together with all the household furniture, horses, hogs and cattle belonging to the said John Bryant.
Wit: none                                                        Signed: John Bryant
Recorded 1 January 1759

p.563 8 November 1757 John Martin of Albemarle County to William Wade of Goochland County, for 5 pounds, 100 acres, being all of the remaining part of the tract called Ben Hoars; adj. said William Wade, Henley, Woodey, the fork of Drinking Hole and crossing Pouncies Road, and Liggon.
Wit: John Jude, Mary Jude, Leonard Henley
Signed: John his $\mathbf{\bar{I}}$ mark) Martin
Recorded 5 March 1759, continued from 6 March 1758 for further proof

p.564 5 February 1759 William Dinguid, (attorney for William Mouatt, administrator of Samuel Gleadowe, deceased, by virtue of a power of attorney dated 9 July 1754) to Benjamin Johnson, for 11 pounds, 100 acres, adj. said Benjamin Johnson, Hardwick and Burditt.
Wit: none
Signed: Wm. Dinguid, attorney for Wm. Mouatt, administrator of the estate of Samuel Gleadowe, deceased.
Recorded 5 February 1759

p.566 21 November 1758 George Freeman and Amos Hix, both of Lunenburg County, to James Ball of Henrico County, for 80 pounds, 216 acres on the branches of Tuckahoe Creek; adj. Randolph and Scraping Branch, and being part of a larger tract granted by patent to George Freeman, deceased, the grandfather of the said George Freeman, and by him left to his son George in his last will and testament and which thereby fell to heirship unto this said George Freeman.
[Note: No explanation is given as to why Amos Hix is a party to this deed.]

Wit: Thomas Alley, Jr., William Alley, Thomas Alley
Signed: George Freeman, Amos Hix
Recorded 5 March 1759

p.567 10 November 1758 William Sims and Susannah, his wife, of the Province of North Carolina, to Zacharias Tait of Hanover County, for 40 pounds, 200 acres on the west side of a branch called the Brook, which tract was conveyed to the said William Sims by John Lipscomb; adj. Wm. Byrd, Esq., William Snead, Nathaniel Bridgwater and others.
Wit: Moses (his M mark) Gentry, William Sharp, Robert Sharp
Signed: William Sims, Susanah Sims
Recorded 5 March 1759

p.569 2 April 1759 Joseph Lewis of Henrico County to John West, and Sarah, his wife, for their natural lives, and to Mary West, daughter of the said John and Sarah, forever, for 23 pounds, 100 acres on the Long Slash, adj. William Nance, William Bowles and John Nance, being part of a patent granted William Lewis; cites that John West intermarried with Sarah Barnes, who had a fortune in slaves to the value of at least 150 pounds, and through his mismanagement or misfortune the whole fortune is nearly exhausted, and to give said John and Sarah a place of residence for their natural lives and in order that their daughter may reap some benefit of her mother's fortune.
Wit: Richard Williamson, Christopher Binns, Joseph (his +++ mark) Hambleton
Signed: Joseph Lewis                                    Recorded 2 April 1759

p.571 9 March 1759 John West and John Pleasants, Jr., to Julius Allen, all of Henrico County, for 120 pounds, three Negroes — Esther, Frank and Jame, said Esther and Jame being in the possession of John West and Frank being in the possession of Mary Whitloe, grandmother of the said John West, and by the will of John Whitloe bequeathed to the said John West upon the death of Mary Whitloe.
Wit: Mark Clarke, Jr., John Barns, Samuel Bridgwater
Signed: John West, John Pleasants, Jr.
Recorded 2 April 1759

p.572 19 April 1759 John Eales of Henrico County to his wife, Elizabeth Eales, all my personal estate as well as my outstanding debts, all and every part to be at her disposal to the intent she may not be charged to the parish where she shall live, as I am intended to travel.
Wit: Christopher John Thomas, John Eales, Jr., Thomas Eales
Signed: John Eales                                      Recorded 7 May 1759

p.573  10 March 1759 John Wood to William Fleming Cocke, both of Henrico County, for 27 pounds, 100 acres, being the plantation of land whereon William Spraggins lived; adj., David Binns, William Fleming Cocke and Thomas Cocke.
Wit: John Pleasants Car, Robert Price, Pleasants Woodson, James Gunn
Signed: John (his Ŧ mark) Wood
Frances, wife of John Wood, relinquished her dower
Recorded 7 May 1759

p.574  17 April 1759 John Eales, Jr., and Elizabeth Eales, to William Price of Goochland County, for 100 pounds, 100 acres on the Deep Run, adj. Edward Pryer, Christopher John Thomas and Richard Cottrell.
Wit: Christopher John Thomas, Peter Clarke, William(his Ⱥ mark) Jones
 Edmund Alley                    Signed: John Eales, Jr., Elizabeth Eales
Recorded 7 May 1759

p.576  7 March 1759 John Brackett to Robert Pleasants, both of Henrico County, 20 pounds, 50 acres adj. Col. Benjamin Harris, Humphrey Smith, the said Pleasants, Turkey Island Creek and the Three Run; being the same land granted by patent to Henry Watkins by date of 23 October 1690 and by his son and heir, Thomas Watkins, sold to the said John Brackett.
Wit: none                                    Signed: John Brackett
Recorded 7 May 1759

p.577  2 June 1759 Luzby Turpin to William Randolph, both of Henrico County, for 80 pounds, 160 acres, being part of the tract said Turpin purchased of Benjamin Burton.
Wit: Alexander Mackie, James Deans, Thomas Eldridge
Signed: Luzby Turpin                         Recorded 6 August 1759

p.578  12 March 1759 James Cocke and William Fleming Cocke to George Scherer, all of Henrico County, for 20 pounds, one lot or half acre of ground in the town of Richmond, being Lot 19 on the plan of the said town.
Wit: William Lewis, Joseph Lewis, Loudwick Warrock
Signed: James Cocke, Wm. F. Cocke
Recorded 6 August 1759

p.579  2 April 1759 Stephen Woodson of Henrico County to his grandchildren, Samuel Bell and Mary Bell, children of George Bell the younger of Louisa County, for love and affection, two Negro slaves, Jacob and Agee, now in the possession of the said George Bell.
Wit: Daniel Price, Robert Spears, Caleb Stone

Signed: Stephen Woodson                    Recorded 6 August 1759

p.580  28 June 1759 Henry Brazeal to John Harwood of Henrico County, for 20 shillings, one acre on the fork of said Brazeal's branch and said Harwood's branch, adj. old Porter's line, beginning at said Brazeal's branch and the old ford. Wit: Thomas Frankling, Drury Brazeal
Signed: Henry Brazeall, Senr.              Recorded 6 August 1759

p.581  10 April 1759 Richard Eppes of Charles City County to Robert Pleasants of Henrico County, for 150 pounds, 490 acres on both sides of White Oak Swamp; adj. Benjamin Jordan and James Binford.
Wit: Mary Eppes, Elizabeth Harwood, William Hardyman
Signed: Richd. Eppes                       Recorded 6 August 1759

p.583  5 March 1759  Dr. Robert Brown of the Town of Norfol[k], Nansemond County [sic], to John Pride, Junr., of the Town of Richmond, Henrico County, for 72 pounds, 10 shillings, one mulatto woman slave, Hannah.
Wit: Thomas Adams, Philip Watson
Signed: Robt. Brown                        Recorded 6 August 1759

p.584  25 April 1759 Commission of John Pride, Jr., as Deputy Clerk of Henrico County, from Thomas Nelson, Esq., upon the powers granted by the Honorable William Adair, Esq., Secretary of the Colony of Virginia, upon application from Thomas Adams, gentleman, Clerk of Henrico County, to act during his absence or indisposition.
Signed: Thos. Nelson                       Recorded 6 August 1759

p.585  3 September 1759 Francis George Stegar of Cumberland County to John Orr of Henrico County, 16 pounds, Lot 61 on the plan of the Town of Richmond, bought of the Honorable William Byrd.                                   Wit: none
Signed: Fran. Geo. (his  F  mark) Stegar
Recorded 3 September 1759

p.586  10 March 1759 Power of Attorney from John Coles and Jane Coles of Henrico County, to our trusty and well beloved brother, Henry Hobson of Cumberland County, to collect for the hire of Major, Jamy and Peter.
Wit: John Pleasants, Junr., William Hatcher
Signed: John Coles, Jn. Coles
Recorded 1 October 1759

p.587 [___] September 1759 William Hughes and Ann, his wife, of Hanover County, to William Harris of Louisa County, for 90 pounds, 450 acres at said Hughes' mill dam on Meredith's Branch and along the Chickahominy Swamp; formerly belonging to Richard Holland.
Wit: none                    Signed: William Hughes, Ann Huegs [sic]
Recorded 1 October 1759

p.588  4 February 1757 Daniel, John, William and Thomas Warriner to their sister, Sarah Warriner, in conformity to the last will and testament of our father, John Warriner, deceased, all our right, title and interest in a Negro boy child, Frank, born of the body of Jane, a Negro woman slave.
Wit: Abraham Trueman, Joseph Warinner, Benjamin Warinner
Signed: Daniel (his d  mark) Warriner, John Warriner, William Warriner,
   Thomas Warriner                         Recorded 1 October 1759

p.589  3 September 1759 Robert Sharp, Jr., to Stephen Woodson, both of Henrico County, for 120 pounds, 100 acres given me by my father, Robert Sharp, adj. Maj. Adams and Capt. Smith.
Wit: none                    Signed: Robt. (his R  mark) Sharp
Susanna, wife of Robert Sharp, Jr., relinquished her dower.
Recorded 1 October 1759

p.590  1 October 1759 Francis Wilkinson and Margaret, his wife, of Henrico County, to William Harris of Louisa County, for 60 pounds, 200 acres on the Chickahominy Swamp (metes and bounds description)
Wit: none                    Signed: Thomas Wilkinson, Margaret Wilkinson
Recorded 1 October 1759

p.592  1 October 1759 William Barns to John Barns, both of Henrico County, for 25 pounds, 100 acres on Gilley's Creek; adj. Joseph Lewis and John Barnes.
Wit: none                    Signed: William (his  X  mark) Barns
Mary, wife of William Barns, relinquished her dower.
Recorded 1 October 1759

p.593  12 October 1759 William Garret and Elizabeth, his wife, of the province of North Carolina, to William Parker, of Henrico County, for 16 pounds, 200 acres adj. Thomas Jordan, Alexander Long, Thomas Randolph and Thomas Perkins; Robert Bullington now living on 100 acres of the 200 acres conveyed.
Wit: Ambros Owen, Edward Parker, George Tirey [Tyree], William Ware
Signed: William (his  +  mark) Garret, Elizabeth (her  +  mark) Garret
Recorded 5 November 1759

p.595  5 January 1760 Thomas Robinson, Jr., to his brother, George Robinson, for 20 pounds, a tract on the branches of Four Mile Creek and being on Clay Branch, the Eastern Run and Daniel's Slash, and adj. Edward Goode.
Wit: Charles Woodson, George Richardson, Samuel Richardson
Signed: Thomas Robinson, Junr.
Jane, wife of Thomas Robinson, Jr., relinquished her dower.
Recorded: 4 February 1760

p.596  24 November 1759 John Ragland, carpenter, to Richard Trueman, planter, both of Henrico County, for 5 pounds, 10 acres, being the lower end of a tract which said John Ragland purchased of Waldugrove Clopton and Unity, his wife; on the Falls Road and adj. Michael Harfield, the said Trueman and Waldugrove Clopton.
Wit: John Trueman, William Gathrite, William Gathrite, Jr., Elizabeth Trueman
Signed: John Raglin                                    Recorded 4 February 1760

p.598  4 February 1760 Josiah Allday to Matthew Herbert, both of Henrico County, for two pounds, 40 acres adj. Herbert and Cocke and on Arthur's Run and Tom Field's Creek and adj. Cox Whitlo; part of a patent granted to my father, John Allday dated 5 March 1747 (metes and bounds description).
Wit: Julius Allin, Richard Crump
Signed: Josiah (his | mark) Alday
Recorded 4 February 1760

p.599  24 November 1759 Deed of Gift from James Cocke of Henrico County to his son-in-law, John Winston, Junr., of Goochland County, for natural love and affection, Lot No. 6 on the plan of the Town of Richmond; being the same lot granted by William Byrd, Esq., to the said James Cocke by deed dated 28 November 1740.
Wit: Edward Curd, Mary Curd, William Winston
Signed: James Cocke                                    Recorded 4 February 1760

p.600  24 August 1759 Henry Bailey to Benjamin Bullington, both of Henrico County, for 15 pounds, 200 acres adj. Peter Bailey, Cox and John Alday; being the tract granted to the said Henry Bailey by Abraham Bailey by deed dated 5 September 1757.
Wit: Matthew Branch, Junr., John Rowland, David Mackie
Signed: Henry Bailey                                   Recorded 4 February 1760

p.601  9 January 1760 David Staples to Capt. John Ellis, both of Henrico County,

for 42 pounds, 10 acres on Deep Run and being the part of Staple's tract whereon his mill now stands, adj. Blackburn and David Hall.
Wit: William Street, Joseph Ellis, Jr., Thomas (his A mark) Alley
Signed: David Staples
Recorded [4 February 1760]; no certificate added

p.603  4 February 1760 Josiah Allday to Edmund Sumpter, both of Henrico County, for 8 pounds, 160 acres adj. Cox Whitlo, Abraham Bailey and Matthew Herbert and which was granted by my father, John Allday, by patent dated
5 March 1747.                                                            Wit: none
Signed: Josiah (his ʃ mark) Allday
Recorded 4 February 1760

p.604  7 January 1760 Peter Mealer to Henry Nixon, both of Henrico County, for 20 pounds, 100 acres on the north side of Cornelius Creek, adj. James Whitlow, Junr., Abraham Bailey and Philip Mayo.
Wit: Mark Clarke, Edmund Sumpter, John Harbord
Signed: Peter Mealer                                    Recorded 4 February 1760

p.605  1 June 1758 Bond of William Dickerson and William Smith to Lewis Burwell Martin, in the amount of 304 pounds, 10 shillings and 10 pence, for the payment of the just sum of 152 pounds 5 shillings and 5 pence to be paid before the 21st of April next ensuing.
Wit: John Shelton, William Harrison
Signed: W. Dickerson & Smith                           Recorded 4 February 1760

p.606  4 January 1759 Hutchins Burton, Sr., of Henrico County to Royall Richard Allen of Middlesex County, 23 pounds, 100 acres on Upnam Brook, adj. William Gordon, John Watson and Thomas Jackson; being the tract formerly belonging to John Childro.
Wit: Richard Burton, David Allen, Julius Burton
Signed: Hutchins Burton, Sr.                           Recorded 4 February 1760

p.607  17 May 1759 Mark Clark to John Pleasants, Junr., both of Henrico County, for 16 pounds and 10 shillings, 90 acres lying on the head of Roundabout Swamp, adj. Joseph Adkins, John Frayser, Hays Whitlow, Robert Scott, Col. William Randolph and Jonothan Williams.
Wit: Charles Gay, William Lester, James Parker
Signed: Mark Clark, Junr                               Recorded 4 February 1760

p.608  12 June 1759 Philip Johnson of James City County to Samuel Gathwright,

Junr. of Henrico County, for 95 pounds, two Negro slaves: a woman named Hannah and her sucking child named Betty.
Wit: Julius Allen, William Gathwright
Signed: Phil. Johnson                                    Recorded 4 February 1760

p.609  8 December 1759 Alexander Long to Josiah Bullington, both of Henrico County, for 800 pounds, all of his real and personal estate, being 189 acres of land,, excepting 50 acres at the upper end of said land joining Burton and Eppes, to be held by the said Long for the term of his natural life, one Negro man slave named Dick, with stock, household furniture and other movables.
Wit: Thomas (his ƒ mark) Jordan, Mark Woodcock, John Redford, Junr.
Signed: Alexander (his  A  mark) Long
Recorded 3 March 1760

p.610  10 December 1759 Deed of Exchange between John Redford to John Redford, his son, both of Henrico County, for the mutual exchange of land and 25 pounds if any ejectment should ensue, 25 acres adj. Bolling, John Redford, Jr., and Chincopen Island line to the son; and 25 acres on Roundabout Swamp, Cranches Ferry Road and Chincopen Island line to the father.
Wit: Josiah Bullington, Alexander (his  A  mark) Long,
John (his  I  mark) Woodcock
Signed: John Redford, John Redford, Junr.
Recorded 3 March 1760

p.612  3 September 1759 John West to William Barnes, both of Henrico County, for 76 pounds, 100 acres, being the land said Barnes now lives on, which did belong to my father, John West, deceased, and joins Luxby Turpin, Richard Renard, Col. William Randolph and John Whitlow, deceased.
Wit: Nicholas Mealow, John Harbord, Benjamin Bullington, William Redford
Signed: John Weast                                       Recorded 1 October 1759
Sarah, wife of John Weast, relinquished her dower and release of dower certified on 3 March 1760.

p.613  3 March 1760 Arthanabue Fair and Mary, his wife, of Albemarle County, to Charles Floyd of Charles City County, for 100 pounds, 244 acres on the branches of Turkey Island Creek, adj. Col. Benjamin Harrison, Stephen Woodson and John Middleton.                                                               Wit: none
Signed: Arthanabue (his  G  mark) Feir, Mary (her ∂ mark) Feir
Recorded 3 March 1760

p.615  3 March 1760 Bond of Julius Allen as inspector of tobacco at the public

warehouse at Shockoe in the amount of 500 pounds;, said Allen being appointed and commissioned as such by the Hon. Francis Fauquier, Lieutenant Governor; sureties being Samuel Duval and Joseph Lewis.
Wit: Thomas Adams
Signed: Julius Allin , Saml. Duval, Joseph Lewis
Recorded 3 March 1760

p.616  1 October 1759 Bond of Philip Mayo as Sheriff of Henrico County in the amount of 500 pounds; being appointed and commissioned as such by the Hon. Francis Fauquier under the seal of the Council dated 17 August last past; sureties being James Cocke and Daniel Price.
Wit: Thomas Adams
Signed: Philip Mayo, James Cocke, Daniel Price
Acknowledged at November Court, 1759            No date of record entered

p.616  7 April 1760 William Nance to James Vallentine, both of Henrico County, for 15 pounds, 93 acres on the road that leads to New Kent, adj. Thomas Boles, John West, Joseph Lewis and John Watson; being part of a patent granted to Michael Jones bearing date of 8 June 1754.
Wit: Joseph Lewis, William Smith, Jr., John Bryan
Signed: William Nance     Mary, wife of William Nance, relinquished her dower.
Recorded 7 April 1760


p.618  17 March 1760 John New, wheelwright, to his son, William New, both of Henrico County, for love and affection, 350 acres, being part of my tract on Genito Branch, the Swamp Road and adj. Robert Cooke, Cole and Mill Creek.
Wit: Benjamin New, John Bryan
Signed: John New                          Recorded 7 April 1760

p.619  2 April 1760 Alexander McCaul, merchant, to Turner Southall, planter, both of Henrico County, for 19 pounds and 10 shillings, 26 acres he bought of Robert Cooke; adj. William Byrd, Esq., John New and Abraham Cowley.
Wit: none                          Signed: Alexander McCaul
Recorded 7 April 1760

p.620  7 April 1760 William New to Turner Southall, both of Henrico County, for 100 pounds, 26 acres, adj. Dasey Southall, William Wood and Abraham Cowley.
Wit: none                          Signed: William (his N mark) New
Recorded 7 April 1760

p.621  29 March 1760 Turner Southall to William New, for 100 pounds, 26 acres adj. William Bird, Mr. New and Abraham Cowley.
Wit: none                                          Signed: Turner Southall
Recorded 7 April 1760

p.622  5 May 1760 Abraham North to William Hall, both of Henrico County, for 20 pounds, 66 acres on Deep Run, being that parcel given to the said Abraham North by his father, William North, by his last will and testament; adj. John Blackburn and Alexander Peterson and crossing Stony Run.
Wit: none                              Signed: Abram (his A mark) North
Susannah, wife of Abraham North, relinquished her dower.
Recorded: 5 May 1760

p.624  4 January 1760 Edward Osborne of Chesterfield County to George Cox of Henrico County, for 322 pounds and 10 shillings, 150 acres, it being that land said Edward Osborne purchased of John Cox; adj. the George Cocke land that he now lives on, Thomas Jerdone and James River.
Wit: Thomas Howlett, Charles Burton, Thomas Howlett, Junr.
Signed: Edward Osborne
Elizabeth, wife of Edward Osborne, relinquished her dower.
Recorded 5 May 1760

p.625  23 April 1760 John Pleasants, Junr. to William Frayser, both of Henrico County, for 16 pounds and 10 shillings, 90 acres on the branches of Roundabout Swamp; adj. Childers, Hays Whitloe, Col. William Randolph, David Breeding and Betty Scott.          Wit: Charles Gay, Priscilla Madderra, Ursula Liptrott
Signed: Jno. Pleasants, Junr.                         Recorded 5 May 1760

p.626  27 February 1760 Col. Richard Randolph, Gent., and Ann, his wife, to (Capt.) John Ellis, all of Henrico County, for 58 pounds, 1 shilling and 2 pence, 105 acres on both sides of Tuckahoe Creek, adj. said Ellis' tract of land whereon he now lives and part of a tract of 945 acres beloning to the said Richard Randolph known as Windsor Forrest (metes and bounds description).
Wit: Henry Ellis, Charles Jordan, Benjamin Clark
Signed: Richard Randolph, Ann Randolph
Recorded 5 May 1760

p.628  27 February 1760 Col. Richard Randolph, Gent., and Ann, his wife, to Henry Ellis, all of Henrico County, for 76 pounds, 17 shilliings and 4 pence, 139 acres on both sides of Tuckahoe Creek, being part of a tract of 945 acres known as Windsor Forrest (metes and bounds description).

Wit: John Woodward, Benjamin Clark, Charles Jordan
Signed: Richard Randolph, Ann Randolph
Recorded 5 May 1760

p.630   27 February 1760 Col. Richard Randolph, Gent., and Ann, his wife, to Thomas Ellis, all of Henrico County, for 179 pounds, 13 shillings and 11 pence, 325 acres on Tuckahoe Creek, being part of a tract of 945 acres known as Windsor Forrest; adj. said Thomas Ellis' own tract whereon he now lives and also adj. Benjamin Duval (metes and bounds description).
Wit: Henry Ellis, Charles Jordan, Benjamin Clark
Signed: Richard Randolph, Ann Randolph
Recorded 5 May 1760

p.632   27 February 1760 Col. Richard Randolph, Gent., and Ann, his wife, to William Ellis, all of Henrico County, for 38 pounds, 14 shillings and three pence, 70 acres on Tuckahoe Creek, being part of a tract of 945 acres known as Windsor Forrest; adj. said William Ellis' own land whereon he now lives.
(metes and bounds description).
Wit: Henry Ellis, Charles Jordan, Benjamin Clark
Signed: Richard Randolph, Ann Randolph
Recorded 5 May 1760


p.634  3 May 1760 John Ellis, Gent., and Elizabeth, his wife, to Jacob Smith, all of Henrico County, for 30 pounds, 366 acres, being part of a tract of 800 acres granted by patent to Obidiah Smith and by him given to his son-in-law and daughter, John Ellis and Elizabeth, his wife (metes and bounds description).
Wit: Thomas Ellis, William Ellis, Henry Ellis, William Street
Signed: John Ellis, Elizabeth Ellis                    Recorded 5 May 1760

p.636  5 December 1759 Robert Childers of Albemarle County, to John Eales, Junr., of Henrico County, for 25 pounds, 150 acres on Meriday's Branch, adj. Holland, Buxton, Miller, Lacy, Ellis and Ford.
Wit: Christopher John Thomas, Peter Clark, William Price
Signed: Robert (his X mark) Childers            Recorded: 2 June 1760

p.637  1 May 1760 William Ellis to John Clarke, both of Henrico County, for 31 pounds, 140 acres on Stony Run, adj. what was formerly Baughone's (Vaughan's?) line, Eales, Simble, Thomas Alley, Junr., said William Ellis' line that divides it from the plantation where Aaron Freeman did live and the plantation sold.
Wit: Christopher John Thomas, Peter Clark, William Price

Signed: William Ellis,
Mary, wife of William Ellis, relinquished her dower.
Recorded 2 June 1760

p.639   11 April 1760 Sackvill Brewer of Hanover County, to William Miller, of Henrico County, for 35 pounds, 130 acres on both sides of the Brook; adj. Richard Hynes and William Kelly.
Wit: John Conway, Jacob Smith, Nathaniel Bridgwater
Signed: Sackvill Brewer                                        Recorded 2 June 1760

p.640   27 July 1759 Matthew Hutcheson of Henrico County to Joseph Clark of Northam Parish, Goochland County, for 20 pounds, 300 acres on the branches of the Brook; adj. John Jones, Breavs Holloway, John Watson, deceased, and Philemon Childers; being the land said Matthew Hutcheson obtained by the will of his father, Matthew Hutcheson, deceased.
Wit: Turner (his  T  mark) Clark, Evan (his  E  mark) Shewmaker,
John (his  J  mark) Clark
Signed: Matthew Hutcheson
Proved  by two witnesses on 4 February 1760 and further proved and recorded at June Court

p.641   2 June 1760 Richard Randolph to Henry Ellis, both of Henrico County;, for 20 shillings, two acres lying on Tuckahoe between the said Ellis' land called Windsor Forrest and his new land.
Wit: John Woodward, Thomas Ellis, Charles Jordan
Signed: Richard Randolph                                       Recorded 2 June 1760

p.642   15 February 1755 Renny Leforce of Goochland County to Sarah Harding of Henrico County for life and then to the children of William Harding that he now has by Sarah Harding, his wife, all right, title and interest in a Negro wench called Sue and a boy called Sesar [Caesar?], which came by the death of Rachel Leforce.
Wit: Thomas Alley, Junr., William Buxton, Sarah  (her B mark)  Burdett
Signed: Rene Laforce
Proved by one witness on 2 June 1760 and further proved and admitted to record on 5 August 1760

p.642   1 October 1759 Bond of John Markham as Surveyor of Henrico County in the amount of 500 pounds; Samuel DuVal and William Smith, sureties.
Wit: Thomas Adams
Signed: John Markham, Saml. DuVal, William Smith
Recorded 1 October 1759

p.643   2 June 1760 Thomas Adams of New Kent County to William Acrill of Charles City County, for 150 pounds, 186 acres on Chickahominy Swamp "bounded according to the known ancient and reputed bounds thereof."
Wit: none                                                            Signed: Thos. Adams
Recorded 7 July 1760

p.644   31 March 1760 Ryland Randolph to William Hatcher, both of Henrico County, for 83 pounds, 41 ½ acres, being part of the Turkey Island tract; adj. Joseph Hobson and Bailey John Pleasants.
Wit: Richard Randolph, John Randolph, Thomas Eldridge
Signed: Ryland Randolph                                Recorded 4 August 1760

p.644   10 May 1760 John Hales to James Binford, both of Henrico County, for 18 pounds, 20 acres on White Oak Swamp; adj. Robert Pleasants, James Binford and John Hales; and along the Main Road to the White Oak Swamp bridge and thence up the said stream.
Wit: Saml. Gathright, William Hobson
Signed: John Hales                                        Recorded 4 August 1760

p.645   4 August 1760 Philip Watson to Miles Taylor, both of Henrico County, for 40 pounds, one half-acre lot on the plan of the Town of Richmond, being Lot 17 on said plan.
Wit: none                                                            Signed: Phil. Watson
Recorded 4 August 1760

p.645   [number duplicated in sequence of pages] 28 June 1760 John Miller to Samuel Duval, both of Henrico County, for 300 pounds, 70 acres on the north side of Deep Run, between the lands of William Buxton, John White, Thomas Conaway, John Shoemaker and Maj. Mayo.
Wit: Christopher Mood, John Bryan, Benjamin Duval.
Signed: John Miller                                        Recorded 4 August 1760

p.646   5 May 1760 John Orr to John Jude, both of Henrico County, for 12 pounds, 103 acres on the eastern branch of Tuckahoe Creek; adj. Leonard Henley, Sr., John Watson, Evan Shoemaker and the said John Jude, and including all the land formerly belonging to Gervis Burditt.
Wit: Leonard Henley, Nathaniel Bacon, Obediah Smith, Timothy Vaughan
Signed: John Orr                                           Recorded 4 August 1760

p.648 [____] 1760 Richard Moor to Robert Moor, his son, for 30 pounds, 33 acres, being all the land that the said Richard Moor now possesses; adj. John Lee, Robert

Pleasants, Frederick Clarke, George Clarke, Isaac White and George Adams.
Wit: George Adams, John Moore
Signed: Richard (his  R  mark) Moor
Recorded 1 September 1760

p.648 Sarah Harding relinquished her dower in the lands conveyed by her husband, William Harding, to John Jude. Priscilla Miller relinquished her dower in the lands conveyed by her husband, John Miller, to Samuel Duval.
Recorded 1 September 1760

p.649  3 June 1758 Deed of Mortgage from Walter Leigh of Cumberland County to Charles Woodson of Henrico County, for 100 pounds with lawful interest to be paid by 10 June 1760, six slaves: Rachel, Fanney, Tom, Anakey, Matilda and Patt. (Released on margin of page by Charles Woodson on 3 May 1762.)
Wit: Edward (his ✚ mark) Matthews, William Reams, Mary (her M mark) Reams
Signed: Walter Leigh                             Recorded 1 September 1760

p.650  31 August 1760 Edmond Alley of Henrico County to David Alley, for two pounds, 50 acres on the Main Road, adj. Thomas Alley, Sr., William Ellis and Rockett.
Wit: Ja. Alley, Richard Burton, David Harris
Signed: Edmond Alley                             Recorded 1 September 1760

p.651  25 August 1760 David Hall and Darkes [Dorcas] Hall, his wife, of Henrico County, to John Price of Goochland County, for 30 pounds, 50 acres adj. John Blackburn, William Hall, Alexander Patterson, Thomas Alley, Staples and Ellis.
Wit: Christopher John Thomas, Samuel Shepard, William Price
Signed: David (his  X  mark) Hall, Dorcas Hall [apparently literate]
Recorded 1 September 1760

p.653  3 November 1760 James Allen to Isham Allen, both of Henrico County, for 40 shillings, 100 acres adj. Thomas Elmore, Littleberry Allen, Martin Martin, Anthony Matthews and Valentine Freeman, deceased; being the land James Allen purchased of Martin Martin.
Wit: none
Signed: James Allen, Elizabeth, wife of James Allen, relinquished her dower.
Recorded: 3 November 1760

p.654  3 November 1760 Isham Allen to Julius Allen, both of Henrico County, for 45 pounds, 137½ acres adj. said Julius Allen, Littleberry Allen, Thomas Elmore and John Watson; being the land that Isham Allen purchased of John Elmore.

Wit: none    Signed: Isham (his \ mark) Allen
Agnes, wife of Isham Allen, relinquished her dower.
Recorded 3 November 1760

p.654 6 October 1760 Valentine Ball of Albemarle County to John Jude of Henrico County, for 70 pounds, 400 acres adj. Col. William Randolph, Col. Byrd, Philip Watson, Benjamin Clarke and Giles Gordon.
Wit: John Hughes, Leonard Henley, William Buxton, James Ball
Signed: Valentine Ball
Recorded 3 November 1760

p.656 6 October 1760 Leonard Henley to Lusby Turpin, both of Henrico County, for 25 pounds, 70 acres on Cornelius Creek at the mouth of Sampson's Slash; adj. Col. Peter Randolph and Josiah Allday.
Wit: Richard Adams, John Redford, John Bryan
Signed: Leond. Henley
Recorded 3 November 1760

p.657 6 October 1760 William Price, son of John, to John Miller, both of Henrico County, for 150 pounds, 100 acres on the Deep Run; adj. Richard Cottrell, Edward Pryor and Christopher John Thomas.
Wit: Christopher John Thomas, Nathaniel Lancaster, Samuel Childers
Signed: William Price    Susannah, wife of William Price relinquished her dower.
Recorded 3 November 1760

p.658 3 November 1760 George Robinson and Margery, my wife, to John Robinson, my son, all of Henrico County, for love, good will and affection, 8 cattle, 20 hogs, 3 feather beds and furniture, 2 iron pots, 3 dishes, 2 basins, 10 plates, 1 chest, 2 boxes and 1 mare.
Wit: Louwick Warreck, John Bryan
Signed: George (his X mark) Robinson, Margery (her I mark) Robinson
Recorded 3 November 1760

p.659 28 July 1760 Charles Floyd of Charles City County to Thomas Rodgers, Junr., both of Henrico County, 40 pounds, 120 acres adj. Col. Benjamin Harrison, Stephen Woodson and John Middleton; being part of the land bought of Arthanatius Fear and Mary, his wife.
Wit: Robert Pleasants, Thomas Bates, W. Harrison, John Williams
Signed: Charles Floyd    Sarah, wife of Charles Floyd, relinquished her dower.
Recorded 3 November 1760

p.661   1 December 1760 William Fleming Cocke to Abraham Cowley, both of Henrico County, for 130 pounds, a tract of land on Chickahominy Swamp at the mouth of Deep Bottom branch; adj. Capt. Joseph Lewis (metes and bounds description).
Wit: none                                                                    Signed: Wm. F. Cocke
Theodosia, wife of William Fleming Cocke, relinquished her dower.
Recorded 1 December 1760

p.662   1 December 1760 Josiah Allday to Lusby Turpin, both of Henrico County, for 80 pounds, two certain separate tracts: 1) 125 acres on the north side of Cornelius Creek; adj. Joseph Bailey, John Allday, Leonard Henley, Peter Randolph, Esq., and Mary Allday, with reservation of about 10 or 12 feet square for a burial place of said Josiah Allday and his descendants; and 2) 10 acres adj. Peter Randolph, Esq., Leonard Henley and said Lusby Turpin.
Wit: Mary Burton, David Womack, John Kendall
Signed: Josiah (his ʃ mark) Allday
Anna, wife of Josiah Allday, relinquished her dower.
Recorded 1 December 1760

p.663  Theodosia, wife of William Fleming Cocke, relinquished her dower in lands sold by her husband to George Scherer by deed of August 1759.
Recorded 1 December 1760

p 664  1 December 1760 John White to Samuel Duval, both of Henrico County, for 41 pounds, 164 acres on the east side of Deep Run; adj. William Buxton, Samuel Duval, John Lancaster and Holland's Estate.
Wit: none                                                                       Signed: John White
Mary, wife of John White, relinquished her dower
Recorded 1 December 1760

p.665   8 November 1760  John Redford, Sr., planter, to his son, William Cocke Redford, both of Henrico County, for great love and affection, 25 acres on Roundabout Swamp, adj. the plantation I now live on, and also adj. John Redford, Jr. and the Chinquapin Island line.
Wit: Mary Redford, Thomas Williams, Mary (her ✚ mark) Williams
Signed: John Redford                                          Recorded on 2 February 1761

p.666   2 March 1761 Bond of Philip Mayo as Sheriff of Henrico County, in the penalty of 1,000 pounds, during pleasure by commission from the Governor under the seal of this colony dated 17 August 1759, with Charles Woodson, his surety.
Wit: Thomas Adams

Signed: Philip Mayo, Charles Woodson                Recorded 2 March 1761

p.667  2 March 1761 William Patman to John Staples, both of Henrico County, for 10 pounds, 50 acres adj. John Watson and John Staples.
Wit: none                                                      Signed: Wm. Pattman
Sarah, wife of William Patman, relinquished her dower
Recorded 2 March 1761

p.668  2 February 1761 Apprenticeship Bond of Joseph Scott of Amelia County and John Scott, his guardian, also of Amelia County, to George Donald of Richmond Town, Henrico County, cabinet maker; said Joseph Scott to be bound to the said Donald for a term of six years from the date hereof.
Wit: Walter Coles, John Coles, Mardun Dr Eventon
Signed: Geo. Donald, Jos. Scott, Jno. Scott                    Recorded 2 March 1761

p.669  2 March 1761 Henry Whitlow of Amelia County to his brother, James Whitlow, for natural love and affection and for his better advancement in the world, 100 acres on both sides of the great meadow of Four Mile Creek; being the land whereon the said Henry Whitlow lately lived.
Wit: Thomas Williams, John Enroughty, Richard Frogmorton
Signed: Henry Whitlow                                          Recorded 2 March 1761

p.669  20 February 1761 (H)Ezekiah Bridgman of Henrico County to David White of Hanover County, for 25 pounds, 50 acres on the New Kent Road; adj. John Harwood, James Cocke and William Rone.
Wit: Joseph Lewis, Samuel Woody, Samuel White
Signed: Ezekiah (his ℮ mark) Brigman
Mary, wife of Hezikiah Bridgman, relinquished her dower.
Recorded 2 March 1761

p.670  5 February 1761 Deed of Lease from Waldegrave Clopton and Unity, his wife, of New Kent County, to George Clopton of Henrico County, for paying to the said Waldegrave Clopton or to the Sheriff of Henrico County the yearly quit rent on the 300 acres of land hereby leased, two tracts: 1) 100 acres commonly called the Middle Ground on the Iron Mine Branch; and 2) 200 acres whereon the said George Clopton now lives; on Bottoms Bridge road and adj. Michael Harfield and Thomas Bottom's Quarter Path.
Wit: John Bacon, William Jones, Nathaniel Tucker
Signed: Waldegrave Clopton        [No signature or release of dower by wife]
Recorded 2 March 1761

p.672  14 March 1761 John North to William Jones, for 25 pounds, 100 acres adj. John Lancaster, said William Jones and Nathaniel Lancaster.
Wit: David Allen, Julius Burton, Samuel Jones
Signed: John (his Ŧ mark) North
Sarah, wife of John North, relinquished her dower.
Recorded 4 May 1761

p.673  29 November 1760 William Hughes of Hanover County, to his son, William Hughes, Jr., for love, good will and affection, 500 acres on Meredith's Branch, a branch of the Chickahominy Swamp, and being the land I bought of Richard Holland and being the land whereon said Holland once lived; adj. Harris and Mill Pond (metes and bounds description).
Wit: Samuel Morris, William Hughes, Archelus Hughes.
Signed: William Hughes                                              Recorded 4 May 1761

p.674  14 February 1761 Francis Whitlow of Amelia County to James Whitlow, Jr. of Henrico Count, for 8 pounds, 100 acres adj. James Whitlow.
Wit: William Whitlow, William Whitlow, Junr., Darby Whitlow
Signed: Francis Whitlow                                             Recorded 4 May 1761

p.675  4 May 1761 Henry Whitlow and James Whitlow, Jr., of Henrico County to James Whitlow, Senr., also of Henrico County, for 31 pounds, 100 acres on both sides of Four Mile Creek; being the lower end of the tract bought by said James Whitlow of William Whitlow and part of the tract whereon said James Whitlow now lives.
Wit: William Whitlow, William Whitlow, Junr., Darby Whitlow
Signed: Henry (his X mark) Whitlow, James Whitlow, Junr.
Lory, wife of James Whitlow, Jr., relinquished her dower
Recorded 4 May 1761

p.676  9 December 1760 Waldegrave Clopton of St. Peter's Parish, New Kent County, to Isaac White of Henrico County, for 40 pounds, 125 acres on Bottom's Bridge Road, Middle Ground Branch, Boar Swamp and Harding's Branch.
Wit: George Adams, John Trueman, Charles White
Signed: Waldegrave Clopton
Unity, wife of Waldegrave Clopton, relinquished her dower.
Recorded 4 May 1761

p.678  3 October 1760 William Lawless to William Henley, both of Henrico County, 50 pounds, 100 acres on the road near the upper end of Henrico County and on two branches of Tuckahoe Creek called Harding's Branch and Peter's

Branch and is the same tract whereon the said Lawless lately lived and which he bought of George Chambers; adj. William Harding, Leonard Henley, John Jude and Rockett.
Wit: John Ellis, William Ellis, Henry Ellis
Signed: William Lawless, Sarah (her X mark) Lawless
Recorded 4 May 1761

p.679 20 March 1761 Samuel Williamson of Hanover County to Dabney Pettus of Louisa County, for 304 pounds, 304 acres on the south side of Trumpet Branch; adj. Samuel Allen, Jr., and the Brook (metes and bounds description).
Wit: Elisha Miller, Cutbirth Williamson, William Miller, John Williamson
Signed: Samuel Williamson                    Recorded 1 June 1761

p.681 6 March 1761 Anthony Haden of Hanover County to his son-in-law, Jacob Ferris, and his daughter, Ruth Ferris, for love and natural affection, one Negro woman named Aggy and her two children, Amey and Sarah, to pass to the children of Jacob and Ruth Ferris upon their deaths.
Wit: George Clopton, Thomas Haden
Signed: Anthony Haden                    Recorded June Court 1761

p.681 3 August 1761 Mathew Hopson to his grandson, Hopson Owen, son of Thomas Owen, all of Henrico County, for natural love and affection and for his better maintenance and performance, 150 acres on the south side of Turner's Run; adj. Joseph Parsons, Senr.                    Wit: none
Signed: Matthew (his X mark) Hobson
[spelled both Hopson and Hobson in the records].
Recorded 3 August 1761

p.682 3 August 1761 Thomas Owen, Sr., to his son, Thomas Owen, Jr., both of Henrico County, for natural love and affection and for better maintenance and performance, 300 acres on the Chickahominy Swamp, adj. Joseph Parsons, John Owen and William Owen; after the decease of the said Thomas Owen (Sr) and not before.
Wit: none                    Signed: Thos. Owen
Recorded 3 August 1761

p.683 3 August 1761 William Barnes to John West, both of Henrico County, for 26 pounds, 100 acres on the branches of Cornelius Creek; being part of the land whereon John West, father of the said John West did live, and adj. Col. William Randolph, Luzby Turpin, Richard Renard, Isham West and the late John Whitloe, deceased.

Wit: John Weaver, John Barnes, Isam West, James Whitlow
Signed: John West   Sarah, wife of John West, relinquished her dower
Recorded 3 August 1761

p.685  7 February 1761 William Turner to John Mosby and John Staples, all of Henrico County, for 5 pounds, 116 acres on Pigpen Branch, being part of a tract that belonged to William Turner, deceased; adj. John Wheeler, Jacob Smith and Nathan Turner.
Wit: Benjamin Wilson, Bremillion Holloway, Francis (his ✝ mark) Cornet
Signed: William (his ✝ mark) Turner
Proved by two witnesses on 4 May 1761
and recorded 3 August 1761 upon further proof

p.686  1 June 1761 Watson Patman to George Jennings, Jr., both of Henrico County, for 8 pounds, 30 acres on Hungry Branch, adj. William Turner.
Wit: none                                             Signed: Watson Patman
Sarah, wife of Watson Patman, relinquished her dower.
Recorded 3 August 1761

p.687  3 July 1761 Thomas Conaway to John Williamson, both of Henrico County, for 5 pounds, 50 acres adj. John Conaway, Holland's line and Nicholas Conaway being part of the land granted by patent to the said Thomas Conaway dated 5 August 1751.
Wit: Robert Williamson, William Miller, Allen Williamson
Signed: Thomas (his  T  mark) Conaway
Recorded 3 August 1761

p.688  3 August 1761 John Conaway to John Williamson, both of Henrico County, for 10 pounds, 100 acres, being part of a piece of land taken up by Thomas Conaway and granted by Thomas Conaway to the said John Conaway on 2 July 1751; adj. John Shoemaker, Richard Eales. Richard Holland's and Thomas Conaway.
Wit: Robert Williamson, William Miller, Allen Williamson
Signed: John Conaway                                  Recorded 3 August 1761

p.689  3 August 1761 Francis West of Hanover County to Robert Elliott of Henrico County, for 5 pounds, Lot G half H on plan of the Town of Richmond near Shockoe Creek, being a lot purchased by James Garner, which lot was escheated in the year 1759 by William Watkins for the said Francis West.
Wit: John Martin, Nicholas Scherrer, George Scherrer
Signed: Francis West   Elizabeth, wife of Francis West, relinquished her dower.

Recorded 3 August 1761

p.690  29 July 1761 Richard Hines of Cumberland County to James Browning of Henrico County, for 50 pounds, 200 acres adj. John Williamson's former line and one John Lankford's former line on the north side of the Main Branch.
Wit: John Williamson, Robert Williamson, Watson Patman
Signed: Richard Ds. Hines , Mary, wife of Richard Hines, relinquished her dower.
Recorded 3 August 1761

p.692  20 March 1761 Power of Attorney from John Martin of Dublin, Ireland, to Hon. William Nelson, Esq., and Lewis Burwell, Esq., of the Colony of Virginia, to ask, demand, sue for and recover in Virginia sums of money due.
Wit: Robert Currey, Daniel Cowman, John (his ✚ mark) Middleton, William (his + mark) Broadway
Signed: Jno. Martin                             Recorded 3 August 1761

p.692  9 July 1761 Luzby Turpin to Abraham Bailey, Jr., both of Henrico County, for 80 pounds, 100 acres adj. William and Richard Cox, Finney and Abram Bailey.
Wit: John Redford, Josiah Redford, Leonard Ward
Signed: Luzby Turpin                            Recorded 3 August 1761

p.694  7 September 1761 John Jude to Leonard Henley, both of Henrico County, for 50 pounds, 200 acres on Deep Branch, adj. Benjamin Clarke, John Clarke, Thomas Lewis and John Gording.
Wit: Richard Adams, George Payne, Peter Clarke
Signed: John Jude        Mary, wife of John Jude, relinquished her dower.
Recorded 7 September 1761

p.695  3 September 1761 John Redford, Senr., to William Cocke Redford, both of Henrico County, for 10 pounds, 20 acres on Roundabout Swamp, being a part of my plantation I now live on, adj. John Redford, Junr.
Wit: none                                       Signed: John Redford
Recorded 7 September 1761

p.696  14 August 1761 William Sheilds of Halifax County to Robert Pleasants of Henrico County, for 40 pounds, 50 acres adj. John Middleton and John Brackett; being the land on which said William Sheilds lately dwelt and which was purchased by John Lewis per deed in the Clerk's Office of the General Court.
Wit: Thomas Bates, Pleasants Jordan, Joseph Goode, Joseph Pleasants
Signed: William Sheilds                  Recorded 7 September 1761

p.697  7 September 1761 John Pleasants & Son, merchants, to Matthew Herbert, all of Henrico County, 13 pounds and 13 shillings, 100 acres, being one-half of the land which Philemon Childers bought of Thomas Bates and conveyed to the said Pleasants by deed dated 1 August 1756; adj. Capt. John Williamson.
Wit: none                                  Signed: John Pleasants & Son
Recorded 7 September 1761

p.699  7 September 1761 Bond of Ryland Randolph as Sheriff of Henrico County, appointed by commission of the Governor dated 21 August last past, in the amount of 1,000 pounds, with Richard Randolph and Bowler Cocke, Jr., his sureties.
Wit: Thomas Adams
Signed: Ry. Randolph, Richard Randolph, Bowler Cocke, Junr.
Recorded 7 September 1761

p.701  21 August 1761 James Ball, and Susannah, his wife, to Richard Cottrell, all of Henrico County, for 82 pounds and 10 shillings, 216 acres on the branches of Tuckahoe Creek; being part of a larger tract granted by patent to George Freeman, deceased, the grandfather of the said George Freeman and by him left to his son, George Freeman, in his last will and testament; adj. Randolph and Scraping Branch.
Wit: Peter Massie, Edmond Allen, Daniel Moore, David Allen
Signed: James Ball, Susanah Ball           Recorded 5 December 1761

p.702  4 January 1762 Abraham Cowley to John Price, both of Henrico County, for 5 pounds, 7 shillings and 6 pence, one-half acre lot in the Town of Westham; being lot 99 in the plan of said town.                                    Wit: none
Signed: Abrahm. Cowley                     Recorded 4 January 1762

p.703  14 September 1761 John Woodson and Francis Peirce to Robert Adkins, all of Henrico County, for 50 pounds and 16 shillings, one Negro girl named Amy.
Wit: Miles Selden, Miles Taylor, Robert Pleasants, Jr.
Signed: John Woodson, Francis (his ✚ mark) Pearce, Junr.
Recorded October Court 1761

p.703  14 September 1761 John Woodson and Francis Peirce to Robert Pleasants, Junr., all of Henrico County, for 82 pounds and 5 shillings, two Negro slaves, viz. Mary, a woman, and Tom, her youngest son.
Wit: Miles Selden, Miles Taylor, Robert Adkins
Signed: John Woodson, Francis (his ✚ mark) Pearce, Junr.
Recorded October Court 1761

p.704  5 October 1761 Col. Richard Randolph, Gent., and Anne, his wife, to

Leonard Henley, all of Henrico County, for 55 pounds, 7 shillings and 6 pence, 400 acres on the branches of Tuckahoe Creek granted to Col. Richard Randolph, deceased, father of the said Richard Randolph. by patent and included in his Windsor Forrest tract; adj. Henry Ellis, John Ellis, Rockett, William Ellis and Thomas Ellis (metes and bounds description).
Wit: none
Signed: Richard Randolph [no signature for wife, nor release of dower]
Recorded 5 October 1761

p.706  1 February 1762 Isaac Breading of New Kent County to William Bowles of Hanover County, for a tract in New Kent County, 174 acres on the Southern Branch; adj. Capt. Joseph Lewis, William Nance, John Watson, Philip Mayo and Jacob Valentine.
Wit: James Allen, James Vollintine, Miles Garthright, Junr.
Signed: Isaac Breeding                           Recorded 1 February 1762

p.707  4 January 1762 Samuel Gording to Robert Gording, both of Henrico County, for 25 pounds, 50 acres on the Brook, adj. John Gording, Samuel Gording, Giles Gording, Robert Gording and Thomas Lewis; according to the patent lines of William Gording, deceased.
Wit: Christopher John Thomas, John (his I mark) Lankester, Leonard Henley
Signed: Samuel (his S mark) Gording
Recorded 1 February 1762

p.709  8 September 1761 John Sheppard, planter, to William Sheppard, planter, for 8 pounds, a tract on the south side of the Chickahominy Swamp, lying at the lower end of the land said John Sheppard now lives on at said swamp and running up the swamp to the mouth of the Miry Branch and thence up the said branch; being the land patented by the said John Sheppard.
Wit: Benjamin Bowles, Robert (his R mark) Webb, Benjamin Sheppard
Signed: John Sheppard                           Recorded 1 February 1762

p.710  1 February 1762 Walter Coles to Alexander Brown, both of Henrico County, for 40 pounds, four acres, bounded on the south by Wiltshire Marrin, southwest by the James River, west by Walter Coles and Robert Cook and east by the Main Road that leads from Rockett's Landing at the the mouth of Gilley's Creek to Richmond Town.
Wit: none                                       Signed: Walter Coles
Recorded February Court 1762

p.711  1 February 1762 Walter Coles to Robert Cook, both of Henrico County, for

8 pounds, lot of one-half acre between the lands of Alexander Brown, the said Walter Coles and the Main Road that leads from the mouth of Gilley's Creek to Richmond Town.
Wit: none　　　　　　　　　　　　　　　　　　　Signed: Walter Coles
Recorded 1 February 1762

p.712　1 February 1762 Bond of John Radford, Jr., as one of the inspectors of tobacco at the Publick Warehouse established at Four Mile Creek, who was appointed by the Honorable Francis Fauquier, Esq., his Majesty's Lieutenant Governor, commander in chief of the colony and dominion of Virginia, in the amount of 500 pounds, his sureties being Thomas Childers, Jesse Burton and Thomas Williams.
Wit: Thomas Adams
Signed: John Radford, Jr., Thomas (his　T　mark) Childrey, Jesse Burton,
Thomas Williams　　　　　　　　　　　　　　Recorded 1 February 1762

p.712　7 December 1761 Bond of Thomas Wilkinson as one of the inspectors of tobacco at the Publick Warehouse established at Shoces (Shockoes), who was appointed by the Honorable Francis Fauquier, Esq., etc., in the amount of 500 pounds, his surety being Robert Williamson.
Wit: Thomas Adams
Signed: Thomas Wilkinson, Robert Williams
Recorded 7 December 1761

p.713　7 December 1761 Bond of Robert Williamson as one of the inspectors of tobacco at the Publick Warehouse established at Byrds, who was appointed by the Honorable Francis Fauquier, Esq., etc., in the amount of 500 pounds.
Wit: Thomas Adams
Signed: Robert Williamson, Thomas Wilkenson
Recorded 7 December 1761

p.714　20 February 1762 Apprenticeship Bond of John Symes, son of Richard Symes, late of Somershire and parish of Huntspill, deceased, to William Wills, of the Town of Richmond, Henrico County, surgeon, to serve from the first day of November last past for and during the term of five years ensuing; it is agreed that if any disputes should arise between them that the same be left to the determination of Robert Goode, and if he should judge that the apprentice is ill-used, the said Wills doth hereby oblige himself to let the said apprentice have liberty to return to England, and that he, the said Wills, will pay his passage.
Wit: none　　　　　　　　　　　　　　　　Signed: Wm. Wills, John Symes
Recorded 1 March 1762

p.715  4 January 1762 Philip Watson to John Kelley, both of Henrico County, 70 pounds, 315 acres adj. Hon. William Byrd, said Philip Watson, Zachariah Tate, Jonathan Bridgwater, William Kelley, Benjamin Clark, John Jude and Parker's Hospen [Horsepen?] Branch.
Wit: none                                        Signed: Phil. Watson
 Elizabeth, wife of Philip Watson, relinquished her dower on 1 March 1762.
Recorded 4 January 1762

p.716  3 April 1762 Nathaniel Vandewall to Francis Franklin, both of Henrico County, for 36 pounds, 100 acres, being the tract and plantation whereon George Robinson of late did dwell; adj. John Burton, Philip Mayo, Eleanor Williams and Barnard Agee.
Wit: Drury Wood, Thomas Williams, Jonathan Williams
Signed: Nath'el Vandewall
Elizabeth, wife of Nathaniel Vandewall, relinquished her dower.
Recorded April Court, 1762

p.717  6 February 1762 Martin Martin, Sr., to Anthony Mathews, both of Henrico County, for 12 pounds and 15 shillings, 50 acres adj. said Anthony Matthews, Hughes' Slash and Isham Allen; being part of the land I purchased of Thomas Harding, deceased.
Wit: George Adams, Ephraim Gathright, John Martin,
Lucy (her  X  mark) Adams
Signed: Martin (his  M  mark) Martin          Recorded 5 April 1762

p.719  5 April 1762 George Donald to John Orr, both of Henrico County, for 26 pounds, 17 shillings and 6 pence, one half-acre lot, being Lot 61 on the plan of the Town of Richmond.
Wit: none                                        Signed: Geo. Donald
Recorded 5 April 1762

p.719  9 October 1742 Bond of Edward Watkins to James Cocke, Gent., for 500 pounds and to put to an end a suit for settling a divisional line; cites that the said James Cocke about two years since commenced a chancery suit in the General Court against the said Edward Watkins for the compelling of the said Edward Watkins to run a divisional line pursuant to an agreement and deed made to the said James Cocke by William and James Watkins; said line is now determined to begin at a black shrub oak between Edward Watkins and Daniel Price, and thence to a maple, and thence to a poplar and a beech on each side of the main stream of Deep Run and thence up Chickahominy Swamp; adj. Edward Curd and Daniel Price; to include Cocke's land purchased of William and James Watkins.

Wit: Andrew Barclay, Samuel Thompson
Signed: Edward (his E mark) Watkins
Recorded 5 April 1762

p.721  13 March 1762 John Law to Joseph Parsons, both of Henrico County, for 200 pounds, 230 acres on the west side of Beechom Branch, adj. John Watkins, John Orange and John Owens.
Wit: Royal Brittain, Joseph (his ✚ mark) Goode, Thomas Owen
Signed: John (his I mark) Law Sarah wife of John Law relinquished her dower.
Recorded 5 April 1762

p.722  22 March 1762 John Winston of Henrico County to George Scherrer of the Town of Richmond in said county, for 60 pounds, one half-acre lot, being Lot 6 on the plan of the Town of Richmond; being the same lot granted by Wm. Byrd, Gent., to James Cocke, Gent., by deed dated 28 November 1740 and by said Cocke given to his son-in-law, the said John Winston, by deed of gift dated 21 November 1759.
Wit: James Vaughan, Nicholas Scherer, John Sanders
Signed: Jno. Winston                                          Recorded 5 April 1762

p.724  27 March 1762 Jonathan Williams to William Frayser, both of Henrico County, for five pounds, 16 acres adj. Benjamin Scott, deceased, said William Frayser, Col. William Randolph, Esq., deceased, and land of said Jonathan Williams on the south side of the Main Road.
Wit: John Teck, Charles Breeding, Susannah (her ʔ mark) Teck
Signed: Jonathan Williams
Hannah, wife of Jonathan Williams, relinquished her dower.
Recorded 5 April 1762

p.725  16 November 1761 Bond of Elizabeth Pleasants, widow and executrix of Joseph Pleasants, deceased, to Joseph Pleasants, both of Henrico County, conditioned upon said Joseph Pleasants' bond to keep various owners in peaceful possession of their lands, three Negroes, viz., Ned, a man, Sarah, a woman and Fanny, a girl of eight years, to be put immediately in his possession, including 1/6 part of Turkey Island fishing place, but said slaves, valued at 240 pounds, to return to her if he or his heirs should bring a suit to recover certain lands; cites bond of same date wherein said Joseph Pleasants is bound to keep sundry persons in possession of various parcels as well as half of Four Mile Creek Mill.
Wit: Tarlton Woodson,
John (his O mark) Toms, John Townley, Robert Toms, Jno. Pleasants
Signed: Elizabeth Pleasants                            Recorded April Court 1762

p.726  16 November 1761 Bond of Joseph Pleasants to Elizabeth Pleasants, widow and executrix of his father, Joseph Pleasants, deceased, for 480 pounds, upon the receipt of three Negroes valued at 240 pounds, for keeping John Pleasants of Bailey's in quiet possession of a certain parcel of land and a mill which his father, Joseph Pleasants, deceased, sold to James Povall Cocke, deceased, and an adjoining parcel of 125 acres; for keeping Joseph Goode, Jr., in quiet possession of 150 acres whereon said Joseph Goode (Jr.), now lives near Four Mile Creek, and which land was sold to Edward Goode, deceased, by his father, Joseph Pleasants, deceased; for keeping in quiet possession all those persons who bought land of Col. Richard Randolph (Sr. and Jr.), commonly called the Greater Survey near White Oak Swamp or on the branches thereof, and being one-half of a tract granted to John Pleasants the Elder bearing date October 1690; for keeping Ryland Randolph in quiet possession of about 150 acres called Turkey, which his father, Joseph Pleasants, sold to Thomas Pleasants, deceased; and any other lands sued for which may bring damage to said father or grandfather's estate; and that his brother, Josiah Pleasants, may have according to his father's will what land he possessed at the time of his death at Four Mile Creek, except 394 acres whereon the said Joseph Pleasants now lives, called the Eastern Run, to be first laid off; said Joseph Pleasants agreeing that if he and any heirs of his body shall enter process at law against any persons now in possession of aforementioned lands and mill, the said three Negroes and their increase shall be returned unto the said Elizabeth; and said Joseph further agrees not to sell or move the Negroes out of Virginia.
Wit: Tarlton Woodson, John (his (====) mark) Toms, John Townley, Robert Toms, Jno. Pleasants
Signed: Joseph Pleasants                    Recorded April Court 1762

p.728  5 April 1762 John Barnes to Thomas Elmore, both of Henrico County, for 20 pounds, 100 acres on Gilley's Creek; adj. Jones and Lewis.
Wit: William Gathright, Junr., Robert Spears
Signed: John Barnes                         Recorded 5 April 1762

p.729  5 April 1762 David Whitlock, and Ann, his wife, of St. Paul's Parish, Henrico (Hanover) County, to Thomas Howerton of Essex County, for 41 pounds, 113 acres on one of the branches of Chickahominy Swamp; adj. Pleasants, Hundley, Watson, Holloway, Lacy and Ellis; said land is part of two patents: one granted to John Watson and the other granted to William Bacon, one being dated 5 September 1749. (metes and bounds description).
Wit: none                    Signed: David Whitlock, Ann Whitlock
Recorded 5 April 1762

p.731  7 November 1761 Benjamin Bullington to Josiah Bullington, both of

Henrico County, for 20 pounds, 200 acres adj. Peter Bailey and John Alday.
Wit: Richard Renard, Abraham Bailey, Junr., Mark Woodcock
Signed: Benjamin Bullington
Elizabeth, wife of Benjamin Bullington, relinquished her dower.
Recorded 3 May 1762

p.732  5 June 1762 Benjamin Clarke, Sr., to Joseph Clarke, for love, good will and affection, after my decease, the land and plantation whereon I now live, but subject to the widowhood of my wife Mary should she live longer than myself, unless she should marry after my decease.
Wit: William Bridgwater, David Clarke, Jonathan Bridgwater
Signed: Benjamin Clarke                                Recorded 7 June 1762

p.733  5 July 1762 William Guttry and Agnes, his wife, of St. Paul's Parish, Hanover County, to Joseph Perrin, blacksmith, for five shillings, 200 acres, adj. William Pattman and John Mosby.
Wit: none
Signed: William (his I mark) Guttray, Agnes (her ✚ mark) Guttray
Recorded 5 July 1762

p.735  7 June 1762 William Fleming Cocke and Theodosia, his wife, and Thomas Wild and Mary, his wife, who was the widow of Pleasant Cocke, deceased, and mother of the said William Fleming Cocke, who joins herein to release her dower, to Miles Selden, Clerk of Henrico Parish, all of Henrico County, for 555 pounds and 15 shillings, 443 acres on the south side of the Chickahominy Swamp and on the main run of said swamp and on the Spring Branch, adj. Abraham Cowley and Daniel Price (metes and bounds description).
Wit: Nathaniel Bacon, Daniel Price, Jr., Philip Mayo
Signed: Wm. Fleg Cocke, Theodosia Cocke, Thomas Wild, Mary Wild
Recorded 5 July 1762

p.737  10 June 1762 Commission of Fortunatus Sydnor as Deputy Clerk of Henrico County from Thomas Nelson, acting under authority of the Honorable William Adair, Secretary of the Colony.
Wit: none                                              Signed: Thos. Nelson
No date of record given

p.738  2 August 1762 William Watson to Julius Allen, both of Henrico County, for 400 pounds, 800 acres adj. Matthew Johnson, Elizabeth Dolton, Richard Williamson and James Valentine, being the land given to the said William Watson by his grandfather, Joseph Watson deceased, and granted by patent dated 15

October 1741 to said Joseph Watson.
Wit: none
Signed: William Watson                    Recorded 2 August 1762

p.739  2 August 1762 John Jude to William Buxton, both of Henrico County, for 55 pounds, 88 acres on Harding's Branch, adj. Leonard Henley and Harwick's orphans.
Wit: none                                 Signed: John Jude
Mary, wife of John Jude, relinquished her dower.
Recorded 2 August 1762

p.740  7 June 1762 Constant Perkins, and Mary, his wife, of Louisa County, to Nathaniel Dennis, son of said Mary Perkins, for love, good wlll and affection, 100 acres on the branches of Tuckahoe Creek; adj. James Allen, William Street, William Ellis, Leonard Henley, Thomas Ellis and William Cottrell; being the same tract Mary Perkins, widow of James Allen, deceased, lived [(on] and bought of John Shoemaker and is the same tract whereon said Nathaniel Dennis now lives.
Wit: Joseph Perkins, Stephen Attkings, Solomon Attkinson
Signed: Constant Perkins, Mary (her  T  mark) Perkins
Recorded 2 August 1762

p.741  14 April 1762 Power of Attorney from James Stewart, late of James River in Virginia but now of London, merchant, to Alexander Stewart, of Somerset County, Maryland, merchant, James McDowell of Warwick, Chesterfield County, merchant, and John Esdale of Rocky Ridge, Chesterfield County, merchant, to ask, demand, sue for and recover all debts in the provinces of Virginia and Maryland.
Wit: Robert Heastie, Alexander Taggart
Signed: James Stewart                     Recorded 2 August 1762

p.743  2 August 1762 John Bryan to George Donald, both of Henrico County, for 80 pounds, Four certain lots containing two acres in a town called Richmond, being lots 100, 99, 86 and 85 in the plan of said town.
Wit: none
Signed: John Bryan    Obedience, wife of John Bryan, relinquished her dower.
Recorded 2 August 1762

p.744  23 October 1760 Dedimus to Thomas Paulette, Samuel Waddy, Robert Anderson and Charles Barrett, Gentlemen, for the release of dower of Martha Brewer, wife of Sackvill Brewer of Henrico County, who by deed of 11 April 1760 conveyed to William Miller of Henrico County 130 acres on both sides of the Brook.                                    Wit: none

Acknowledgment taken by Chs. Barret and Thos. Paulette on 2 December 1760.
Recorded 4 October 1762

p.745  18 September 1762 John Sheppard to Joseph Sheppard, both of Henrico County, for 50 pounds, 200 acres to be laid off at the upper end of the land whereon I now live.
Wit: Benjamin Bowles, William Sheppard, Benjamin Sheppart
Signed: John Sheppard                              Recorded 4 October 1762

p.746  4 October 1762 Thomas Pleasants of Goochland County, son of Joseph Pleasants the Elder, deceased, to John Staples of Henrico County, for 30 pounds, 200 acres on the Long and Hungry Branch, which land is part of a larger tract granted unto John Watson by patent dated 22 February 1724 and was conveyed by him to the said Thomas Pleasants by deed dated 5 September 1726 (metes and bounds description).
Wit: John Pleasants, William Kelley, James Pleasants
Signed: Thos. Pleasants
Elizabeth, wife of Thomas Pleasants, relinquished her dower.
Recorded 4 October 1762

p.748  7 June 1762 William Buxton to Samuel Duval, both of Henrico County, for 150 pounds, 150 acres on the east side of Deep Run, adj. John White (now in possession of Samuel Duval), William Buxton, John Lacey, Tom Miller and John Eales (metes and bounds description).
Wit: Robert Smith, Richard Cottrell, Stephen Pankey, Junr.
Signed: William Buxton
Joyce, wife of William Buxton, relinquished her dower on 4 October 1762.
Recorded 2 August 1762

p.749  3 October 1760 William Lawless to William Henley, both of Henrico County, for 50 pounds, 100 acres, being on the road near the upper end of Henrico County, and on two branches of Tuckahoe Creek called Harding's Branch and Peters' Branch and being the same tract where said Lawless lately lived and which he bought of George Chambers; adj. William Harding, Leonard Henley, John Jude and Rocketts.
Wit: John Ellis, William Ellis, Henry Ellis
Signed: Wm. Lawless, Sarah (her X mark) Lawless
Recorded 4 May 1761

p.751  6 September 1762 Philip Mayo to Samuel Duval, both of Henrico County, for 40 pounds, 30 acres between the lands of Edward Pryar and Samuel Duval's

land that he bought of John Miller and William Buxton, together with all coal mines and other appurtenances.
Wit: none  Signed: Philip Mayo
Recorded 6 September 1762

p.751  29 September 1761 Bond of James Ligon and Judith Ligon, his wife, to John Ligon, son of the said Judith, for 1,000 pounds, cites that by the death of John Stuart, late of Henrico County, brother of the said Judith Ligon, said Judith with Sarah Ward and Mary Stuart, sisters to the said John Stuart, deceased, are now possessed of two tracts of land–one in Henrico County and one in Cumberland County–and with James Ligon have all agreed tp a partition of the said lands by which partition the land in Cumberland is allotted to Judith on condition that she and her husband execute bond that land will descend to John Ligon in fee upon the death of his mother.
Wit: Archibald Cary, Leonard Ward
Signed: James Ligon, Judith Ligon
Recorded 6 September 1762

p.752  13 April 1762 Godfrey Piles of the Parish of St. Patrick, Prince Edward County, to James Alley of Henrico County, for 20 pounds, 110 acres on the north side of the road at Deep Run Chapel, being the tract whereon said Godfrey Piles formerly lived; adj. Thomas Alley, Junr., John Shewmaker, and Peter Clark.
Wit: Thomas (his A mark) Alley, Nathaniel Dennis, John Street, Rachel Dennis
Signed: Godfrey Piles  Recorded 6 September 1762

p.754  1 October 1762 Daniel Price and James Cocke to Edward Curd, all of Henrico County, for 200 pounds, 200 acres on Meeting House Spring, adj. said Price, Cocke, Curd, Harrord and Watkins (metes and bounds description).
Wit: William Smith, John Harwood, Junr.
Signed: Daniel Price, James Cocke
Mary, wife of James Cocke, relinquished her dower
Recorded 1 November 1762

p.755  16 February 1762 Dedimus issued by Thomas Adams, Clerk of Henrico County Court to William Cabell, James Nevell and Ambrose Lee, Gent., for the relinquishment of dower of Susanna, wife of Valentine Ball, in the conveyance of 400 acres to John Jude.
Acknowledgment taken by W. Cabell, Junr., and James Nevil
Recorded 1 November 1762

p.756  10 November 1761 Nicholas Mealer of Lunenburg County to James

Whitlock of Henrico County, for 52 pounds and 10 shillings, 200 acres near Cornelius Creek, adj. James Whitlow, Burton and Caterpillar Branch.
Wit: Nathaniel Whitlock, George Clopton, Benjamin Raglin, Hannah Whitlock
Signed: Nicholas Mealer   Ann, wife of Nicholas Mealer, relinquished her dower.
Recorded 1 November 1762.

p.758   17 September 1762 John Pleasants, heir-at-law of his father, Thomas Pleasants, deceased, to John Pleasants, Charles Woodson, Robert Pleasants, Robert Pleasants, Junr., Thomas Pleasants, Junr., Thomas Bates, Charles Keesee, James Ladd, John Crew, Joseph Ellyson, David Johnson, Edward Stabler and Charles Woodson, Junr., Trustees, for five shillings, one acre on the south side of White Oak Swamp, adj. the land of James Binford and is the remaining part of a tract of land sold to John Hales and is the same whereon the Meeting House of the people called Quakers now stands; and also two acres bought by John Pleasants, great grandfather to the said John and [from?] William Hatcher on the James River near Four Mile Creek, being the same whereon the Curles Meeting House of the aforesaid people called Quakers now stands, and was given by the said John Pleasants (deceased) by his last will and testament in trust and for the use and convenience of the said people in the discharge of their publick worship and as a burying ground; now the trustees being dead, and said John Pleasants, as heir of his great grandfather and for the better promotion of the Christian religion and being one of the said Quakers does convey the three acres to the said trustees forever; cites that when said trustees shall be reduced to three or less in number, they shall convey same parcels to ten or more friends or trustees .
Wit: none                                                Signed: Jno. Pleasants, Junr.
Recorded 6 December 1762

p.760   4 December 1762 David Allen to Samuel Jones, both of Henrico County, for five pounds, 15 acres, being at the head of a branch of Deep Run called Plumtree Branch and is part of the same track that David Allen lives on; adj. said Samuel Jones and Benjamin Jones.
Wit: William (his W mark) Miller, Cremillion Holloway, Benjamin Jones
Signed: David Allen
Mary, wife of David Allen, relinquished her dower.
Recorded 6 December 1762

p.761   20 February 1760 John West of Henrico County to John Barnett, for four pounds, one feather bed and furniture, one iron pot and all the remainder part of my estate.
Wit: Daniel Binns, Christopher Binns, John Davis
Signed: John Weast                                       Recorded 6 December 1762

p.762  3 December 1762 David Allen to Benjamin Jones, both of Henrico County, for 10 pounds, 60 acres at the head of a branch of Deep Run called Plumtree Branch and is part of the same tract that David Allen lives on; adj. William Jones and Samuel Jones (metes and bounds description).
Wit: Julius Burton, William (his  W  mark) Jones, Samuel Jones
Signed: David Allen
Mary, wife of David Allen, relinquished her dower.
Recorded 6 December 1762

p.764  10 September 1762 Robert Williamson, executor of John Williamson, deceased, to David Allen of Henrico County, for 15 pounds, 125 acres whereon the said David Allen now lives, adj. William Jones, John North, Thomas Randolph, Nicholas Childers and Samuel Jones.
Wit: Thomas Thorp, William (his  W  mark) Jones,
Samuel (his  S  mark) Jones, Junr
Signed: Robert Williamson                    Recorded 6 December 1762

p.765  10 January 1763 John Jude to Jesse Smith, both of Henrico County, for 65 pounds, 200 acres on Deep Branch, adj. Col. QWilliam Randolph, Burton, Benjamin Clark, Gording and a branch of the lower Westham.
Wit: William Street, Leonard Henley, Junr., Markham Ware
Signed: John Jude
Mary, wife of John Jude, relinquished her dower
Recorded 7 February 1763

p.766  5 July 1762 Indemnity Bond of William Fleming Cocke as Deputy Sheriff under Philip Mayo to Bowler Cocke, Junr., Richard Adams and Abraham Cowley, all of Henrico County, sureties for Philip Mayo, late Sheriff of Henrico County, 15 slaves, viz.: Farthing, Caesar, Agg, Naneo, Bett, Sue, Sarah, Nelsey, Hannah, Phillis, Beck, Hannah, David, Ned and Ursley in trust for all trouble or damage that may arise to them or any of them on account of their securityship.
Wit: Miles Selden, Philip Watson, William Smith
Signed: Wm. F. Cocke                         Recorded 7 February 1763

p.768  7 February 1762 Thomas Cocke of Goochland County to Daniel Price of Henrico County, for 10 pounds, 50 acres granted by John Robertson, deceased, to Thomas Cocke by deed dated 13 November 1749.
Wit: John Harwood, Junr., Samuel Price, James Cocke, Junr.
Signed: Thos. Cocke                          Recorded 7 February 1763

p.769  7 February 1763 John Jude to George Jude, both of Henrico County, for 40

pounds, 103 acres on Harding's Branch, adj. Evan Shoemaker ad Henley.
Wit: none
Signed: John Jude   Mary, wife of John Jude, relinquished her dower.
Recorded 7 February 1763

p.770  1 January 1763 William Henley of Henrico County to William Wade of Goochland County, for 3 pounds and 8 shillings, 20 acres, being part of the land William Henley bought of Henry Woody; it being all the land the said Henley holds in Cox's patent and joins the said Wade's land.
Wit: William Buxton, Leonard Henley, Junr., Benjamin Johnson
Signed: William Henley, Mary Henley
Recorded 7 February 1763

p.771  28 February 1763 William Taylor, eldest surviving son and heir-at-law of William Taylor, late of Henrico County, deceased, to William Robinson, son of Thomas Robinson of Henrico County, for 22 pounds and 10 shillings, two tracts of land which were possessed by William Taylor, father of William Taylor, one tract being 22 acres adj. Thomas Robinson, John Fussell, William Hobson and the head of the Western Branch; the other tract being 15 acres adj. Thomas Robinson, John Childers and Fussell.
Wit: James Lindsay, Thomas (his R mark) Robinson,
Elijah (his X mark) Childers
Signed: William (his X mark) Taylor
Recorded 7 March 1763

p.773  7 January 1763 Thomas Robinson of Henrico County, to his son, William Robinson, for true love and natural affection and for advancing in this world, 50 acres on the waters of Four Mile Creek, being the plantation whereon I now dwell and was purchased by me from Thomas Childers, a life right being retained.
Wit: Charles Woodson, James Lindsay, George Robinson,
William (his X mark) Taylor
Signed: Thomas (his R mark) Robinson
Recorded 7 March 1763

p.774  1 March 1763 Abraham Bailey to Roger Cock Bailey, both of Henrico County, for love and affection and maintenance, 140 acres near Cornelius Creek whereon I now live on Mirey Run.
Wit: Nicholas Giles, John Enroughty, Hallary Mosley
Signed: Abraham Bailey                                   Recorded 7 March 1763

p.774 31 January 1763 James Webb of Orange County, province of North Carolina,

to Gerrard Ellyson of Henrico County, for 10 pounds, 62 acres on the south side of the Chickahominy Swamp, for the term of 99 years from date hereof, being the land devised to said James Webb under the will of his father, John Webb, deceased,, and to be held for 99 years as if granted by patent; said Gerrard not to be answerable for any action of waste whatsoever admitted.
Wit: Thomas Wooldridge, William Shepard, Sr., Elijah (his ✚ mark) Moxley
Signed: James (his  mark) Webb
Continued for further proof 7 February 1763 and recorded 7 March 1763

p.776 15 August 1762 Daniel Price and Mary, his wife, of Lunenburg County, and John Price and Hannah, his wife, of Henrico County, to Thomas Williamson of Henrico County, for 150 pounds, 100 acres on the south side of the Brook at the mouth of Timber Branch; adj. Jacob Smith, John Price, William Snead and Nathaniel Bridgwater.
Wit: Jonathan Patterson, Harwood Bacon, Benjamin Estes, David Allen, William (his W mark) Jones, Samuel Williamson
Signed: Daniel Price, Mary Price, John (his I mark) Price,
Hannah (her H mark) Price
Continued for further proof 7 February 1763 and recorded 7 March 1763

p.777 7 March 1761 Bond of Thomas Wilkinson as one of the inspectors at the tobacco warehouses at Shockhoes in Henrico County, in the amount of 500 pounds, being appointed by Lieutenant Governor Francis Fauquier; his sureties being Nathaniel Wilkinson, Robert Williamson and William Fleming Cocke.
Wit: Fortu: Sydnor
Signed: Thos. Wilkinson, Nat. Wilkinson, Robt. Williamson, Wm. F. Cocke
Recorded 7 March 1763

p.778 5 November 1761 Walter Lee of Lunenburg County to Ephraim Garthwright of Henrico County, for 40 pounds, 70 acres near White Oak Swamp on Pick a della (Pickadillo) Branch and Long Branch; adj. Benjamin Jordan, Robert Pleasants, George Adams and the Main Road.
Wit: Robert Moore, James Lindsay, William Faris, Ephraim Garthwright
Signed: Walter Lee                      Recorded 7 December 1761
Agnes, wife of Walter Lee, relinquished her dower on 1 April 1763


p.779 4 April 1763 Thomas Miller to Samuel Duval, both of Henrico County;, for 50 pounds, 100 acres, being on the tract whereon the said Thomas Miller now lives on Drinkinghole Branch, adj. John Carey, John Lacey and Christopher John Thomas and adj. tracts said Samuel bought of William Buxton and Edward Pryer.

Wit: none                                Signed: Thos. (his I mark) Milar
Elizabeth, wife of Thomas Miller, relinquished her dower.
[Recorded] 1 April 1763

p.781 2 April 1763 Bond of Turner Southal as one of the inspectors of tobacco warehouses at Shockoes in Henrico County, appointed as such by Lieut. Governor Francis Fauquier, in the amount of 300 pounds, with his sureties being Samuel Duval and Dasey Southal, both of Henrico County.            Wit: none
Signed: Turner Southal, Samuel Duval, Dasey Southal
Recorded 2 May 1763

p.781 27 April 1763 Edmund Sumpter to James Lindsay, both of Henrico County, 12 pounds, 144 acres between Tom Field Creek and Cornelius Creek; adj. Cox Whitlow, Matthew Harbert and Abraham Bailey.
Wit: John Childers, John Childers, Jr., William (his + mark) Robinson
Signed: Edmund Sumpter                            Recorded 2 May 1763

p.782 10 February 1763 Edward Pryer to Samuel Duval, both of Henrico County, for 400 pounds, 200 acres, being the land whereon the said Edward Pryer now lives; adj. land said Samuel bought of Philip Mayo and William Buxton and adj. Thomas Miller, Christopher John Thomas, Peter Clark and John Shoemaker.
Wit: George Pettus, Thomas Boyd, Jesse Smith, Edward Boyd
Signed: Edward (his Ǝ mark) Pryer
Sarah, wife of Edward Pryer, relinquished her dower.
Recorded 2 May 1763

p.784 29 March 1763 John Clark and Peter Clark to Samuel Duval, all of Henrico County, for 250 pounds, 100 acres on the west side of Deep Run, being the land whereon the said John and Peter Clark now liveth; adj. land said Samuel bought of Edward Pryor, John Shoemaker, Godfrey Piles, the Main Road, John Pimble, Thomas Eales and Thomas Alley (metes and bounds description).
Wit: Andrew Jameson, John Boyd, Walter (his ᙬ mark) Crewes, Turner Southall
Signed John(his Ǝ mark) Clark, Peter Clark
Sarah, wife of John Clark, and Mary Ann, wife of Peter Clark,
relinquished their dowers.                            Recorded 2 May 1763

p.786 17 November 1762 David Staples of Henrico County and William Ford of Amelia County, to Joseph Brown of Henrico County, for a Negro named Jacob paid and delivered to them by Joseph Brown , 150 acres on the north side of the Deep

Run; adj. Thomas Randolph, Samuel Shepard, Richard Cottrell, Nathaniel Dennis and Thomas Alley (metes and bounds description).
Wit: Leonard Henley, Thomas Lewis, John (his X mark) Gording
Signed: David Staples, (no signature, William Ford)
Recorded 2 May 1763

p.787 2 May 1763 Bond of Ryland Randolph as Sheriff of Henrico County, being commissioned by the governor under the seal of the colony and under date of 21 August 1761, in the amount of 1,000 pounds, with John Fleming, his surety.
Wit: Thomas Randolph, Benjamin Bryan
Signed: Ry. Randolph, Jno. Fleming                Recorded 2 May 1763

p.788  6 June 1763 James Lindsey to Samuel Garthright, for one pound, two acres between the branches of Four Mile Creek and White Oak Swamp, beginning at the line of the Eastern Run between said Lindsey and Garthright and thence up the run to the first slash.
Wit: none
Signed: James Lindsey                Recorded 6 June 1763

p.789  6 June 1763 John Winn of Hanover County to Nathaniel Holeman of Henrico County, for 80 pounds, 400 acres on the Chickahominy Swamp; granted by patent to the said John Winn (metes and bounds description).
Wit: none
Signed: John Winn                Recorded 6 June 1763

p.790 [----] 1763 William Patman to James Allen, for 200 pounds, 201 acres, one acre of which is for the use of a mill formerly built by the said William Patman; adj. John Williamson, deceased, and being on George's Branch, Rocky Branch and Board [?] Branch.
Wit: none
Signed: William Patman, Sarah, wife of William Patman, relinquished her dower.
Recorded 6 June 1763

p.790 [----] 1763 William Patman to James Allen, for 200 pounds, 201 acres, one acre of which is for the use of a mill formerly built by the said William Patman; adj. John Williamson, deceased, and being on George's Branch, Rocky Branch and Board [?] Branch. [repeat of above]
Wit: none
Signed: William Patman Sarah, wife of William Patman, relinquished her dower.
Recorded 6 June 1763

p.792  6 June 1763 James Cocke, Sr., to James Cocke, Jr. for better securing the payment of a certain sum of money owed to John Pleasants by James Cocke, Sr., and for natural love and affection, three tracts containing 863 acres–two containing 485 acres and being on the Chickahominy Swamp adj. Edward Watkins and Edward Curd and Deep Run, and one tract containing 378 acres adj. Daniel Price, James Cocke, Sr., John Robertson and John Harwood; the aforesaid sum being 138 pounds 17 shillings and 10 pence paid by James Cocke, Jr. to discharge the said mortgage. A release made a part of this instrument by John Pleasants was witnessed by Mark Clark and Thomas Bacon.
Wit: Daniel Price, Jr., Daniel Harwood, Joseph Price
Signed: James Cocke                                    Recorded 6 June 1763

p.793  6 June 1763 James Cocke, Jr., to Daniel Price, Jr., both of Henrico County, for 100 pounds, 378 acres on Reedy Branch, adj. said Cocke, John Robinson, John Harwood and Daniel Price
Wit: James Cocke, Daniel Harwood, Joseph Price
Signed: James Cocke, Junr.                             Recorded 6 June 1763

p.795  6 June 1763 Samuel Garthright, Junr., to James Lindsay, both of Henrico County, for three pounds, six acres between the branches of Four Mile Creek and White Oak Swamp; adj. James Lindsay's line on Turcas Branch.
Wit: none
Signed: Samuel Garthright                              Recorded 6 June 1763

p.796  Receipt of 1,004 pounds 4 shillings 4 pence farthing paid by Harding Burnley on his bond to James Shelton, deceased:

| | | | |
|---|---|---|---|
| 17 May 1758 | 366 pounds | 0 shillings | 0 pence |
| 16 Jun 1759 | 412 pounds | 0 shillings | 0 pence |
| 21 Jun 1759 | 126 pounds | 4 shillings | 4¼ pence |
| 29 Nov 1760 | 100 pounds | 0 shillings | 0 pence |

Paid and satisfied in the proportions and the times above mentioned, Jno. Fleming, Executor, and acknowledged by him on 6 June 1763.
Recorded 6 June 1763

p.796  10 November 1762 John Weaver to William Nance, both of Henrico County, 70 pounds, 100 acres adj. William Fleming Cocke near a branch of Gilley's Creek, David Binns, Lewis and John Barnes (metes and bounds description).
Wit: Turner Southall, John Weast, John Barnes
Signed: John Weaver                                    Recorded 6 June 1763

p.797  4 July 1763 Andrew Radford to William Frayser, both of Henrico County,

for 75 pounds, 130 acres on the Spring Branch, adj. John Frayser and Miry Run. Wit: John Redford, Jr., Charles Lewis, William Smith
Signed: Andrew Radford                                    Recorded 4 July 1763

p.798  24 March 1763 John Barnes to Thomas Elmore, both of Henrico County, for 37 pounds and 10 shillings, 92 acres on Gilley's Creek, adj. John Leason and John Watson (metes and bounds description).
Wit: Richard Hooper, William Garthright, Junr., Jean Ann Garthright
Signed: John Barnes                                       Recorded 4 July 1763


p.800  4 July 1763 Abraham Cowley and Ann, his wife, of Dale Parish, Chesterfield County, to (The Reverend) Miles Selden, Clerk of Henrico Parish, for 400 pounds, 200 acres on the south side of the Chickahominy Swamp, on the Main Road, adj. Joseph Lewis and the run of the Chickahominy.
Wit: Charles Lewis, Joshua Stores, Samuel Duval
Signed: Abraham Cowley, Ann Cowley
Recorded 4 July 1763

p.802  4 July 1763 George Richardson of St. James Parish, Goochland County, to Thomas Calder of Henrico County, for 16 pounds, for half-acre lot on the plan of the Town of Richmond, being Lot 57 on the plan of the said town.
Wit: John Branfford, Nicholas Scherer, Bernard Markham
Signed: George Richardson
Recorded First Monday in July, 1763

p.803  4 July 1763 Henry Martin, Pouncey Anderson and Richard Holland, executors of Michael Holland, deceased, under will dated 10 October 1746, to Samuel Duval, of Henrico County, for 28 pounds and 7 shillings, for 587 acres adj. John Lankester, said Samuel Duval, Thomas Conaway, Cottrell, John Puryear, William Harris and Thomas East (metes and bounds description).
Wit: Samuel Williamson, John Orr, Turner Southall
Signed: Henry Martin, Pouncey Anderson
[no signature or acknowledgment for Richard Holland]
Recorded 4 July 1763

pages 805-806 [an inventory for the Estate of
John Williamson the Younger, deceased, recorded 6 July 1763]

p.807  7 July 1763 Samuel Allen and Elizabeth Allen of Lunenburg County, to Peter Elmore of Henrico County, for 150 pounds, 160 acres purchased of John

Williamson, deceased; adj. Dabney Pettus, Thomas Conaway and James Browning.

Wit: Robert Williamson, Izard Bacon, Samuel Williamson, Allen Williamson, Harwood Bacon
Signed: Samuel (his S mark) Allen [not signed by Elizabeth Allen]
Recorded 1 August 1763; Elizabeth, wife Samuel Allen, relinquished her dower on 3 December 1763

p.808  1 August 1763 William Patman to James Eubank, both of Henrico County, for 12 pounds, 50 acres on Rocky Branch;  adj. William Brittain, James Eubank and William Patman.
Wit: Jonathan Bridgwater, Thomas Lewis
Signed: William Patman  Sarah, wife of William Patman, relinquished her dower.
Recorded 1 August 1763

p.809  17 December 1762 John Orring and Judah, his wife, to Francis Owing of Henrico County, for 15 pounds, 30 acres adj. David Ford, John Cornett, John Orring and Watson.
Wit: Benjamin Bowles, Richard Allen, John Bowles
Signed: John (his + mark) Orring
Judah, wife of John Orring, relinquished her dower.
Recorded 1 August 1763

p.809  5 September 1763 John Staples to David Clarke, both of Henrico County, for 15 pounds, 100 acres on Piney Branch; adj. William Patman, David Clarke, Thomas Stewerton, Thomas Howerton and Susannah Watson.
Wit: Benjamin Clarke, William Kelley, John Williams
Signed: John (his + mark) Staples
Judith, wife of John Staples, relinquished her dower.
 Recorded 5 September 1763

p.811  7 September 1763 Bond of Turner Southall as one of the inspectors of tobacco at the Publick Warehouse established at Shockoes Warehouse, in the amount of 500 pounds, with Dasey Southal and James Ball as his sureties, under a commission of appointment by the Hon. Lieut. Gov. Francis Fauquier, Esq.
Wit: Fortu: Sydnor
Signed: Turner Southall, Dasey Southal, James Ball
No date of record

p.811  3 October 1763 Jessee Burton to John Burton, both of Henrico County, for 110 pounds, 150 acres on a branch of the Roundabout Swamp; adj. Col. Richard

Eppes, Josiah Bullington, William Randolph, John Scoearts(?) and Jessee Burton.
Wit: William Donald, John Price, Jno. Pleasants, Junr.
Signed: Jessee Burton
Mary, wife of Jessee Burton, relinquished her dower.
Recorded 3 October 1763

p.812  3 October 1763 Bond of Joseph Lewis as one of the inspectors of tobacco at the Publick Warehouse established at Shockoes Warehouse, in the amount of 500 pounds, with Richard Randolph his surety, under a commission of appointment by the Hon. Lieut. Gov. Francis Fauquier, Esq.　　　　　　　　　　Wit: none
Signed: Joseph Lewis, Richard Randolph
Recorded 3 October 1763

p.813  10 October 1763 William Boles to John Oakley, both of Henrico County, for 15 pounds, 100 acres on the north side of the New Kent Road; adj. James Volentine, John West, Jacob Valentine and said New Kent Road.
Wit: Philip Mayo, James Whitlow, Lory Whitlow
Signed: William (his  X  mark) Boles
Elizabeth, wife of William Boles, relinquished her dower.
Recorded 7 November 1763

p.814  7 November 1763 John Mosbey and John Staples to Andrew Patterson, all of Henrico County, for 15 pounds, 120 acres on Pigpen Branch; adj. Daniel Turner, Jacob Smith and John Wheeler.
Wit: William Donald
Signed: John Mosby, John (his  +  mark) Staples
Lucy, wife of John Mosby; Judith, wife of John Staples, relinquished their dowers.
Recorded 7 November 1763

p.815  31 October 1763 Edmond Humphrey and Mary Humphrey, his wife, of the Parish of St. James [sic], Henrico County, to David Boles, of the same parish and county, for 35 pounds, 200 acres, being part of a patent dated [blank]; adj. Nathaniel Holman on the west side of Beale's path and John Thompson (partial metes and bounds description).
Wit: John Harlow, Nathaniel Holman, Elijah (his  +  mark) Liggan
Signed: Edmond (his  A  mark) Humphrey, Mary Humphrey
Recorded 7 November 1763


p.816  7 November 1763 William Henley to William Lawless, for 50 pounds, 124 acres adj. Benjamin Johnson, the old mill pond, Henley's Spring Branch, Wade,

John Martain's patent, Cocke's patent and Austin Wooddy; being part of the land said Henley bought of Henry Wooddy.
Wit: none
Signed: William Henley, Mary Henley
Mary, wife of William Henley, relinquished her dower.
Recorded 7 November 1763

p.817  7 November 1763 Joseph Binns to David Binns, Junr., both of Henrico County, for 25 pounds, 54 acres on the north side of Gilley's Creek; adj. said David Binns and the line formerly Thomas Robinson's and James Hilton.
Wit: Samuel Ligon, Christopher Binns
Signed: Joseph (his ✚ mark) Binns, Judith (her X mark) Binns
Recorded 7 November 1763

p.818  7 November 1763 David Binns, Junr., to Joseph Binns, both of Henrico County, for 30 pounds, 70 acres on the north side of Gilley's Creek; it being the land formerly belonging to Peter Binns and Demetrious Binns; adj. Miles Selden, William Nance, Thomas Elmore and James Hilton.
Wit: Samuel Ligon, Christopher Binns
Signed: David Binns, Milret (her ∫ mark) Binns
Recorded 7 November 1763

p.820  7 November 1763 Bond of Isaac Younghusband as Sheriff of Henrico County, by a commission of the Hon. John Blair dated 11 October 1762 under the seal of the colony, in the amount of 1,000 pounds, with Samuel Duval and Alexander McCaul, his sureties.
Wit: F. Sydnor
Signed: Isaac Younghusband, Samuel Duval, Alexr. McCaul
Recorded 7 November 1763

p.820  28 March 1763 Richard Rockett of Lunenburg County and John Rockett, the latter by Richard Rockett, his attorney-in-fact, to Patrick Coutts of Henrico County, for 50 pounds, 720 acres on Peters' Branch, 250 acres thereof purchased by said Richard Rockett of his brother, Ware Rockett, by deed of 11 April 1751, 240 acres devised to the said Richard Rockett under the will of his father, Baldwin Rockett and 240 acres devised to the said John Rockett under said will.
Wit: Alexander McCaul, Robert Brown, Walter Coles, Loudwick Warrock
Signed: Richard Rockett
Recorded 7 November 1763

p.821  13 October 1763 Nathaniel Lankester to William Jones, both of Henrico

County, for 150 pounds, 180 acres, adj. John Miller, Richard Cottrell, John Lankester and William Jones.
Wit: Christopher John Thomas, David Allen, William Allen Lankester
Signed: Nathaniel Lankester
Hope, wife of Nathaniel Lankester, relinquished her dower.
Recorded 7 November 1763

p.823  6 September 1762 William Henley to Austin Woody, both of Henrico County, for 7 pounds, 50 acres, beginning at a corner pine in John Martin's patent and adj. Samuel Ligon; it being a tract William Henley bought of William Harding.
Wit: none                    Signed: William Henley, Mary Henley
Mary, wife of William Henley, relinquished her dower.
Recorded 7 November 1763

p.823  5 November 1763 Robert Williamson to William Smith, Gent., both of Henrico County, for 35 pounds, 87 acres adj. said William Smith (metes and bounds description).
Wit: Henry Stokes, Elisha Miller, Martin Burton
Signed: Robert Williamson                    Recorded 4 January 1764

p.825  24 May 1763 Deed of Mortgage from James Vaughan of Henrico County to Alexander McCaul of the Town of Richmond, Henrico County, for payment of 279 pounds, 12 shillings and one half-penny, with interest from date hereof by 30 October next, upon default in payment, four Negroes, viz., Bett and Agg, wenches, with all their increase, and Will and Bob, fellows.
Wit: John S. Eippen, John Walker, William Wallace
Signed: Jas. Vaughan                    Recorded 2 January 1764

p.826  5 November 1763 William Buxton and Joyce, his wife, to Peter Clarke, all of Henrico County, for 75 pounds, 88 acres, adj. Leonard Henley and Hardwick's orphans and on Harding's Branch.
Wit: none
Signed: William Buxton, Joice (her X mark) Buxton
No date of record given

p 827  20 December 1763 Benjamin Johnson and Alee, his wife, of Hanover County, for 5 shillings and natural affection, to our son, Benjamin Johnson and Elizabeth, his wife, part of 150 acres now in possession of them and by a line agreed on by said Benjamin and Michael Johnson, my son; which tract was purchased of William Street by deed, all cattle, horses, hogs and sheep now in his possession, and also one-third of the Negroes now in possession of said son

Benjamin Johnson and wife, to be equally divided among my three children, Michael, Benjamin and Sarah Johnson.
Wit: Robert Anderson, Henry Anderson, Stephen (his S mark) Lacy
Signed: Benjamin (his B mark) Johnson, Alee (her ✚ mark) Johnson
Recorded 2 January 1764


p.828  20 December 1763 Benjamin Johnson, Sr. and Alee, his wife, of Hanover County, for 5 shillings and natural affection, to our son, Michael Johnson, 130 acres now in his possession, which tract was purchased of William Lafoon by deed.
Wit: Robert Anderson, Henry Anderson, Stephen (his S mark) Lacy
Signed: Benjamin (his B mark) Johnson, Alee (her ✚ mark) Johnson
Recorded 2 January 1764

p.829  5 November 1763 William Smith, Gent., to Martin Burton, both of Henrico County, for 30 pounds, 77 acres, part being taken off of Smith's former tract of land and part taken out of a parcel of land with the said Smith lately purchased of Mr. Robert Williamson (metes and bounds description).
Wit: William Smith, Junr., Richard Timberlake, Lucy (her + mark) Hibdon
Signed: William Smith
Recorded 2 January 1764

p. 831  1 February 1764 Thomas East to William Miller, both of Henrico County, for 25 pounds, 100 acres adj. John Lankester, Junr., Francis Cooke and William Hughes (metes and bounds description).
Wit: Richard Timberlake, William Donald, Daniel Price, Junr.
Signed: Thomas (his X mark) East
Aggy, wife of Thomas East, relinquished her dower.
Recorded 6 February 1764

p.832  30 December 1763 John Enroughty to James Hallock, both of Henrico County, for 70 pounds, 50 acres adj. Richard Sharp, the late George Williamson, deceased, and the main run of Four Mile Creek.
Wit: Daniel Stone, Robert Dumbar, Edward (his ✚ mark) Enroughty
Signed: John Enroughty, Martha (his ✚ mark) Enroughty
Recorded 6 February 1764

p.833  6 February 1764 Bond of Benjamin Duvall as Surveyor of Henrico County, during pleasure by a commission dated 21 January last, in the amount of 500 pounds, his sureties being Isaac Younghusband and John Redford.     Wit: none
Signed: Benjamin Duvall, Isaac Younghusband, Jno. Redford

Recorded 6 February 1764

p.834  5 March 1764 John Fussell to William Robinson, both of Henrico County, for 17 pounds, 20 acres on the Great Branch and Spring Branch; adj. William Hobson and said Fussell.
Wit: none                                              Signed: John Fussel
Mary, wife of John Fussel, relinquished her dower.
Recorded 5 March 1764

p.835  9 January 1764 Curthburt Williamson of Lunenburg County, to Robert Williamson of Henrico County, for 300 pounds, 340 acres on the Brook and on the Timber Branch (metes and bounds description).
Wit: Martin Burton, Samuel Williamson, Allen Williamson, Dabney Pettus
Signed: Cut. Williamson                        Recorded 5 March 1764

p.836  19 August 1763 Deed of Mortgage from Thomas Williams to Richard Adams, both of Henrico County, for 27 pounds, 8 shillings and 11 pence to be paid on first of January next, one bay horse, one mare and colt begat by Young Silver Eye, one young mare two years old, six herd of black cattle, ten sheep, thirteen hogs, two feather beds and furniture and all the rest of his household goods.
Wit: Thomas Calder, Samuel Griffin
Signed: Thomas Williams                        Recorded 5 March 1764

p.837  [-----] Deed of Mortgage from David Breeding of Henrico County to Richard Adams, for 12 pounds, 18 shillings, 8 pence and one half-penny to be paid by 10 April next, one Negro boy named John and five head of black cattle.
Wit: Samuel Griffin                            Signed: David Breeding
Recorded 5 March 1764

p.838  9 August 1763 Abraham Childers of Henrico County and Henry Childers (not in caption of deed and therefore residence not given) to John Pleasants, Sr., of Henrico County, for 150 pounds, cites that Abraham Childers, father of the said Abraham Childers and Henry Childers, by indenture of 7 August 1756 mortgaged unto the said John Pleasants and Robert Pleasants, then co-partners in trade, a tract of 50 acres within the place called the Roundabout as collateral for a debt then due the said Pleasants, and the said Abraham Childers by his last will and testament did give to his son Abraham the said 50 acres, reserving a life estate to his son Henry; that without making a provision to discharge the said debt, the said Abraham and Henry Childers sell said 50 acres to said Pleasants.
Wit: Thomas Bates, Charles Woodson, Junr., Thomas (his ✚ mark) Scott, Nicholas (his X mark) Scott, Francis (his ✚ mark) Scott

Signed: Abraham (his ✢ mark) Childers, Henry (his H mark) Childers
Recorded 1 October 1764

p.839 9 August 1763 Frederick Childers and Abram Childers to Robert Pleasants, all of Henrico County, for 20 pounds, cites that Abraham Childers, father of the said Frederick, by indenture of 7 August 1756 did mortgage unto John and Robert Pleasants, besides other land, a tract of 77 acres lying near the Gravely Hill, adj. Joseph Woodson and said Robert Pleasants, as collateral for a debt due from Abraham Childers, Sr., to said Pleasants, and said Abraham did give to his son Frederick said 77 acres, reserving part thereof to a branch by Sarah Scott's, to keep the land he then lived on and by the same gave his son Abraham timber fencing and firewood, but said Abraham departed this life and discharged said mortgage, said Frederick is willing to sell the land for payment of the debt.
Wit: Thomas Bates, Charles Woodson, Junr., Francis (his ✢ mark) Scott, Nicholas (his X mark) Scott
Signed: Frederick Childers, Abraham (his ✢ mark) Childers
Partially proven on 5 March 1764 and continued for further proof and recorded on 2 September 1764

p.841 3 September 1763 David Alley and Elizabeth Alley, his wife, to Thomas Ginnitt, for 25 pounds, 50 acres adj. Thomas Alley, Junr., William Ellis, Richard Rockett and the Main Road.
Wit: Edmund Alley, Nathaniel Dennis, Robert (his ⸮ mark) Ginnet
Signed: David Alley, Elizabeth (her E mark) Alley
Recorded 5 March 1764

p.842 24 February 1764 Jesse East to Thomas Williams, both of Henrico County, for 24 pounds, 50 acres adj. Robert Maddox, John Williams, William Porter and Thomas Rogers; being part of the land formerly belonging to Edward East, deceased.
Wit: George Adams, Peyton Smith
Signed: Jesse (his ⸮ mark) East                    Recorded 2 April 1764

p.843 28 March 1764 Deed of Mortgage from Peter Bailie of Henrico County to James Lyle of Chesterfield County, for the payment of 23 pounds, 18 shillings and 5 pence with lawful interest from the date hereof to be paid on 1 April 1765, 200 acres adj. Herbert, Cocke, Peter Randolph, Henry Cox and John Aldway (metes and bounds description).
Wit: John S. Eippen, Robert Murray, John Tallock
Signed: Peter Bailey                    Recorded 2 April 1764

p.844  30 March 1764 James Woodfin to his son, John James Woodfin, both of Henrico County, for love and good will, 100 acres between the branches of Four Mile Creek and White Oak Swamp; adj. Thomas Matthews, Joseph Pleasants (formerly), the Piney Branch, the Eastern Run near the mouth of the Clay Branch, Daniel's Path near the fording place and Benjamin Childers.
Wit: James Lindsey, George Robinson, William (his X mark) Robinson
Signed: James Woodfin, Darcus, wife of James Woodfin, relinquished her dower.
Recorded First Mon. in April 1764

p.845  12 December 1763 John Hutchens to Thomas Bates, for 13 pounds, 11 shillings and 6 pence, two beds and furniture, one cow and calf, one dozen pewter plates, two basins, two dishes, one black mare named Swallow, two chests, two iron pots and one cupboard.
Wit: Edward White
Signed: John Hutchins                                            Recorded 2 April 1764

p.846  6 February 1764 Jacob Burton and Mary, his wife, and Jesse Burton and Mary, his wife, to Richard Adams, all of Henrico County, for 60 pounds, 400 acres adj. Robert Burton (formerly), the Deep Run, Joseph Mayo (formerly) and Robert Burton; said tract granted to Benjamin Burton by patent dated 30 July 1742.
Wit: William Smith, Edward Curd, Samuel Griffin, Richard White
Signed: Jacob Burton, Jesse Burton
(no signatures nor relinquishments of dower by wives)
Recorded 2 April 1764

p.847  2 April 1764 Bond of William Pike for an ordinary at the place lately kept by John Middleton, in the amount of 50 pounds, with John Royster, his surety.
Wit: Fortu. Sydnor
Signed: William Pike, John Royster
Recorded First Mon. in April 1764

p.848  6 February 1764 Bond of Isaac Younghusband as Sheriff of Henrico County upon appointment under a commission of the Hon. John Blair, Esq., in the amount of 500 pounds, with Robert Pleasants and Alexander McCaul, his sureties.
Wit: Fortu. Sydnor
Signed: Isaac Younghusband, Robert Pleasants, Jr., Alexander McCaul
Recorded 7 November 1763

p. 849  4 June 1763 Apprenticeship Contract between Joseph Fontaine, late of Charles City County to George Donald, cabinetmaker, of the Town of Richmond, for Fontaine to be bound to Donald for six years from the date hereof; to be taught

the trade and mystery of a cabinet and chair maker.
Wit: none                                    Signed: Geo. Donald, Joseph Fontaine
Recorded 4 July 1763

p.849   30 December 1762 Benjamin Burton of Henrico County to James Lyle, merchant, of Chesterfield County, for 192 pounds and 10 shillings, one half-acre lot in the Town of Richmond, being Lot 52 on the plan of said town, and also one Negro man slave named Prince, one named Harry and one Negro woman slave named Jean with her increase, one small bay horse about 7 years old not branded, one roane mare, one black and white cow, one red and white cow, six feather beds and furniture, one large copper kettle, 15 pewter dishes, 5 doz. pewter plates, one square table of cherry, four tables, two desks of black walnut, three leather chairs, one doz. rush bottom chairs, one corner cupboard of walnut and one corner cupboard of pine painted.
Wit: John Tillock, Robert Murray
Signed: Benja. Burton                             Recorded 1 August 1763

p.851   26 February 1763 Turner Southall to Elizabeth Pleasants, both of Henrico County, for 100 pounds, one Negro man slave Ned.
Wit: Anderson Peers, Samuel (his X mark) Gehee
Signed: Turner Southall
Recorded First Mon. in September 1763

p.851   7 May 1764 John Oakley to James Vollintine, for 16 pounds, 50 acres adj. Nance, the Southern Branch, the New Kent Road and said James Valentine.
Wit: Fortu. Sydnor                      Signed: John (his ✚ mark) Oakley
Recorded 7 May 1764

p.852   29 March 1764 Martin Martain, Senr., to his son, John Martain, both of Henrico County, for 30 pounds, 34 acres at the mouth of the Spring Branch of the said Martin Martin on the main Western Run to the mouth of Porter's Spring Branch.
Wit: George Adams, William Gravitt
Signed: Martin (his M mark) Martin              Recorded 7 May 1764

p.853   29 March 1764 Martin Martin, Senr., to his son, James Martain, both of Henrico County, for love and good will, 33 acres at the mouth of the Spring Branch on the main Western Run and adj. John Martin, John Bracket, William Jenkins, deceased, and William Porter.
Wit: George Adams, William Gravitt
Signed: Martin (his M mark) Martin              Recorded 7 May 1764

p.854   7 May 1764 William Harris to Isaac Winston, both of Henrico County, for 250 pounds, 650 acres on the south side of the Chickahominy Swamp, adj. said swamp and William Hughes' mill dam on Meredith's Branch (metes and bounds description).
Wit: Peter Massie, William Donald, John Harris
Signed: William Harris
Henrietta, wife of William Harris, relinquished her dower.
Recorded 7 May 1764

p.856   6 December 1763 Robert Webb, Jr., and Christian, his wife, to William Webb of Henrico County, for 18 pounds, 57 acres adj. William Morris, Robert Webb, William Harris and William Hughes; being the same tract that he had of his father, Robert Webb.
Wit: Christopher John Thomas, Charles (his ✚ mark) Webb,
David (his ✚ mark) Ginnins, Robert (his R mark) Webb
Signed: Robert (his ✚ mark) Webb, Christian (her C mark) Webb
Recorded 7 May 1764

p.857   10 December 1763 Nathan Turner of Halifax County to Andrew Patison of Henrico County, for four pounds, 50 acres on Pigpen Branch and part of a larger tract which formerly belonged to William Turner, deceased.
Wit: Pearce Griffing, Shadrick Atkins, George Ginins
Signed: Nathan Turner, Elizabeth (her ᙢ mark) Turner
No date of record given

p.859   4 June 1764 Bond of Daniel Stone for keeping an ordinary at Pleasants, in the amount of 50 pounds, with John Royster, his surety; to provide good holsome and cleanly lodging and diet and stable and fodder nor on the Sabbath day suffer or permit any person to tipple or drink more than is necessary.
Wit: Fortu. Sydnor                    Signed: Daniel Stone, John Royster
Recorded First Mon. in June 1764

p.859   4 June 1764 Daniel Fitzpatrick of Hanover County to Robert Chapple of Hanover County, for 25 pounds, 200 acres adj. Samuel Duvall, Benjamin Bowles, Benjamin Sheppard and John Ryalls.
Wit: Leonard Henley, John Conaway, Jesse Smith
Signed: Daniel (his X mark) Fitzpatrick                    Recorded 4 June 1764

p.860   15 May 1764 William Fleming Cocke and Theodosia, his wife, of Cornwall Parish, Lunenburg County, to Samuel Mitchell, of Richmond Town, Henrico County, blacksmith, for 36 pounds, two half lots in the said town,

being Lots 32 and 46.
Wit: Elisha White, Edward Curd, Junr., William Price
Signed: William F. Cocke, Theodosia Cocke
Theodosia Cocke's relinquishment of dower taken pursuant to a dedimus directed to David Caldwell and Elisha White, Gent., from Fortunatus Sydnor dated 10 May 1764. Recorded 4 June 1764

p.862  27 January 1764 Julius Allen to William Morris, both of Henrico County, for 60 pounds, 123 acres adj. Samuel Childress, Miles Garthright and Anthony Matthew; being the land which Julius Allen purchased of Samuel Garthright, Junr.
Wit: Christian Allen, Matthew (his X mark) Johnson
Signed: Julius Allen                               Recorded 4 June 1764

p.863  (----) 1763 John North and Sarah, his wife, to Thomas North, for 30 pounds, 100 acres adj. John Lankester, Anthony North, Old House Branch, Thomas North, Thomas Randolph, David Allen and William Jones.
Wit: Christopher John Thomas, Abraham (his A mark) North, William Allen Lankester, Anthony North
Signed: John (his E mark) North, Sarah (her 2 mark) North
Recorded 3 October 1763

p.864  24 February 1764 James Cocke, Gent., and William Fleming Cocke, grandson and heir-at-law to the said James Cocke, to Joseph Hobson, planter, all of Henrico County, for 110 pounds, 400 acres known as Hell Garden, which land was formerly purchased by John Pleasants the Elder, of Robert Woodson, Sr., and Henry Rowen and was conveyed by the said John Pleasants unto James Cocke, and Elizabeth [Pleasants Cocke], his daughter, the wife of the said James Cocke by deed dated 16 May 1692 and afterward by the said Elizabeth and her son, the said James, the party to these presents, conveyed to the said Joseph Hobson, by deed of exchange dated 1 September 1740.
Wit: Daniel Price, Jr., John Price, Fortunatus Sydnor, Samuel Mitchell
Signed: James Cocke, Wm. Fg. Cocke                  Recorded 2 July 1764

p.866  16 April 1764 Deed of Mortgage from John Ellis and John Lancaster of Henrico County to Peter Randolph, Esq., Richard Randolph, Thomas Mann Randolph, Richard Adams, James Buchanan, Alexander Baine, Charles McPherson, Ninian Minzier, Philip Mayo and Alexander McCaul, Gent., for 150 pounds with interest from the date hereof to be paid on or before the first of October next ensuing, the collateral being ten Negro slaves, vizt.: Caesar, Peter and Hampshire, men, Lucy and Jane, women, belonging to the said John Ellis; and Peter, a man, Pegg, a woman, and Rachel, Sall and Phebe, children, belonging to the said John

Lancaster, with the future increase of the females.
Wit: John Kippen, John Old, William Wilson, William Wallace
Signed: John Ellis, John (his ⁊ mark) Lancaster
Recorded 2 July 1764

p.867  2 July 1764 Benjamin Goode of Henrico County to John Goode of Chesterfield County, for 15 pounds, 25 acres on the east side of Four Mile Creek, with the plantation house, orchards and all appurtenances, with life estate reserved.
Wit: none                         Signed: Benjamin (his B mark) Goode
Recorded 2 July 1764

p.868  30 July 1764 Deed of Mortgage from Elisha Miller of Henrico County to Alexander McCaul of Richmond, merchant, for the payment of 68 pounds 3 shillings and 9 pence with lawful interest by the first of October next ensuing, collateral being three Negroes, vizt.: a fellow named Phill and a wench named Anaky and her child Hannah.
Wit: Hector McAlester, William Wilson, John Old
Signed: Elisha Miller                         Recorded 2 July 1764

p.869 2 July 1764 John Owen of Henrico County to Thomas Prosser of Cumberland County, for 280 pounds, 300 acres adj. Parson, William Owen and Hobson (metes and bounds description).
Wit: none                         Signed: John (his ✚ mark) Owen
Mildred, wife of John Owen, relinquished her dower.
Recorded 2 July 1764

p.871  7 May 1764 Richard Randolph and John Randolph, executors of William Hatcher, late of Henrico County, to William Hobson, for 26 pounds, 100 acres near the head of Bailey's and Grindall's runs and bounded as by deed from Tarleton Woodson, late of Henrico County, to James Hatcher, brother of the said William Hatcher, deceased, bearing date 3 April 1738; cites will of William Hatcher, in which he directs that the residue of his estate be sold and that part of the said residue is this tract of 100 acres, which was put up for public sale and bid was made by the said William Hobson.
Wit: James Vaughan, Miles Taylor, Abraham Cowley
Signed: Richard Randolph, John Randolph
Recorded 6 August 1764

p.872  26 July 1764 George Pike to William Pike, both of Henrico County;, for 50 pounds, 30 acres, being the plantation whereon the said William Pike now lives, adj. Humphrey Smith, Thomas Binford and William Pike.

Wit: George Adams, Charles Carter, Benjamin Curtis
Signed: George Pike
Recorded 6 August 1764
Marginal notation: Delivered to Robert Pleasants, merchant, 12 October 1770, who bought the land of Pike.

p.874   10 April 1764 Deed of Mortgage from Jonathan Williams to Richard Adams, both of Henrico County, for the payment of 20 pounds with lawful interest from date hereof on or before the first of June next ensuing, collateral being 34 acres, all of that tract whereon the said Jonathan Williams now lives, together with one grey horse, two cows, two feather beds and furniture, one gun, one whip, one saw, one set of shoe tools and the rest of his estate.
Wit: Samuel Griffin, Richard Smith, Miles Taylor
Signed: Jonathan Williams                    Recorded 7 August 1764

p.875   4 July 1764 Apprenticeship Contract between Richard Adams, Gent., churchwarden, who with Richard Randolph, churchwarden, pursuant to the order of the Henrico County Court, has bound Sarah Scott, orphan, from the date hereof until she shall arrive at the age of 21, and Elizabeth Woodson, her mistress, who agrees to allow sufficient meat, drink, lodging and apparel and to teach to read and write.                    Wit: William Lewis
Signed: Richard Adams, Elizabeth Woodson
No date of record given

p.875   1 September 1764 David Jennings to Abram Chappel, both of Henrico County, for 11 pounds, 50 acres adj. Samuel Duval, Benjamin Bowles and William Morris.
Wit: William Kelley, William Adkinson, George Wood
Signed: David (his + mark) Jennings           Recorded 3 September 1764

p.876   18 August 1764 George Adams to Ephriam Garthright, both of Henrico County, for 40 pounds, 50 acres adj. said Ephriam Garthwright, Benjamin Jordan, John Carter and Robert Moore.
Wit: Ephriam Garthright, Junr., Ansel Garthright, James Austin
Signed: George Adams
Lucy, wife of George Adams, relinquished her dower on 2 June 1766.
Recorded 3 September 1764

p.878   30 June 1764 Deed of Mortgage from Elisha Miller to James Buchanan, both of Henrico County, for the payment of 148 pounds and 4 shillings with lawful interest from the date hereof before the first day of December next, collateral being

four Negroes, to-wit: Abigail and Frank, young wenches, and Stepney and Simon, two boys, with the increase of the wenches.
Wit: Fortunatus Sydnor, Shad. Vaughan, Hector McAlester
Signed: Elisha Miller
No date of record given

p.879  3 September 1764 Robert Mosby of Henrico County to Benjamin Bowles of Hanover County, for 20 pounds, 21 acres adj. Hunt and Shepherd on the Chickahominy Swamp (metes and bounds description).
Wit: Robert Hunt, David Wade, John Bowles
Signed: Robert Mosby                    Recorded 3 September 1764

p.881  17 April 1764 John Wheeler and Roland Wheeler to Benjamin Bowles, for 9 pounds, 100 acres (from John Wheeler) and 50 acres (from Roland Wheeler) included in one bounds as 150 acres; adj. Turner, Jennings and Morris (metes and bounds description).
Wit: Robert Hunt, David Wade, John Bowles
Signed: John (his ɪ mark) Wheeler, Rowland Wheeler
Recorded 3 September 1764

p.882  11 June 1764 John Shoemaker to John Gleen, both of Henrico County, for 25 pounds, 180 acres adj. Samuel Duval, James Conaway, James Alley and James Alley, Junr.
Wit: Benjamin Bowles, Benjamin Pulliam, Benjamin Mosby, Frank Cornet
Signed: John Shewmaker                    Recorded 3 September 1764

p.884  11 March 1758 Bill of Exchange from Richard Walley to John Pleasants and Son or order, for 123 pounds one shilling and two pence sterling at thirty days drawn on Thomas Holdsworth, merchant in Dartmouth, for 122 pounds 5 shillings and 8 pence current money of Virginia, to be placed to the account of the ship Mary.                                                    Wit: none
Handwriting of Richard Walley affirmed by Robert Pleasants, Quaker, before Richard Adams, justice of the peace, on 24 August 1764.
Recorded October Court 1764

p.885  10 April 1764 James Valentine to Jesse Hogg, both of Henrico County, for 6 pounds, 25 acres adj. William Bowles, the New Kent Road and Julius Allen; being part of a tract granted by patent to Michael Jones.
Wit: John (his + mark) Oakley, William ( his I mark) Bowles,
Nicholas (his X mark) Vallentine                Signed: James Volletine
Recorded 1 October 1764

p.886  1 October 1764 Apprenticeship Contract between William Bridgwater to Thomas Hombs, carpenter and joyner, to learn his art or mistery and to serve from date hereof for four years; not to contract matrimony, play cards or haunt ale houses.  Wit: Richard White, Drury Breazeal
Signed: William (his  X  mark) Bridgwater, Thos. Hombs
Recorded 1 October 1764


p.886  17 March 1764 Deed of Mortgage from Jessee Burton to James Vaughan, both of Henrico County, for the payment of 122 pounds and 14 shillings with lawful interest from date hereof at or upon the 15th of October next; collateral being 500 acres whereon said Burton's mother now lives, being in reversion; adj. the estate of William Randolph, deceased, Richard Epps and the estate of John Howard, deceased; and a Negro fellow Ben now in the possession of Elizabeth Burton, but the property of said Jessee Burton in reversion.
Wit: Joseph Lewis, Miles Taylor, Matthew Vaughn
Signed: Jessee Burton  Recorded 1 October 1764


p.888  17 March 1764 Jessee Burton and Elizabeth Burton, both of Henrico County, to James Vaughan, for 122 pounds and 14 shillings, one Negro fellow named Jacob, the late property of Benjamin Burton, deceased.
Wit: Joseph Lewis, Miles Taylor, Daniel Harwood
Signed: Jessee Burton, Elizabeth (her  EB  mark) Burton
Recorded 1 October 1764


p.889  1 May 1764 John Williams of Henrico County to Nicholas Lankester, for 30 pounds, 200 acres, being the same tract that Philemon Williams bought of William Harding.
Wit: Christopher John Thomas,
 William (his  ✚  mark) Cauthorn, William Allen Lankester
Signed: John Williams  Recorded 1 October 1764


p.890  24 September 1764 James Whitlow, Senr., to John Enroughty, both of Henrico County, for 34 pounds, 130 acres, beginning at the great meadow of Four Mile Creek at the first branch of the south side; adj. David Breeding, William Whitlow, John Parker and John Clark.
Wit: James Hallock, Charles Breeding, Sarah (her  ✚  mark) Strange
Signed: James (his  E  mark) Whitlow
Edith, wife of James Whitlow, relinquished her dower.
Recorded 5 November 1764


p.891  5 November 1764 Walter Coles to Samson Matthews of Augusta County, for

130 pounds, one certain lot and storehouse in the Town of Richmond, formerly in the possession of Messrs. Coles, Mouatt, Gladowe & Co., and sold in May 1762 at public sale by William Dinguid, attorney for William Mouatt, only surviving partner of Messrs. Coles, Mouatt, Gladowe & Co., by the consent of Walter Coles, heir-at-law to the said John Coles, who it has since found has the only and sole right of conveyance.
Wit: none                                                                               Signed: Walter Coles
Recorded 5 November 1764

p.892 2 July 1764 Andrew Castlen to George Scherrer, for 12 pounds, 50 acres adj. Alexander Robertson, Samuel Liging, William Dueguid and John Harwood.
Wit: Shad. Vaughan, Groves Harding, Richard Crouch
Signed: Andrew Castlen                                      Recorded 5 November 1764

p.893 5 November 1764 Apprenticeship Contract between Littleberry Epperson and Robert Duval, both of Henrico County, by the consent of the Henrico County Court Epperson to serve two years from 16 October last.
Wit: none                                Signed: Littleberry Epperson, Robert Duval
Recorded 5 November 1764

p.893 1 May 1764 Deed of Lease from Mary Burton, late widow of Gillee Gromarrrin of Henrico County, deceased, and now widow of David Burton, deceased, and Wiltshire Marrin, otherwise called Wiltshire Gromarrin, eldest son and heir of the said Gillee Gromarrin, to Samuel Duval, for fifteen years from hence; 15 pounds to be paid on 1 January yearly; and 20 pounds years for the last five years; 200 acres on the west side of Gillead's Creek, adj. John New, Richard Adams, and Margret Brown and the James River; being part of demised land known as Rocket's Landing and all the landings and fishing places, with liberty to erect warfs and with full liberty of fishing and hunting, except a place of level land on the top of a hill now in the possession of Thomas Cardwell containing about 20 acres. Duval shall build at his own expense substantial houses and wharfs at the full value of 200 pounds.
Wit: Colwel Pool, Lewis Roper, Martha Holmes, Olive (his ✚ mark) Thomas
Signed: Mary Burton, Wiltshire Marrin, Samuel Duval
Recorded 5 November 1764

p.897 2 September 1765 Thomas Jordan (the father) to Thomas Jordan (the son), both of Henrico County, for 65 pounds, 100 acres on the Roundabout Swamp; adj. Robert Bullington, Thomas Man Randolph, William Parker, Milner Redford and John Redford.
Wit: Josiah Bullington, Mark Woodcock, William Rabon

Signed: Thomas Jordan Martha, wife of Thomas Jordan, relinquished her dower.
Recorded 5 September 1765

p.898  3 December 1764 Joseph Goode to James Lindsey, both of Henrico County, for 50 pounds, 200 acres between Daniel's Path and Deep Run; adj. William Clark and Childers' Branch.
Wit: none                                                                Signed: Joseph Goode
Recorded 3 December 1764

p.899  6 August 1764 Loudwick Warrock and Mary, husband and wife, to John Orr, all of Henrico County, for 140 pounds, one lot and one-half, containing three-fourths of an acre in the Town of Richmond, being Lot 49 and half lot being part of Lot 35; they are the lots on which the said Worrock now lives, and the other half lot being where the said Orr now lives.
Wit: James Lyle, Robert Brown, Drury Wood
Signed: Loudwick Warrock
(no signature nor release of dower by Mary Warrock)
Recorded 5 November 1764

p.900  30 October 1764 John Williams to Thomas Williams, his son, both of Henrico County, for 92 pounds, 92 acres, being part of the tract whereon the said John Williams now lives; adj. Robert Maddox, Jesse East and Col. Richard Randolph and near the road that leads from Bottom's Bridge and Woodson's Ferry. Wit: George Adams, William (his  e  mark) Martain
Signed: John (his JW mark) Williams
Recorded 5 November 1764

p.902  3 December 1764 Joseph Goode to Thomas Goode, both of Henrico County, for 11 pounds and 10 shillings, 40 acres at the Wolf Slash; adj. Thomas Pleasants, James Lindsey, Robert Goode and Edward Goode.
Wit: none                                                                Signed: Joseph Goode
Recorded 3 December 1764

p.903  30 November 1764 John Fussell to William Robinson, both of Henrico County, for 25 pounds and 10 shillings, 30 acres between the branches of Four Mile Creek and White Oak Swamp; adj. William Hobson and Grindall's Branch.
Wit: James Lindsay, James Woodfin, Thomas Evans
Signed: John Fussell                                    Recorded 3 December 1764

p.904  29 November 1764 John Williams to Solomon Fussell and his wife of Henrico County, in consideration of a bond for several performances to him, the

said John Williams and his wife, or the survivor of them, for the term of 16 years, 50 acres on the north side of the road that leads from Bottom's Bridge to Woodson's Ferry; adj. Robert Maddox.
Wit: George Adams, John Fussell
Signed: John Williams   Mary, wife of John Williams, relinquished her dower.
Recorded 3 December 1764

p.905 1 January 1764 Bill of Sale for George Clarke to John Childers, son of John Childers, all of Henrico County, for 100 pounds, one bed and furniture, three head of cattle, one mare and saddle, one lamb, eight head of hogs and all the rest of my movable estate, also the tract of land and plantation where I now live. 110 pounds with interest to be paid on 21 January 1766 for the redemption of the land and premises.
Wit: none                                         Signed: Geo. Clarke
Recorded 4 February 1765

p.905 11 June 1764 Merry Carter of Bedford County to Thomas Starke of Henrico County, for 4 pounds and 10 shillings, one half-acre lot in a certain town called Beverly Town, Town of Westham, being Lot 110 on the plan of said town.
Wit: Lewis Ball, William (his X mark) Day, Thomas Largeon
Signed: Merry Carter                              Recorded 4 February 1765

p.906 1 March 1765 Thomas North of Amelia County to Nicholas Amos of Henrico County, for 70 pounds, 171 acres on the branches of Deep Run; adj. Anthony North, John Lancaster's Spring Branch called by the name of Old House Branch, William Jones, Randolph and Roland Blackburn.
Wit: William Street, Thomas Pemble, Thomas Ellis
Signed: Thomas (his ✚ mark) North
Dorothy, wife of Thomas North, relinquished her dower
Recorded 4 March 1765

p.908 6 February 1765 James Alley to David Hall, both of Henrico County, for 65 pounds, 100 acres on Stony Run; being the same tract of land whereon the said James Alley now lives and which he bought of his father, Thomas Alley; adj. Flaxpond Branch, Thomas Alley, David Staples, Nathaniel Dennis and William Street.
Wit: William Street, John Street, Samuel Alley, David Allin
Signed: James Alley                               Recorded 4 March 1765

p.910 8 December 1765 Matthew Bridgman to David White, both of Henrico County, 15 pounds, 20 acres on a branch of Gilley's Creek on the road that leads

from Bottoms Bridge to Richmond Town.
Wit: Joseph Lewis, William (his W mark) Snead, John Strong
Signed: Matthew (his M mark) Bridgman
Mary, wife of Matthew Bridgman, relinquished her dower.
Recorded 4 March 1765

p.911  1 April 1765 James Conway to James Cawthon, Junr., for 15 pounds, 68 acres adj. Edmund Alley, Thomas Alley, John Glen, Thomas Conway and Nicholas Conway.
Wit: John Ellis, Hezekiah Puryear
Signed: James (his C mark) Conway
Ann, wife of James Conway, relinquished her dower.
Recorded 5 April 1765

p.912  1 April 1765 John Williams to John Homes, both of Henrico County, for 12 pounds, 6 shillings and 6 pence, 180 acres near the branches of White Oak Swamp; being part of 360 acres granted by patent to the said Williams dated 13 August 1744 (the other part sold by the said John Williams to John Martin).
Wit: Robert Pleasants, Robert Povall, Frederick (his I mark) Clarke
Signed: John Williams                                    Recorded: 1 April 1765

p.914  1 April 1765 James Lindsey to Thomas Evans, both of Henrico County, for 7 pounds, 25 acres adj. William Hobson, William Taylor and the path from James Woodfin's.
Wit: none                                         Signed: James Lindsey
Recorded: 1 April 1765

p.915  20 March 1765 Michael Gawin of Cauts County, North Carolina, to David Gawin of Henrico County, for 40 pounds, 400 acres adj. William Harlow and Farrar's Branch (metes and bounds description.).
Wit: David Bowles, John Thompson, John Gawin
Signed: Michael (his M mark) Gawin
Recorded 1 April 1765

p.917  30 April 1765 Renunciation of Susannah Puryear of the will of her late husband, Peter Puryear, by being dissatisfied.
Wit: Richard Cottrell, William Jones
Signed: Susanna Puryear                               Recorded 6 May 1765

p.917  6 May 1765 Andrew Patison to Drury Wood, both of Henrico County, for 18 pounds, 170 acres, being a tract of land he bought of John Mosby, John Staples

and Nathan Turner; adj. Richard Allen, Marriott, William Turner, Pig Pen Branch, Jacob Smith, Wheeler and Benjamin Bowles.
Wit: John Pride, Jr., Benjamin Bryan
Signed: Andrew Patterson
Elizabeth, wife of Andrew Patterson, relinquished her dower.
Recorded 6 May 1765

p.919  11 April 1765 James Cocke of Henrico County to his grandson, William Fleming Cocke, for love and affection, 287 acres on Chicahominy Swamp; adj. Daniel Price, Junr.
Wit: John Pride, Jr., Benjamin Burton, William Tulloh
Signed: James Cocke                                          Recorded 6 May 1765

p.920  11 April 1765 William Fleming Cocke of Henrico County to Abraham Cowley of Chesterfield County, for 150 pounds, 362 acres on Chickahominy Swamp; adj. the Reverend Miles Selden, Daniel Price, Jr., and David Binns.
Wit: John Pride, Jr., Benjamin Burton, William Tulloh
Signed: Wm. Fleg. Cocke                                      Recorded 6 May 1765

p.921  6 May 1765 Nicholas Conway to John Cawthorn of Goochland County, for 9 pounds, 50 acres adj. James Cawthorn, John Williamson, deceased, Richard Cottrell, Junr., and Richard Rockett.
Wit: William Alley, Jeremiah Johnson
Signed: Nicholas Conway
Hannah, wife of Nicholas Conway, relinquished her dower.
Recorded 6 May 1765

p.922  6 May 1765 Waldegrave Clopton and Unity, his wife, of New Kent County, to Thomas Watkins of Cumberland County, for 22 pounds and 10 shillings, 30 acres on the south side of Bottoms Bridge Road; adj. land formerly belonging to Thomas Bottom, the main run of Chickahominy Swamp and Richard Whitlock.
Wit: none                                            Signed: Waldegrave Clopton
[no signature nor release of dower for wife]            Recorded 6 May 1765

p.924  3 October 1766 Henry Mitchell of Sussex County, Edward Osborne, Christopher Branch, Robert Goode and Josiah Tatum of Chesterfield County, Branch Tanner and Thomas Branch Wilson of Amelia County and John Goode of Mecklenburg County to George Cox of Haddihaddox, Henrico County, for 2,357 pounds, 448 acres on the James River; adj. Eppes, Burton and Perkins. Wit: Thomas Friend, Leonard Ward, Seth Ward, Junr., Nathaniel Friend
Signed: Henry Mitchell, Edward Osborne, Robt. Goode, Josiah Tatum, Branch

Tanner, Christr. Branch, T.B. Wilson, John Goode, Mary Page Tanner, wife of Branch Tanner; Elizabeth Osborne, wife of Edward Osborne; Martha Branch, wife of Christopher Branch; Sarah Tatum, wife of Josiah Tatum; relinquished their dowers. Priscilla Mitchell, wife of Henry Mitchell, examined by John Mason and Benjamin Wyche, Sussex justices, on 19 March 1767 for her release, pursuant to a dedimus; and Elizabeth, wife of Thomas Branch Wilson, was to be examined by William Crawley and John Booker, Amelia justices, also pursuant to a dedimus, but no return is noted here.
Recorded 1 December 1766

p.928 26 April 1765 Thomas Bottom and Rebecca, his wife, of Henrico County, to Waldegrave Clopton of New Kent County, for 60 pounds, 30 acres on the south side of Bottoms Bridge Road, the main run of Chicahominy Swamp and Richard Whitlock.
Wit: George Clopton, Jenny Clopton, William Bassett
Signed: Thos. Bottom   [no signature nor release of dower for wife]
Recorded 6 May 1765

p.929 21 March 1765 Josiah Clark to Robert Pleasants of Curles, both of Henrico County, for 40 pounds, 33 acres on the north side of White Oak (Swamp); adj. said Pleasants on the south, on the east by Bear Hill Swamp, on the north by Frederick Clark and on the west by Robert Ferris; being the land given by William Clark, deceased, to his son Josiah by his last will and testament dated 23 August 1756.
Wit: Henry (his H mark) Childers, Charles Carter, Thomas Bethall,
George (his ✚ mark) Clark, William (his ℭ mark) Bethall, Robert Moore
Signed: Josiah (his X mark) Clark
Recorded 6 May 1765

p.930 3 June 1765 Richard Adams to Nicholas Scherer, both of Richmond, Henrico County, for 10 pounds, 5 acres on the east side of Shockoe Creek, beginning at the said creek at the lower end of Scherer's tract of land purchased of William Byrd, Esq.                                                                                                   Wit: none
Signed: Richard Adams                                                Recorded 3 June 1765

p.931 2 February 1765 David Hall to Benjamin Brown, both of Henrico County, for 84 pounds, 94 acres near Deep Run; being said parcel which said Hall bought of William Harding and which said Harding bought part of (from) Joseph Tanner Whiteman and part of (from) Joseph Freeman; being bounded on the south by Tuckahoe Creek and on the east or lower part by Thomas Randolph and on the west or upper part by Benjamin Duval.
Wit: Edmund Alley, Nathaniel Dennis, Samuel Alley, Joseph Brown

Signed: David (his X mark) Hall     Recorded 3 June 1765

p.932  1 April 1765 William Morris to Richard Adams, both of Henrico County, for 19 pounds and 11 shillings, 123 acres lying on the head of Bulls Branch; adj. Anthony Matthews, Miles Gathright and Samuel Childers; being the land said Morris bought of Julius Allen and whereon he now lives.
Wit: T. Watkins, John Pride, Jr., George Underwood, John Martin, James Ladd
Signed: William Morris
Partially proven by 2 witnesses 3 June 1765 and continued for further proof.

p.933  17 March 1765 Thomas Eales to James Vaughan, James Gunn and James Ball, all of Henrico County, for 40 pounds, 200 acres on the north side of Deep Run; being the lad given to the said Thomas Eales by deed from his father, John Eales; adj. Edward Reaves, John Simcoks and the Deep Run.
Wit: Benjamin Bryan, Miles Taylor, Fortunatus Sydnor
Signed: Thomas Eales     Recorded 3 June 1765

p.934  3 June 1765 Nicholas Scherer to Richard Adams, both of Richmond, Henrico County, for 15 pounds, one half-acre lot in said Town of Richmond, being Lot 51 in the plan of said town.
Wit: none     Signed: Nicho. Scherer
Recorded 3 June 1765

p.935  2 February 1765 Deed of Mortgage from John Williams to Richard Adams, both of Henrico County, for the payment of 16 pounds and 12 shillings, with interest, on the 10th of October next, one bay horse branded R, four head of cattle, four sheep, two feather beds and all the rest of his household goods.
Wit: Samuel Griffin, George Underwood, W. Smith
Signed: John Williams     Recorded 3 June 1765

p.935  9 May 1765 Power of Attorney from William Fisher of the City of Philadelphia, merchant, at present at Curles in Henrico County, Virginia, by virtue of another power of attorney executed by James Harford of the City of Bristol, merchant, surviving partner of Joseph Robson, merchant of the said city, deceased, sworn to before Richard Farr, mayor of the said city, to Robert Pleasants and Thomas Bates of Henrico County, to recover debts due the said James Harford, surviving partner.
Wit: Richard Randolph, James Coupland, Robert Pleasants, Jr.
Signed: William Fisher     Recorded 3 June 1765

p.937   11 January 1765 John Randolph of Curles, son of Thomas Randolph, to Robert Pleasants, both of Henrico County, for 550 pounds, 50 acres near the mouth of Four Mile Creek, being the same land whereon William Hatcher, deceased, did dwell and by his last will and testament gave to the said John Randolph on certain conditions. [Bond for 1,000 pounds from John Randolph to Robert Pleasants dated 11 February 1765 appended, confirming that Randolph pursuant to the said will will pay Edith Turpin, Elizabeth Hix, Sarah Wadlow and Susannah Wadlow each 50 pounds.]
Wit: Richard Randolph, Rolfe Eldridge, R.K. Meade, Thomas Eldridge, Richard Baugh, Bolling Eldridge, Ryland Randolph
Signed: John Randolph                             Recorded 3 June 1765

p.939   26 April 1765 Robert Scott to William Frazier, both of Henrico County, for 35 pounds, 100 acres whereon the said Robert Scott now dwelleth; adj. Hayse Whitlow, Robert Pleasants and said William Frazier.
Wit: Betsy Webster, Benjamin Jordan, Junr., Pleasants Jordan
Signed: Robert (his R mark) Scott                 Recorded 1 July 1761

p.940   1 July 1765 James Whitlock to Thomas Casson, both of Henrico County, for 10 pounds, 50 acres on the head of White Oak Swamp; adj. Tandam Slash, Whitlow and Adams.
Wit: George Underwood, Robert Elliott, Valentine Tucker
Signed: James Whitlock Sarah, wife of James Whitlock, relinquished her dower.
Recorded 1 July 1765

p.941   1 July 1765 Leonard Henley of Henrico County to his son, Leonard Henley, for the fatherlike love I bare unto my son and five shillings, 197 acres in Henrico and Goochland counties; adj. William Henley, Strangemen Hutchings, John Jude and Benjamin Johnson.
Wit: none                                         Signed: Leond. Henley
Recorded 1 July 1765

p.941   1 July 1765 Thomas Bethell of Henrico County to his son, Thomas Bethell, Jr., for natural love and affection and five shillings, one-half of the tract of land I now live on containing 180 acres; adj. Abraham Trueman, William Mays, Julius Allen and William Warrener.
Wit: none                              Signed Thomas (his T mark) Bethell
Recorded 1 July 1765

p.942   7 June 1765 Bowler Cocke the Elder of Charles City County, Gent., to his son, Bowler Cocke the Younger of Amelia County, for natural love and affection

and five shillings, 100 acres, being part of 900 acres formerly belonging to John Cocke, deceased, but has for four years past and upwards been in the quiet possession of the said Bowler Cocke the Younger; adj. on the west by Theodorick Baker and John Carter and on the north by the main run of Chickahominy Swamp.
Wit: William West, John Wayles, Henry Talmon, John Hylton, Robert Necks, John Brickhil.
Signed: Bowler Cocke                                                  Recorded 1 July 1765

p.943  12 December 1764 William Shepherd and Joseph Shepherd to Benjamin Shepherd, all of Henrico County, for 200 pounds, all of the land which John Shepherd possessed at the time of his death, being about 600 acres, lying between the lands of said William Shepherd and Joseph Shepherd in Henrico County.
Wit: Benjamin Bowles, John Bowles, Philip Webber, James Ryall
Signed: William Sheppard, Joseph Sheppard
Recorded 5 August 1765

p.944  9 February 1765 William Ellis to William Street, both of Henrico County, for 14 pounds, 54 acres on the branches of Tuckahoe Creek granted to the said William Ellis by patent dated 30 January 1741; adj. John Shewmaker (now Nathaniel Dennis) and Richard Randolph (now Leonard Henley) (metes and bounds description).
Wit: John Ellis, David Allen, William Allen Lankester,
Thomas (his  X  mark) East
Signed: William Ellis                                                 Recorded 5 August 1765

p.945  5 August 1765 Richard Adams, merchant of Henrico County, and Elizabeth, his wife, to Joshua Storrs, for 400 pounds, 184 acres at a place called Pickquanockque, commonly known by the name of Locust Neck.
Wit: none                                                            Signed: Richd. Adams
Recorded 5 August 1765

p.946  30 July 1765 William Barnes to Richard Renard, both of Henrico County, for 15 pounds, 50 acres on the branches of Cornelius Creek; adj. Richard Whitloe, John Whitloe, deceased, Isham West and said Richard Renard.
Wit: Luzby Turpin, Michael Turpin
Signed: William (his  X  mark) Barnes
Recorded 5 August 1765

p.947  5 August 1765 Zachariah Tait of Louisa County to John Price of Henrico County, for 50 pounds, 200 acres on the west side of a branch of the Brook called Jordan's Branch; adj. Col. Byrd, William Snead, Nathaniel Bridgwater and John

Kellie; said tract was conveyed to William Sims by John Lipscomb and afterwards conveyed to Zachariah Tait by William Sims.
Wit: none
Sarah, wife of Zachariah Tait, relinquished her dower.
Recorded 5 August 1765

p.949  27 August 1765 Mathew Hobson to his granddaughter, Judith Owen, for love, good will and natural affection, one Negro girl called Phebee; but if said Judith should die before she attains the age of 18, then said Negro girl and her increase to be equally divided between Hobson Owen, William Owen, Thomas Owen, Jr., Mary Owen and Sarah Owen.
Wit: Samuel Parsons, Nathaniel Clarke, Robert Sharp
Signed: Mathew (his X mark) Hobson
Recorded 2 September 1765

p.950  26 August 1765 Bond for 1,000 pounds, and report of Robert Pleasants, son of John, to Robert Pleasants, son of Thomas, and Thomas Pleasants, Jr., son of John, who take upon them to act in behalf of Exum Pleasants, an infant, in resolving the claim of John Pleasants, deceased, late of Bailey's, Henrico County, to one-third part of a tract of land in Goochland County, being the lands given by Dorothy Pleasants to her son Joseph Pleasants by deed of gift dated 22 July 1718, the said John Pleasants bequeathing to his son Exum Pleasants. an infant, his said right in the lands before same was completed; Charles Woodson, Fleming Bates and Peter Warren being arbitrators in this settlement.
Wit: Daniel Stone, Richard (his X mark) Dean, James Fawcett
Signed: Robert Pleasants                    Recorded 2 September 1765

p.951  27 August 1765 Thomas Owen to his son, Thomas Owen, Junr., both of Henrico County, for love, goodwill and affection, one Negro boy named Ben; but if said Thomas Owen, Junr., should die before he attains the age of 21, Negro boy Ben is to be given to Hobden Owen, William Owen, Mary Owen and Sarah Owen.
Wit: Samuel Parsons, Nathaniel Clark, Robert Sharp
Signed: Thomas Owen                          Recorded 2 September 1765

p.951  2 September 1765 William Faris to his son, William Faris, for love and goodwill, 200 acres on the north side of White Oak Swamp; adj. Daniel Warriner, Senr., Benjamin Warriner, William Faris, Senr., William Bottom, James Austin and William Faris, son of John Faris.
Wit: Samuel Gathright, Jr., Ephraim Gathright, William Gathright, Jr.
Signed: William (his ⋀ mark) Fearis, Snr.
Recorded 2 September 1765

p.952  2 September 1765 William Fearis, Senr., to his son, Sherwood Fearis, both of Henrico County, for true love and natural affection, 75 acres on the north side of White Oak Swamp, beginning at the lower side of the main run of said swamp; adj. Robert Pleasants, Robert Fearis, William Bottom and William Fearis, Junr., son of the said William Fearis.
Wit: Samuel Gathright, Jr., Ephraim Gathright, William Gathright, Jr.
Signed: William (his ⋀ mark) Fearis, Snr.
Recorded 2 September 1765

p.953  29 August 1765 Isaac Winston of Henrico County to Fontaine Owen, son of Thomas Owen and Anne, his wife, one Negro girl named Tempey, now in the possession of his father, Thomas Owen, and her future increase.
Wit: Isaac Winston, Junr., Peter Winston, William Winston
Signed: Isaac Winston                    Recorded 2 September 1765

p.954  2 September 1765 Richard Truman of Henrico County to son-in-law, William Faris, Junr., and my daughter, Martha Faris, his wife, for love and good will, one Negro girl named Fanny and her increase.
Wit: Samuel Gathright, Jr., Ephriam Gathright, William Gathright, Jr.
Signed: Richard (his X mark) Trueman
Recorded 2 September 1765

p.954  27 August 1765 Thomas Owen, to his daughter, Sarah Owen, both of Henrico County, for love, good will and affection, one Negro girl named Rachel; but if said daughter Sarah should die before she attains the age of 18, said slave Rachel to be equally divided between Hobson Owen, William Owen, Thomas Owen, Jr. and Mary Owen.
Wit: Nathaniel Clarke, Samuel Parsons, Robert Sharp
Signed: Thomas Owen                    Recorded 2 September 1765

p.955  27 August 1765 Thomas Owen to his son, William Owen, both of Henrico County, for love, good will and affection, two Negro boys named Harry and Isom, but if said William should die before he attains the age of 21, said Negro boys to be equally divided between Hobson Owen, Thomas Owen (Jr.), Mary Owen and Sarah Owen.
Wit: Samuel Parsons, Nathaniel Clarke, Robert Sharp
Signed: Thomas Owen                    Recorded 2 September 1765

p.956  27 August 1765 Thomas Owen to his daughter, Mary Owen, both of Henrico County, for love, good will and affection, one Negro girl named Ursley; but if said Mary should die befire she attains the age of 18, said slave to be equally divided

between Hobson Owen, William Owen, Thomas Owen, Junr., and Sarah Owen.
Wit: Samuel Parsons, Nathaniel Clarke, Robert Sharp
Signed: Thomas Owen     Recorded 2 September 1765

p.956  2 September 1765 Bond of Turner Southall as one of the inspectors of tobacco at the publick warehouse established at Shockoe in Henrico County, in the amount of 500 pounds, with Samuel Duval and John Royster as his sureties.
Wit: none
Signed: Turner Southall, Saml. Duval, John Royster
Recorded 2 September 1765

p.957  29 September 1765 Ann Skinner of Henrico County to her two sons, Thomas Skinner of Williamsburg, York County, and William Skinner of Henrico County, an apprentice, for love and affection, six pewter places of the smaller size, one pewter basin of the smaller size and one box iron and heaters to son Thomas; and my house and lot in Richmond Town, being Lot 71 purchased of Andrew Castle in Hanover County, one cow and calf and my other household furniture to son William.
Wit: John Bryan     Signed: Ann (her ✚ mark) Skinner
Recorded 7 October 1765

p.957  29 December 1764 Power of Attorney from John Elam of Leeds, County of York, Great Britain, merchant, to Joshua Storrs upon James River and George Ellis bound to him as an apprentice, late of the same place, to take and accept all goods, wares, merchandise consigned to them or either of them and to sell and dispose of same "in my name" for ready money.
Wit: Peter Dickonson, Thomas Bolland
Signed: John Elam (with Thomas Bolland before Sam Davenport, Esq.,
   mayor of Leeds)     Recorded 7 October 1765

p.960  7 October 1765 William Pike to Robert Pleasants, both of Henrico County, for 100 pounds, 75 acres at the fork of Long Bridge Road and Bottoms Bridge Road, known as Pike's Ordinary, and purchased by the late George Pike and by his last will and testament given to his two sons, William and George Pike; bounded by Thomas Binford, Humphrey Smith, Daniel Warriner, Junr., and the said Robert Pleasants and on which the said Pike now dwelleth.
Wit: none     Signed: William Pike
Signed: Zachariah Tait, Sarah (her ✚ mark) Tait
Recorded 7 October 1765

p.961  9 August 1765 John Pleasants to Edward White, both of Henrico County, for

20 pounds, 19 acres near the branches of Four Mile Creek; adj. Richard Sharp, George Williamson, deceased, the late Frogmorton and the late Joseph Pleasants; land John Pleasants purchased of Richard Blaws.
Wit: Thomas Bates, John (his ✚ mark) Holmes, Lewis Hancock
Signed: John Pleasants                                     Recorded 7 October 1765

p.962  10 July 1765 John Pleasants, Senr., to Nicholas Scherer, both of Henrico County, for 100 pounds, one-half acre lot in the Town of Richmond, being Lot 20, which said Pleasants bought of William Byrd, Esq.
Wit: Edward Curd, Samuel Mitchell, George Scherer
Signed: John Pleasants                                     Recorded 7 October 1765

p.963  9 May 1765 Nicholas Amos to Thomas Ellis, both of Henrico County, for 70 pounds, 171 acres on the branches of Deep Run; being the same land Amos lately purchased of Thomas North; adj. Anthony North, John Lankester's Spring Branch called the Old House Branch, Randolph and Roland Blackburn.
Wit: William Street, Robert Shephard, Jesse Ellis, William (his X mark) Flowers
Signed: Nicholas (his ⊔ mark) Amos
Recorded 7 October 1765

p.964  7 October 1765 Thomas Atchison of the Town of Portsmouth, Norfolk County, merchant, to John Rose, son and devisee of the Reverend Robert Rose, deceased, for 7 pounds, Lot No. N on the plan of the Town of Richmond; cites that said Atchison sold to Robert Rose in his lifetime one of his lots in the Town of Richmond for 7 pounds, which was paid, but said Rose died before a deed was executed; Rose left said lot to his son John by his last will and testament.
Wit: Alexander McCaul, John Kippen
Signed: Thos. Atchison                                     Recorded 7 October 1765

p.965  7 October 1765 Randall Depriest to Robert Duval, both of Henrico County, an apprenticeship contract, in which Depriest binds his son William Depriest to said Duval for nine years, from 5 March last past, to be taught the trade of a house carpenter joiner and to pay William Depriest 28 pounds at the end of his service.
Wit: none                          Signed: Randall Depriest, Robert Duval
Recorded 7 October 1765

p.966  8 October 1765 Drury Wood to William Cornett, both of Henrico County, for 6 pounds and 5 shillings, 25 acres adj. Jacob Smith, John Wheeler and William Turner.
Wit: none                                                  Signed: Drury Wood
Recorded 7 October 1765

p.967 7 October 1765 William Cock Redford to Josiah Bullington, both of Henrico County, for 12 pounds, 6 acres on Branches Ferry Road and the Roundabout Swamp; adj. Robert Bullington.
Wit: Thomas Jordan, Junr., Mark Woodcock, John (his I mark) Woodcock
Signed: William Cock Redford                    Recorded 7 October 1765

p.968 4 November 1765 Bond of Joseph Lewis as Sheriff of Henrico County, in the amount of 1,000 pounds, during pleasure by commission from the Governor under the seal of the colony dated 29 October last past, with Nathaniel Bacon and Daniel Price, Junr., his sureties.
Wit: Thomas Adams
Signed: Jos. Lewis, Daniel Price, Nathaniel Bacon
Recorded 2 June 1766

p.968 2 June 1766 Bond of Joseph Lewis as Sheriff of Henrico County for the collection of all quitrents, fines, forfeitures, etc., in the amount of 500 pounds; with Nathaniel Bacon and Daniel Price, Junr., his sureties.
Wit: Fortunatus Sydnor
Signed: Jos. Lewis, Daniel Price, Nathaniel Bacon
Recorded 2 June 1766

p.969 2 June 1766 Bond of Joseph Lewis as Sheriff of Henrico County for the colleciton and payment of taxes, in the amount of 1,000 pounds, with Nathaniel Bacon and Daniel Price, Junr., his sureties.
Signed: Jos. Lewis, Daniel Price, Nathaniel Bacon
Recorded 2 June 1766

p.969 26 October 1765 Samuel Childres to Christian Allen, both of Henrico County, for 20 pounds, 40 acres on Bulls Branch; adj. Julius Allen, William Gathright and the said Samuel Childres.
Wit: William Morris, James (his ✚ mark) Turner, Isham (his I mark) Allen
Signed: Samuel Childres                    Recorded 2 June 1766

p.970 14 May 1766 William Gathright and Judah Gathright, his mother, to Philip Watson, all of Henrico County, for 240 pounds, 215 acres on the south side of the Chickahominy River, which tract was granted to the said William Gathright by the last will and testament of his father, Miles Gathright, deceased; adj. Julius Allen, William Morris, Miles Gathright, John Gathright, son of William Gathright, deceased, and the main run of the said river, or swamp.
Wit: James Buchanan, John McKeand, William Donald
Signed: Wm. Gathright, Judah (her ✚ mark) Gathright

Recorded 2 June 1766

p.971  28 June 1765 Peter Randolph, Esq., of Henrico County, to Arthur Hopkins of the Parish of St. Anne's, Albemarle County, for 26 pounds, 17 shillings and 6 pence, several lots, each containing half an acre in the Town of Beverly, being Lots 91, 9, 36 and 59.
Wit: Charles Clarke, John Hopkins
Signed: Peter Randolph                                    Recorded 7 July 1766

p.971  23 June 1766 John Price to his son, William Price, for love, good will and affection, 64 acres, being all of the tract of land whereon I now live and all of my Negroes: a Negro girl named Doll, a Negro girl named Bett and a Negro girl named Moll, and their increase, all of my household goods, and all my stock (cattle, horses, sheep and hogs).
Wit: James Davis, Edward Barnett, Thomas Ginnett, William Loving
Signed: John (his ƚ mark) Price                           Recorded 7 July 1766

p.972  7 July 1766 Abraham Cowley and Ann, his wife, of Dale Parish, Chesterfield County, to Miles Selden, Clerk of the Parish, Henrico County, for 150 pounds, 362 acres on the south side of the Chickahominy Swamp; adj. Daniel Price, Reedy Branch, Spraggins (formerly) and the Main Road.
(metes and bounds description).
Wit: Charles Lewis, Jr., William Lewis, Groves Harding
Signed: Abraham Cowley, Ann Cowley
Recorded 7 July 1766

p.973  2 June 1766 Jonathan Williams to William Spencer, both of Henrico County, for 25 pounds, 34 acres on the county road; adj. William Scott, John Scott, Darby Whitlow, Nathaniel Whitlow, David Breeding and Col. William Randolph, deceased.
Wit: none
Signed: Jonathan Williams, Hannah (her + mark) Williams
Hannah, wife of Jonathan Williams, relinquished her dower.
Recorded 7 July 1766

p.975  9 June 1766 James Woodfin to John James Woodfin, both of Henrico County, for 18 pounds, 44 acres, being part of the land whereon the said James Woodfin now lives; adj. said James Woodfin, James Lindsey, William Taylor and the said John James Woodfin.
Wit: Thomas Bates, Benjamin (his B mark) Childres, John (his [blank] mark) Hutchings, Junr.

Signed: James Woodfin                                       Recorded 4 August 1766

p.975   12 November 1765 William Webb of Halifax County, planter, to John Norvell of Hanover County, planter, for 20 pounds, 60 acres, being all of that plantation tract which said William Webb now possesses, bound according to the known and reputed bounds.
Wit: Archbill Snead, William Morris, Joseph Sheppard, John Stevens
Signed: William (his  X  mark) Webb
Recorded 4 August 1766

p.977   4 August 1766 Nicholas Giles, Sr., to William Clopton, both of Henrico County, for 6 pounds, 12 acres on Cornelius Creek; adj. said William Clopton and said Nicholas Giles.
Wit: none                                                  Signed: Nicholas Giles
Recorded 4 August 1766

p.977   4 August 1766 John Martin and Jane, his wife, to Richard Adams, all of Henrico County, for 30 pounds, 180 acres in the fork of White Oak Swamp and on the branches thereof; being one moiety of a tract granted to John Williams and by the said Williams sold to the said John Martin.                    Wit: none
Signed: John (his  +  mark) Martin, Jane (her  +  mark) Martin
Recorded 4 August 1766

p.978   12 November 1766 Robert Webb and Leticia, his wife, of Henrico County, to John Norvell of Hanover County, for 40 pounds, 140 acres adj. Benjamin Shepherd, Thomas Bowles, Hughes and William Morris.
Wit: John Stevens, Archbill Snead, William Morris, Joseph Sheppard.
Signed: Robert (his  R  mark) Webb, Leticia her  ✚  mark) Webb
Recorded 4 August 1766

p.979   6 June 1766 Benjamin Childres to John James Woodfin, both of Henrico County, for 45 pounds, 66 acres, being part of the land whereon the said Benjamin now lives; adj. Thomas Matthews, deceased, the said Woodfin, James Woodfin, William Taylor and said Childers.
Wit: Thomas Bates, Ann Trotter, Jacob F. Randolph, Elizabeth Jordan
Signed: Benjamin (his B mark) Childers
Receipt dated 6 June 1766 of John Pleasants and Robert Pleasants for 45 pounds paid them by Benjamin Childers (per the hands of John James Woodfin) in part of a debt due them from said Childers mentioned in a deed of mortgage dated 15 August 1757 of record; they join in deed to release the 66 acres from the lien.
Recorded 4 August 1766

p.981  4 August 1766 Bond of Thomas Starke to keep an ordinary as Westham, in the amount of 50 pounds, with John Price, his surety.
Wit: none                                          Signed: Thomas Starke, John Price
Recorded 4 August 1766

p.981  22 July 1766 Deed of Mortgage from William Bryan to Benjamin Bryan, attorney-at-law, both of Henrico County, for 54 pounds, 17 shillings and 11 pence with lawful interest to be paid to the said Benjamin Bryan on or before 10 April next ensuing, and for said Benjamin Bryan to act as his surety for the payment of 48 pounds, 18 shillings and 5 pence, collateral being two Negro slaves, Abraham and Dick, and the profits of their labors, one bay mare and colt, two cows and calf, one bed and furniture, six leather bottom chairs, two sows and 7 pigs.
Wit: James Wilson, Mary Bryan, Mary Gunn, James Gunn
Signed: William Bryan, Benja. Bryan
Recorded 1 September 1766

p.982  5 October 1766 William Adkisson to Matthew Hobson, both of Henrico County, for 35 pounds, 100 acres on the Long and Hungry Branch, which said 100 acres was given by deed recorded; adj. John Mosby, Watson Patman and David Atkisson.
Wit: Benjamin Bryan, Thomas Prosser
Signed: William Adkisson,
Susanna, wife of William Adkisson, relinquished her dower.
Recorded 3 November 1766

p.983  3 November 1766 James Martin to Samuel Gathright, Sr., both of Henrico County, for 33 pounds, 30 acres beginning at the mouth of a branch where it comes into the Westin Run; adj. Col. Richard Randolph, William Porter, deceased, John Brackett, John Martin and Martin Martin.
Wit: Benjamin Bryan, Daniel Stone, Anselm Gathright
Signed: James Martin
Elizabeth, wife of James Martin, relinquished her dower.
Recorded 3 November 1766

p.984  3 October 1766 Richard Trueman to my loving friend, James Austin, and his wife, Mary (and the heirs of her body lawfully begotten), all of Henrico County, for good will and affection, one young Negro wench named Nann and her increase.
Wit: John Dollard, John Trueman, Abraham Trueman
Signed: Richd. Trueman                           Recorded 3 November 1766

p.985  30 September 1766 William Adkisson, planter, to Thomas Bowles, planter,

159

both of Henrico County, for 5 pounds, 45 acres on Poplar Branch, adj. Frank Cook and William Morris.
Wit: Pierce Griffin, William Morris, John Grinstead
Signed: William Adkisson, Susanna Adkisson
Susanna, wife of William Adkisson, relinquished her dower.
Recorded 3 November 1766

p.986  4 October 1766 John Frayser to William Frayser, both of Henrico County, for 40 pounds, 90 acres on the Main Road; adj. said John Frayser and said William Frayser.
Wit: William (his  +  mark) Childres, William Frayser, Jr., William Frayser Younger
Signed: John Frayser,
Susanna, wife of John Frayser, relinquished her dower.
Recorded 3 November 1766

p.988  26 August 1766 William Childres to William Frayser, both of Henrico County, for 34 pounds, 100 acres, bounded on the north by Darby Whitloe and said William Frayser, on the west by John Scott and William Scott and on the south and east by Joseph Akins.
Wit: Hannah White, Sally Pleasants, Thomas Pleasants, Jr.
Signed: William (his  X  mark) Childers
Susanna, wife of William Childers, relinquished her dower
Recorded 3 November 1766

p.989  11 July 1766 Susannah Burton, widow and executrix of Hutchens Burton, deceased, to William Allen Burton, son of the said Hutchens Burton, for 37 pounds and 3 pence, two Negro slaves: Peter, a boy; and Milley, a girl, and her increase, six head of black cattle, six head of sheep and one black horse branded.
Wit: Fortunatus Sydnor, Christian Allen
Signed: Susannah (her  +  mark) Burton
Recorded 3 November 1766

p.989  9 October 1766 Samuel Liggon, Sr., to his son, John Liggon, both of Henrico County, for diverse good causes and especially love and good will, 89 acres on Gilley's Creek, being part of a tract of land said Samuel Ligon, Sr., holds by patent dated 5 July 1751; adj. Alexander Moss and Alexander Robinson.
Wit: George Adams, Richard Crouch, Thomas Calder, William Powell
Signed: Samuel (his ₣ mark) Liggon
Recorded 3 November 1766

p.990  3 November 1766 Martin Martin, Sr., to Samuel Garthright, Sr., both of

Henrico County, for 37 pounds, 30 acres, beginning at the mouth of a branch that divides said Martin's land from that of his son, James Martin, and which runs into the Western Run joining Col. Richard Randolph and running to Martin's Spring Branch which divides the land of the said Martin from that of his son, John Martin, thence up branch and thence along the said John Martin and said James Martin.
Wit: Benjamin Burton, Daniel Stone, Anselm Garthright
Signed: Martin (his  MM  mark) Martin
Barbara, wife of Martin Martin, relinquished her dower.
Recorded 3 November 1766

p.991  15 October 1766 David Hall of Henrico County to James Alley of Orange County, North Carolina, for 100 pounds, 100 acres on the south side of Stony Run; adj. Thomas Alley, Joseph Brown, Nathaniel Dennis and William Street.
Wit: Burgis Harralson, Michael Dickson, John Street, Samuel Alley,
Thomas Alley                                           Signed: David Hall
Partly proved on 3 November 1766 and continued to 2 March 1767, when fully proved and admitted to record.

p.992  3 November 1766 Bond of Samuel Gathright, Junr., as one of the inspectors of tobacco at the Four Mile Creek warehouse, by commission of the Governor, in the amount of 500 pounds, with Samuel Gathright, Senr., his surety.
Wit: Fortunatus Sydnor                    Signed: Samuel Gathright, Junr.
Recorded 3 November 1766

p.993  2 February 1767 Apprenticeship Contract between William Allen, a mulatto, and Christian Allen, both of Henrico County, for 6 pounds and 10 shillings, the said William Allen agrees to serve Christian Allen six years from the date hereof as a true and faithful servant.
Wit: John Howard, Junr., David White, William Cooke
Signed: Chrsn. Allen, William (his  ✚  mark) Allen
Recorded 2 February 1767

p.993  2 July 1763 Deed of Lease from the Hon. William Byrd, Esq., of Westover, Charles City County, to Fortunatus Sydnor, of Richmond Town, Henrico County, for the rent and easements herein, 302 acres on the James River known as Eppes and adjoining Belvidere Branch and the Main Road on Shockoe Hill [the Island C mentioned on the plan drawn by Peter Fontaine, Gent., not included]; for the term of 21 years from 25 December last past, and for the payment every year of 32 pounds and 13 shillings on the first of January.
Wit: Peter Randolph, Benjamin Bryan, James Gunn, C. Gist
Signed: W. Byrd, Fortu. Sydnor

Recorded 2 February 1767

p.996  29 April 1763 Obadiah Smith to Richard Timberlake, both of Henrico County, for natural love and affection and for his better maintenance and livelihood, 20 acres on the Miry Branch; adj. John Smith, the Main Road, the Spring Branch and Adams.
Wit: Martin Burton, John Smith, Junr., William Timberlake
Signed: Obadh. Smith
Date of record not given; (re-recorded on page 1000, also on a date not given, adding Joseph Smith as a neighboring landowner in the description).

p.996  4 February 1765 Bond of Isaac Younghusband as Sheriff of Henrico County, by commision of the Governor under the seal of the colony, in the amount of 176,228 pounds of tobacco, with Samuel Duval and John Pleasants, Jr., his sureties.
Wit: none
Signed: Isaac Younghusband, Samuel Duval, Jno. Pleasants, Junr.
Recorded 4 February 1767

p.997  1 December 1766 James Britton to his son, Lyddall Britton, both of Henrico County, for natural love and affection, 204 acres whereon the said James Britton now lives, reserving unto himself and his wife, Sarah Britton, a life estate therein.
Wit: none                                Signed: James (his I B mark) Brittain
Recorded 1 December 1766

p.997  7 November 1766 Order of Manumission from the Council of Virginia, the Governor present, in response to the petition of Alexander McCaul and many others setting forth the extraordinary service, merit and fidelity of a Negro man named Joe, lately the property of Robert Burton of Henrico County and now belonging to the said Alexander McCaul, and praying that he may have his freedom; Board finds that said slave is highly deserving of his liberty and orders that said Alexander McCaul has cause to manumit said slave.
Signed: N. Walthoe, Clerk of Council
Recorded on motion of Alexander McCaul 1 December 1766

p.998  29 November 1764 John Williams to Soloman Fuzel, both of Henrico County, for his bond for several promises to him, the said John William and his wife, a lease for the term of 16 years, to said Fuzel and his wife, of 50 acres on the north side of the road that leads from Bottom's Bridge to Woodson's Frrry; adj. Robert Maddox.
Wit: George Adams, John Fuzel
Signed: John Williams, Mary, wife of John Williams, relinquished her dower.

Recorded 3 December 1764

p.998 1 April 1765 James Lindsey to Thomas Evans, both of Henrico County, for 7 pounds, 25 acres adj. William Hobson, William Taylor and a path leading from James Woodfin's to William Robinson's.
Wit: none　　　　　　　　　　　　　　　　　　　Signed: James Lindsey
Recorded 1 April 1765

p.999 16 March 1763 Pouncey Anderson of Hanover County and Henry Martin of Albemarle County, executor of the last will and testament of Michael Holland, deceased, of record in Hanover County, to Francis Cook, for 20 pounds, 200 acres adj. John Lankester, said Holland and John Hughes.
Wit: Turner Southall, Christopher John Thomas, William Harris, Richard Cottrell
Signed: Pouncey Anderson [Henry Martin's signature omitted]
Date of record not given

p.1001 5 August 1765 Bond of Julius Allen for building a bridge 12 feet wide across the main run of Chickahominy Swamp, at a place known as Bailey's Bridge; to be finished on 8 October next and to be kept up for eight years; adj. the Reverend Miles Selden and Joseph Lewis on the south and adj. William Macon on the north; with Robert Spears, his surety.
Wit: John Hales, Samuel Griffin, James Cocke, Jr.
Signed: Julius Allen, Robert Spears　　　　　　Date of record not given

p.1002 28 February 1767 Robert Moore to Ephraim Gathright, both of Henrico County, for 65 pounds, 30 acres on the north side of White Oak Swamp, a the mouth of the Long Branch and along the road; adj. the widow White and Bear Hill; being the land given to the said Robert by his father, Richard Moore.
Wit: John Dollard, Ephraim Garthright, William Garthright
Signed: Robert Moore, Susannah, wife of Robert Moore, relinquished her dower.
Recorded 2 March 1767

p.1003 6 April 1767 Miles Gathright, Junr., of New Kent County, to Robert Spears of Henrico County, for 100 pounds, 133 acres on the south side of Bear Swamp, which land was decreed to the said Miles Gathright, Junr., by his father, William Gathright, in his last will and testament dated 18 September 1762; beginning at Trueman's path on the Bear Road, and adj. Robert Spears, Bear Swamp, Miles Gathright, Sr., and John Gathright.
Wit: Miles Gathright, Senr., William Gathright, Junr., Joseph Gathright
Signed: Miles Gathright, Junr.　　　　　　　　　Recorded 6 April 1767

p.1004  5 April 1767 Anthony Redford to Nottoway Parish, Amelia County, to John Markham of Bath Parish, Chesterfield County, for 100 pounds, 10 acres known as Piny Point on the north side of the James River opposite Warwick Warehouses; adj. Thomas Mosely, John Giles and down a steep bottom called John Giles' Spring Bottom.
Wit: F. Watkins, Luzby Turpin, John Royster
Signed: Anthony Redford, Mary, wife of Anthony Redford, relinquished her dower by a dedimus directed to Robert Munford, William Crawley, John Booker and Richard Jones, Gent., dated 6 April 1767 from Thomas Adams, Clerk, taken by William Crawley and Robert Munford on 20 April 1767 recorded 4 May 1767.
Recorded 6 April 1767

p.1006  10 November 1766 Thomas Canter Still to Thomas Ginnett, both of Henrico County, 10 pounds, 68 acres near Deep Run Church; adj. Edmund Alley, John Glen, John Williamson and John Cawthorn.
Wit: William Henley, Peter Clarke, David Bowles, Benjamin Johnson
Signed: Thos. Canter (his T mark) Still, Linder Still
Recorded 4 May 1767.

p.1007  4 May 1767 William Henley of Henrico County to Thomas East of Chesterfield County, for 40 pounds, 100 acres on both side of the Country Road; adj. William Harding, Wallis, Rockett's Crossing, Henley, Fig Branch and Harding's Branch; being a tract said Henley brought of William Lawless.
Wit: none                    Signed: William Henley, Mary Henley
Recorded 4 May 1767

p.1008  4 May 1767 Thomas Alley of Henrico County to his son, David Alley, for love, good will and affection...after my deceased and the decease of my wife, Frances Alley, 50 acres on the south side of Stony Run, being the tract whereon I now live; adj. James Alley, Stony Run, William Price and Joseph Brown.
Wit: Jesse Clark, William Street, John Johnson, John (his H-H mark) Clark
Signed: Thomas (his A mark) Alley
Recorded 4 May 1767

p.1009  2 December 1766 Bill of Sale from Walter Dick of Henrico County to Lewis Hancock, for 4 pounds and 5 pence and the cost of a suit due unto Robert Pleasants (agreeable to a judgment of the Henrico Court and an execution thereof issued against me some time ago which I acknowledge to be justly due) together with the cost of a scape warrant which the said Lewis Hancock this day hath taken upon himself and satisfied, one bed and furniture, two iron pots, one copper saucepan, half dozen plates, two dishes, two basins, two pewter porringers, one

spinning wheel and other tangible personal property.
Wit: Thomas Bates                Signed: Walter (his WD mark) Dick
Recorded 1 June 1767


p.1010  18 April 1767 Mary Eppes and Richard Eppes of Charles City County to Robert Pleasants, merchant, of Henrico County, for 150 pounds, 400 acres on both sides of White Oak Swamp, formerly the property of Richard Cocke which was given to his daughter Mary by deed dated 2 June 1735 of record.
Wit: Thomas Bates, John Ellyson, Samuel Parsons
Signed: Mary Eppes, Richd. Eppes            Recorded 1 June 1767

p.1011  29 January 1767 Richard Timberlake, cabinet maker, to Joshua Storrs, merchant, both of Henrico County, for 45 pounds, 25 acres, being the land which was given to the said Richard Timberlake by deed from Obadiah Smith Wit: John Pleasants, Jacob Pleasants, George Ellis, Archibald Pleasants
Signed: Richard Timberlake
Mary, wife of Richard Timberlake, relinquished her dower.
Recorded 1 June 1767

p.1012  4 May 1767 Francis George Stegar of Cumberland County to William Wills, surgeon, of the Town of Richmond, Henrico County, for life, with remainder to Melicent Abner, sometimes called Melicent Wills, daughter of the said William Wills, and Harruet Lettuck, or to the survivor should either die without heirs of their bodies, and should both die without heirs, then to Sally Scherer, daughter of George Scherer, for 45 pounds, two lots or half acres of land in the Town of Richmond, shown on the plan of the said town as numbers C.D.
Wit: James Vaughan, Nicholas Scherer, George Scherer, Christopher Pryor
Signed: Francis George (his F mark) Stegar
Recorded 1 June 1767

p.1014  2 March 1767 Hon. Peter Randolph, Esq., heir and surviving executor of Beverly Randolph, Esq., deceased, to William Wills, surgeon, of the Town of Richmond, for his life, with remainder to Melicent Abner, otherwise called Melicent Wills, daughter of the said William Wills, and to the said William Wills' heirs should the said Melicent die without heirs of her body, for 70 pounds, three lots in the Town of Richmond, or half acres of land, being lots 30, 43 and 44 on the plan of the said town, which lots one Robert Weatherly, deceased, in his lifetime mortgaged for a sum he owed said Beverly Randolph and which was not paid; heirs of said Weatherly are barred or foreclosed of all equity of redemption by a decree of the County Court of Henrico.

Wit: Alexander McCaul, James Buchanan, John Esdale
Signed: Peter Randolph                                    Recorded 1 June 1767


p.1015  1 June 1767 Alexander Robinson of Henrico County to his son, Samuel Robinson, for 5 shillings and natural love and affection, 75 acres on the branches of Gilley's Creek; being land purchased of John Robinson by deed dated 4 December 1752.
Wit: none                      Signed: Alexander (his X mark) Robinson
Recorded 1 June 1767

p.1016  1 June 1767 Alexander Robinson of Henrico County to his son, William Robinson, for 5 shillings and natural love and affection, 157 acres, according to the known and reputed bounds thereof; being the land purchased of George Dabney by deed of record.
Wit: none                      Signed: Alexander (his X mark) Robinson
Recorded 1 June 1767

p.1016  14 March 1767 Edward Goode, Senr., of Henrico County, to John Goode, son of Benjamin Goode, for 25 pounds and 10 shillings, 50 acres at William Frayser's line at the mouth of the Deep Run, adj. to the other lands of John Goode to William Frayser's land on Four Mile Creek and along said creek.
Wit: Thomas Bates, Francis Sharp, Samuel Parsons
Signed: Edward (his X mark) Goode
Mary, wife of Edward Goode, relinquished her dower.
Recorded 1 June 1767

p.1018  Dedimus for examination of Elizabeth Wilson, wife of Thomas Branch Wilson, (of Amelia County) from Thomas Adams, Clerk, dated [- January 1767, taken by William Crawley and John Booker, Gent., on 3 March 1767; and dedimus for examination of Priscilla Mitchell, wife of Henry Mitchell, of Sussex County from Thomas Adams, Clerk, dated (-) January 1767, taken by John Mason and Benjamin Wyche, Gent., on 19 March 1767 recorded 6 April 1767; pertain to a conveyance from Henry Mitchell, Edward Osborne, Robert Goode, Josiah Tatum, Branch Tanner, Christopher Branch, Thomas Branch Wilson and John Goode to George Cox for 448 acres.

p.1019  5 July 1767 Thomas Ginnitt and Ruth, his wife, to Nicholas Connoway, all of Henrico County, for 15 pounds, 66 acres adj. John Glen, Edmund Alley, Thomas Ginnitt and John Williamson, deceased.
Wit: William Lawless, William Price

Signed: Thomas Ginnett, Ruth (her ✢ mark) Ginnitt
Recorded 7 July 1767

p.1020  5 July 1767 Joseph Parsons of Henrico County, to his children, William, Sarah, Josiah, Mary, Ursulah, Elizabeth, Woodson, Agnes and Judith, for natural love and affection, Negro slaves, and the increase of the female Negroes; Abram to William Parsons, Mima to Sarah Parsons, Stephen to Josiah Parsons, Aggy to Mary Parsons, Jenny to Ursulah Parsons, Moses to Woodson Parsons, Carter to Elizabeth Parsons, Dooke to Agnes Parsons and Isaac to Judith Parsons.
Wit: Thomas Owen, Thomas Thorp              Signed: Jos. Parsons
Recorded 3 August 1767

p.1021  1 August 1767 Joseph Parsons of Henrico County to his sons, William and Josiah Parsons, for natural love and affection, 464 acres on Chickahominy Swamp.
Wit: none                                   Signed: Jos. Parsons
Recorded 3 August 1767

p.1022  3 August 1767 John Pleasants to his granddaughter, Susanna Pleasants, for the love I bear, One Negro girl named Patt.
Wit: Jesse Pleasants, Archibald Pleasants
Signed: John Pleasants                      Recorded 3 August 1767

p.1022  3 August 1767 Deed of Gift from John Pleasants, carpenter, of Henrico County to his two daughters, Mary Pleasants and Susanna Pleasants, for the love I bear, two Negro girls: Naomi to daughter Mary and Silve to daughter Susanna and to the survivor should either die, and if both should die, then said Negroes shall return to me or my heirs.
Wit: none                                   Signed: John Pleasants, Carpr.
Recorded 3 August 1767

p.1023  7 January 1767 John Allday to Luzby Turpin, both of Henrico County, for 20 shillings per acre, 65 acres on Cornelius Creek, at Joseph Bailey's Ford.
Wit: William Clopton, Francis Redford, James Redford
Signed: John Allday                         Recorded 3 August 1767

p.1023  15 March 1767 James Alley of Rowan County, North Carolina, to Edmund Alley, David Alley and Nathaniel Dennis, all of Henrico County, for 60 pounds, 100 acres on Stony Run, beginning at two corner ashes on said run; adj. Thomas Alley, Joseph Brown, Nathaniel Dennis and William Street.
Wit: William (his ✗∽ mark) Willis, Samuel Alley, Jacob Johnson,
Susanna (her ∽ mark) Teek.

Signed: James Alley                                    Recorded 3 August 1767

p.1024  29 July 1767 John Blackburn, planter, to Royal Richard Allen, both of Henrico County, for a sum not given, 93 acres on the south side of Deep Run at David Staples' Mill; being the land left by Rowlin Black, deceased, to be sold to discharge his just debts; running from the mill that David Staples built, up the Deep Run to the mouth of Quioccason Run and adj. Nicholas Amos, Thomas Randolph and John Ellis.
Wit: William Ally, David Allen                         Signed: John Blackburn
Recorded 3 August 1767

p.1025  25 March 1767 James Alley of Rowan County, North Carolina, to David Alley of Henrico County, for 20 pounds, 109 acres on the branches of Deep Run and on the Main Road; adj. Samuel Duval, John Glen and William Alley.
Wit: Edmund Alley, Nathaniel Dennis, Samuel Alley
Signed: James Alley                                    Recorded 3 August 1767

p.1026  8 December 1766 James Alley of Orange County, North Carolina, to Burgis Harrelson and David Hall, for 118 pounds, 100 acres on Stony Run, beginning at two corner ashes on Stony Run; adj. Thomas Alley, Joseph Brown, Nathaniel Dennis and William Street.
Wit: James Gregory, Garet Gutry, Ezekiel Harralson,
Alisheba or Lichaba (her ✚ mark) Harralson
Signed: James Alley                                    Recorded 3 August 1767

p.1027  8 December 1766 James Alley of Orange County, North Carolina, to Burgis Harrelson and David Hall, of the same county, for 118 pounds, 109 acres on the north side of the Main Road that leads by Deep Run Chappel; adj. Samuel Duval, John Glen and William Alley.
Wit: James Gregory, Garet Guttry, Ezekiel Harralson,
Alistraba (her ✚ mark) Harralson.
Signed: James Alley                                    Recorded 3 August 1767

## Conclusion of Deed Book 1750-1767

## Begin HENRICO COUNTY DEED BOOK, 1767-1774

p.1  8 September 1766 Gerard Walker, brother of Henry Walker, deceased, of the Parish of Hale in the County of Cumberland [in Great Britain], yeoman; Ann Walker, sister of Henry Walker, deceased, now the wife of William Noble, of

Egremont in the said County of Cumberland, millwright; and Henry Walker, father of Henry Walker, deceased, of said parish, yeoman; to Roger Atkinson, in consideration of the payment of debts owed by the decedent, hereby release all of their right in various tracts of land owned by the decedent; cites that Henry Walker, late of the Town of Petersburg, County of Dinwiddie, Colony of Virginia, merchant, by his last will and testament dated 2 April 1764, directed his executors (Roger Atkinson and Robert Newsum) to sell all of his lands for the best price; said lands consisting of one tract lately purchased of George Nicholas, one tract lately purchased of John Edwards and another tract of Sterling Thornton (for which he has no deed but has paid the consideration); a small lot on Brickhouse Run and four lots in the Town of Petersburg. The testator was justly indebted to his father, Henry Walker, in the sum of 283 pounds and 15 shillings for money lent and also for 30 pounds due his brother, Gerard Walker.
Wit: Benson Fearon, Thomas Stephenson, James Wennington (the last being one of the masters extraordinary of the High Court of Chancery and a Notary Public of Whitehaven)
Signed: Gerard Walker, William Noble, Ann Noble, Henry Walker
Recorded 3 August 1767

p.6  31 August 1767 James Tyree of Hanover County to William Tyree, both of Henrico County, for 15 pounds, 113 acres, being ½ of the tract of land which David Tyree purchased of David Whitlock; adj. land of William Tyree.
Wit: Nathaniel Bacon, Nathaniel Wilkinson, Izard Bacon
Signed: James (his 𝒥𝒟 mark) Tyree
Recorded 7 September 1767

p.7  2 June 1767 Joseph Goode to Thomas Goode, both of Henrico County, for 40 pounds, 200 acres on the Great Branch of Four Mile Creek; adj. William Clarke and James Lindsay, being part of a tract granted to Edward Goode by patent dated 30 July 1742 (metes and bounds description).
Wit: J. Pleasants, Jr., M. Everton, Daniel Stone
Signed: Joseph Goode                          Recorded 7 September 1767

p.9  27 August 1767 Joseph Bailey to Luzby Turpin, both of Henrico County, for 0 pounds, 30 acres on Cornelius Creek; adj Richard Reanard, Luzby Turpin, Bridge Branch and Hollow Spring Branch.
Wit: William Allen Burton, Michael Turpin
Signed: Joseph Bailey                         Recorded: 7 September 1767

p.10  13 August 1767 Henry Bailey of Albemarle County and John Goff of Amherst County to Peter Clarke of Henrico County, for 16 pounds, 50 acres on Harding's

Branch; adj. Peter Clarke, Leonard Henley, Jr., and Benjamin Johnson. Wit: Christopher John Thomas, Richard Cottrell, John Lankester, Mary Cottrell.
Signed: Henry (his H mark) Bailey, John Goff
Recorded 7 September 1767

p.12  5 September 1767 John Orr to Robert Brown, both of the Town of Richmond, Henrico County, for 30 pounds, Lot No. 4 on the plan of the Town of Richmond, adj. the other lots of said Richard Brown.
Wit: Alexander McCaul, John Farquharson, John Edmundston
Signed: John Orr, wife of John Orr, (unnamed) relinquished her dower
Recorded 7 September 1767

p.14  12 March 1767 Thomas Howerton of Henrico County to Richard Farrar of Goochland County, for 60 pounds, 227 acres at the head of the northern branch of The Brook; same tract of land whereon the said Thomas Howerton now lives and which he bought of David Whitlock; adj. David Clarke, John Staples, Jesse Smith and Tyree.
Wit: William Street, William his ✚ mark) Willis, Sutton Farrar, William Cornett, William (his ✚ mark) Miller, Suttun Farrar
Signed: Thos. Howerton, Gerzle Howerton           Recorded 7 September 1767

p.16  21 September 1767 Richard Trueman of Henrico County to Thomas Baker, Junr., and Elizabeth, his wife, of Chesterfield County, for love, good will and affection I have and do bear to my loving friend, one young Negro girl named Patt and her increase.
Wit: John Dollard, John Trueman, Sarah Trueman
Signed: Richd. Trueman                               Recorded 5 October 1767

p.17  5 October 1767 John Conaway of Henrico County to Augustine Smith of Essex County, for 20 pounds, 125 acres adj. the Brook on the northside, William Miller, James Browning, William Kelley, William Bridgwater, Nathaniel Bridgwater and Peter Elmore; except one acre joining the mill and eight square feet of ground where the said John Conaway's father and mother are buried.
Wit: Jonathan Bridgwater, Zachariah King, William Bridgwater
Signed: John Conway   Elizabeth, wife of John Conway, relinquished her dower
Recorded 5 October 1767

p.18  13 April 1767 John Trueman of Henrico County and William Trueman of Chesterfield County to Christian Allen of Henrico County, for 80 pounds, 200 acres which was granted to Valentine Trueman, deceased, by patent; adj. Julius Allen,

Isham Allen and Thomas Elmore.
Wit: Drury Brazeal, Miles Gathright, James (his X mark) Swepson
Signed: John Trueman, William Trueman
Partly proved on 3 August 1767
further proved and admitted to record on 5 October 1767

p.20  7 December 1767 Memucan Hunt of Granville County, North Carolina, to James Ryall of Henrico County, for 60 pounds, 220 acres on the Chickahominy Swamp at the Deep Bottom opposite Benjamin Bowles; adj. Chappel, Ryall, Winston and Mosby.                                                            Wit: none
Signed: Memucan Hunt                              Recorded 7 October 1767

p.23  25 September 1767 Deed of Mortgage from Julius Burton of Henrico County to Patrick Coutts, James Buchanan and Alexander McCaul, for five shillings and for the better security of the payment of 120 pounds with interest from date hereof and due at or upon the first of December next ensuing, 400 acres and four Negro slaves: Hampton, a fellow; Cis, a wench; Sye and Joe, two boys; with their increase.
Wit: Henry B. Lightfoot, Charles Lewis, Jr., Edmund Sweeny, Benjamin Brown
Signed: Julius Burton                              Recorded 7 December 1767

p.24  7 December 1767 Robert Williamson to Robert Price, both of Henrico County, for 360 pounds, 420 acres, beginning at Cuthbert Williamson's spring; adj. Brook Road, Jacob Smith and Timber Branch (metes and bounds description).
Wit: none                                         Signed: Robert Williamson
Susanna, wife of Robert Williamson, relinquished her dower.
Recorded 7 December 1767

p.26  7 December 1767 John Raglin and Judith, his wife, to John Truman, all of Henrico County, for 35 pounds, 95 acres on Boar Swamp whereon I now live; adj. Richard Trueman, Michael Hartfield, Thomas Bottom and Abraham Trueman.
Wit: Waldegrave Clopton, Abraham Trueman, William Trueman,
John Dollard, W. Gathright, Jr.
Signed: John Raglin, Judith, wife of John Raglin, relinquished her dower.
Recorded 7 December 1767

p.29  [----] 1767 William Parker to Darby Whitlow and Nathan Whitlow, all of Henrico County, for 60 pounds, 190 acres adj. James Whitlow, Junr., Abraham Bailey, John Whitlow and William Whitlow, Jr.
Wit: Francis Parker, John (his X mark) Clark
Signed: William Parker    Mary, wife of William Parker, relinquished her dower.
Recorded 7 December 1767

p.31  11 November 1767 Darby Whitlow to William Frayser, both of Henrico County, for 40 pounds, 95 acres adj. Benjamin Goode, William Whitlow, Jr., William Spencer, John Scott and other lands of the said William Frayser.
Wit: Thomas Bates, Samuel R. Brooke, Henry Segrief,
Philemon (his ✚ mark) Childers
Signed: Darby Whitlow, Mary, wife of Darby Whitlow, relinquished her dower.
Recorded 7 December 1767

p.34  13 November 1767 Henry Hobson of Halifax County to William Hobson of Henrico County, for 450 pounds, 556 acres adj. John Williams, deceased, Col. Richard Randolph, Thomas Pleasants, Junr., Samuel Hobson and other lands of said William Hobson.
Wit: Robert Pleasants, Thomas Binford, James (his ✚ mark) Childers,
 Thomas (his ♂ mark) Goode, Thomas Bates
Signed: Henry Hopson                                    Recorded 7 December 1767

p.37  12 November 1767 Carter Braxton, Esq., of King William County to James Vaughan of Henrico County, for five pounds, Lot 154 in a Town called Beverly Town.
Wit: Richard Adams, William Griffin, Anderson Rers
Signed: Carter Braxton                                  Recorded 7 December 1767

p.38  7 December 1767 Bond of Benjamin Duval as Sheriff of Henrico County by a commission dated 20 October last past from the Governor, in the amount of 1,000 pounds, with Samual Duval and John Ellis his sureties.
Wit: none                     Signed: Benj. Duval, Saml. Duval, John Ellis
Recorded 7 October 1767

p.39  7 December 1767 Bond of Benjamin Duval as Sheriff, for the collection of quitrents, fines and forfeitures, in the amount of 500 pounds, with Samuel Duval and John Ellis, his sureties.
Wit: none                     Signed: Benj. Duval, Saml. Duval, John Ellis
Recorded 7 December 1767

p.40  7 December 1767 Bond of Benjamin Duval as Sheriff, to collect and pay the taxes by law required, in the amount of 1,000 pounds, with Samuel Duval and John Ellis, his sureties.
Wit: none                     Signed: Benj.Duval, Saml.Duval, John Ellis
Recorded 7 December 1767

p.41  18 September 1767 William Taylor to Thomas Evan, both of Henrico County,

for 2 pounds, 12 shillings and 6 pence, three acres between the branches of Four Mile Creek and White Oak Swamp on the Western Branch; adj. William Hobson, James Woodson and William Robinson.
Wit: James Lindsey, John Lindsey, William (his ✚ mark) Robinson
Signed: William (his ✚ mark) Taylor              Recorded 1 February 1768

p.42  1 February 1768 William Ford, planter, to Hopson Owen, planter, both of Henrico County, for 70 pounds, 75 acres granted by patent to William Ford, father of said William Ford, dated 1 August 1734 (metes and bounds description).
Wit: none                                    Signed: William Ford
Rachel, wife of William Ford, relinquished her dower.
Recorded 1 February 1768

p.44  7 March 1768 John Pleasants & Son of Curles in Henrico County to William Childers of Goochland County, for 36 pounds, 160 acres adj. Julius Allen, Anthony Matthews and William Morris; cites mortgage of Joseph Childers, deceased, to John Pleasants & Son dated 30 November 1756, which was foreclosed and land herein described was sold at Henrico Court to the said William Childers, the highest bidder.
Wit: Samuel Childers, James Sharp, Charles Lewis
Signed: John Pleasants & Son                 Recorded 4 April 1768

p.46  18 November 1767 William Cock Redford to Josiah Bullington, both of Henrico County, for 40 pounds, 40 acres on the Roundabout Swamp; adj. John Redford, Sr., John Redford, Jr. and said Bullington; being the same tract granted by John Redford, Sr., to the said William Cock Redford.
Wit: Joseph Redford, Frederick Childers, Philip Yates Jobson
Signed: William Cock Redford
Partly proved on 4 April 1768 and continued for further proof and admitted to record on 21 May 1768

p.48  7 November 1767 John Conaway to Charles Snead of Henrico County, for 15 pounds, a water grist mill and one acre of land on the north side of Uphnam Brook excepted in the deed made from John Conway to Augustine Smith dated 5 October 1767.
Wit: Peter Elmore, Jonathan Bridgwater, Daniel Kelley, Nathaniel Bridgwater
Signed: John Conaway, Elizabeth (her E mark) Conaway
Recorded 4 April 1768

p.49  4 April 1767 William Wills of the Town of Richmond, Henrico County, to his daughter, Melisent Wills, alias Melisent Abney, for natural love and affection and

five shillings, after his death, eight slaves: one Negro woman named Jenny and Peg and her children named Dublin and Molly; a Negro boy named Mat, son of Frank; a Negro girl named Rose, daughter of Fanny; and two Negro girls, Betty and Cloe, daughters of Grace.
Wit: Nicholas Scherer, James Bowyer, William Harrison
Signed: Wm. Wills                                                      Recorded 4 April 1768

p.50  3 March 1768 John Raglin to Julius Allen, both of Henrico County, in consideration of a deed from the said Julius Allen to the said John Raglin for a parcel of land whereof the said John Raglin doth confess himself contented, all right and title Raglin hath in the estate of his brother, Gideon Raglin, deceased.
Wit: James Sharp, Tommas Snead, Mary Stokes
Signed: John Raglin                                                    Recorded 4 April 1768

p.51  3 May 1768 Abraham Cowley of Chesterfield County to Turner Southall of Henrico County, for 16 pounds, 16 acres adj. said Turner Southall and Richard [--?--].
Wit: none                                                              Signed: Abraham Cowley
Recorded 3 May 1768

p.53  26 December 1767 Robert Pleasants, merchant, to Benjamin Jordan, both of Henrico County, for 300 pounds, 300 acres on the north side of White Oak Swamp, being part of a larger tract said Robert Pleasants bought of Mary and Richard Eppes and all of the land adjoining that he bought of Josiah Clark; bounded on the east by said Jordan, on the south by White Oak Swamp, on the west by Robert Ferris and on the north by Ephraim Gathright.
Wit: Robert Pleasants, Jr., Susanna Pleasants, Thomas Bates, William Davis
Signed: Robert Pleasants                                               Recorded 2 May 1768

p.54  2 May 1768 Thomas Vaughan of Henrico County to Shadrack Vaughan of Goochland County, for 62 pounds, the reversion, after the death of my mother, Elizabeth Vaughan, in whose possession they are at present five Negro slaves: Leadenhall, David and Sue and her children, Bett and Matt, with their future increase.
Wit: Dabney Carr, James Galt, Gabriel Galt
Signed: Jas. Vaughan                                                   Recorded 2 May 1768

p.55  27 October 1767 Thomas Cardwell to Drury Braezeal, both of Henrico County, for 45 pounds, one Negro woman named Tamer and her increase.
Wit: John Harwood, Samuel Harwood, Lucy (her ✚ mark) Hibdon
Signed: Thomas Cardwell                                                Recorded 6 June 1768

p.56  6 June 1768 John Fussel to Noble Jordan, both of Henrico County, for 35 pounds, 75 acres on Bailey's Run and Grindall's Run; adj. Thomas Childrey, William Hobden and William Robinson.
Wit: none                                                                Signed: John Fussel
Recorded 6 June 1768

p.58  6 June 1768 William Winston to Ludwell Britton, both of Henrico County, for 74 pounds, 7 shillings and 6 pence, 105 ½ acres on Hues [Hughes?] Branch; adj. James Britton, James Jones, Mosby and William Winston (metes and bounds description).
Wit: James Ryall, William Goode, Archibald Payne
Signed: Wm. Winston                                         Recorded 6 June 1768

p.59  2 December 1766 Boundary Settlement between John Pleasants and Jacob Pleasants respecting their lands on Horse Swamp at the main Chickahominy Swamp devised by Joseph Pleasants the Elder unto Joseph, father of the said Jacob and the said John, by his last will and testament; defined by arbitrators Thomas Pleasants and Robert Pleasants, Jr.
Wit: Jesse Pleasants, Peter Gregory
Signed: Thos. Pleasants, Robert Pleasants, Jr.
Recorded 6 June 1768

p.60  4 June 1768 Thomas Pleasants and Elizabeth, his wife, of the Parish of St. James Northam, Goochland County, to Richard Adams of Henrico County, for 40 pounds, 340 acres granted unto George Riddell of the Town and County of York by patent dated 10 March 1756 and by him sold to said Thomas Pleasants and one Lewis Parham, deceased, late of Prince George County, as joint tenants, by deed dated 30 April 1760 and recorded in the General Court.
Wit: George Davers, Groves Harding, Thomas Poindexter
Signed: Thos. Pleasants, Elizabeth Pleasants
Recorded 6 June 1768

p.62 6 June 1768 Thomas Man Randolph, Gent., of Goochland County, to Samuel Shepard of Henrico County, for 87 pounds and 10 shillings, 175 acres on the Deep Run, part of a greater tract of land belonging to the said Thomas Man Randolph; beginning at a corner white oak marked W.R. and running thence along Samuel Shepard's line and also adj. Benjamin Brown's line (being a line established by Obediah Smith for damages done by Thomas Randolph's Mill Pond unto David Hall) and Joseph Brown's line (metes and bounds description).
Wit: none                                                          Signed: Thos. M. Randolph
Recorded 6 June 1768

p.64  4 July 1768 John Price of Henrico County to his son, Samuel Price, for natural love and affection and for better maintenance and livelihood, 200 acres on Watson's Path; adj. Col. Byrd's line and being part of the land I now live on.
Wit: none                                                                  Signed: John Price
Recorded 4 July 1768

p.65  4 July 1768 John Price of Henrico County to his son, James Price, for natural love and affection and for better maintenance and livelihood, 100 acres on Jordan's Branch; adj. William Byrd, Esq., William Sneed, Nathaniel Bridgwater and John Kelley and being the land said John Price purchased of Zachariah Tate.
Wit: none                                                                  Signed: John Price
Recorded 4 July 1768

p.67  17 July 1767 Settlement of dispute between John Hicks, who intermarried with Isabella, the daughter of John Shepherd, deceased, and the executors of the said Shepherd, cites that the arbitrators, after reviewing said Shepherd's will and other papers, are of the opinion that the devise of a slave was vacated by his disposing of the said slave and others to his sons and hereby direct the executors to pay said Hicks one pound and five shillings, that being the balance of 32 pounds, his proportional share.
Wit: none                                    Signed: John Henry, Nathaniel Wilkinson
Recorded 1 August 1768 on motion of Benjamin Shepard.

p.68  1 August 1768 John Gathright to William Gathright, both of Henrico County, for 10 pounds, 50 acres on the Deep Run along the line between myself and son John Gathright to Niles Branch.
Wit: David Cation, John Moore                           Signed: John Gathright
Recorded 1 August 1768

p.69  1 August 1768 John Mosby to David Ford, both of Henrico County, for three pounds, five acres adj. French Cornet and said Ford and Mosby.
Wit: William Ford, William Cornet, Thomas Thorp
Signed: John (his X mark) Mosby
Recorded 1 August 1768

p.71  12 October 1767 Deed of Mortgage between George Raborne, Sr., to Robert Pleasants, Jr., and Thomas Pleasants, Jr., all of Henrico County, to secure 36 pounds, 8 shillings and 5 pence with lawful interest thereon and also 5 shillings, one Negro man named Peter, one bay mare with her colt, five head of cattle and one feather bed and furniture.
Wit: Peggy Pleasants, John Burton

Signed: George (his ✚ mark) Raborne
Recorded 1 August 1768

p.73  20 February 1768 Thomas Pleasants, Jr., to George Robertson, for 20 pounds, 56 acres, being part of a tract of 2,626 acres patented by John Pleasants the Elder, who by his will gave his sons, John and Joseph Pleasants, and the heirs of their bodies, the said 2,626 acres, and that said John Pleasants died soon after making said will; that after the death of the son John, his son and heir Thomas came into that share, and after the death of the said Joseph, his son and heir Joseph came into his father's share. Said 56 acres bounded as by deed from Edward Goode to James Woodson.
Wit: Robert Pleasants, Jr., Anselm Gathright,
William (his ✚ mark) Robinson
Signed: Thomas Pleasants, Jr.                                    Recorded 1 August 1768

p.75  16 January 1768 John Childers of Henrico County to his son, John Childers, for love and good will, 75 acres between Grindall's Run and the Western Branch; adj. John Fussel and the Myrtle Branch.
Wit: none                                                              Signed: John Childers
Recorded 1 August 1768

p.76  5 June 1755 James Anderson to William Ratterly, for 4 pounds, one shilling and 6 pence due from the said James to the said William, which is hereby discharged, and the sum of [blank] due from the said James to George Carrington, assignee of John Thom, by judgment and to be undertaken and discharged by the said William, attorney-at-law for the said George Carrington, a lot in Richmond Town purchased by the said James of Edward Abbot and on which the said James now dwells.
Wit: William Wills, James Vaughan, William Paslay
Signed: James (his IA  mark) Anderson
Recorded 1 August 1768

p.77  5 September 1768 John Royster to Robert Pleasants of Curles, both of Henrico County, for 81 pounds, 200 acres on the north side of the road that leads from Woodson's Ferry to the Long Bridge; adj. William Hobson, Robert Maddox and Samuel Gathright, Jr.; being the tract said Royster purchased of Robert Pleasants, Executor of John Williams, deceased, by deed dated 5 August [1768] at publick sale.
Wit: none                                                              Signed: John Royster
Recorded 5 September 1768

p.78  5 August 1768 Robert Pleasants, Executor of John Williams, deceased, late of Henrico County, to John Royster of Henrico County, for 81 pounds, 200 acres on the north side of the road that leads from Woodson's Ferry to the Long Bridge; cites will of John Williams dated 24 July 1766, directing sale of this land to the highest bidder.
Wit: none  Signed: Robert Pleasants
Recorded 5 September 1768

p.80  10 August 1768 Robert Pleasants of Curles to James Binford, both of Henrico County, for 72 pounds, 106 acres on the south side of White Oak Swamp; bounded on the east by John Hales, on the south by Benjamin Harrison and on the west by said James Binford; being the land purchased of John Robinson by deed dated 16 April 1767.
Wit: Daniel Stone, Thomas Binford, John Binford, William Binford
Signed: Robert Pleasants  Recorded 5 September 1768

p.81  2 August 1768 Thomas Williams to Benjamin East, both of Henrico County, for 40 pounds, 50 acres, being where the Path crosses the Western Run from William Porter's to said Thomas Williams'; adj. Thomas Rogers, Robert Maddox, Col. Richard Randolph and the Western Run.
Wit: John Ballard, Samuel Gathright, Junr., Elizabeth (her ✚ mark) Jolley
Signed: Thomas (his ᔑ mark) Williams, Mary, wife of Thomas Williams, relinquished her dower.
Recorded 5 September 1768

p.83  10 July 1765 Thomas Mann Randolph of Tuckahoe, Goochland County, to Archibald Cary, of Ampthill, Chesterfield County, for 25 pounds, 150 acres beginning at Tuckahoe Bridge and thence down the creek to the mouth of George's Branch and thence down the main road.
Wit: Thomas Randolph, James Murray, Mary Eldridge
Signed: Thos. M. Randolph  Recorded 5 September 1768

p.84  24 April 1766 Power of Attorney from Samuel Sedgley, Esq., William Heilhouse and William Randolph, merchants and partners, all of the City of Bristol, to Richard Randolph, Esq., of James River, Colony of Virginia, to sue for, recover and receive debts due.
Wit: Henry Bengsugh, Daniel Burges; acknowledged before Isaac Baugh, Esq., mayor of the City of Bristol
Signed: Saml. Sedgley, William Helhous, William Randolph
Recorded 5 September 1768

p.88   10 August 1768   Renunciation of Sarah Williams of legacy provided her under the will of her late husband, John Williams.
Wit: John Dollard, Benjamin Est
Signed: Sarah (her ✚ mark) Williams
Recorded 5 September 1768

p.88   3 October 1768 Anthony North of Cumberland County to Royal Richard Allen of Henrico County, for 45 pounds, 75 acres adj. John Lankaster, Sr., William Hall, Royal Richard Allen and Nicholas Amos.
Wit: John Sanders, F. Sutton, Jr., Robert Williamson
Signed: Anthony North,    Lucy, wife of Anthony North, relinquished her dower.
Recorded 3 October 1768

p.89   11 October 1768 William Whitlow, Jr., and Nathan Whitlow to Mark Woodcock, all of Henrico County, for 33 pounds, 100 acres on Four Mile Creek; adj. William Frazier, William Spencer and David Breeding; being the same land given by Darby Enroughty by deed of gift to the said William and Nathan, his grandsons.
Wit: Richard Whitlow, William (his ✚ mark) Whitlow, Darby Whitlow
Signed: William Withlow, Junor, Nathan Whitlow
Recorded 3 October 1768

p.91 Certification from Joseph Lewis, Gent., one of his majesty's justices of the peace, for land entered for Benjamin Duval, Surveyor of Henrico County, joining James Cocke, Jr., Thomas Watkins, Daniel Price and the main run of Chickahominy Swamp, surveyed 13 September 1765.
Signed: Jos. Lewis
Recorded 3 October 1768 on motion of Benjamin Duval, Gent., county surveyor

p.91   16 April 1768 John Redford to Luzby Turpin, both of Henrico County, for 280 pounds, 120 acres on Roundabout Swamp; bounded on the east by Milner Redford; on the north by Kingsland Road, the Little Roundabout, Robert Pleasants and a corner of the land said Redford gave his son John; on the west by John Redford, Jr., and the land given to William Redford; and on the south by the main run of Roundabout Swamp; being all of the land whereon said Redford now dwelleth.
Wit: Robert Pleasants, John Hutchens, Ann (her *m* mark) Adkins
Signed: John Redford
Recorded 3 October 1768

p.93   10 October 1768 William Morriss to Miles Gathright, Senr. both of Henrico

County, for 55 pounds, 123 acres adj. said Miles Gathright, Philip Winston, deceased, Julius Allen, Joseph Childers, deceased, and Anthony Matthews
Wit: George Adams, Robert Spear, W. Gathright, Jr.
Signed: William Morriss,   Jane, wife of William Morriss, relinquished her dower.
Recorded 7 November 1768

p.95  18 July 1768 John Sanders to Samuel Mitchell, for 58 pounds, one Negro man, Patrick. Wit: William Brett, Samuel Ege.
Signed: John Sanders
Recorded 7 November 1768

p.96  22 October 1768 Alexander Moss of Cumberland County to George Donald of the Town of Richmond, Henrico County, for 130 pounds, 250 acres, being the land Moss purchased of Joseph Mayo, deceased; adj. John New, Samuel Liggon, John Harwood and Moses Bridgwater.
Wit: Dick Holland, Gabriel Galt, Joseph Fontaine
Signed: Alex. Moss                          Recorded 7 November 1768

p.97  7 November 1768 Jesse Burton and James Vaughan to John Burton, all of Henrico County, for 14 pounds, 13 shillings and 4 pence, 20 acres; cites that Jesse Burton executed a deed of conveyance to John Burton dated 3 October 1763 for 150 acres, but subsequently granted a mortgage to James Vaughan using the residue adjacent to the said 150 acres as collateral; a survey has since found 20 acres to be an overplus of the said 150 acres, and James Vaughan joins in this deed to convey said 20 acres as shown on plat done by Benjamin Duval, county surveyor, dated 20 April 1764.
Wit: John Price, Thos. Bates, William Clopton
Signed: Jesse Burton, Jas. Vaughan             Recorded 7 November 1768

p.100  5 November 1768 Samuel Shepard to Benjamin Duval, both of Henrico County, for 5 pounds and 5 shillings, 14 acres on Deep Run, and being part of a parcel which Samuel Shepard bought of Thomas Randolph, Gent.; beginning at Flat Branch on Randolph's line which comes from the river (metes and bounds description).
Wit: Thomas Ellis, Benjamin Brown, William Street
Signed: Samuel Shepard                      Recorded 7 November 1768

p.102  3 October 1768 John Orrange to John Walton, both of Henrico County, for five pounds, ten acres on both sides of the new road; adj. John Watson, deceased, Samuel Parsons, Jonathan Duglass and John Orrange
Wit: none

Signed: John (his ✚ mark) Orrange, Judith (her ✚ mark) Orrange,
Judith, wife of John Orrange, relinquished her dower.
Recorded 7 November 1768

p.104   21 November 1768 Nathaniel Vandewall and Ann, his wife, to John Harwood, Junr., all of Henrico County, for 135 pounds and 17 shillings, 104 ½ acres, being part of a larger tract whereon the said Nathaniel Vandevall now lives and is the same land whereon Benjamin Watkins at present lives; bounded on the south by Drury Brazeil, on the north by Edward Curd and on the west by a new line.
Wit: John Harwood, Nathan Bell, Zebulon (his ✚ mark) Franklin
Signed: Nathaniel Vandewall
Ann, wife of Nathaniel Vandevall, relinquished her dower on 2 Jan 1769.
Recorded 7 December 1768

p.105   24 November 1755 Bond of Samuel Morris and Dennitt Abney, both of Hanover County, in the amount of 100 pounds, to Nathaniel Wilkinson of Henrico County, to resolve a dispute between the parties as to the main run of the Chickahominy Swamp (being the division of their lands), and they mutually agree to submit all matters to Isaac Winston, Henry Stoakes, John Owen, Ben Timberlake, James Anderson and John White, Gent., or a majority thereof, to be delivered to either of the parties in writing by the first of December next ensuing. Arbitrator's Report dated 24 November 1755 states that the swamp as it runs from the Great Dam Beaver Pond against the land of John Ellis includes lands awarded to Nathaniel Wilkinson, who holds deed from John Bacon. Bacon was patentee of the land to the fork of the swamp at several small beaver dams below Bacon's Bridge, being the northeast branch issuing out of Izard's Pond.
Bond Signed: Saml. Morriss, Denitt Abney
Report Signed: Isaac Winston, Jr., Henry Stokes, John (his ✚ mark) Owen, Ben Timberlake, James Anderson
Recorded 7 December 1768

p.106   7 August 1768 Peter Elmore to Dabney Pettus, both of Henrico County, for 150 pounds, 160 acres purchased of Samuel Allen, late of Henrico County, and lying between the lands of said Pettus, Augustine Smith and James Browning.
Wit: Martin Burton, Stephn. G. Letcher, William Burton, Julius Sharpe
Signed: Peter Elmore                                    Recorded 2 January 1769

p.108   18 August 1767 John Bolling, Gent., of Goochland County, to Robert Brown of the Town of Richmond, Henrico County, for 36 pounds, Lot 3 on the plan of the Town of Richmond; adj. a lot of Miles Taylor and other lots of the said Robert

Brown.
Wit: Richard Hogg, Robert Baine, Robert Buchanan, John Woodson,
Alexander McCaul  Signed: John Bolling
Partly proved on 7 December 1767 and continued for further proof and recorded on 2 January 1769.

p.110  14 December 1768 Norvel Burton to John Stark, infant son and heir of Thomas Stark, deceased, both of Henrico County, for 45 pounds, 90 acres, of which the said Thomas Stark died seized and possessed, lying between the two Westhams, adj. Robert Carter Nicholas, Esq., Julius Burton and Hutchens Burton; and being all that tract which Hutchens Burton, deceased, devised unto the said Norvel Burton by will. [No explanation disclosed how tract passed from Starke to Burton, or vice versa, but it is likely that Thomas Starke, deceased, never received a deed for the property and that is why said tract is being convey to his infant].
Wit: Benjamin Woodroof, Cliffin Woodroff, John Hodges, John Sharp
Signed: Norvell Burton  Recorded 2 January 1769

p.111  7 December 1768 Burgis Harralson and David Hall, both of Orange County, North Carolina, to Nathaniel Dennis of Henrico County, 50 pounds, 100 acres, less one acre for an old mill, on the main Stony Run; adj. William Street, Nathaniel Dennis, Joseph Brown and Thomas Alley.
Wit: David Alley, Isham Martin, Thomas (his A mark) Alley
Signed: Burgis Harralson, David (his ✢ mark) Hall
Recorded 6 February 1769

p.113  5 December 1768 Burgis Harralson and David Hall, both of Orange County, North Carolina, to David Alley of Henrico County, for 10 pounds, 109 acres on the Main County Road; adj. Samuel Duval, John Glenn and William Alley; being the land formerly belonging to Godphra Piles.
Wit: Nathaniel Dennis, Isham Martin, William (his + mark) Willis,
Thomas (his A mark) Alley, Sr.
Signed: Burgis Harralson, David (his ✢ mark) Hall
Recorded 6 February 1769

p.115  5 September 1753 John Williamson of Henrico County to William Battersby of Cumberland County, for 79 pounds, three lots lying in the Town of Richmond, being the lower part of the lots marked IG on the plan of the said town, and also Lots K and H.  Wit: Giles Letcher, Langston Bacon, Joseph Hopkins
Signed: John Williamson
Partly proved on 1 August 1767 and continued for further proof and
Recorded on 6 February 1769

p.116  3 December 1768 Stephen Spurlock and Agness, his wife, to Michael Johnson, all of Henrico County, for 10 pounds and 15 shillings, 60 acres at the head of an eastern branch of Tuckahoe known as Wildcat Branch; adj. said Johnson, William Lawless, Benjamin Johnson, Philemon Williams and the road called Pouncey's Tract.
Wit: David Bowles, Leonard Henley, Jr., Benjamin Johnson
Signed: Stephen Spurlock, Agness (her + mark) Spurlock
Recorded 6 February 1769

p.118  6 March 1769 Samuel Hobson of Cumberland County to William Hobson of Henrico County, for 100 pounds, 100 acres adj. Thomas Pleasants on the south, Thomas Childrey on the west and the said Hobson on the north and east.
Wit: none                                                     Signed: Samuel Hobson
Recorded 6 March 1769

p.120  6 March 1769 Joseph Allen of Charlotte County to John Mosby of Henrico County, for 27 pounds, 200 acres on both sides of the Northam; adj. John Ford, Joseph Merritt, Richard Allen, Roland Blackburn, deceased, and John Mosby.
Wit: none                                                       Signed: Joseph Allen
Recorded 6 March 1769

p.121  6 March 1769 William Hobson to William Robinson, both of Henrico County, for 75 pounds, 111 acres between the branches of Four Mile Creek and White Oak Swamp; adj. Thomas Evans, William Robinson, John Fussel (formerly) and James Lindsey.                                                     Wit: none
Signed: William (his M mark) Hobson, Lucy (her + mark) Hobson,
Lucy, wife of William Hobson, relinquished her dower.
Recorded 6 March 1769

p.123  1 November 1768 William Byrd, Esq., of Charles City County, to William Wills, surgeon, of Richmond in Henrico County and to his reputed daughter, Millicent Wills, alias Abney, for their natural lives, for yearly rents of 6 pounds on or before the first of January every year, 200 acres now in the possession of the said Wills.
Wit: John Pankey, David Patterson, J.W. Eppes, B. Watkins
Signed: W. Byrd, Peyton Randolph, John Page, Chas. Carter
[last three not recognized in the caption to this deed.]
Recorded 6 March 1769

p.124 6 February 1769 David Allen to Nicholas Conaway, both of Henrico County, for 36 pounds, 150 acres on the Main County Road; adj. Richard Rockett, Conaway

and William Alley.
Wit: none                                          Signed: David Allen
Mary, wife of David Allen, relinquished her dower.
Recorded 6 March 1769


p.125  6 February 1769 Nicholas Conaway to William Ellis, both of Henrico County, for 24 pounds, 65 acres on the branches of the Chickahominy Swamp; adj. Jacob Johnson, Edmund Alley and John Glenn.
Wit: R. Richard Allen, David Allen, William Alley, John Ellis
Signed: Nicholas (his $\mathcal{U}$ mark) Conaway
Hannah, wife of Nicholas Conaway, relinquished her dower.
Recorded 6 March 1769


p.127  29 September 1768 William Spencer to Alexander Young, both of Henrico County, for 20 pounds, 34 acres on the Main Road; adj. William Frayser, William Scott, John Scott, Darby Whitlow, Nathan Whitlow, David Breeding and William Randolph, deceased.
Wit: John Ellyson, Thomas Pleasants, Jr., Daniel Stone
Signed: William (his W mark) Spencer
Elizabeth, wife of William Spencer, relinquished her dower.
Partly proved on 3 October 1768 by John Ellyson's affirmation, he being a Quaker, and continued for further proof on 6 March 1769, with affirmation by Thomas Pleasants, Jr., also a Quaker.


p.129  1 February 1769 Joseph Hopkins, Senr., of Chesterfield County, and Robert Pleasants of Henrico County, to Joseph Hopkins, Jr., of Chesterfield County, for 20 pounds, two lots or half acres of land in the Town of Richmond marked F and E on the plan of the said town.
Wit: John Puller, George Blaydes, Daniel Moore
Signed: Joseph Hopkins, Sr. [No explanation given of why Robert Pleasants is a party to this deed, also no signature or acknowledgment.]
Recorded 6 March 1769


p.131  3 April 1769 John Hobson of Cumberland County to Thomas Childrey of Henrico County, for 100 pounds, 100 acres, bounded on the west, north and east by William Hobson and on the south by Bailey's Run, which divides it from the land of Thomas Pleasants, Jr.
Wit: Alexander Ferguson, David Crumpler, Rachel (her $\mathcal{E}$ mark) Coward
Signed: John Hobson                              Recorded 3 April 1769


p.132  3 April 1769 Henry Martin and Pouncey Anderson, executors of Michael

Holland, deceased, of Hanover County to William Puryear of Henrico County, for 10 pounds, 100 acres on a branch of the Chickahominy Swamp called Allen's Branch; being part of a larger tract granted by patent unto the aforesaid Michael Holland and by him in his last will and testament directed to be sold by his executors; adj. David Bowles, John Thomason, Stephen Spurlock, and Peter Puryear (metes and bounds description).
Wit: none                                       Signed: Pouncey Anderson
[No signature or acknowledgment for Henry Martin]
Recorded 3 April 1769

p.134 31 March 1769 Bowler Cocke the Elder of Shirley to his son, Bowler Cocke, Jr., of Bremo, for natural love and affection and for 10 shillings, 37 Slaves: old Bob, Hannah, Betty, Harry, Judy, Fanny, Ciss, Billy, Suckey, little Harry, young Bob, Frank, Godfrey, little Bob, Anthony, Jenny, Nancy, Jack, Aggy, Abraham, little Caesar, Ned, Cupid, Jack, Fortune, Cyphax, Arthur, Tommy (a smith), Davy (a shoemaker), old Jack, old Jenny, Tommy, Neby, Cuffy, Langston, Katey and Caesar.
Wit: Henry Talman, William West, Daniel S. Hylton
Signed: Bowler Cocke                            Recorded 3 April 1769

p.136  6 March 1769 James Vaughan, James Gunn and James Ball to Thomas Pemble, all of Henrico County, for 40 pounds, 200 acres on the north side of Deep Run; being the same parcel bought of Thomas Eales; adj. Edward Reaves and John SimCocks.
Wit: Samuel Williamson, Drury Breazeal, David Alley
Signed: James Vaughan, James Gunn, James Ball
Partly proved on 6 March 1769 and continued for further proof and admitted to Record on 3 April 1769

p.138  24 May 1749 Receipt of John Curd and Elizabeth, his wife, being their acknowledgment of having received of the executors of Edward Curd, deceased, their full share of his estate.                        Wit: Richard Curd
Signed: John Curd, Elizabeth Curd
Recorded 5 June 1769

p.139  20 May 1749 Receipt of John Richardson and Mary, his wife, being their acknowledgment of having received of the executors of Edward Curd, deceased, their full share of his estate.
Wit: Isham Richardson, Richard Curd
Signed: John (his X mark) Richardson, Mary Richardson
Recorded 5 June 1769

p.139  24 May 1749  Receipt of Richard Curd and Sarah , his wife, being their acknowledgment of having received of the executors of Edward Curd, deceased, their full share of his estate.
Wit: John Curd
Signed: Richard Curd  [Not signed by Sarah Curd]
Recorded 5 June 1769

p.140  3 June 1749  Receipt of Samuel Allen and Elizabeth, his wife, being their acknowledgment of having received of the executors of Edward Curd, deceased, their full share of his estate.
Wit: Simon (his X mark) Wootton, Nathaniel (his 𝗅𝗇 mark) Bridgwater
Signed: Samuel (his S mark) Allen, Elizabeth (her E mark) Allen
Recorded 5 June 1769

p.140  4 December 1752  John McBride and Mary, his wife, being their acknowledgment of having received of the executors of Edward Curd, deceased, their full share of his estate.
Wit: Jon. Oliver, Benjamin (his B mark) Sadler
Signed: John McBride, Mary (her M mark) McBride
Recorded 5 June 1769

p.141  5 June 1769  William Alley to Loudwick Warrock, both of Henrico County, for 8 pounds, a lot in the Town of Richmond, being Lot 76 on the plan of the said town.
Wit: Samuel Parsons, George Woodson, Samuel R. Brooks
Signed: William Alley                                    Recorded 5 June 1769

p.141  20 May 1769  Milner Redford to John Pleasants the Elder, both of Henrico County, for 24 pounds, 30 acres on Roundabout Swamp; adj. other land of the said John Pleasants and William Parker.
Wit: Thomas Pleasants, Jr., Thomas Eldridge, Henry (his mark) Clarke
Signed: Milner Redford                                    Recorded 5 June 1769

p.143  5 June 1769  William Ellis to Joseph Clarke, both of Henrico County, for 45 pounds, 100 acres on Stony Run; adj John Sincock, John Clarke and Alexander Patterson.           Wit: John Clarke, Jesse Smith, Jonathan Bridgwater
Signed: William Ellis                                     Recorded 5 June 1769

p.144  15 April 1769  Joseph Clarke to Nathaniel Clarke, both of Henrico County, for 45 pounds, 300 acres on the south side of Uphnam Brook; adj. John Clarke, Leonard Henley, John Kelley, George Kelley and Jackson's Horsepen Branch.

Wit: Jonathan Bridgwater, Thomas Lewis, John Clarke
Signed: Joseph Clarke                                           Recorded 5 June 1769

p.145  3 June 1769 John Pleasants to Ryland Randolph, both of Henrico County, for 5 shillings, 60 acres adj. the land of Richard Randolph called Green's Quarter, Solomon Fussel, Thomas Williams and Samuel Gathright; being the same land said Pleasants purchased of Pleasants Cocke and for which he obtained a decree of the Henrico County Court to confirm the same.
Wit: Daniel Stone, Thomas Betts, John Burton, Thomas Bethell
Signed: John Pleasants                                          Recorded 5 June 1769

p.146  5 June 1769 Robert West to Luzby Turpin, both of Henrico County, for 40 pounds, 100 acres on Cornelius Creek; adj. said Luzby Turpin, Isham West, Richard Renard and Richard Whitlow.
Wit: Loudwick Warrock, George Woodson, Samuel Parsons
Signed: Robert West                                             Recorded 5 June 1769

p.147  12 May 1769 William Byrd, Esq., of Westover, Charles City County, Presley Thornton of Northumberland County, Peyton Randolph of York County, John Page of Gloucester County, Charles Carter of Lancaster County and Charles Turnbull, Gent. of Dinwiddie County, to Edward Carter and Peter Field Trent of Albemarle County, for 5 pounds, 100 acres, which land was drawn a prize in the said William Byrd's lottery and numbered 744.
Wit: Archibald Cary, Joshua Storrs, James Buchanan, Robert Donald, John Esdale
Signed: John Page, Peyton Randolph, Charles Carter
Recorded 5 June 1769

p.148  5 June 1769 Apprenticeship Contract between John Salmons, an infant of Henrico County, to Thomas Harris of Hanover County, for the said infant to be taught the art and mystery of the carpenter's trade, by consent of the Henrico County Court and by the consent of his mother, Ann Salmons.
Wit: none
Signed: John (his I mark) Sammons, Thomas Harris
Recorded 5 June 1769

p.149  13 February 1769 Thomas Ginnet to John Reins, both of Henrico County, for 25 pounds, 50 acres adj. William Ellis, Richard Rockett, William Alley and by the Main Road that leads to Richmond Town.
Wit: Samuel Duval, Jr., Thomas Phillips, Leonard Henley, Jr.
Signed: Thomas Ginnitt, Ruth, wife of Thomas Ginnett, relinquished her dower.

Recorded 6 June 1769

p.150   21 November 1768 Alexander Robinson, Jr., and Susannah, his wife, to Thomas Colder, all of Henrico County, for 50 pounds, 100 acres adj. John and Thomas Robinson; being the tract given to Alexander Robinson, Jr., by his father, Alexander Robinson, Sr., by deed dated 5 April 1753, which land was given to the said Alexander Robinson, Sr., by his father, Thomas Robinson.
Wit: John Price, Daniel Price, William Robertson
Signed: Alexander (his ✚ mark) Robinson, Susannah (her X mark) Robinson
Recorded 5 June 1769

p.151   28 April 1769 Robert Chappell and Agnes, his wife, of Prince Edward County, to James Ryall of Henrico County, for 25 pounds, 200 acres, being part of a tract known as Patrick's tract; adj. Samuel Duvall (formerly the property of Thomas Owen), John Sheppard, Ralph Hunt and John Ryall.
Wit: none.                                                      Signed: Robert Chappell
[No signature or relinquishment of dower by Agnes Chappell]
Recorded 5 June 1769

p.153   27 February 1769 Protest against damages from Christian Muller, Royal Danish Secretary and Notary Public, who states that James Briggs, master of Briggs Brothers, bound from Virginia to Lisbon and Joseph Briggs, mate, John Lynch, carpenter, William Hanly, boatswain, Richard Smith and William Whitehead, seamen, on board said brig, who on oath declared that on the 2nd of this month they left Virginia in the aforesaid Briggs' Briggs Brothers, bound for Lisbon, loaded with wheat and flour, according to the tenor of their charter party, Misters Storrs and Ellis, merchants in Virginia and owners of the aforesaid cargo; that they met with a large gale of wind which continued for six days and were obliged to sail half-mast with their deck constantly full of water; the 11th the vessel sprung a leak and considerable damage occurred and the wheat was entirely damaged; the remains of the vessel and cargo were placed in the hands of Mr. Kennedy and Mr. Fartane to be disposed of to best advantage.
Wit: none                                                            Signed: C. Muller
Ordered to be recorded at the request of Mr. Storrs and Mr. Ellis
Recorded 5 June 1769

p.155   6 June 1769 William Lawless to Michael Johnson, both of Henrico County, for 32 pounds and 10 shillings, 134 acres on the branches of Eastern Tuckahoe; adj. Benjamin Johnson, William Henley, William Wade, Augustine Woody, William Harding and Michael Johnson.
Wit: David Bowles, Elijah Bowles, Benjamin Johnson

Signed: William Lawless                    Recorded 3 July 1769

p.156  3 July 1769 Ann Skinner and William Skinner of Chesterfield County to Loudwick Worrock of the Town of Richmond, Henrico County, for 17 pounds, Lot 71 on the plan of the Town of Richmond.
Wit: J. Sutton, Jr., Richard Crouch, Samuel Mitchell
Signed: Ann (her  X  mark) Skinner, William Skinner
Recorded 3 July 1769

p.157  10 December 1768 Nathaniel Lancaster and Hope, his wife, of Goochland County, to William Rowe, Sr., of Hanover County, for 25 pounds, a tract of land adj. Spurlock, Shewmaker, David Bowles and Thomason.
Wit: William Dandridge, William Donald, Robert Wilson
Signed: Nathaniel Lankester, Hope (her  ✚  mark) Lankester
Recorded 7 August 1769

p.159  29 July 1769 William Jones to William Allen Lankester, for 8 pounds, 6 shillings and 8 pence, 25 acres adj. said Lankester at Old House Branch.
Wit: Christopher John Thomas, John Lankester, Mary Thomas
Signed: William (his  X  mark) Jones
Recorded 7 August 1769

p.160  10 June 1769 Ryland Randolph, Gent., to William Gathright, both of Henrico County, for 321 pounds and 10 shillings, 311 3/4 acres on the Western Run; adj. William Hobson, Solomon Fussell, Thomas Williams and Thomas Jolley. Wit: Joseph Warinner, Benjamin Warinner,
Daniel (his ⊢─┤ mark) Warrinner, Samuel Gathright
Signed: Ryland Randolph
Recorded 7 August 1769

p.162  11 February 1769 John Lankester to his son, William Allen Lankester, for 110 pounds, 100 acres on Deep Run, being the land whereon I now live and five Negroes Pegg, Rachel, Sarah, Charles and Peter.
Wit: Leonard Henley, David Allen, Jesse Smith, William Henley
Signed: John (his ⊢─┤ mark) Lankester
Recorded 7 August 1769

p.163  5 August 1769 Anthony Mathews and Anne, his wife, to Anselm Gathright, all of Henrico County, for 23 pounds, six Negroes: Phillis, Gwin, Jane, Fanny, Harry and Moll. Wit: Julius Allen, George Adams, Ephraim Gathright
Signed: Anthony Mathews, Anne (her  ✚  mark) Mathews

Recorded 7 August 1769

p.163  5 August 1769 Deed of Gift from Anselm Gathright to Susanna Mathews, daughter of Anthony Mathews, for divers good causes, one Negro girl named Fanny, about six years old, and her increase.
Wit: Julius Allen, George Allen, Ephraim Gathright
Signed: Anselm Gathright                                   Recorded 7 August 1769

p.164  7 May 1769 William Hughes, Jr., of Amherst County to Martin Burton of Henrico County, for 150 pounds, 150 acres on a branch of the Chicahominy Swamp called Meredith's Branch; adj. Winston (metes and bounds description).
Wit: Nathaniel Wilkinson, Robert Williamson, John Tinsley, William Tyree
Signed: William Hughes                                     Recorded 7 August 1769

p.166  7 August 1769 Robert Williamson, executor of the Estate of John Williamson, deceased, to William Ellis, both of Henrico County, for 12 pounds, 150 acres on the branches of Chickahominy Swamp; adj. John Glenn, Samuel Duval, Richard Cottrell, Jacob Johnson and Nicholas Conaway; being part of a tract of land granted by patent unto Thomas Conaway, and this said parcel was sold by Thomas Conaway and John Conaway to John Williamson in his lifetime and directed to be sold under his last will and testament.
Wit: John Clarke, Thomas Lewis, John Ellis, Junr.
Signed: Robt. Williamson                                   Recorded 7 August 1769

p.168  7 August 1769 Bond of Isaac Winston, planter, of Hanover County, to Obadiah Smith of Chesterfield County, trustee for my daughter, Elizabeth Winston, in the amount of 600 pounds; said daughter to be paid the sum of 300 pounds on the day she shall come of age or marry.
Wit: none                                                  Signed: Isaac Winston
Recorded 7 August 1769

p.168  7 August 1769 Deed of Gift from Isaac Winston, planter, of Hanover County, to daughter, Elizabeth Winston, for natural love and affection, a Negro girl named Jane, daughter of Tamer, together with her future increase, to be delivered the day daughter shall marry or come of age.
Wit: none                                                  Signed: Isaac Winston
Recorded 7 August 1769

p.169  7 August 1769 Deed of Gift from Obadiah Smith, planter, of Chesterfield County, to granddaughter, Elizabeth Winston (daughter of my daughter Elizabeth, deceased, and Isaac Winston), for natural love and affection, a Negro girl named

Nell now in possession of said Isaac Winston, together with her future increase, to be delivered the day granddaughter shall marry or come of age, but if granddaughter should die before then, said Nell to return to the said Obadiah Smith.
Wit: none  Signed: Obadiah Smith
Recorded 7 August 1769

p.169 7 August 1769 Bond of Obadiah Smith, planter, of Chesterfield County, to Isaac Winston of Hanover County, trustee for my granddaughter, Elizabeth Winston, in the amount of 2,000 pounds, said granddaughter to be paid the sum of 300 pounds, with legal interest, on the day she shall come of age or marry; 100 pounds with interest from 27 February 1767, 100 pounds with interest from 27 February 1768 and 100 pounds with interest from 27 February 1769; cites that son-in-law, Isaac Winston, relinquished his claim to 300 pounds promised him per marriage contract with Elizabeth Smith, now daughter of Obadiah Smith; obligation of the bond to be void if granddaughter should die.
Wit: none  Signed: Obadiah Smith
Recorded 7 August 1769

p.171 10 June 1769 Capt. James Cocke of Henrico County to George Donald of the Town of Richmond in said county, for 20 pounds, Lot 21 on the plan of the Town of Richmond.
Wit: David Cation, John McKindley, James Buchanan
Signed: James Cocke  Recorded 7 August 1769

p.172 1 May 1769 Francis West and Elizabeth, his wife, one of the daughters of John Bransford, deceased, John Bransford, Thomas Dunn and Barbary, his wife, one of the daughters of John Bransford, deceased, and James Bransford, said John Bransford and James Bransford being executors of the estate of the said John Bransford, deceased, to Loudwick Worrock of the Town of Richmond, for 60 pounds, Lot 58 on the plan of the Town of Richmond.
Wit: Richard Crouch, John Liggon, Samuel Mitchell
Signed: Francis West, John Bransford, Thomas Dunn (his signature verified by Charles Allen, Lewis Roper and William Harrison), Jas. Bransford, Sarah Bransford (wife of John Bransford), Judith Bransford (wife of James Bransford), Barbara Dunn.  Recorded 7 August 1769

p.173 4 January 1769 Release of Mortgage from Richard Adams for land sold to Miles Gathright from William Morriss, for 5 shillings.
Wit: William Griffin, Elizabeth Strachan, Catherine Powers, Dorothy Thomas
Signed: Richd. Adams  Recorded 7 August 1769

p.174  2 September 1769 William Smith to Martin Burton, both of Henrico County, for 300 pounds, 250 acres adj. Robert Williamson, Allen Williamson, John Smith, Robert Sharp, Stephen Woodson, Obadiah Smith's Estate and said Martin Burton.
Wit: William Lewis, Mary Lewis, John (his ✚ mark) Rane
Signed: William Smith, Susanna, wife of William Smith, relinquished her dower.
Recorded 4 September 1769

p.175  31 August 1769 John Cawthon and Margaret, his wife, of Goochland County, to William Ellis, Sr., of Henrico County, for 8 pounds and 5 shillings, 50 acres on the branches of Chickahominy Swamp; adj. Richard Cottrell, Jr., Ware's line (commonly known by the name of Watson's line), Edmund Alley and the said William Ellis.
Wit: Peter Clarke, Samuel Robert Brookes, Anderson Piers
Signed: John Cawthon, Margaret Cawthon
Recorded 4 September 1769

p.177  13 May 1769 Richard Hooper to Elizabeth Porter, both of Henrico County, to settle all differences for a marriage "suddenly intended," 30 acres on Gilley's Creek, adj. Alexander Robertson and others; one feather bed and furniture, half a dozen pewter plates, two pewter dishes, half a dozen table knives and forks, two iron pots and one pine chest.
Wit: John Price, Mary Price, John Price, Junr.
Signed: Richard Hooper                      Recorded 4 September 1769

p.178  4 September 1769 Josiah Bullington to William Cocke Redford, both of Henrico County, for 2 pounds, 2 acres adj. John Redford, deceased, William Cocke Redford and Kingsland Road.
Wit: none                                    Signed: Josiah Bullington
Sarah, wife of Josiah Bullington, relinquished her dower.
Recorded 4 September 1769

p.179  26 April 1769 Isaac Coles to Richard Adams of the Town of Richmond, Henrico County, for 500 pounds, 10 lots in the Town of Richmond, being Lots 78, 79, 80, 91, 92, 93, 94, 105, 107 and 108 on the plan of the said town.
Wit: Neil Campbell, John Edmondstone, Jasper Halket, Robert Brown
Signed: Isaac Coles                          Recorded 4 September 1769

p.180  2 October 1769 Charles Crenshaw of Hanover County to his daughter, Susanna Crenshaw, for love and affection, a Negro girl named Alley and all her increase forever.
Wit: Daniel Price, Jr., Izard Bacon

Signed: Charles Crenshaw                    Recorded 2 October 1769

p.180  2 October 1769 Nathaniel Bacon, Senr., of Henrico County, to Susannah Crenshaw, daughter of Charles and Sarah Crenshaw, for love and affection, one Negro girl named Judy and all her increase forever.
Wit: Daniel Price, Jr., Izard Bacon
Signed: Nathl. Bacon                         Recorded 2 October 1769

p.180  2 October 1769 Bond of Charles Lewis, Sr., and Susanna Lewis, his wife, of Henrico County, to Colwell Pettipool and Mary, his wife, of Cumberland Parish, Lunenburg County, in the amount of 2,000 pounds, pursuant to a mutual agreement for the division of two tracts of land in Henrico County which became the property of Susanna Marrin, who intermarried with the said Charles Lewis, and Mary Marrin, who intermarried with the said Colwell Pettipool, beneficiaries under the will of Gilleygron Marrin, deceased, which two tracts belonged to Wiltshire Marrin, son and heir-at-law of the said Gilleygron Marrin, which tracts were divided by Thomas Prosser between them. Said Colwell and Mary Pettipool are to be allotted (1) 320 acres on the James River below Roper's Fishing Place and adj. Mayo (metes and bounds description); and (2) 408 acres on the James River adj. Isaac Younghusband (metes and bounds descript.).
Wit: none                    Signed: Charles Lewis, Susannah Lewis
Recorded 2 October 1769

p.182  2 October 1769 Bond of Colwell Pettipool and Mary Pettipool, his wife, of Cumberland Parish, Lunenburg County, to Charles Lewis and Susanna, his wife, of Henrico County, in the amount of 2,000 pounds, pursuant to a mutual agreement cited in the preceding deed. Said Charles and Susanna Lewis are to be allotted (1) 320 acres on the James River adj. Gilley's Creek (metes and bounds description); and (2) 400 acres on the James River at the mouth of Thomas Field's creek (metes and bounds description).
Wit: none                        Signed: Colwl. P Pool, Mary P Pool
Recorded 2 October 1769

p.183  6 November 1769 Bond of George Cox as Sheriff of Henrico County, with Bowler Cocke, Jr., and Leonard Ward, Gent., his sureties, in the amount of 1,000 pounds, pursuant to a commission under the hand and seal of Norborne Baron de Botetourt, Esq., Lieutenant Governor General of this Colony of Virginia, bearing date 28 October last past.
Wit: Fortunatus Sydnor
Signed: George Cox, B. Cocke, Jr., Leond. Ward
Recorded 6 November 1769

p.184  6 November 1769 Bond of George Cox as Sheriff of Henrico County for collecting the quitrents, fines, forfeitures, in the amount of 500 pounds, with Bowler Cocke, Jr., and Leonard Ward, Gent., his sureties.
Wit: Fortunatus Sydnor
Signed: George Cox, B. Cocke, Jr., Leond. Ward
Recorded 6 November 1769

p.185  6 November 1769 Bond of George Cox as Sheriff of Henrico County to collect and pay taxes required, in the amount of 1,000 pounds, with Bowler Cocke, Jr., and Leonard Ward, his sureties.
Wit: Fortunatus Sydnor
Signed: George Cox, B. Cocke, Jr., Leond. Ward
Recorded 6 November 1769

p.186  30 October 1769 Power of Attorney from Stephen Woodson of Henrico County to my trusty friend, Benjamin Johnson, of Hanover County, a general authority to bargain, sell, deliver or buy and receive for me...
Wit: Thomas Johnson, David Johnson, John Mackghee [all Quakers]
Signed: Stephen Woodson                    Recorded 6 November 1769

p.187  21 May 1769 Thomas Anderson, Executor of Nicholas Mealor, deceased, of St. James Parish, Lunenburg County, to William Mealor, orphan and one of the residuary legatees of the said Nicholas Mealor, deceased, for 40 shillings and for William Mealor being one of the children of said Nicholas Mealor, deceased, a tract in Henrico County [no description].
Wit: Boling Cox, Thomas Cox, Philip Miler, Peter Malor
Signed: Thomas Anderson                    Recorded 6 November 1769

p.188  28 October 1769 William Byrd and Mary, his wife, of Westover, Charles City County, Presley Thornton of Northumberland County, Peyton Randolph of the City of Williamsburg, John Page of Gloucester County, Charles Carter, Esq., of Lancaster County and Charles Turnbull of Dinwiddie County, Gent., to David Pattison of Chesterfield County, for 290 pounds, 300 acres, bounded as laid down and expressed in a plan produced at the drawing of the lottery called Byrd's Lottery, distinguished as Nos. 819, 820 and 822.
Wit: Joshua Storrs, Jacob Pleasants, George Ellis, Turner Southall, Alexander Banks, Thomas Prosser
Signed: W. Byrd, Presley Thornton, Peyton Randolph, John Page, Chas. Carter
[not signed by Mary Byrd and Charles Turnbull]
Recorded 6 November 1769

p.188  28 October 1769 William Byrd and Mary, his wife, of Westover, Charles City County, Presley Thornton of Northumberland County, Peyton Randolph of the City of Williamsburg, John Page of Gloucester County, Charles Carter, Esq., of Lancaster County and Charles Turnbull of Dinwiddie County, Gent., to David Pattison of Chesterfield County, for 290 pounds, 300 acres, bounded as laid down and expressed in a plan produced at the drawing of the lottery called Byrd's Lottery, distinguished as Nos. 819, 820 and 822.
Wit: Joshua Storrs, Jacob Pleasants, George Ellis, Turner Southall, Alexander Banks, Thomas Prosser
Signed: W. Byrd, Presley Thornton, Peyton Randolph, John Page, Chas. Carter [not signed by Mary Byrd and Charles Turnbull]
Recorded 6 November 1769

p.190  28 October 1769 William Byrd and Mary, his wife, of Westover, Charles City County, Presley Thornton of Northumberland County, Peyton Randolph of the City of Williamsburg, John Page of Gloucester County, Charles Carter, Esq., of Lancaster County and Charles Turnbull of Dinwiddie County; Gent., to John Pleasants, carpenter, of Henrico County, for 190 pounds, 200 acres, bounded as laid down and expressed in the plan of Byrd's Lottery, distinguished as Nos. 798 and 803.
Wit: Joshua Storrs, Jacob Pleasants, George Ellis, John Markham, Thomas Bates, Turner Southall, David Patteson
Signed: W. Byrd, Presley Thornton, Peyton Randolph, John Page, Chas. Carter [not signed by Mary Byrd and Charles Turnbull]
Recorded 6 November 1769

p.191  28 October 1769 William Byrd and Mary, his wife, of Westover, Charles City County, Presley Thornton of Northumberland County, Peyton Randolph of the City of Williamsburg, John Page of Gloucester County, Charles Carter, Esq., of Lancaster County and Charles Turnbull of Dinwiddie County, Gent., to William Ellis of Southampton County, for 5 pounds, for a ticket in the lottery called Byrd's Lottery, No. 5378, for 100 acres distinguished as No. 834.
Wit: George Ellis, Thomas Prosser, David Patterson, Alexander Banks, Alexander Baine, Jacob Pleasants
Signed: W. Byrd, Presley Thornton, Peyton Randolph, John Page, Chas. Carter [not signed by Mary Byrd and Charles Turnbull]
Recorded 6 November 1769

p.192  15 June 1769 Hon. William Byrd of Westover, Charles City County, Hon. Peyton Randolph, and Hon. John Page of Gloucester, to Francis Watkins of Prince Edward County, for 505 pounds, 400 acres in four lots situate on James River,

being numbers in the lots of the hundred acres drawn in William Byrd's Lottery as 749, 750, 752 and 753.
Wit: John Hailes, Thomas Pimble, Thomas Watkins, Jr., Julian Allen, James Sharp, Charles Allen
Signed: W. Byrd, Peyton Randolph, John Page
Recorded 6 November 1769

p.193  28 October 1769 Hon. William Byrd and Hon. Presley Thornton, Hon. Peyton Randolph, Hon. John Page, Charles Carter and Charles Turnbull, as surviving trustees of the said W. Byrd by instrument recorded in the General Court, to John McKeand of Henrico County, for 100 pounds, a lot between Byrd's Warehouse and the tenement called McKeand's Tavern, containing half an acre of land as shown on plat lately made by Capt. James Gunn which is hereto annexed.

[Plat appears on page 194].
Wit: David Patteson, James Buchanan, Joshua Storrs, Turner Southall, Thomas Prosser
Signed: W. Byrd, John Page, Chas. Carter
Recorded 6 November 1769

p.195  15 September 1768 William Buxton and Joyce Buxton, his wife, of Buckingham County, to Peter Clarke of Henrico County, for 70 pounds, 88 acres adj. Leonard Henley, the Main Road, Harding's Branch and my own line.
Wit: Nathaniel Lankester, Charles Cottrell, John Lankester, Benjamin Cottrell
Signed: Wm. Buxton, Joyce (her X mark) Buxton
Partly proved on 3 April 1769 and continued for further proof and
Recorded on 6 November 1769

p.196  6 November 1769 John Ellis, Gent., to Samuel Shepard, both of Henrico County, for 42 pounds, 17 acres on Deep Run, adj. Joseph Brown, John Blackburn and Thomas Randolph, and having upon it an old mill at present out of repair; said mill being first built by David Staples and formerly known as Old Staple's Mill and afterwards sold by the said David Staples unto the said Ellis.
Wit: Michael Johnson, William Allen Lankester, Joseph Brown
Signed: John Ellis                                    Recorded 6 November 1769

p.197  6 November 1769 John Hopkins, Junr., of Chesterfield County, to John McKeand of Henrico County, for 112 pounds, two lots, each containing one-half acre in a certain town called Richmond as laid off below Shockoe Creek in the County of Henrico, which lots are marked by "F" and "E" on the plan of the said town.

Wit: none  Signed: Joseph Hopkins, Jr.
Elizabeth, wife of John Hopkins, Jr., relinquished her dower.
Recorded 6 November 1769

p.198 11 November 1769 George Clarke to Isaac Echo, both of Henrico County, for 36 pounds, 33 acres adj. Robert Faris, Frederick Clarke and Ephraim Gathright.
Wit: George Adams, Frederick (his X mark) Clarke, John Whitlock
Signed: George (his X mark) Clarke, Susanna, wife of George Clarke, relinquished her dower.  Recorded 4 December 1769

p.199 3 May 1769 Bond of William Wills of the Town of Richmond, Henrico County, to Samuel Mitchell of the same County and Town, for 500 pounds, for a pledge of relinquishment in 100 acres on the Deep Run and for any claim of Millicent Wills, alias Millicent Abney, his daughter, in said 100 acres; said William Wills hath leased 200 acres for life and for the life of his respected daughter, which land is to go to the longer liver, and 100 acres is being transferred to said Samuel Mitchell.  Wit: Turner Southall, Robert Bain, James Vaughan
Signed: [not signed]  Recorded 4 December 1769

p.200 7 November 1769 Apprenticeship Contract between Thomas Ratchford, late from London, to James Vaughan of Henrico County, in consideration of 11 pounds paid to John Carter by James Vaughan for the passage of the said Ratchford to Virginia, a term of three years and eleven months from the date hereof, but if said Thomas Ratchford should depart from his master's business, he shall serve two days for every day's departure and Vaughan shall provide sufficient meat, drink, lodging, clothing and washing
Wit: none  Signed: Thomas (his X mark) Ratchford, Jas. Vaughan
Recorded 4 December 1769

p.201 16 September 1754 Agreement between Elizabeth Randolph, widow of Beverley Randolph, Esq., late of Henrico County, deceased, and Hon. Peter Randolph, Esq., eldest brother and heir-at-law of the said Beverley Randolph, deceased, of the same county, and remainderman under the will of the said decedent, in consideration of 200 pounds sterling annually, with the first payment to be made 1 April 1756 and on the first of April every year afterwards, for said willingness of Elizabeth Randolph to release lands, slaves and personal estate to the said Peter Randolph by 25 December next, which she is entitled to for life under the said will of her late husband; said Peter Randolph further agrees that on or before 25 December, he will sell to the said Elizabeth all his right in the following slaves: Rachael and her 5 children: Sally, Gabriel, Robert, Sam and Sukey, and Agnes and her 3 children: Johnny, Absalom and Frank, which slaves belonged to the said

Elizabeth before her intermarriage with the said Beverley Randolph, and will further permit the said Elizabeth to possess a woman named Ary and a boy named Malo for her life and then said slaves and their increase are to be returned to the said Peter and those claiming under him; and he will also give by 25 December next a silver teapot, coffee pot, milk pot, marrow spoon, punch strainer and silver cup intended for her by direction of her grandmother, and table linens and sheets, two feather beds with blankets and quilts belonging to them, and a chariot and horse now used by her.
Wit: Phil Watson, Philip Rootes, Junior, Thomas Aselby
Signed: Elizabeth Randolph, Peter Randolph
Recorded 5 February 1770

p.202  14 November 1769 William Mealor of Mecklenburg County to Matthew Herbert of Henrico County, for 20 pounds, 200 acres on Cornelius Creek; adj. James Whitlow, Nixon, Mayses and Bullington; being part of a certain tract which belonged to his father, Nicholas Mealor.
Wit: Thomas Williams, Thomas Harbord, William Harbord, Francis Kemp Signed: William Mealer
Recorded 5 February 1770

p.203  23 May 1769 Alexander McCaul of the Town of Richmond, Henrico County, and John Pride, Junr., of Amelia County, to John Liggon of the Town of Richmond, Henrico County, for 57 pounds, a lot in the Town of Richmond numbered G half H on the plan of the said town, being collateral under a deed of trust dated 6 August 1766 made to the said McCaul and Pride, or either of them, by Robert Elliott, who then dwelt on the banks of Shockoe Creek on said lot, which the said McCaul and Pride were empowered to sell upon default, and which lot was escheated in 1759 by William Watkins for Francis West and by West sold to Robert Elliott. Wit: John Edmondstone, Samuel Mitchell, Richard Crouch
Signed: Alexr. McCaul                    Recorded 5 February 1770

p.204  5 February 1770 Apprenticeship Contract between Josiah Parsons, son of Joseph Parsons, deceased, of Henrico County, and pursuant to his father's will and by consent and choice of the executor, hath put himself as an apprentice to John Harris of Hanover County, carpenter, to learn the art and mystery of building houses, house joynery, etc. from the date hereof until he arrives to the age of 21.
Wit: none                    Signed: John Harris, Josiah Parsons
Recorded 5 February 1770

p.205  9 May 1769 William Byrd, Esq., of Charles City County, to William Wills and his daughter, Millicent Wills, alias Abney, of the Town of Richmond, notes his

agreement that Wills shall continue to occupy Lot No. 788 as a part of 200 acres on Deep Run heretofore leased to the said Wills by deed of lease dated 1 November 1766, recognizing that Lot No. 786, being 100 acres of said land, has been sold by the said Byrd to Samuel Mitchell .
Wit: David Patteson, Samuel Mitchell, Edmund Vaughan
Signed: W. Byrd
Partly proved on 4 December 1769 and continuedfor further proof and Recorded on 5 March 1770

p.206  5 March 1770 Peter Winston, planter, of Henrico County to my brother, Isaac Winston, for natural love and affection, four Negroes: Cuffy, Isaac, Sue and Harry and their increase.
Wit: none                                                                          Signed: Peter Winston
Recorded 5 March 1770

p.207  9 December 1769 Thomas Casson and Margaret, his wife, of Henrico County, to Richard Bennett of Hanover County, for one horse bridle and saddle of the value of 14 pounds, 50 acres adj. Tandam Slash, Parker, Whitlow and Adams; being the land Casson bought of James Whitlock.
Wit: William Lewis, Samuel Williamson, Miles Gathright
Signed: Thomas (his  C  mark) Casson, Margaret (her  X  mark) Casson
Recorded 5 March 1770

p.208  31 March 1770 William Bacon to Thomas Wilkinson, both of Henrico County, for 150 pounds, 16 shillings, 60 1/3 acres on Miry Run, being part of a larger tract given by the last will and testament of John Bacon, late of New Kent County, to his son, William (metes and bounds description).
Wit: Thomas Owen, John Bacon, Izard Bacon, John Skelton, Edward Curd,Jr.
Signed: Wm. Bacon         Mary, wife of William Bacon, relinquished her dower.
Recorded 5 March 1770

p.209 6 February 1770 Miles Gathright and Elizabeth, his wife, to James Sharp, all of Henrico County, for 200 pounds, 335 acres on the north fork of Boar Swamp; adj. William Gathright, a line of blazed trees made by my father for a dividing line between my brother, William Gathright, and myself, William Childers, Julius Allen, Anthony Matthews and Mayo's land.
Wit: Jacob Ferris, Thomas Watkins, Jr., Robert Gunn, William Gathright, Jr.
Signed: Miles Gathright, Elizabeth (his  X  mark) Gathright
Recorded 7 May 1770

p.210 Hannah Elmore, wife of Peter Elmore, came into court and relinquished her

dower in land conveyed by her husband to Dabney Pettus.
Recorded 7 May 1770

p.210 18 December 1769 William Ellis and Jane, his wife, of Southampton County, to Richard Timberlake of Henrico County, for 15 pounds, 100 acres, being a lot drawn by William Ellis in Col. William Byrd's Lottery, No. 834.
Wit: Jacob Pleasants and George Ellis, Quakers, John Brooke
Signed: William Ellis
Partly proved on 5 February 1770 and continued for further proof and Recorded on 7 May 1770

p.211 27 November 1769 Samuel Liggon of Henrico County to John Williams of Goochland County, for 60 pounds, 200 acres adj. William Wade, David Gwine, William Harlow, Richard Loving and William Price.
Wit: Pleasant Willis, William Price, William (his X mark) Liggon
Signed: Samuel (his X mark) Liggon
Recorded 7 May 1770

p.212 2 April 1770 Deed of Trust from Frederick Clarke to Richard Adams, both of Henrico County, for 11 pounds 11 shillings and 9 pence, 33 ½ acres, adj. Isaac Echo on the north, Benjamin Jordan on the south, Ephraim Gathright on the east and west; being the land given him by his father, William Clarke and whereon the said Frederick Clarke now dwells.
Wit: Henry B. Lightfoot, Dabney Miller, William Faris
Signed: Frederick (his X mark) Clark
Recorded 7 May 1770

p.213 4 April 1770 Drusiller Jenkins of Henrico County to her daughter, Ann Jenkins, otherwise called Ann Daley, wife of Joseph Daley of Henrico County, for love and affection and tender regard, two cows and one yearling now in my possession, and to granddaughter, Sally, or Sarah Daley, daughter of the aforesaid Ann, one cow yearling.
Wit: George Hicks, William Craighton, Elizabeth Creighton
Signed: Drusiller (her X mark) Jenkins
Recorded 7 May 1770

p.214 14 December 1769 Robert Pleasants to William Binford, both of Henrico County, for 250 pounds, 250 acres on the south side of White Oak Swamp; adj. James and Thomas Binford on the east, Thomas and Daniel Warriner on the west and the said Robert Pleasants on the south; being all the land on the south side of the swamp that Robert Pleasants purchased of Mary and Richard Eppes.

Wit: Thomas Pleasants, Jr., James Binford, Robert Povall, James Cureton
Signed: Robert Pleasants    Recorded 7 May 1770

p.215  12 November 1769 Dedimus for Susanna Hughes, wife of William Hughes, Jr., directed to George Stovall, Jr., and James Dillard of Amherst County, regarding deed to Martin Burton of Henrico County for 500 acres from Hughes; said writ issued by Thomas Adams, Clerk; said Susanna examined on 19 May 1770.
Signed: George Stovall, Jun., James Dillard
Recorded 4 June 1770

p.216  10 December 1769 James Thomas to John Hodges, both of Henrico County, for 10 pounds, one half-acre lot in the Town of Westham, being Lot 110; adj. the lots of Thomas Starks, deceased.
Wit: Turner Southall, John Price, Barrett Price
Signed: James (his X mark) Thomas
Recorded 4 June 1770

p.217  5 June 1770 Dedimus for Elizabeth Adams, wife of Richard Adams, directed to William Lewis and William Smith, Gent., of Henrico County, regarding deed to Joshua Storrs for 164 acres; said writ issued by Thomas Adams, Clerk.
Signed: Thomas Adams

p.218  [-?-] April 1770 Power of Attorney from Samuel Mitchell of the Town of Richmond, Henrico County, to trusty friends, Thomas Prosser and Turner Southall of Henrico County, to ask, demand, recover or receive and pay all demands as they shall find just.
Wit: Samuel Harwood, John Price    Signed: Samuel Mitchell
Recorded 5 June 1770

p.219  5 May 1770 William Byrd and Mary, his wife, of Westover, Charles City County, Peyton Randolph of the City of Williamsburg, John Page of Gloucester County, Charles Carter of Lancaster County, and Charles Turnbull of Dinwiddie County, to David Patteson of Chesterfield County, for 300 pounds, two lots containing 200 acres as expressed in a plan produced at the drawing of Byrd's Lottery and distinguished in said plan as Nos. 821 and 773.
Wit: Joshua Storrs and George Ellis, Quakers, John Orr
Signed: W. Byrd  Partly proved on 5 June 1770 and continued for further proof and recorded on 6 August 1770

p.220  5 March 1770 Robert Pleasants to Alexander Bailey, both of Henrico

County, for 26 pounds, pursuant to a foreclosure, 50 acres; cites that David Breeding, for the better security of the payment of the sum due John and Robert Pleasants, merchants, executed a deed of mortgage for said 50 acres dated 10 March 1761, that the partnership between John and Robert Pleasants expired years ago and the said debt due from David Breeding became the property of Robert Pleasants by a mutual agreement and a decree of the Henrico County Court entered in October 1769, and the property was sold for foreclosure on 8 January last to the highest bidder, Abraham Bailey.
Wit: Luzby Turpin, Lewis Roper, David Mackie
Signed: Robert Pleasants                              Recorded 6 August 1770

p.221  21 December 1769 Robert Frogmorton of Halifax County to Richard Frogmorton of Henrico County, for 40 pounds, 50 acres, being the land whereon Richard Frogmorton now lives.
Wit: Robert Pleasants, Jr., Charles Hughes and Noble Jordane, Quakers, and Thomas Bates
Signed: Robert (his X mark) Frogmorton               Recorded 6 August 1770

p.222  14 January 1769 Augustine Wooddy of Henrico County to Joseph Faudree of Goochland County, for 10 pounds, 50 acres, adj. William Wade and Martin's patent.    Wit: William Henley, Hezekiah Henley, John Wade, Joseph Lively
Signed: Augustine (his A mark) Wooddy, Susannah (her R mark) Wooddy
Recorded 6 August 1770

p.223  4 September 1768 Stephen Woodson to William Parsons, Josiah Parsons, Woodson Parsons, Sarah Parsons, Mary Parsons, Ursley Parsons, Elizabeth Parsons, Agness Parsons and Judith Parsons, for good will and affection and 5 shillings, to Woodson Parsons 100 acres of land at Piccanocqucy; to William, Josiah and Woodson Parsons all my land at Malvern Hills containing 300 acres, to be divided in three equal parts; and 20 Negroes, horses, cattle, hogs, sheep and household furniture to be equally divided between said nine grantees.
Wit: William Goode, Joseph Parsons (since deceased), Nathaniel Hood
Signed: Stephen Woodson
Recorded 6 August 1770

p.224  24 May 1770 David Allen to Thomas Ginnett, both of Henrico County, 27 pounds, 100 acres, adj. R. Richard Allen, Mat Herbert, Robert C. Nicholas and William Gordon and the Great Branch.
Wit: none                                             Signed: David Allen
Recorded 3 September 1770

p.225 31 March 1770, Williamsburg: Receipt for Sheriff's collection of officers fees and dues forwarded by the Clerk of Henrico County Court by the hands of Lyddal Bacon on Benjamin Duvall's bond as Sheriff dated 7 December 1767.
Wit: Lyddal Bacon  Signed: John Randolph
Recorded 3 September 1770

p.226 1 October 1770 Apprenticeship Contract between Nathaniel Royster, orphan of John Royster, deceased, to William Stone, both of Henrico County, by consent of the Henrico County Court and by his guardian, John Hales of Henrico County, the said Nathaniel Royster doth bind himself to the said William Stone to learn the art of a house carpenter till he shall arrive at the age of 21, he now being 16 years and 9 months.  Wit: none
Signed: Nathaniel Royster, William Stone, Jr.
Recorded 1 October 1770

p.228 28 September 1770 William Harlow of Hanover County to John Faris and Lucy, his wife, of Henrico County, 15 pounds, 50 acres on the south side of the Chickahominy River bequeathed to the said William by his father, Thomas Harlow in his last will and testament; bounded by Richard Lovell, John Williams, David Goings and Esau Ferris.
Wit: Zephaniah Tait, Thomas Robinson, Sr.
Recorded 1 October 1770

p.229 1 October 1770 Robert Pleasants to John Brackett, both of Henrico County, for 120 pounds, 75 acres, known as the Ordinary, lying in and about the forks of the Long and Bottoms Bridge roads; bounded on the south by Humphrey Smith, on the west by Daniel Warriner, on the north by the land lately sold by the said Pleasants to William Binford and on the east by Thomas Binford; being the same tract purchased by Pleasants of William Pike.
Wit: none  Signed: Robert Pleasants
Recorded 1 October 1770

p.230 1 October 1770 John Brackett to Robert Pleasants, both of Henrico County, for 170 pounds, 170 acres, adj. 60 acres sold by Pleasants by deed dated 7 May 1759 and also other land of the said Pleasants whereon Charles Keesse now lives, the lands of Humphrey Smith and Robert Povall; being the same land whereon said Brackett now dwells, formerly granted unto Henry Watkins by patent dated 20 November 1679 and by his son and heir, Thomas Watkins, sold to the said Brackett.
Wit: none  Signed: John Brackett,
Elizabeth, wife of John Brackett, relinquished her dower.
Recorded 1 October 1770

p.231  3 September 1770 Patrick Coutts, merchant, of the Town of Richmond, to Isaac Younghusband, of Henrico County, for 150 pounds, all of the said Patrick Coutts' right, title and property interest in 700 acres, which was sold to him from Richard Rockett for himself and as attorney for his brother, John Rockett.
Wit: none                                       Signed: Patrick Coutts
Recorded 1 October 1770

p.232  15 October 1770 John Jordone of Henrico County to his son, Noble Jordone, for divers good causes and for 5 shillings, 13 head of cattle, 23 hogs, 10 head of sheep, one dunn colored mare, 2 horse colts and one bed and furniture.
Wit: Thomas Bates, John Dollard
Signed: John (his JJ mark) Jordone
Recorded 5 November 1770

p.233  18 July 1769 Sarah Comron of Boston, Suffolk County, Massachusetts, widow of John Comron, late of Boston, Gent., and Dr. James Loyd and Sarah, his wife, daughter and sole heir-at-law of the said John Comron, to Alexander Baine of Richmond Town, Henrico County, for 30 pounds, two lots containing about ½ acre in Richmond Town marked B and O on the plan of the said Town, which said John Comron purchased of Wm. Byrd, Esq., by deed dated 5 June 1741.
Wit: William Griffin, John Hyldon, Jr., Patrick Coutts, William Carson, Richard C. Anderson
Signed: Sarah Comron, James Loyd,
Sarah Loyd; acknowledged before Elias Hutchenson, the Subscriber First Justice of the Court of Common Pleas.
Partly proved on 6 November 1769 and continued for further proof and admitted to record on 5 November 1770.

p.234  3 September 1770 George Donald and Dorothea, his wife, to Alexander Baine, all of Henrico County, for 140 pounds, one certain square of land in the Town of Richmond containing four lots of ½ acre each, numbered 100, 99, 86 and 85 on the plan of the said town, and lying opposite the lots where the said George Donald now lives on the southeast, opposite John Bransford's and Thomas Calder's lots on the southwest, opposite Thomas Atcheson's lots on the northwest and opposite Richard Adams' lands on the northeast; being the lots Donald purchased of John Bryan by deed dated 2 August 1762.
Wit: Samuel DuVal, George Wood, Robert Duval, Peter Lyons, William DuVal, John Sutton, Jr.
Signed: Geo. Donald, Dorothea Donald
Recorded 5 November 1770

p.235  18 October 1770 William Porter of Southam Parish, Cumberland County, to John Warriner of Henrico County, for 55 pounds, 100 acres on a branch of the Western Run called Maddox's Branch; adj. Thomas Williams, William Gathright, Turkey Island Road, Humphrey Smith, Daniel Warriner and the road that leads to Richmond Town.
Wit: Samuel Gathright, John Gathright, John Warriner, Jr.
Signed: William Porter
Rebecca, wife of William Porter, relinquished her dower.
Recorded 5 November 1770

p.236  5 November 1770 Bond of Thomas Owen as the third inspector at Byrd's Warehouse, in the amount of 500 pounds, with Thomas Prosser and Alexander Baine, his sureties, to perform the office of an inspector agreeable to the act of Assembly and an act made and entitled an act to amend the staple of tobacco and for preventing frauds in his Majesty's customs.           Wit: Peter Hon, Jr.
Signed: Thomas Owen, Thomas Prosser, Alexander Baine
Recorded 5 November 1770

p.237  3 December 1770 John Pleasants to his son, Joseph Pleasants, both of Henrico County, for natural love and affection, 50 acres, being part of the tract whereon John Pleasants now lives, including the house and plantation whereon the said Joseph Pleasants now lives; on Horse Swamp and adj. Joshua Storrs.
Wit: none                                                                Signed: John Pleasants
Recorded 3 December 1770

p.238  3 December 1770 John Talbot of Bedford County to The Reverend Miles Selden, executor of Philip Mayo, deceased, of Henrico County, for 75 pounds, one Negro man named Joe, for the use of the estate of Philip Mayo, deceased.
Wit: Jerman Baker                                                  Signed: John Talbot
Recorded 3 December 1770

p.239  3 December 1770 William Childers, son of Joseph Childers, deceased, to Julius Allen, Sr., both of Henrico County, for 14 pounds and 5 shillings, 28 acres on the west side of Bull's Branch; adj. said Childers, James Sharp, Philip Watson, deceased, and said Julius Allen; being the parcel of land that Benjamin DuVal, deceased, surveyed for Christian Allen, deceased, and being part of the tract formerly belonging to Joseph Childers, deceased, and was by him mortgaged to Robert Pleasants, merchant at Curles.
Wit: Samuel Price, Dabney Pettus, Abra (his  C  mark) Childers
Signed: William Childers                                  Recorded 3 December 1770

p.240  20 November 1770 Isaac Coles of Halifax County to Nicholas Scherer and George Scherer, both of the Town of Richmond, for 110 pounds, 175 acres on the south side of Gilley's Creek adj. John New (metes and bounds description), which land was devised to Isaac Coles under the will of his father, John Coles and by him purchased of Robert Mosby and Henry Stokes by deed of record in the General Court of this colony.
Wit: Turner Southall, Miles Taylor, Samuel Ege, Thomas Frankling
Signed: Isaac Coles                                    Recorded 3 December 1770

p.241  16 November 1770 James Jones to Ludwell Britain, both of Henrico County, for 20 pounds, 50 acres adj. Matthew Hobson, Robert Mosby, Ludwell Britain and James Britain.
Wit: Thomas Prosser, James (his B mark) Britain, Benjamin Mosby, John Lipscomb
Signed: James Jones                                    Recorded 7 January 1771

p.242  9 June 1770 Nathaniel Dennis of Henrico County to Burges Harrelson of Orange County, North Carolina, for 50 pounds, 100 acres, except one acre at an old mill, on the main Stoney Run; adj. William Strait, Nathaniel Dennis, Joseph Brown and Thomas Alley.
Wit: David Alley, John Dennis, Thomas (his A mark) Alley
Signed: Nathaniel Dennis, Rachel Dennis
Recorded 7 January 1771

p.243  3 December 1770 Robert Gordon and Giles Gordon of Chesterfield County to Leonard Henley of Henrico County, for 75 pounds, 150 acres on a branch of Westham and Upram Brook; adj. Thomas Lewis, said Gordons, John Gordon and Jesse Smith.
Wit: Jonathan Bridgwater, John Hodges, Obadiah Smith
Signed: Robert Gordon, Giles (his X mark) Gordon, Ann and Kitty, wives of Robert and Giles Gordon, relinquished their rights of dower.
Recorded 4 February 1771

p.244  12 November 1770 Deed of Mortgage from George Donald of Town of Richmond to James Buchanan and Neil Campbell both of Henrico County, for 1000 pounds and for all sums due them as my sureties, six Negro slaves, Isaac, Aberdeen, Frank, Cloe, Harris and Anne; and 250 acres on Gilley's Creek, lots and houses in Richmond Town, corn fodder, stocks of cattle, hogs, sheep and horses, household furniture, beds, plates, book and debt bonds and notes.
Wit: Benjamin Pollard, Jasper Halket, William Cuthbert
Signed: Geo. Donald

Recorded 4 February 1771

p. 245 (-?-) November 1770 Power of Attorney from George Donald of the Town of Richmond to James Buchanan and Neil Campbell, all of the Town of Richmond, Henrico County, to enter into possession of his property, to execute deeds, to collect debts, etc.
Wit: Benjamin Pollard, Jasper Halket, William Cuthbert
Signed: Geo. Donald                                    Recorded 4 February 1771

p.246 27 September 1770 William Cocke Redford to Josiah Bullington of Henrico County, for 50 pounds, 10 shillings, 82 acres on Roundabout Swamp; adj. Thomas Mann Randolph.
Wit: Archibald (his A mark) Philbord, Mark Woodcock, Moses Hampton
Signed: William Cock Redford                           Recorded 4 February 1771

p.247 20 December 1770 John Holmes to James Childers, both of Henrico County, for (-?-) pounds, 50 acres, being part of a larger tract granted to John Williams by patent bearing date 13 August 1744 and by him conveyed by deed to the said John Holmes; bounded on the northwest by Richard Williamson, west by Richard Adams, south by John Hobson and east by the other part of the tract whereon said John Holmes now lives.
Wit: none                               Signed: John (his X mark) Holmes
Recorded 4 February 1771

p.248 25 January 1771 William Parker to Isaac Sharp, both of Henrico County, for 5 shillings, one Negro boy, Caesar.
Wit: Joseph Parker, Obedience (her X mark) Lester
Signed: William Parker                                 Recorded 4 February 1771

p.249 4 February 1771 William Parker of Henrico County to Benjamin Parker of Bertie County, North Carolina, for 10 shillings, a Negro wench named Betty.
Wit: Joseph Parker, William Sharp
Signed: William Parker                                 Recorded 4 February 1771

p.250 Deed (not identified) as to Charles Carter, Esq., proved by oath of Fortuanatus Sydnor and William Mitchell, two witnesses thereto, for partial proof on 7 January 1771; and further proved by James McDowell, the other witness thereon, as to Charles Carter, Esq., and by Turner Southall and James Sharp, two witnesses thereof, as to Peyton Randolph, Esq., on 4 February 1771; and further proved by Daniel Price and Turner Southall, the other witnesses thereto, as to Peyton Randolph and recorded on 4 March 1771.

p.250  30 December 1767 Frederick Clark to Benjamin Jordan, both of Henrico County, for 13 pounds and 18 shillings, 20 acres adj. Ephraim Gathright, George Clark and other land of the said Frederick Clark and the land which the said Benjamin Jordan purchased of Robert Pleasant.
Wit: Thomas Bates [Quaker], Ephraim Gathright, James Austin
Signed: Frederick (his I mark) Clark
Recorded 4 March 1771

p.252  21 September 1770 Dedimus from Thomas Adams, Clerk, to Nathaniel Ridley and William Blunt of Southampton County for the relinquishment of dower from Jane Ellis, wife of William Ellis, regarding deed of 18 December 1769 to Richard Timberlake for 100 acres.
Executed by Ridley and Blunt on 24 November 1770.
Recorded 4 March 1771

p.253  6 August 1770 Jonathan Williams to John Hopson both of Henrico County, for 10 pounds, 23 acres on Roundabout Swamp; adj. parcel said John Hopson bought of Constantine, John Burton, Francis Bowman's spring and Maj. Francis Eppes.
Wit: Hays Whitlow, Joseph Whitlow          Signed: Jonathan Williams
Sarah, wife of Jonathan Williams, relinquished her dower.
Recorded 4 March 1771.

p.254  29 November 1770 Deed of Mortgage from John Martin to Pleasants & Bates, both of Henrico County, for 30 pounds, 90 acres adj. Thomas Jolly, William Gathright, John Warriner, Robert Pleasants and Robert Povall.
Wit: Lancelot Stone, Giles Stone
Signed: John (his M mark) Martin
Recorded 4 March 1771

p.255  4 March 1771 Robert Cooke of Henrico County to Fortunatus Sydnor and Elizabeth, his wife, for 9 pounds, a half-acre lot near Richmond Town; adj. Alexander Brown, Walter Coles and the main road that leads from the mouth of Gilley's Creek to Richmond Town.
Wit: none                    Signed: Robert (his ∕⊘ mark) Cooke
Recorded 4 March 1771

p.257  19 November 1770 Jonathan Williams to John Burton, both of Henrico County, for 70 pounds, 106 acres on Roundabout Swamp; adj. Thomas Mann Randolph, Josiah Bullington, John Hobson, Christopher Branch, Peter Randolph and Hays Whitlow, as per patent.

Wit: Thomas Bates, George Crawford, Francis Parker, Samuel Matthews, Giles Stone
Signed: Jonathan Williams,
Sarah, wife of Jonathan Williams, relinquished her dower.
Recorded 4 March 1771

p.258  4 March 1771 Apprenticeship Contract between William Bullington to Robert Duval, both of Henrico County, and by consent of the Henrico County Court and by consent of the guardian appointed by the Court, to be bound to the said Duval from the 13th day of this month to be trained as a house carpenter and joyner.
Wit: none            Signed: William Bullington, Robert Duval, Abraham Bailey
Recorded 4 March 1771

p.259  5 December (1770) Apprenticeship Contract between John Lipcomb of Hanover County to Thomas Prosser and Alexander Peterfield Trent, merchants, of his own free will and accord doth bind himself to learn their art, trade and mystery of a merchant from the day of the date hereof until he shall arrive at the age of 21 years.                                                                                    Wit: none
Signed: John Lipcomb, Thos. Prosser, Alexander Peterfield Trent
Recorded 1 April 1771

p.260  25 October 1770 David Gowin and Elizabeth, his wife, of Henrico County, to Edward Barnett of Hanover County, for 21 pounds, 100 acres in the forks of Farrar's Branch; adj. John Harlow and Nathan Dunaway.
Wit: David Bowles, Randal Loving, James Matthews
Signed: David (his  D  mark) Gowin  Elizabeth, wife of David Gowin, relinquished her dower.
Recorded 1 April 1771

p.262 16 April 1771 Susannah Burton of Henrico County to her daughter, Susannah Price, for mother-like love, one Negro boy named Toney.
Wit: Leonard Henley, Richard Burton, Richardson Henley
Signed: Susanna (her  X  mark) Burton
Recorded 4 May 1771

p.262  6 May 1771 Thomas Dunn to James McDowell, both of Henrico County, for 20 pounds, 2 shillings and 10 pence, one masted pilot boat about 300 bushels burthen with all her anchors and rigging thereto belonging, two feather beds and furniture, one walnut table, two pine tables, six flag-bottomed chairs and other personal property.
Wit: J. Pleasants, George Weir                                    Signed: Thos. Dunn

Recorded 6 May 1771

p.263 1 January 1771 Power of Attorney from William Mitchell of the subberts of Londonderry, Ireland, innkeeper, to his son, Robert Mitchell, mariner, now in Richmond Town, Henrico County, to receive legacies from executors under the will of Samuel Mitchell, deceased, late of the Town of Richmond; cites that said Samuel Mitchell, by his will dated 7 April 1770, devised to his son, the said William Mitchell, 400 acres of land which was purchased of William Byrd, Esq., numbered 786, 789, 790 and 791, adj. Samuel DuVal and which last lot was purchased from James Buchanan; will also bequeathed 2 Negroes, Patrick, a blacksmith, and Jack, a wagoner, 5 horses, a wagon, the smith's tools and one-half of the vessel and cargo owned in partnership with George McDonald (which half amounted to 400 pounds); the joint executors being Turner Southall, Thomas Prosser and Edward Curd.
Wit: Charles Campbell, Thomas Lock, John Count (acknowledged by Count before Robert Fairly, mayor of Londonderry, on 7 January 1771)
Signed: Wm. Mitchell                                    Recorded 6 May 1771

p.266 6 May 1771 Apprenticeship Contract between Leonard Henley, orphan of Turner Henley, about 16 years of age, and Jesse Smith, planter; said orphan to be apprenticed to Smith until he be 21 years of age; by consent of Leonard Henley, guardian, and the Henrico County Court.
Wit: none                           Signed: Jesse Smith, Leond. Henley
Recorded 6 May 1771

p.267 6 May 1771 Apprenticeship Contract between Markes Vandevall, orphan of Nathaniel Vandevall, deceased, and by consent of his mother, to Zachariah Rowland; orphan to be apprenticed for the term of three years in the occupation of a merchant.
Wit: none                    Signed: Markes Vandevall, Zachariah Rowland
Recorded 6 May 1771

p.268 30 October 1770 Francis Cook of Roan County, North Carolina, to John Lankester of Henrico County, for 25 pounds, 200 acres adj. John Lankester and Hughes (metes and bounds description).
Wit: Christopher John Thomas, Major (his X mark) Holloway, Peter Clarke, Jacob Smith
Signed: Francis Cook                                    Recorded 6 May 1771

p.269 18 March 1771 Joseph Clarke of Henrico County to R. Richard Allen, for 25 pounds, 100 acres on Stony Run Creek; adj. John Clarke, Thomas Alley, Alexander Paterson and Richard Cottrel.

Wit: David Allen, Samuel (his S mark) Allen, Joseph Brown
Signed: Joseph Clark
Clarke's wife, unnamed, relinquished her dower.
Recorded 6 May 1771

p.271   13 January 1767 Mary Bryan, widow and relict of Benjamin Bryan, deceased, to James Gunn, who has since intermarried with Mary Bryan, daughter of the said widow, for 32 pounds (which he had paid to Alexander Spain & Co.), a life interest in 6 Negro slaves: Dinah, Rose, Lucy, Betty, Venus and Pegg and their increase; cites bond of James Gunn to Alexander Buchanan payable October next for a debt due from the said Mary Bryan, widow, which was taken in execution for to Spain & Co. for the said sum
Wit: Turner Southall, Groves Harding, Drury Breazeal
Signed: Mary Bryan                               Recorded 6 May 1771

p.272   13 January 1767 Mary Bryan, widow and relict of Benjamin Bryan, deceased, to Hannah Bryan, for love and affection, her maintenance and support and especially for 51 pounds, 8 shillings and 9 pence, a life interest in all household furniture of what kind so ever, which belonged to said Benjamin Bryan in his lifetime, and 8 Negro slaves: a fellow named Frank (of Wincher ?), Anna, Beck, Sylvia, and children Anthony, Smith, Febey [Phoebe] and Jone [Joan]. Reversion in above to her two daughters, Hannah Bryan and Mary Gunn.
Wit: Turner Southall, Groves Harding, Drury Breazeal
Signed: Mary Bryan                               Recorded 6 May 1771

p.274   8 November 1770 Hutchings Burton of Mecklenburg County to William Burton of Cumberland County, for 500 pounds, 390 acres on Westham Creek, adj. Mr. Randolph (metes and bounds description).
Wit: Charles Burton, Mark Moor, Julius Burton
Signed: Hutchings Burton                         Recorded 3 June 1771

p.274   5 March 1771 John Sutton Farrar to Richard Cotterell, both of Henrico County, for 41 pounds, 227 acres on the branches of Chickahominy Swamp; adj. David Clark, William Staples, crossing Long and Hungry Branch, Jesse Smith and Tyree.              Wit: Nathaniel Dennis, John Dennis, Nathaniel Dennis
Signed: John Sutton Farrar
Susanna, wife of John Sutton Farrar, relinquished her dower.
Recorded 3 June 1771

p.277   3 May 1771 Richard Randolph and Ryland Randolph to Robert Pleasants, son of Thomas Pleasants, all of Henrico County, for 902 pounds and 10 shillings,

340 acres, being part of the Turkey Island tract sold by the last Peter Randolph, Esq., unto the said Ryland Randolph and commonly known as Green's Quarter; bounded by [n?] the middle of [by?] the county road from Williamsburg to Richmond, the boundary of the lands of Ryland Randolph on the south, by James Powell Cocke on the east, by Thomas Jolly on the northeast, by William Gathright on the north and by Bowler Cocke on the west.
Wit: Richard Kidder Meade, John Eldridge, Thomas Eldridge
Signed: Richard Randolph, Ryland Randolph
p. 296: Partly proved on 3 June 1771, acknowledged by Richard Randolph and Recorded on 5 August 1771

p.279  2 May 1771 William Childress to Richard Wade, both of Goochland County, for 65 pounds, 132 ½ acres, being the land said Childress purchased of John Pleasants & Son and part of the same tract of land that his father, Joseph Childress, deceased, lived on; adj. Julius Allen, Anthony Matthews, James Sharp.
Wit: Robert Wade, Rebekah Wade
Signed: William Childress,
Ann (her X mark) Childress, Ann, wife of William Childress, relinquished her dower.                                                                            Recorded 3 June 1771

p.280  28 June 1771 Abraham Bailey to his son, David and wife Jean, and to his grandson, Johnston Bailey, being the son of the said David and Jean Bailey, for love and affection and 5 shillings, a Negro lad named Will now in the possession of son, David Bailey in trust to Caleb Johnston and Samuel Johnston, Jr., for the benefit and use of my son, his wife and my grandson, said slave not to be sold but to remain in the family and ultimately to belong absolutely to said grandson.
Wit: Abraham Bailey, Jr., Peter Bailey
Signed: Abraham Bailey                                                       Recorded 5 August 1771

p.282  5 August 1771 Ann Randolph, of Henrico County, widow and relict of William Randolph, late of the said county, deceased, to Peter Randolph, son of the said Ann Randolph, for 5 shillings, her interest in 100 acres on the main road from Warwick to Four Mile Creek, where the back line of the tract known as Wilton crosses the said road near a place called Cox's Old Field, thence along the road towards Varina Ferry, thence to a slash, thence along Burton, thence north to the road that leads from Warwick Ferry to Four Mile Creek.
Wit: Robert Walker, Parrobe Boswell, Archibald Cary, Thomas Fleming
Signed: Ann Randolph                                                         Recorded 5 August 1771

p.283  5 August 1771 William Owen, Thomas Cheatham, Joseph Bass and John Fowler, executors of Christopher Cheatham, deceased, of Chesterfield County, for

145 pounds, 100 acres on Miery Run; adj. Thomas Wilkinson, Watkins and Prosser (metes and bounds description).
Wit: Peter Fitzgerald, Charles Lewis, Jr., Miles Taylor, John Forsee, Jr.
Signed: William Owen, Thos. Cheatham, Jo. Bass, John Fowler,
Sarah, wife of William Owen, relinquished her dower.
Recorded 5 August 1771

p.286  4 March 1771 Jonathan Williams to John Burton of Henrico County, for 40 pounds, 50 acres adj. John Pleasants, James Hallock, William Frayser and John Frayser; being the land Jonathan Williams purchased of John Frayser.
Wit: Robert Pleasants, Thomas Pleasants, Jr.,Thomas Pleasants Jordan, Ben Jordan [Quakers]
Signed: Jonathan Williams                    Recorded 5 August 1771

p.288  5 August 1771 James Powell Cocke and Elizabeth, his wife, to Ryland Randolph, all of Henrico County, for 5 shillings, 21 acres on the Brook; adj. said Randolph (metes and bounds description); and 23 poles on the north side of the great road leading from Williamsburg to Richmond; adj. said Cocke (metes and bounds description).
Wit: Robin Povall, John Sturdivant
Signed: James Powell Cocke, Elizabeth Cock
Recorded 5 August 1771

p.290  5 August 1771 Ryland Randolph and Richard Randolph to James Powell Cocke, all of Henrico County, for 550 pounds, 233 acres on the great road leading from Williamsburg to Richmond (metes and bounds description).
Wit: none                    Signed: Ry. Randolph, Richard Randolph
Recorded 5 August 1771

p.291  5 August 1771 Power of Attorney from Andrew Edmondson, merchant, late of Richmond Town, to Robert Baine and John Edmondson, merchants, of Henrico County, to sue for, recover and receive all debts.
Wit: William Clarke, Emanuel Walker, John McLeam
Signed: Andrew Edmonds                    Recorded 5 August 1771

p.293  19 February 1771 John Sutton Farrar and Susanna, his wife, Samuel Williamson, Allen Williamson, Thomas Williamson, James Browning and Anne, his wife, William Miller and Elizabeth, his wife, Groves Harding and Sarah, his wife, Harwood Bacon and Mary, his wife, William Allen Lankaster and Judah, his wife, and Lucy Williamson, residuary legatees under the will of John Williamson deceased, to Charles Snead of Henrico County, for 30 pounds, 170 acres on

George's Branch; adj. Henry Stoakes, Watson, Patrick and Patman (metes and bounds description); being entered for with the surveyor and the works assigned by the said John Williamson to William Patman, notwithstanding the said assignment a patent has since issued in the name of the said John Williamson and agreeable to the will of the said William Patman.
Wit: Daniel Kelley, Robert Snead
Signed: John Sutton Farrar, Susanna (her ✚ mark) Farrar, James (his ✚ mark) Browning, Ann (his + wife) Browning, William Miller, Elizabeth (her X mark) Miller, Allen Williamson, Samuel Williamson
(Not signed by Thomas Williamson and last seven grantors in the caption.)
Recorded 5 August 1771

p.296 31 July 1771 William Alley to daughter, Jane Battersby, both of Henrico County, and to her two sisters, Sophia and Elisabeth, should she die without issue, for love, good will and affection, one Negro girl named Eve and her increase.
Wit: William Kennedy, Micajah Chilo [Chiles?]
Recorded 6 August 1771

p.297 10 August 1770 Deed of Mortgage from Thomas Booth of Henrico County to James Lyle of Chesterfield County, for the payment of 152 pounds, 7 shillings and 3 pence due 1 May 1771, the collateral being 9 Negro slaves: Bobb, Joe, Will, Isaac, Daniel, Tom, Alse, Eve and young Alse; and interest in 6 Negro slaves: Harry, Cesar, Phill, Judy, Molly and Dinah and their increase since my father's death and now being in my mother's possession as her dower.
Wit: James Lockhart, Robert Barbour
Signed: Thomas Booth                    Recorded 3 June 1771

p.299 7 October 1771 James Whitlow to his son, James Whitlow, for natural regard and affection, 100 acres adj. Edward Whitlow, John Enroughty, John Parker, Richard Bennet and John Whitlow.
Wit: none                    Signed: James (his ✚ mark) Whitlow
Recorded 7 October 1771

p.300 7 October 1771 Moses Bridgwater and Eleanor, his wife, of Henrico County to William Bridgwater of Lunenburg County, for 5 shillings, 65 acres adj. John Clarkson, Mayo and Samuel Liggon.
Wit: Abraham Bailey, Elliott Lacy, Joseph Brown
Signed: Moses Bridgwater
Eleanor, wife of Moses Bridgwater, relinquished her dower.
Recorded 7 October 1771

p.302 7 October 1771 Moses Bridgwater and (Eleanor) his wife of Henrico County, and William Bridgwater, Jr., of Lunenburg County, to John Clarkson of Henrico County, for life, and then to his son, Charles Clarkson, for 5 shillings, 50 acres adj. Liggon (metes and bounds description).
Wit: Abraham Bailey, Joel Childers, Junr., Joseph Brown
Signed: Moses Bridgmater, William Bridgwater
Eleanor, wife of Moses Bridgwater, relinquished her dower.
Recorded 7 October 1771

p.304 7 October 1771 William Bridgwater, Jr., of Lunenburg County, to Moses Bridgwater of Henrico County, for 5 shillings, 65 acres adj. said William Bridgwater and Mayo near Gilley's Creek.
Wit: Abraham Bailey, Elliott Lacy, Joseph Brown
Signed: Wm. Bridgwater                                    Recorded 7 October 1771

p.306 7 October 1771 Apprenticeship Contract between John Royster, orphan, of Henrico County, with the consent of his guardian, James Sharp, and Samuel Arnold, house carpenter and joiner, of Henrico County; said orphan to serve said Arnold as an apprentice for a term of five years from the date hereof. Wit: none
Signed: John Royster, Samuel Arnold, James Sharp
Recorded 7 October 1771

p.308 7 October 1771 Bond of Robert Price, with Peter Winston and Robert Povall, his sureties, in the amount of 500 pounds, to qualify as one of the inspectors of tobacco at the publick warehous known as Byrd's Warehouse; appointed by the Hon. William Nelson, his Majesty's President and Commander in Chief of the Colony and Dominion of Virginia.                                    Wit: none
Signed: Robert Price, Peter Winston, Robert Povall
Recorded 7 October 1771

p.309 7 October 1771 Bond of Samuel Price, with Obadiah Smith of Chesterfield County and Charles Lewis, his sureties, in the amount of 500 pounds, to qualify as one of the inspectors of tobacco at the publick warehouse known as Byrd's Warehouse; appointed by the Hon. William Nelson, his Majesty's President and Commander in Chief of the Colony and Dominion of Virginia.                Wit: none
Signed: Samuel Price, Oba. Smith, Charles Lewis
Recorded 7 October 1771

p.310 8 October 1771 Bond of Neil Campbell and James Buchanan, his surety, merchants, in the amount of 1,000 pounds, to erect and build and continue to build so as to completely finish by or before 10 April next on the lots commonly known

by the name of Howling's Tenements at Shockoes in the Town of Richmond and County of Henrico and mentioned in the Acts of Assembly for ...the relief of the sufferers by the loss of tobacco damage by the last fresh and set apart for the building of warehouses...to contain at least 1,600 hogsheads of tobacco with strong doors, locks, bolts and hinges as shall be sufficient. Wit: none
Signed: Neil Campbell, James Buchanan
Recorded 8 October 1771

p.311  18 March 1771 Indenture Tripartite among Martha Miller, widow and relict of John Watson of Henrico County, deceased; Robert Bolling, Jr., of Buckingham County, Gent., and Susannah, his wife, one of the daughters of the said John Watson, deceased, and a residuary legatee; and Thomas Prosser of Henrico County, merchant; cites that John Watson was possessed of a tract of 1,061 acres on a branch called the Brook and by his last will and testament dated 10 March 1749 devised to his wife, said Martha Watson (now Martha Miller), the plantation whereon he did live, and 541 acres, being part of the said tract of 1,061 acres, for her natural life, and that the rest of his estate, real and personal, to be equally divided between his wife and his two daughters, Elizabeth and Susannah Watson, each to possess a 1/3 interest in the same; said Thomas Prosser to have immediate interest in the two undivided 1/3 interests in the 520 residuary acres, but dwelling house now occupied by Martha Miller to be hers for life.
Wit: Matthew (his ✚ mark) Hopson, Francis (his ✚ mark) Cornett, Nathaniel Clarke, John Timberlake, Peter Feild Trent, Elizabeth Trent, Alexander Trent, John Scott, William Gay
Signed: Martha Miller, R. Bolling, Susanna Bolling
Recorded 1 April 1771
Dedimus for examination of Susannah Bolling, dated 3 June 1771, directed to George Hooper, William Cannon and Jeremiah Whitney, Gent., of
Buckingham County, from Thomas Adams, Clerk of Henrico County, was executed by the three justices of the peace on 9 July 1771 for her relinquishment of dower and recorded 2 December 1771.
[ Note: The above abstract is noteworthy in that it identifies the parentage of the second wife of Robert Bolling, Jr., of Chellow in Buckingham County. The marriage bond survives among the records of Amherst County, but her kinship to John and Martha Watson of Henrico County is divulged only by the above record. J. A. Leo LeMay in his excellent study, Robert Bolling Woos Anne Miller (Charlottesville: University of Virginia Press, 1990), makes the observation that because of the obscurity of Susanna Watson among records, her social status was probably beneath that of Bolling's first wife, Mary Burton.  The above deed, confirming Captain John Watson as a planter of considerable means, would refute that conclusion and would also underscore our dilemma in drawing conclusions

about our ancestors when records to not survive to tell us the real story. GMW]

p.320  2 December 1771  Bond of Nathaniel Wilkinson as Sheriff of Henrico County, with Edward Curd, Martin Burton and Richard Adams, his sureties, in the amount of 1,000 pounds, appointed by commission of the Earl of Dunmore, the Governor, under the seal of the Colony dated 20 October last.    Wit: none
Signed: Nathaniel Wilkinson, Edward Curd, Martin Burton, Richard Adams
Recorded 2 December 1771

p.321  2 December 1771  Bond of Nathaniel Wilkinson as Sheriff of Henrico County, with Edward Curd, Martin Burton and Richard Adams, his sureties, in the amount of 500 pounds, to collect all quitrents, fines and forfeitures.    Wit: none
Signed: Nathaniel Wilkinson, Edward Curd, Martin Burton, Richard Adams
Recorded 2 December 1771

p.322  2 December 1771  Bond of Edward Curd as one of the inspectors of tobacco at the warehouses established at Shockoes on James River; by commission from his Excellency the Governor, Earl of Dunmore, with Nathaniel Wilkinson and Richard Adams, sureties, in the amount of 500 pounds.    Wit: none
Signed: Edward Curd, Nat Wilkinson, Richard Adams
Recorded 2 December 1771

p.323  3 September 1771  George Donald and Dorothea, his wife, to Ellexander Baine, all of Henrico County, for 140 pounds, a certain square of land in the Town of Richmond containing four lots of one-half acre each and numbered on the plan of the said town as 100, 99, 86 and 85; lying opposite the lots on the southeast where the said George Donald lives, and opposite John Bransford and Thomas Calder to the southwest, and opposite Thomas Atkinson's lots on the northwest, and opposite Richard Adams' land on the northeast; being the same lots George Donald purchased of John Bryan by deed dated 2 August 1762.
Wit: Samuel DuVall, George Wood, Robert DuVal, Peter Lynn,
William DuVall, John Sutton, Junr.
Signed: Geo. Donald, Dorothea Donald
Recorded 2 December 1771

p.327  13 November 1771  William Kelly, Sr., to his son, William Kelly, Jr. for five shillings and natural love and affection, 70 acres on the south side of the Brook; adj. George Kelly, William Kelly and William Miller.
Wit: Jonathan Bridgwater, William Miller, William Bridgwater
Signed: William (his W mark) Kelly
Recorded 2 December 1771

p.332  2 December 1771 John Staples to William Staples, both of Henrico County, for fatherly love and affection, 100 acres, being the land and plantation whereon said William Staples doth now live and part of the land said John Staples purchased of Thomas Pleasants.
Wit: Izard Bacon, Thomas Bacon, John Bacon
Signed: John (his  J  mark) Staples                    Recorded 2 December 1771

p.333  2 December 1771 Apprenticeship Contract of Samuel Williamson of Henrico County to bind Thomas Williamson, orphan of John Williamson, deceased, to William Harrison, cabinet maker, of Amelia County, to learn the trade and mystery of cabinet making and to serve from the date hereof until said Thomas Williamson shall arrive at the age of 21.
Wit: James Vaughan, William Allen Lankester
Signed: Samuel WmSon, Thomas WmSon, Wm. Harrison
Recorded 2 December 1771

p.335  2 January 1772 Patrick Coutts, Esq., to William Randolph, Esq., both of Henrico County, for 100 pounds, 100 acres "distinguished in the scheme of the lottery called Byrd's Lottery by number 793; deed to said Coutts recorded in the General Court.
Wit: none                                              Signed: Patrick Coutts
Recorded 2 March 1772

p.337  7 August 1771 Richard Poynter and Elizabeth, his wife, of Charles City County, to William Griffin, Gent., of King and Queen County, for 40 pounds, four lots in or near the Town of Richmond, being the lots formerly belonging to William Mills Taylor, deceased, and left by his will to the said Richard Poynter.
Wit: Silvanus Gregory, Thomas Smith, Will Tyree
Signed: Richd. Poynter, Elizabeth (her  X  mark) Poynter
Recorded 2 March 1772

p.338  2 December 1771 Alexander Baine, merchant, to Dr. James Currie, for 400 pounds, a lot in the Town of Richmond at the falls of the James River, being that part of the said town known as Shockoes, and was one of the tenements in the Hon. William Byrd's Lottery and known by the name of Rosser's Tenement, number 336, which the said Baine purchased of the said Byrd by deed recorded in the General Court; also two lots containing one-half acre on the easternmost side of Shockoe Creek and on the southwest side of the Main Street, marked A and B on the plan of the said town, which said Baine purchased of Sarah Courin, James Lloyd and Sarah Lloyd by deed recorded in Henrico County Court.
Wit: Archibald Bryce, Jacob Pleasants, James McDowell, Joseph Pleasants, John

McKeand  Signed: Alexander Baine
Recorded 2 March 1772

p.340 [----] 1772 Peter Bailey and Frances, his wife, to Robert DuVall, all of Henrico County, for 70 pounds, 200 acres adj. Herbert, Peter Randolph, Henry Cox and John Alday (metes and bounds description).
Wit: none  Signed: Peter Bailey, Frances Bailey
Recorded 2 March 1772

pp.344-358 1 March 1766 Power of Attorney from Alexander Baine, merchant, to David Ross of Goochland County, Baine, finding it convenient to remove to Great Britain or elsewhere beyond the sea, empowers Ross to make good his engagements to the first and lawful creditors the sums of money due them; cites 17,368 pounds due to Mr. James Dunlop and to Misters Alexander Spain, Andrew Blackburn and Andrew Syme of the City of Glasgow, merchants, assignees, upon trust of the said James Dunlop, for which said Baine hereby acknowledges to have received a full receipt and discharge from said Dunlop and John Cumming, Misters Spain, Blackburn and Syme, said assignees, but first reserving 700 pounds thereof for use of the said Baine and for the salary of the said David Ross for executing the power of attorney with understanding to collect said Baine's debts and to dispose of his affects, hereinafter mentioned as parcels of land to sell and dispose of at any time and manner as he thinks proper: 1) 1,530 acres in Bedford County near the Peaks of Otter, which Baine purchased of Tucker Woodson by deed recorded in the General Court; 2) 125 acres in Louisa County purchased from David Cosby; 3) another tract in Louisa County purchased from Edward Webb; 4) 200 acres in Goochland County on both sides of Beaverdam Creek purchased from Capt. John Cannon by deed not yet recorded; 5) 220 acres in Goochland County on Beaverdam Creek whereon Goochland Court House now stands, 50 acres of which was purchased of Jeremiah Read and the remaining 170 acres purchased in company with David Ross from David, Mary and Nancy Clarkson; 6) 667 acres in Hanover County on Chickahominy River purchased from William Massie under an agreement with said Massie in his handwriting herewith delivered for conveying to said Baine a good and sufficient deed; 7) four lots of ground in the Town of Richmond purchased from George Donald by deed recorded in the General Court; and also granting authority to said David Ross to foreclose on the collateral granted in various mortgages:
1) sundry slaves and other affects conveyed by Phillip Kenson by deed of mortgage recorded in the General Court to which said Kenson would be entitled at the death of his grandmother-in-law; 2) one Negro woman named Nan conveyed by Mary Clarkson by instrument herewith delivered; 3) a tract in Goochland County and sundry other affects conveyed by Will Harris; 4) one Negro boy conveyed by John

Hill by instrument herewith delivered, said boy still in Hill's possession; 5) a tract in Bedford County conveyed by instrument herewith delivered; 6) two tracts in Louisa County on the northside of the South Anna River conveyed by Thomas East; 7) a tract in Goochland County and sundry slaves (debtor not indicated); 8) a tract in Goochland County and sundry other affects conveyed by Benjamin Sadler of that county; 9) sundry goods and chattels conveyed by James Dickinson by instrument herewith delivered; 10) a tract in Goochland County conveyed by John Clarkson to secure debts, which deed was afterwards destroyed by said Clarkson and the title thereon depends on a suit in chancery pending in Goochland County Court; 11) a deed of mortgage from Richard Baldwin and Elizabeth, his wife, for their proportion in a division of the slaves and personal estate of John Clarkson, deceased, to which they are entitled at the death of Mary Clarkson under the last will and testament of said John Clarkson recorded in Goochland County Court; 12) a tract of land on the branches of Lickinghole Creek in Goochland County and sundry slaves conveyed by James George, Sr.; 13) an entry on a tract in Albemarle County later taken up in the name of William Rutherford and to be entered in the Surveyor's Book, and may issue therefrom in the name of said Alexander Baine; 14) a tract in Goochland County conveyed by Thomas Alberto; 15) a deed for sundry slaves (Harry and Cupid, fellows; Viney and Betty, wenches) from Col. Charles Barrett; 16) 1,200 acres of land in Augusta County and five Negro slaves conveyed by Alexander Boyd; 17) sundry goods and chattels conveyed by John Prewit of Goochland County; 18) a Negro girl in possession of Francis Killey and conveyed in bond for her value and security; 19) a tract of land in Goochland County conveyed by Francis Killey; 20) a tract of land at the southwest of Little Mountains in Albemarle County conveyed by Thomas Smith; 21) two other tracts in Albemarle County conveyed from William Hammock; and 22) a tract belonging to Nicholas Mills conveyed by deed of mortgage.
Wit: John McKeand, Charles Clarke, William Donald, John Davies, William Mitchell
Signed: Alex. Baine                                   Recorded 3 March 1772

p.358  2 March 1772 Matthew Bridgman to Richard Hooper, Jr., both of Henrico County, for 15 pounds, 25 acres whereon the said Matthew Bridgman now lives; being all of the land said Bridgman purchased of John Robinson.
Wit: none                           Signed: Matthew (his ll mark) Bridgman
Recorded 3 March 1772

p.360  2 March 1772 William Perkins to George Cox, Gent., both of Henrico County, for 450 pounds, 100 acres adj. Elizabeth Perkins and said George Cox.
Wit: Miles Selden, Abraham Cowley, Thomas Pleasants, Jr.
Signed: William Perkins                               Recorded 2 March 1772

p.362  31 October 1771 Jesse Burton and James Vaughan to Lisbit Turpin, all of Henrico County, for 73 pounds and 9 shillings, 130 acres, being all of the remaining part of the land given to the said Jesse Burton by his father Benjamin Burton, deceased; adj. William Randolph, deceased, John Burton and Christopher Branch.
Wit: Miles Taylor, Joseph Redford, Joseph Goode
Signed: Jesse Burton, Jas. Vaughan
Recorded 2 March 1772

p.365  9 March 1772 John Price and Mary, his wife, to Majer Hallaway, all of Henrico County, for 30 pounds, 100 acres on the Brook; adj. Bremillon Hallaway, William Tyree, Samuel Jones, Ralph Humphry and Mathew Hutcheson.
Wit: Samuel Price, Dick Holland
Signed: John Price, Mary (her  M  mark) Price
Recorded April Court 1772

p.366  9 March 772 Richard Randolph to Edward Wade, both of Henrico County, for 40 pounds, 300 acres on the waters of White Oak Swamp; adj. Julius Allen and Thomas Goode.
Wit: none                                    Signed: Richard Randolph
Recorded April Court 1772

p.368  [21 April] 1772 The Reverend Miles Selden to David White, both of Henrico County, for 76 pounds and 10 shillings, 108 acres on Reedy Branch; being part of the land said Selden purchased of Abraham Cowley; adj. Daniel Price and Spraggins (formerly) (metes and bounds description).
Wit: Mary Selden, James Hardman
Signed: Miles Selden                          Date of record not given

p.370  Isaac Echo and Lucy, his wife, to William Faris, son of John, all of Henrico County, for 38 pounds, 33 acres, bounded on the north by Robert Faris, on the east by Ben Jordan and Frederick Clarke, on the south by said Jordan and Robert Faris and on the west by said Robert Faris; being the land purchased by Isaac Echo from George Clarke.
Wit: Thomas Pleasants, Junr., John Dollard, Thomas (his  V  mark) Childress, Jr., Federick (his  I  mark) Clarke, Tarleton Woodson, Junr., Nathaniel Whitlock, Samuel Parsons.
Signed: Isaac (his  ✚  mark) Echo, Lucy (her  ✚  mark) Echo
Date of record not given

p.372  29 November 1771 David Alley to Samuel Alley, both of Henrico County, for 19 pounds, 85 acres on the north side of the main county road; adj. Samuel

Duvall, John Gleen, David Allen and William Alley.
Wit: Thomas (his A mark) Alley, Richard Cottrel, Jacob Cottrel
Signed: David Alley                                             Date of record not given

p.373  21 April 1772 Pouncey Anderson and Henry Martin, executors of Mitchell Holland, deceased, to Joseph Shepherd of Henrico County, for 36 pounds, 360 acres adj. Thomas Conaway; being part of a greater tract of land and by the last will and testament of Mitchell Holland, deceased, to be sold by his executors. (metes and bounds description)
Wit: Benjamin Shepherd, William Morris, William (his ✚ mark) Morris, Jr.
Signed: Pouncey Anderson, Henry Martin
Date of record not given

p.375  4 May 1772 John Wood of Henrico County to William DuVal, attorney of law, for 100 pounds, 100 acres, being the same tract said John Wood received and enjoyed by deed of gift from his father, Thomas Wood, deceased; situated at a little branch that empties into Shockoes Creek near Ege's meadow and adj. Samuel DuVal.
Wit: Giles Carter, Thomas Wood, Samuel DuVal, Jr.
Signed: John (his ✚ mark) Wood                                 Date of record not given

p.379  18 July 1772 Deed of Mortgage from Robert Cooke to Geo. Kippen & Co., merchants of Glasgow, for the payment of 106 pounds, 8 shillings and 3 pence with lawful interest from 17 July 1772; collateral being one Negro man slave named Essex, one Negro girl named Nell, lately purchased of Mr. Minzies, and 12 head of cattle, and their future increase.
Wit: George Sexton, William Mitchell, Neil Campbell
Signed: Robert (his R mark) Cooke                               Date of record not given

p.380  2 April 1772 John Kelly to Jonathan Bridgwater, both of Henrico County, for 25 pounds, 100 acres on Parker's Horse Pen Branch; adj. William Kelly, George Kelly, Benjamin Clarke, said John Kelly and James Price.
Wit: Daniel Gorden, Anguish (his ✚ mark) McDowall, Joseph Clarke
Signed: John Kelly, Agness Kelly                                Date of record not given

p.381  3 August 1772 James Browning and Anne, his wife, to William Miller, all of Henrico County, for 50 pounds, 100 acres on Upham Brook; adj. Charles Smth, William Miller, Augustine Smith and James Browning.
Wit: Jonathan Bridgwater, William Kelley, William Bridgwater,
Daniel Kelley                        Signed: James (his ✚ mark) Browning
[no signature or release of dower from wife indicated]

Date of record not given

p.382  2 May 1772 James Currie to William Miller, both of the Town of Richmond, Henrico County, to William Kennedy, for 70 pounds, lots in the Town of Richmond marked A R on the plan of the said town; being the lots James Currie purchased of Alexander Bain.
Wit: Joseph Pleasants, James McDowall, George Donald
Signed: James Currie                                                  Date of record not given

p.384  6 July 1772 Deed of Gift from John New to his son, William New, for natural love and affection, 350 acres with a water grist mill thereon and the profits thereof, being all of the tract I purchased and exchanged with Benajamin Harrison, Esq., and six Negro slaves: Cuffie, Sheeba, Bob, Philis, Hannah and Lucy and their increased.
Wit: Turner Southall                                                  Signed: John New
Recorded July Court 1772

p.385  1 June 1772 James McDowell, merchant, to Mrs. Judith Young, both of Henrico County, for 200 pounds, 4 and 6/16ths acres, being a parcel of land whereon she now lives, situated at Shockoe and being part of a certain tenement purchased by McDowell of William Byrd, Esq., by the name of McDowell's Tenement, by deed recorded in the General Court; adj. Thomas Turner, James McDowell and Shockoe Creek (metes and bounds description).
Wit: none                                                          Signed: James McDowell
Recorded June Court 1772

p.386  28 December 1772 Robert Bolling, Jr., of Chellow in Buckingham County, to Mrs. Martha Miller for life, and then to Anne Miller, daughter of the said Martha Miller, for 50 pounds, the use of a Negro girl called Patience who has lived for some time past with the said Martha Miller.
Wit: Thomas Prosser, Henry Whites, David Miller
Signed: [Robert] Bolling Junior                                    Date of recorded not given

p.387  6 July 1772 Judy Bryan to her two children, Archer and Nancy, for natural love and affection, Moll, Sue and Sarah and their future increase, equally to be divided between them, but reserving the wench Moll to the said Judy Bryan for life.
Wit: none                                                Signed: Judy (her ✚ mark) Bryan
Recorded July Court 1772

p.387  30 December 1771 John Robinson of Orange County, North Carolina, son of Thomas Robinson of the same province, to Thomas Stone of Henrico County,

for 5 pounds, 65 acres adj. Thomas Stone, Colder and Joseph Binns, on a branch and a creek.
Wit: David White, William Stone, Richard (his R mark) Williams
Signed: John Robinson                                    Date of record not given

p.388  3 January 1772 David Alley and Elizabeth, his wife, to John Glen, all of Henrico County, for 6 pounds and 10 shillings, 25 acres on the north side of the main county road; adj. John Glen and William Alley.
Wit: William Alley, John (his ✚ mark) Miller, Sr., Joseph (his W mark) Lankester
Signed: David Alley, Elizabeth Alley                     Date of record not given

p.390  3 June 1772 Edward Whitlow to Thomas Jordan, both of Henrico County, for 50 pounds, 104 acres on Cornelius Creek; adj. William Whitlow, John Enroughty, James Whitlow, Jr., and John Whitlow.
Wit: Thomas Bates, John (his X mark) Parker
Signed: Edward Whitlow                                   Date of record not given

p.391  5 May 1772 Power of Attorney from James Currie to my trusty and loving friend, James McDowell, both of the Town of Richmond, Henrico County, to contract for and to dispose of any part of my estate within the Colony of Virginia.
Wit: none                                          Signed: James Currie
Recorded May Court 1772

p.393  4 May 1772 Deed of Mortgage from Robert West to Daniel L. Hilton, both of Henrico County, for 70 pounds, 100 acres in Chesterfield County, adj. Robert Cary; being the same line which John Branch nows lives on, and one Negro man slave named Joe; after 25 December 1773 to be sold for the best price if in default.
Wit: David Ross, James Webster, Tarleton Woodson, Junr.
Signed: Robert West                                      Date of record not given

p.394  4 May 1772 John Norvell and Mary, his wife, to Henry White, all of Henrico County, for 65 pounds, 203 acres adj. Thomas Bowler, William Morris and Benjamin and Joseph Shepherd.
Wit: none              Signed: John Norvell, Mary (his ✚ mark) Norvell
Date of record not given

p.400  5 October 1772 Gideon Freeman and Sarah, his wife, of Amelia County, to James Eubank of Henrico County, for 55 pounds, 100 acres on Rocky Branch, delivered to the said Freeman and wife by the last will and testament of William Patman, deceased; adj. William Brittan, John Grinstead and Thomas Thorp (metes

and bounds description).
Wit: Pierce Griffing, Jonathan Bridgwater
Signed: Gidian Freeman, Sarah (her ✚ mark) Freeman
Date of record not given

pp.401-405  24 September 1772 Deed of Settlement Margaret Wilkinson, widow of Thomas Wilkinson, deceased, of Henrico County, and William Clark, inspector, of Hanover County, to Nathaniel Wilkinson, Gent., of Henrico County, for 5 shillings, all of the said Margaret's undivided moiety of a proportion of the slaves and personal property in her husband's estate, subject to the conditions of his last will and testament dated 31 March 1769; cites that said Thomas Wilkinson departed this life March last, without issue, possessed of about 40 slaves and a valuable personal estate which has not been divided between his said widow and brothers and sisters according to the said will; cites impending marriage between Margaret Wilkinson and William Clark, and if it takes effect, Clark is to receive only the rents and profits; estate is to be equally divided among her children, if any should be born from this impending marriage, when she and Clark are deceased, and if Margaret should die without children, the said estate shall remain in the care of Andrew Balfour and James Balfour, brothers of the said Margaret Wilkinson, and be equally divided between them, but the moiety that goes to Andrew Balfour shall remain with him for life and then go to his living children at his death, but if he should die without issue, to go to the said James Balfour and his heirs.
Wit: Thomas Prosser, Geddes Winston, Peter Winston, Bartlet Davis
Signed: Maraget Wilkinson, Wm. Clark
Recorded October Court 1772

p.406  21 October 1772 Deed of Mortgage from Thomas Pimble, ferryman in Henrico County, to John Leitch, merchant in Warwick, Virginia, for the payment of 100 pounds, 1 shilling and 11 pence with lawful interest from 10 September 1772, to be paid by 1 January 1773 or collateral to be sold for the best price after giving 10 days publick notice; collateral being 200 acres on Deep Run, adj. John Pimble, Samuel DuVal and Richard Cottrell.
Wit: Robert Boyd, David Leitch, Alexander Baine, James Parrlie

Signed: Thomas Pimble                    Recorded November Court 1772

p.407  30 October 1772 John Wales, Gent., of Charles City County, Giles Harding of Goochland County and Sarah Harding, mother of the said Giles Harding and widow of William Harding, deceased, to Joseph Ellis of Henrico County, for 150 pounds, 200 acres on Peter's Branch and Harding's Branch, branches of Tuckahoe Creek; adj. Joseph Ellis' own land whereon he now lives, Jacob Smith, Jr., Thomas

Fenton and John Jude (metes and bounds description).
Wit: Jacob Smith, Stephen Ellis, Mager Holloway
Signed: Giles Harding, Sarah Harding
(No signature or acknowledgment for John Wales)
Recorded 2 November 1772

p.409  2 October 1772 Thomas Robinson and George Robinson, both of Henrico County, to St. George Robinson, for 17 pounds and 10 shillings, 25 acres on Clay Branch; adj. Samuel Gathright.
Wit: Jonathan Williams, Moses Woodfin
Signed: Thomas Robinson
[No signature or acknowledgment for George Robinson]
Date of record not given

p.410  4 April 1772 John Sutton Farrar and Susanna, his wife, to James Allen, for 20 pounds, their interest in one Negro wench named Lucy and her increase, who was to be sold pursuant to the will of William Patman at the death of his wife and equally divided among his five children: Agness Tharp, wife of Thomas Tharp; Elizabeth Morris, wife of William Morris; Sarah Freeman, wife of Gideon Freeman; Mary Allen Patman and Susanna Patman, who has since the death of her father married John Sutton Farrar.
Wit: William Allen Burton, Matthew Hopson, James (his ✚ mark) Drake
Signed: John Sutton Farrar, Susanna (her ✚ mark) Farrar
Date of record not given
[Note: This deed recorded on page 410 seems to show unequivocally that John Sutton Farrar's wife, Susanna was definitely a Patman. The deed recorded on page 293 at first glance would ordinarily be interpreted to suggest that Susanna was a Williamson. Yet that deed also makes reference to William Patman. Susanna is identified only as a residuary legatee under the will of John Williamson. I would conclude that Elizabeth Miller, Mary Bacon and Judah (Judith) Lankaster were definitely Williamsons, but the deed on page 410 would discount Susanna as being one. It is interesting that her sisters are not mentioned on page 293. GMW]

p.411  3 September 1772 John Whitlow and Elizabeth, his wife, to Richard Thurman, all of Henrico County, for 60 pounds, 100 acres on Cornelius Creek; adj. Matthew Herbert, James Whitlow, Richard Bennett, James Whitlow, Jr. and Thomas Jurdan.
Wit: John Roper, Dudley (his M mark) Wade, James Whitlow
Signed: John Whitlow, Elizabeth (her ✚ mark) Whitlow
Recorded 3 November 1772

p.413  12 September 1770 Deed of Mortgage from Thomas Booth of Henrico County to Patrick Coutts of the Town of Richmond, for the payment of 416 pounds, 1 shilling and 3 pence to be paid by 22 September 1773 or collateral to be sold for the best price after giving 10 days publick notice; collateral being 100 acres which said Thomas Booth bought in the Hon. William Byrd's Lottery and by a deed recorded in the General Court, and also 9 Negroes–Bob, Joe, Will, Daniel, Aley, Evy, Aley (mulatto), Thom and Isaac, and reversion in 5 Negroes, names at present unknown, with all their increase, which were left to the said Thomas Booth under the will of his father and which his mother now holds in her possession for life, also two horses and wagons and other personal property..
Wit: Richard Adams, James Wall, John Miller
Signed: Thomas Booth        Recorded November Court 1772
Notation: Original deed is filed among the papers in a suit, Coutts' Exors. v. Booth, Dec'd., March Court 1795.

p.416  23 October 1772 Deed of Mortgage from Joseph Brown to George Kippen & Co., merchants of Glasgow, for the payment of 55 pounds, 6 shillings and 10 pence with lawful interest thereof from 25 October 1772, collateral being 150 acres whereon the said Joseph Brown now lives; adj. John Blackburn, Thomas Mann Randolph and Richard Cottrell; which tract was purchased by said Joseph Brown of David Staples, and also 8 head of cattle.
Wit: Francis Bailie, Gilliam Cuthbert, Ben Pollard, Neill Campbell
Signed: Thomas Brown        Recorded November Court 1772

p.418  23 March 1772 Benjamin Walrond to Robert Mitchell, both of Henrico County, for 35 pounds, 90 acres lying near the main road that leads from Westham to Deep Run Church; adj. Robert Carter Nicholas, Esq., Jesse Smith, Julius Burton and Giles Gorden; being the same tract purchased by Benjamin Walrond of Hutchens Burton.
Wit: William Brett, Parks Smith, John Jones
Signed: Benjamin Walrond        Date of record not given

p.420  6 October 1772 Deed of Mortgage from John Parks, Sr., of Surry County, North Carolina, to George Kippen & Co., merchants of Glasgow, for the payment of 87 pounds, 5 shillings and 7 pence with lawful interest thereon to be paid by 1 April 1773 or collateral to be sold for the best price after giving 10 days public notice; collateral being two Negro slaves, James, a fellow and Lucy, a wench, and her future increase.
Wit: Benjamin Pollard, Robert Brown, James Lyle, Neill Campbell
Signed: John Parks, Senr.        Recorded 3 November 1772

p.422  7 December 1772 William Tyree to Dabney Pettus, both of Henrico County, for 50 pounds, 226 acres on the branches of Upfram Brook; adj. Robert Bolling, Bermelion Holloway, Major Holloway, Samuel Jones, Benjamin Jones, Charles Cottrell, John Lacy and Richard Cottrell (which the said Richard purchased of Farrow); said 226 acres being ½ the tract which David Whitlock purchased of William Bacon.
Wit: James Sharp, John Warriner, Ephraim Gathright, Junr.
Signed: William (his W mark) Tyree          Recorded December Court 1772
Notation: Delivered Mr. Pettus this deed, 29 March 1775, John Beckley.

p.423  31 October 1772 Richard Freeman of Henrico County to his son, John Freeman, for love and good will, one Negro boy named Jesse.
Wit: John Warriner, Jr., Ephraim Gathright, Junr., William (his + mark) Bethel
Signed: Richard (his R mark) Freeman
Recorded December Court 1772

p.424  31 October 1772 Richard Freeman of Henrico County to his daughter, Anna Warriner, for love and good will, one Negro girl named Jane.
Wit: John Warriner, Jr., John Truman, Ephraim Gathright, Junr.
Signed: Richard (his R mark) Freeman
Recorded December Court 1772

p.424  31 October 1772 Richard Freeman of Henrico County to his daughter, Rebeckah Bethel, for love and good will, one Negro girl named Rachel.
Wit: John Warriner, Jr., Ephraim Gathright, Junr., John Freeman
Signed: Richard (his R mark) Freeman
Recorded December Court 1772

p.425  31 October 1772 Richard Freeman of Henrico County to his daughter, Agnes Gathright, for love and good will, one Negro boy named Peter.
Wit: John Warriner, Jr., John Trueman, Jr., William (his + mark) Bethel
Signed: Richard (his R mark) Freeman
Recorded December Court 1772

p.426  7 December 1772 John Boles of Hanover County to William Burton of Henrico County, for 19 pounds, 150 acres on a branch called Turner's Run; adj. Gennings Morris (metes and bounds description).
Wit: Nathaniel Clarke, [--?--] Bacon, John Timberlake
Signed: John Boles                              Recorded December Court 1772

p.427  12 May 1772 William Byrd of Westover, Charles City County, Presley

Thornton of Northumberland County, Peyton Randolph of the City of Williamsburg, John Page of Gloucester County, Charles Carter of Lancaster County and Charles Turnbull of Dinwiddie County, Gentlemen, to Thomas Watkins, Jr., of Henrico County, for 11 pounds, three half-acre lots in the Town of Richmond, being numbers 572, 553 and 513 on the plan of said town.
Wit: David Patteson, Richard Martin, John Pankey
Signed: W. Byrd, Peyton Randolph        Recorded December Court, 1772

p.428  7 December 1772 John Parrot Steger and Sarah, his wife, of Cumberland County, to Shilldrake Brown of St. Paul's Parish, Hanover County, for 50 pounds, 85 acres about four or five miles below Richmond Town on both sides of the New Kent Road that leads from Richmond Town; adj. Jacob Valentine, Alexander Robertson, Mayo and Bailey's Branch.
Wit: Gabriel Galt, Samuel Ege, R. Brown, Richard Thurman
Signed: John Parrot Steger     [no signature or relinquishment of dower for wife]
Recorded December Court, 1772.

p.430 [-?-] April 1772 John Amoss to Hugh Moody, both of Henrico County, for 30 pounds, 50 acres adj. Daniel Warren and Humphrey Smith [metes and bounds description]; granted to the said John Amoss by patent dated 15 August 1764.
Wit: George Clopton, William Clopton, Elizabeth (her ✚ mark) Smith
Signed: John (his X mark) Amoss       Recorded December Court, 1772.

p.432  10 April 1772 Deed of Mortgage from Joel Childress to John, Robert and Thomas Pleasants, merchants, all of Henrico County, for the payment of 23 pounds, 1 shilling and 10 pence payable by 10 April 1773, the collateral being one dun colored mare five years old got by a horse of Isaac Sharpe, 6 head of cattle, 11 head of hogs with their respective increase, 2 feather beds and all their furniture, one trunk, one frying pan, etc.
Wit: Richard Sharpe, Milner Redford, Mark Woodcock
Signed: Joel (his  X  mark) Childress
Recorded January Court, 1773

p.434  7 September 1772 John Goode of Chesterfield County to Edward Whitlow of Henrico County, for 28 pounds, 50 acres at the mouth of Deep Run and up the run to the Deep Bottom; adj. said Goode and Four Mile Creek; being 50 acres purchased of Edward Goode.
Wit: John (his ✚ mark) Baker, Edward (his ✚ mark) Clarke
Signed: John Goode                Recorded January Court, 1773

p.435  2 October 1772 Patrick Coutts, Gent., merchant, to Archibald Bryce,

merchant, both of Henrico County, for 60 pounds, two half-acre lots in the Town of Richmond, known on the plan of Col. William Byrd's Lottery by the numbers 354 and 349, and conveyed to the said Patrick Coutts by William Byrd, John Page and Peyton Randolph by deed recorded, General Court dated 6 November 1771.
Wit: none                                                                         Signed: Patrick Coutts
Recorded December Court 1772

p.436 12 May 1772 Hon. William Byrd of Westover, Charles City County, Presley Thornton, Esq., Peyton Randolph, John Page, Charles Carter and Charles Turnbull, Esq., surviving trustees, in execution of the trust in them reposed by a judgment made to them by the said William Byrd, Esq., which was proved and recorded in the General Court, to Samuel Overton of Hanover County, for 700 pounds, 100 acres, being number 741 on the plan of Byrd's Lottery, except 7 ½ acres sold to John Buchanan, with all edifices and buildings, etc.
Wit: David Patteson, Bernard Markham, John Pankey
Signed: W. Byrd, Peyton Randolph                Recorded June Court 1772

p.437 28 September 1772 Deed of Mortgage from Giles Carter of Henrico County to Drury Wood, for the payment of 77 pounds with interest thereon before first day of November next, one Negro boy named Aaron and horses and wagon with gear.
Wit: James Whitlock, John Wood
Signed: Giles Carter                                    Recorded April Court 1773

p.439 9 October 1771 Deposition in response to a dedimus directed by Thomas Adams, Clerk, to Richard Randolph and John Hales, Gent., to examine Elizabeth, wife of James Powal Cocke, for the release of her dower in a deed to Ryland Randolph dated 5 August 1771.
Wit: none                                       Signed: Richard Randolph, John Hales
Date of recordation not given

p.440 6 April 1773 Richard Hogg and Mary Lindsey, wife of Campbell Lindsey, to Turner Southall and Abraham Cowley, for 180 pounds, in trust for the said Mary Lindsey and her heirs, to be free of contrasuit of her husband, lots in the Town of Richmond numbered 7 and 21 and all the buildings thereon, which the said Richard Hogg purchased of George Donald by deed dated 3 September 1771.
Wit: none
Signed: Richard Hogg, Mary (her ✚ mark) Lindsey, Turner Southall, Abraham Cowley                                    Recorded April Court 1773

p.442 5 April 1773 Alexander Patterson and Secily, his wife, of Henrico County, to Miles Gathright of St. Peter's Parish, New Kent County, for 100 pounds, 86 acres

on Stoney Run; adj. Royall Richard Allen (metes and bounds description).
Wit: Thomas Martin, Junr., William Gathright, Joseph Gathright
Signed: Alexander (his ℔ mark) Patterson, Sicily (her ✚ mark) Patterson
Recorded April Court 1773

p.444  5 April 1773 Deed of Gift from John Carter of Henrico County to his grandchildren John Carter Walton, Mary Walton and Elizabeth Walton, children of his daughter Frances Walton of Charlotte County, for love and affection, to grandson John Carter Walton a Negro girl Jane and her increase; to granddaughter Mary Walton a Negro girl Judith and her increase; and to granddaughter Elizabeth Walton a Negro girl Lucretia and her increase.
Wit: none                                                      Signed: John Carter
Recorded April Court 1773

p.445 24 September 1772 Maraget Wilkinson, widow, with the consent of William Clark, with whom she is to intermarry, to Nathaniel Wilkinson, both of Henrico County, for 5 shillings and for such sum of money as Thomas Prosser, Nathaniel Wilkinson and Martin Burton or any two of them shall fix and ascertain on or before 25 January next ensuing as to the value of Maraget Wilkinson's dower in 447 acres, being the whole tract whereon Thomas Wilkinson died seized and possessed, farms and lets to the said Nathaniel Wilkinson her 1/3 interest in said tract, with houses and appurtenances.
Wit: Thomas Prosser, Geddes Winston, Peter Winston, Bartlet Davis
Signed: Maraget Wilkinson, Wm. Clark
Date of record not given

p.446 15 March 1773 John Pemble to William Miller, both of Henrico County, for 50 pounds, 100 acres on the Main Road; adj. Samuel DuVall, John Price and William Alley.
Wit: Christopher John Thomas, John Lankester, John Miller, Mary Thomas
Signed: John B. Pemble                         Recorded April Court 1773

p.447 26 June 1772 Deed of Mortgage from Daniel Allen to Messrs. Prosser and Trent, merchants and partners, all of Henrico County, to secure payment of 42 pounds, 7 shillings and 4 pence now due, collateral being 100 acres on Northen Swamp; adj. John Mosley, Drury Allen, Samuel Duvall, Gent., and James Royall; being the land whereon the said Daniel Allen now lives.
Wit: John P. Sutton, Jr., John Lipscomb, Matthew Hobson
Signed: Daniel Allen                         Recorded February Court 1773

p.449 23 March 1773 Thomas Stegar and Hans Stegar, executors of the last will

and testament of Francis George Stegar, deceased, to Alexander Baine, merchant, for 225 pounds, two acres or four lots in the Town of Richmond on the southwest side of the main street opposite the lots late in occupation of Dr. William Wills, deceased; being lots 1, 2, 15 and 16 on the plan of the said town, which Samuel Gicheffele, late of the Town of Richmond, died seized and possessed, and which on his death escheated to our late sovereign, George II, and was granted to the said Francis Stegar by patent dated 13 June 1755, Williamsburg, and who, by his last will and testament dated 14 January 1769 and recorded in the County Court of Cumberland, directed his executors (his son, John Parrot Stegar, refused to qualify as co-executor) to sell said lots and pay his debts.
Wit: George Muter, William Dandridge, George Carrington, Jr., William Fleming             Signed: Thomas Stegar, Hans Stegar
Recorded June Court 1773

p.450  20 June 1771 Joseph Perrin to Peter Elmore, both of St. Paul's Parish, Hanover County, for 50 pounds, 200 acres on Northern Creek, being the tract of land formerly belonging to John Bow and by him conveyed to Henry Perrin and by the said Perrin to his son Joseph; adj. John Mosely and William Patman.
Wit: William Q. Owen, Junr., John Timberlake, Lya Britton, Gideon Ragland
Signed: Jos. Perrin             Recorded February Court 1773

p.451  9 May 1772 John Woodson, Jr., of Cumberland County to Samuel Richardson of Prince Edward County, for 218 pounds and 15 shillings, 175 acres near Four Mile Creek; adj. Robert Pleasants (metes and bounds description).
Wit: Joseph Goode, Robert Sharp
Signed: John Woodson, Junior             Recorded April Court 1773

p.454  12 May 1772 William Byrd of Westover, Charles City County, Presley Thornton of Northumberland County, Peyton Randolph of the City of Williamsburg, John Page of Gloucester County, Charles Carter of Lancaster County, Esqs. and Charles Turnbull of Dinwiddie County, Gent., to Joseph Watkins of Goochland County, for 65 pounds, fourteen half-acre lots in the Town of Richmond, as laid down in a plan produced at the drawing of the lottery called Byrd's Lottery, distinguished as lots numbered 626, 627, 628, 629, 630, 589, 587, 567, 568, 549, 550, 551, 446 and 415; said plan remaining of record in the County Court of Henrico.
Wit: David Patteson, Bernard Markham
Signed: W. Byrd, Peyton Randolph             Recorded December Court 1772

p.455  1 September 1772 Deed of Mortgage from Peter Strachan of Henrico County to John Johnson of Hanover County and Archibald Gowan of King William

County, attorneys-in-fact for Andrew Cochran, Robert Donald & Co., for John Murdock & Co. and for John McDowall, merchants in Glasgow; cites that Strachan owes 115 pounds, 13 shillings and 3 pence to Cochran, et als, and 526 pounds to McDowall, for a total indebtedness of 723 pounds, 10 shillings and 3 pence to be paid by 1 April 1773; collateral being nine slaves: Lucy, Venus and her child Lucy, Gilly, George, Hannah, Pompey, Neptune and Dennis; as many as necessary to be sold at publick auction to settle accounts after 1 April 1773.
Wit: George Muter, William Barrett
Signed: Peter Strachan                    Recorded April Court 1773

p.457  12 December 1772 Richard Chamberlane and Mary, his wife, and Richard Crump and Susanna, his wife, of New Kent County, to Nathaniel Wilkinson of Henrico County, for 92 pounds and 5 shillings, 82 acres, being their proportion of the tract of land whereon Thomas Wilkinson lived, which he purchased of Isaac Winston, containing 287 acres.                    Wit: Tur. W. Hudson,
Epaproditus (his a mark) Howl, Daniel Crump, William Hudson
Signed: Richd. Chamberlayne, Mary Chamberlayne, Richard Crump,
Susanna Crump                    Recorded April Court 1773

p.458  27 February 1773 Release from James Buchanan and Neil Campbell to George Donald, all of Henrico County, for all the money for which we stood as security for the said George Donald on his leaving the colony in 1770 and also for every transaction which gave rise to a conveyance or mortgage which said Donald made dated 12 November 1770; releases six Negro slaves: Isaac, Aberdeen, Frank, Cloe, Kemp and Venus; and 250 acres on Gilley's Creek, houses and lots in Richmond Town, stocks of cattle, hogs and sheep, household furnishings, bonds, notes, book debts and all other items included in said conveyance.
Wit: George Muter, Benjamin Pollard, George Seaton, David Cation
Signed: James Buchanan, Neil Campbell
Recorded 5 April 1773

p.458  1 February 1773 Deed of Mortgage from William Kennedy to George Donald, both of Henrico County, for the payment of 176 pounds, 1 shilling, 9 pence and one farthing, with interest, to be paid by ye first November next ensuing, collateral being a lot in the Town of Richmond described by letters A and B on the plan of the said town; being part of the said parcel of land which Kennedy now occupies and has lately built on, which includes all the land hereby described except the west end of the said lot lately sold to Robert Mitchell; to be sold by publick auction if in default, given said Kennedy ten days notice of such sale.
Wit: Thomas Hogg, George Muter, James Vaughan
Signed: William Kennedy                    Recorded April Court 1773

p.460  11 February 1773 Daniel Price of Henrico County to his son, Charles Price, for true love and natural effection, 400 acres which was conveyed to the said Daniel Price by deed from William Byrd, Esq., dated 2 May 1771.
Wit: none                                          Signed: Daniel Price
Recorded April Court 1773

p.461  19 February 1773 John Clarkson and Susanna, his wife, to George Donald, all of Henrico County, for 100 pounds, 50 acres whereon the said Clarkson now lives.
Wit :   John Woodson, James Vaughan, Moses Bridgewater,Benjamin Pollard
Signed: John (his ✚ mark) Clarkson, Susanna (her ✚ mark) Clarkson
Recorded April Court 1773

p.462  5 April 1773 John Jude and Mary, his wife, to William Gathright, all of Cumberland County, for 250 pounds, 300 acres on the east side of the eastern branch of Tuckahoe Creek; adj. Thomas East, "the old road on Clark's line," the County Line, Jude, Jacob Smith, Joseph Ellis and Old Mill Branch; which land said John Jude bought of William Harding and Thomas Hughes.
Wit: John Harris, James Austin, Joseph Gathright
Signed: John Jude, Mary Jude                       Recorded April Court 1773

p.463  28 July 1772 John Dalton to Julius Allen, Sr., both of Henrico County, for 25 pounds, 50 acres adj. said Allen, Matthew Johnson, Charles Allen, Isham Allen and Elizabeth Dalton; being part of the land said Elizabeth Dalton purchased of said Allen and which she gave to her said son, John Dalton.
Wit: George Adams, Elizabeth Lewis, Ann Watson
Signed: John Dalton                              Recorded February Court 1773

p.465  1 April 1773 Benjamin Jordan, Sr., and Lydia, his wife, to William Gathright, son of Ephraim Gathright, all of Henrico County, for 15 pounds and 20 shillings, 16 acres on the north side of White Oak Swamp; adj. the Little Branch, Robert Farris, Fedrick Clark and Duck's Branch.
Wit: Anselm Gathright, William Moore, Robert Jordan
Signed: Benjamin Jordan, Lydia Jordan
Recorded April Court 1773

p.466  3 April 1773 Ninian Menzies to Robert Baine, both merchants of the Town of Richmond, Henrico County, for 88 pounds, 7 shillings and 3 pence, the interest of Menzies in a certain parcel in the Town of Richmond purchased by them in an indenture dated 5 November 1770 of record in the General Court from the Hon. William Byrd and others, surviving trustees, distinguished in Byrd's Lottery by the

name of Storres and Ellis' tenement, numbered in the plan as lot number 329.
Wit: none                                           Signed: Ninian Menzies
Recorded April Court 1773

p.468   30 October 1772 Joseph Binns and Obedience, his wife, to Isham Allen, all of Henrico County, for 85 pounds, 126 acres on Gilley's Creek; adj. the Reverend Miles Selden, William Nance, Thomas Elmore, Christopher Binns and Thomas Stone.
Wit: Daniel Harwood, Joseph Price, Lesha Harwood
Signed: Joseph (his  X  mark) Binns, Obedience Binns
Recorded May Court 1773

p.469   2 May 1773   Joseph Watkins of Goochland County to Drury Wood of Henrico County, for 15 pounds, 2 ½ acres of land in the Town of Richmond and laid down and expressed in a plan produced at the drawing of Byrd's Lottery by numbers 630 and 415.
Wit: none                                           Signed: Joseph Watkins
Recorded May Court 1773

p.470   5 April 1773 John Oakley to John Clarkson, both of Henrico County, for 39 pounds and 10 shillings, 50 acres adj. James Valentine, William Bowles, deceased and Nance; being the land purchased by said Oakley of said Bowles.
Wit: Samuel Price, William Stone, James Price
Signed: Jno. (his  ✚  mark) Oakley, Martha (her  X  mark) Oakley
Martha, wife of John Oakley, relinquished her dower.
Recorded May Court 1773

p. 470   5 April 1773 John Oakley to John Clarkson, both of Henrico County, for 39 pounds and 10 shillings, 50 acres adj. James Valentine, William Bowles, deceased and Nance; being the land purchased by said Oakley of said Bowles.
Wit: Samuel Price, William Stone, James Price
Signed: Jno. (his  ✚  mark) Oakley, Martha (her  X  mark) Oakley
Martha, wife of John Oakley, relinquished her dower.
Recorded May Court 1773

p.471   11 January 1773 David Binns and Mildred, his wife, to William Stone, all of Henrico County, for 19 pounds, 10 shillings and 5 pence, 25 ½ acres adj. said Stone and Binns (metes and bounds description).
Wit: George Adams, Jesse Crump, Samuel (his  X  mark) Robinson
Signed: David Binns, Martha(her  X  mark)Binns
Recorded June Court 1773

p.473   31 May 1773 Roger Cock Bailey to Thomas Williams, both of Henrico County, for 7 pounds and 10 shillings, 12 acres on Cornelius Creek; adj. a small tract once owned by Luzby Turpin, said Roger Cock Bailey and Nicholas Giles, Junr.   Wit: John Pemble, Thomas Pemble, John Redford
Signed: Roger Cock Bailey   Recorded 7 June 1773

p.474   24 May 1773 John Parrot Steger to Hans Steger, both of Cumberland County, for 10 pounds, an island in the James River with sands and banks thereunto belonging, being 12 acres opposite Cole's Warehouses; against Richmond Alexander Brown's land and the division between Burton's and Marrin's land (metes and bounds description); granted to Francis George Steger by patent dated 13 June 1755.
Wit: John Pankey, William Richardson, John Murrer
Signed: John Steger   Recorded 7 June 1773

p.475   19 February 1773 Moses Bridgewater and Elenora, his wife, to George Donald, all of Henrico County, for 100 pounds, 66 acres adj. John New, Thomas Calder, Francis Frankling and the said George Donald.
Wit: Benjamin Pollard, John Woodson, James Vaughan
Signed: Moses Bridgewater, Elenora (her ✚ mark) Bridgewater
Recorded 7 June 1773

p.476   1 February 1773 Thomas Calder to William Stone, both of Henrico County, for 107 pounds, 100 acres, being that tract said Thomas Calder purchased of Alexander Robinson, Jr., by deed dated 21 November 1768.
Wit: William Burton, Christopher Binns, Thomas Stone
Signed: Thos. Calder   Recorded June Court 1773

p.478   27 January 1773 William Mitchell, late of Londonderry, Ireland, to his son, Robert Mitchell, both of the Town of Richmond, for 130 pounds, two Negro man slaves: Jack, a wagonner, and Patrick, a blacksmith, who were devised to me by my son, Samuel Mitchell, deceased, late of the Town of Richmond, Henrico County, as shown by his will duly probated in said county.
Wit: James Vaughan, Miles Taylor, George Scherer, John Peterson
Signed: Wm. Mitchell   Recorded: July Court 1773

p.479   26 January 1773 William Kennedy to Robert Mitchell, both of the Town of Richmond, for 50 pounds, a certain tenement on the south side of the Main Street in the Town of Richmond; being the lower or west part of two lots distinguished on the plan of the said town as A and B and divided by a line in the front of the two lots equal distance from each corner and running to the back of the lots parallel with

the Cross Street on the east side of the said lots.
Wit: James Patterson, James Vaughan, Miles Taylor
Signed: William Kennedy                    Recorded July Court 1773

p.480  25 September 1772 Robert Pleasants of Curles to Richard Sharpe, both of Henrico County, for 21 pounds and 10 shillings, 21 ½ acres on or near the branches of Four Mile Creek; adj. Richard Sharpe, Joseph Pleasants, Richard Frogmorton and George Williamson; being the same land Edward White died seized of and for want of heirs became escheat and was granted to the said Robert Pleasants by patent dated 20 June last past.
Wit: William Frayser, John Eldridge, Robert Pleasants, Jr.
Signed: Robert Pleasants                   Recorded July Court 1773

p.482  6 July 1773 Cox Whitlow of Chesterfield County to Loudwick Worrock of Henrico County, for 100 pounds, 200 acres adj. Philip Mayo, deceased, Mathew Hubbard, James Lindsey and Abraham Bailey.
Wit: Richard Cocke, James Watt
Signed: Cox Whitlow                        Recorded July Court 1773

p.483  9 June 1772 Deed of Mortgage from Thomas Eldridge to Pleasants & Bates, all of Henrico County, for the payment of 88 pounds, 2 shillings and 3 pence with legal interest on or before 1 June 1774; collateral being four Negroes: Jenny, Harry, Jenny and Moll, 21 head of horned cattle, two horses, six feather beds and furniture, and all household furniture.
Wit: George Woodson, F. Woodson
Signed: Thomas Eldridge
Recorded September Court 1773

p.484  8 July 1773 Deed of Mortgage from Hugh Moody to Pleasants & Bates, all of Henrico County, for the payment of 30 pounds, the judgment of court, by 7 January next; collateral being 50 acres purchased of John Amos and on which the said Amos now lives; one grey mare called Phoenix; two feather beds and furniture, one brown cow, one yearling and one calf, one grey sow and nine shoats.
Wit: none                                  Signed: Hugh Moody
Recorded September Court 1773

p.485  6 September 1773 Josiah Pleasants of Charles City County to John Pleasants of Henrico County, for 100 pounds already paid to the mother of the said Josiah Pleasants and 25 pounds also paid her; cites that Joseph Pleasants, deceased, by his last will and testament bearing date 27 October 1758 devised to his son Josiah in fee simple 192 acres near Four Mile Creek near a place called Matthews' Mill, adj.

Edward Matthews, Richard Sharp and others; that Elizabeth Pleasants, widow, entered into an agreement when the said Josiah was a minor with Robert Pleasants, Jr., with her sons, Jesse and Jacob Pleasants being her sureties for the payment of 100 pounds payable in two years after the conveyance of the land and 25 pounds payable three years after the conveyance; that the said Elizabeth, Jesse and Jacob would produce a deed to be made to the said Robert; that the said Elizabeth is now dead and that she received the consideration money, but that the will did also devise to the said Josiah a much more valuable estate in land and Negroes upon his complying with the said agreement upon his arriving at the age of 21; that the said Josiah is now willing to comply with the said agreement, having possessed himself of said land and Negroes; and that said Robert intended the land for John Pleasants, then also a minor, and has requested the said Josiah to make said conveyance to the said John.
Wit: Robert Pleasants, Junr., Edmund Swinney, Edward East
Signed: Josiah Pleasants                    Recorded September Court 1773

p.488  17 May 1773 Samuel Sheppard and Elizabeth, his wife, to Royall Richard Allen, all of Henrico County, for 110 pounds to be paid and wholly satisfied by 25 December next, all of their useful and necessary utensils and furniture with 17 acres on both sides of the Deep Run Tail; adj. Joseph Brown, William Willis, John Blackburn, Royal Richard Allen and Col. Thomas Randolph.
Wit: William DuVal, attorney, Archibald C. Brice, William Burton
Signed: Saml. Shephard, Eliz. Shephard
Recorded September Court 1773

p.489  30 August 1774 Royal Richard Allen and Frances, his wife, to Miles Gathright, all of Henrico County, for 37 pounds and 10 shillings, 100 acres on Stoney Run; adj. land said Gathright bought of Alexander Patterson and the land of Richard Cottrell, John Clark and David Alley.
Wit: David Alley, Isaac Peek, Nathaniel Dennis
Signed: R. Richard Allen, Frances Anne Allen
Recorded 20 August 1773

p.490  2 March 1773 Deed of Mortgage from John Staples to James Buchanan & Co., all of Henrico County, 83 pounds, 11 shillings and 8 pence with lawful interest to be paid by 1 August 1774; collateral being 150 acres on Piney Branch and Hungry Branch; adj. William Jennings, Morris and Griffin; includes all of the plantation whereon the said John Staples now lives, also six head of black cattle and two bay mares with all their increase.
Wit: Nathaniel Wilkinson, James Miller, John McKindley, Alexander Buchanan
Signed: John (his ✚ mark) Staples             Recorded September Court 1773

p.492  2 August 1773 James Woodfin to his son George Woodfin, for true love and natural affection, 140 acres on the Eastern Run; being the plantation whereon I now dwell; adj. Lindsay and John Woodfin; being part of the land I purchased of James Pleasants.
Wit: John James Woodfin, Moses Woodfin, John Robertson, Charles Matthews
Signed: James Woodfin                                  Recorded September Court 1773

p.493  19 March 1773 Richard Hogg and Zach. Rowland of the Town of Richmond, Henrico County, to William Clopton of Hanover County, for 294 pounds and 5 shillings, one-half acre of land in the Town of Richmond known as Lot number 357 on the plan of the said town; whereon they now live and keep store, with all houses, outhouses, gardens, etc.
Wit: George Rowland, Markes Vandewall, George Clopton
Signed: Hogg & Rowland                                 Recorded September Court 1773

p.494  22 February 1773 John Orange to Samuel Parsons, both of Henrico County, for 50 pounds, 160 acres whereon the said John Orange now lives, granted by patent to the said John Orange remaining of record in the Secretary's Office; but reserving a life estate in same to the said John Orange and his wife; adj. Thomas Prosser, John Walton, Samuel Parsons, John Cornit and Francis Cornit.
Wit: Hobson Owen, Nathaniel Clark, William Burton
Signed: John (his ✚ mark) Orange, Judith (her ✚ mark) Orange
Recorded September Court 1773

p. 495 [-?-] 1773 John Sanders of the Town of Richmond, Henrico County, to Fortunatus Sydnor of Henrico County, for 50 pounds, one full lott of blacksmith's tools, the body carriage and wheels of a double riding chair now in the said John Sanders' shop at Capt. Gunn's.
Wit: Zach. Rowland, Markes Vandewall
Signed: John Sanders                                   Recorded October Court 1773

p.495 [-?-] 1773 William Barnes to his son, Anderson Barnes, both of Henrico County, for diverse good causes and valuable considerations, my land whereon I now live at my decease, one feather bed and furniture and other personal property when son arrives at the age of 21.
Wit: John Turpin, Thomas Williams, Robert West
Signed: William (his ✚ mark) Barnes
Recorded October Court 1773

p.496  4 October 1773 Samuel Williamson, surviving executor of John Williamson, Jr., deceased, and Robert Cook and Anne, his wife, to Abraham Cowley, all of

Henrico County, for 251 pounds, 317 acres now belonging to Robert Cook and whereon he now lives; adj. Turner Southall, James Gunn, Thomas Franklin and lands of Drury Brazeal, deceased; being the land conveyed in trust to the late John Williamson, Jr., to secure payment of 149 pounds; Cook defaulted in said payment, and it was ordered by the Henrico County Court that property be sold to satisfy said indebtedness, and the said Cowley being the highest bidder.
Wit: none                                                  Signed: Saml. Williamson
Recorded October Court 1773

p.497  4 October 1773 Charles Allen to Isham Allen, both of Henrico County, for 155 pounds, 110 acres on Matthews' Spring from the Great Branch; adj. Julius Allen, the Main Road that leads from the Seven Pines, and the said Isham Allen (metes and bounds description).
Wit: George Adams, Lister Harwood
Signed: Chas. Allen                              Recorded October Court 1773

p.498  7 December 1772 Francis Eppes, of Chesterfield County, great grandson of Francis Eppes the Elder, to Archd., or Archer Branch, infant son of Christopher Branch, late of the said County, for 2,000 pounds already paid and at the request of John Archer and Henry Branch, both of Chesterfield County, executors of the said Christopher Branch, the tract known as Longfield on the James River, containing 908 acres; which land was purchased of several persons: John Davis, by deeds of lease and release dated 13 September and 1 October 1697; 340 acres part thereof purchased of Henry Wood by indenture dated 7 May 1722; 300 acres other part thereof purchased of John Davis by indenture dated 13 January 1724; 200 acres and the remainder being 68 acres was by the last will and testament of Francis Eppes, deceased, entailed, and on 7 November 1769 at a session of the General Assembly Francis Eppes, the party to this deed, obtained an act for docking the entail of 400 acres, which act has since received the royal assent and said 400 acres has now become vested in the said Francis Eppes in fee simple; cites that said Christopher Branch purchased the whole of the above tract called Longfield for 2,000 pounds and departed this life before any legal conveyance was executed, and by his last will and testament directed said tract to be the proper use of his son, Archer Branch.
Wit: James Robertson, Benjamin Branch, Jno. Fisher, Henry Archer
Signed: Francis Eppes, Jno. Archer, Jr., Henry Branch
Recorded October Court 1773

p.499  7 May 1772 Hon. William Byrd of Westover, Charles City County, Hon. John Page, Peyton Randolph, Charles Carter and Charles Turnbull, Esq., to Thomas Prosser and Alexander and Peter Feild Trent, merchants and partners, of Henrico County, for 60 pounds, a lot in the Town of Richmond adj. the lot whereon the old

publick warehouse stands and bounded by Ninian Menzies tenement and Chambers' lot; containing 25 square poles (metes and bounds description).
Wit: Andrew Chalmer [?], Zach. Rowland, David Patteson, Richard Hogg
Signed: W. Byrd, Peyton Randolph, Chas. Carter
Recorded October Court 1773

p.500 (-?-) 1773 John Parker and Sarah, his wife, to John Thurman, all of Henrico County, for 24 pounds, 55 acres, being part of the land whreon the said John Parker now lives; adj. Darby and Whitlow.
Wit: Wyatt Starke, John Chappel          Signed: John (his  X  mark) Parker
[No signature or relinquishment of dower for Sarah Parker]
Recorded October Court 1773

p.502 4 October 1773 John Dolton and Mary, his wife, to Julius Allen and Mary, his wife, all of Henrico County, for 15 pounds, 50 acres, it being the land given the said John Dolton by his mother, Elizabeth Dolton, which she purchased of Julius Allen.
Wit: John Casants, Nicholas Davis, Jonathan Pleasants
Signed: John Dolton, Mary (her  ✚  mark) Dolton
Recorded October Court 1773

p.502 11 September 1773 Boundary Agreement between John Smith and Jacob Pleasants; cites that their lands are divided by the Cattail Branch, but for the better security of them in their property, they have agreed to make a line of marked trees on the branch as a perpetual boundary between them and their heirs.
Wit: William Burton, John Smith, John Wood, Martin Burton, John Smith Jr.
Signed: John Smith, Jacob Pleasants          Recorded November Court 1773

p.503 24 October 1773 Wade Netherland and Anne, his wife, to Thomas Harwood, all of Henrico County, for 361 pounds, 328 acres on the south side of the Chickahominy Swamp; adj. Capt. Joseph Lewis, Claude Netherland and Caleb Stone; being the tract which devolved to the said Netherland by the last will and testament of Richard Williamson, deceased (metes and bounds description).
Wit: John Price, Samuel Harwood, William Lewis
Signed: Wade Netherland, Ann Netherland
Recorded November Court 1773

p.504 1 November 1773 Josiah Bullington and Sarah, his wife, to Pangran Parrabo Boswell, all of Henrico County, for 50 pounds, 200 acres adj. Peter Bailey and John Allday; being the same tract granted by Abraham Bailey to his son Henry Bailey by deed dated 5 September 1757.

Wit: none  Signed: Josiah Bullington, Sarah Bullington
Recorded November Court 1773

p.505 17 March 1773 Deed of Mortgage from William Clopton of Henrico County to James and Robert Donald & Co., merchants in Glasgow, for the payment of 85 pounds, 17 shillings and 5 pence, with lawful interest from 8 June 1773, collateral being a Negro boy named Dick, which I bought of the Estate of Walter Clopton; terms being that after 17 July 1773, as soon as they shall think proper or upon request of the debtor, which of these two circumstances shall first happen, the said Negro to be sold to the highest bidder for the best price to satisfy said indebtedness.
Wit: Patrick Peluter, Daniel Weisiger, Archibald Maralester, John Murchie, Simon Frayser  Signed: William Clopton
Recorded November Court 1773

p.506 6 December 1773 Drury Allen and Sarah, his wife, to Robert Sharpe, all of Henrico County, for 61 pounds, 100 acres on the Northern Run, between John Mosby, Daniel Allen, Samuel DuVall, Aaron Lucas and Joseph Merrit.
Wit: none  Signed: Drury Allen, Sarah Allen
Recorded December Court 1773

p.507 19 November 1773 Abraham Bailey to Peter Bailey, both of Henrico County, for 100 pounds, 100 acres adj. Joseph Bailey, William Randolph, deceased, and Abraham Bailey, deceased.
Wit: Roger Cocke Bailey, Thomas Williams, Darby Whitlow
Signed: Abraham Bailey  Recorded December Court 1773

p.508 22 November 1773 John Goode and Sarah, his wife, of Chesterfield County, to John James Woodfin, of Henrico County, for 70 pounds, 75 acres on Four Mile Creek; adj. Edward Clark, John James Woodfin (being the land Woodfin purchased of Edward Whitlow) and Edward Goode; excepting the burying ground.
Wit: Richard Frogmorton, George Woodfin, John (his *John* mark) Robinson
Signed: John Goode, Sarah Goode
Recorded December Court 1773

p.509 6 December 1773 John Wilkinson and Judith, his wife, of New Kent County, to Nathaniel Wilkinson, of Henrico County, for 55 pounds and 11 shillings, two tracts containing 213 acres, and being their proportions of all the land which Thomas Wilkinson died seized and possessed, excepting the claim of William Clarke in right of dower of Margaret Clarke, his late wife.
Wit: none  Signed: John Wilkinson, Judith Wilkinson
Recorded December Court 1773

p.510  4 October 1773 Deed of Mortgage from Gideon Patteson to Lewis Ball and Daniel Hylton, for the payment of 75 pounds, with lawful interest from 25 December 1773, collateral being one Negro girl named Kate, with her future increase; terms being that after 25 December 1773 or as soon as said Ball and Hylton think proper or said Patteson shall request it, whichever of these two circumstances shall first happen, said Negro to be sold to the highest bidder for the best price.
Wit: William White, Joseph Harris, James Miller
Signed: Gideon Patteson                Recorded December Court 1773

p.511  2 August 1773 Darby Whitlow and Mary, his wife, to Pangran Parrabo Boswell, both of Henrico County, for 50 pounds, 100 acres on Cornelius Creek; adj. Nathan Whitler, Robert DuVal, Bullington, James Whitlow and Henry Jordan.
Wit: John Turpin, Michael Turpin, John Roper
Signed: Darby Whitlow, Mary Whitlow
Partly proved at October Court 1773 and recorded December Court 1773

p.511  2 August 1773 Darby Whitlow and Mary, his wife, to Pangran Parrabo Boswell, both of Henrico County, for 50 pounds, 100 acres on Cornelius Creek; adj. Nathan Whitler, Robert DuVal, Bullington, James Whitlow and Henry Jordan.
Wit: John Turpin, Michael Turpin, John Roper
Signed: Darby Whitlow, Mary Whitlow
Partly proved at October Court 1773 and recorded December Court 1773

p.512  13 August 1773 William Miller and Sarah, his wife, to Martin Burton, all of Henrico County, for 50 pounds, 100 acres adj. John Lankester and Martin Burton (metes and bounds description).
Wit: John Pleasants, John Pleasants, carpenter, William Stone, John Fariss, James Allen, William Burton, Richardson Henley, John Burton
Signed: William (his X mark) Miller, Sarah (her X mark) Miller
Recorded January Court 1774

p.513  2 May 1773 Edmond Alley and Landy Lindsey of Henrico County to David Harris, for 5 pounds and 10 shillings, one grey mare about ten years old.
Wit: Blacey Tulley, Francis Tulley
Signed: Edmond Alley, Landy Linsey
Recorded January Court 1774

p.513  9 July 1773 Thomas Pleasants, Jr., to John Brownley of Henrico County, for ten shillings and the conditions hereafter expressed, being the lease of part of the plantation known as Bailey's for six years, to commence from 1 January 1774, and

being the land which has been cleared, leading from Bottom's Bridge to Woodson's Ferry (excepting the tenements already in possession of Judith Childers), provided Brownley does not tend Indian corn for more than three years in regular rotation nor clear any more land except for the necessity of firewood and fencing without Pleasants' permission.
Wit: Jacob Carter, John Pleasants, Jr.
Signed: Thomas Pleasants, Junr., John Brownley
Recorded January Court 1774

p.514 25 November 1773 William Byrd of Westover, Charles City County, Peyton Randolph of Williamsburg, John Page of Gloucester County, Charles Carter of Lancaster County, Esqs., and Charles Turnbull of Dinwiddie County, to Fortunatus Sydnor of Henrico County, for 366 pounds, four tickets in the lottery called Byrd's Lottery, being numbers 8661, 1586, 4550 and 5039, against each of which was drawn a prize of 100 acres distinguished in the plan by numbers 762, 764, 765 and 766; also three other tickets in the said lottery numbered 9033, 6784 and 9145, against each of which was drawn a prize of one-half an acre in the Town of Richmond and numbered on the plan of the said town as Lots 417, 431 and 487.
Wit: Carter Braxton, George Webb, Turner Southall, Samuel Price, Patrick Coutts, Thomas Adams                                                                Signed: W. Byrd
Recorded January Court 1774

p.516 7 February 1774 Marriage Agreement between William Gathright and Agnes Gathright, both of Henrico County, in which the said William Gathright relinquishes any claim to five Negroes: Pompey, Stephen, Martin, Beth and Tamar and their increase; which slaves were left to the said Agnes by her father, Samuel Gathright, deceased.
Wit: none                                                                Signed: Wm. Gathright
Recorded January Court 1774

p.517 23 February 1774 Bill of Sale from Richard Holland, late of London and son of Henry Holland, Esq., of said city, and now of the Province of Maryland, to Patrick Coutts, of the Town of Richmond in Virginia, for 700 pounds, the ship or vessel called the Royal Exchange, in the James River at the moorings of Bermuda Hundred, Thomas Woodford, master; and bound for the port of London, of the burthen of 280 tons or thereabouts, together with masts, sailyards, cables, etc.
Wit: John Brooke, T. Woodford, James Watt, Reuben Coutts
Signed: Richard Holland                                         Recorded March Court 1774

p.519 12 November 1773 Deed of Mortgage from John George Hopson, planter, of Henrico County, to William Cunningham & Co., merchants of Glasgow, for the

payment of 10 pounds, 15 shillings and 9 pence, with interest from 24 May last; collateral being 40 acres whereon said John George Hopson now lives; ad. Syer Bullington, John Burton and Christopher Branch, deceased.
Wit: George Lindsey, Jonathan Anderson, Simon Paterson
Signed: John George (his  H  mark) Hopson,
William Henderson (agent for William Cunningham)
Recorded March Court 1774

p.520  13 December 1773 Deed of Mortgage from James Vaughan of Henrico County to Henderson, McCaul & Co., merchants of Glasgow, for the payment of 500 pounds before 1 April 1776, collateral being six Negro slaves: Big Will, Will and Tom, men; Betty, Agie and Kate and their increase; and two lots of land each containing 100 acres which I purchased from Col. William Byrd and distinguished in his lottery by numbers 805 and 806; after 1 April 1776, as soon as they may think proper or said Vaughan shall request it, any or all of said collateral to be sold to the highest bidder for the best price to satisfy said indebtedness.
Wit: William Mitchell, William Cutberth, Neil Campbell
Signed: James Vaughan                                  Recorded 7 March 1774

p.522  7 March 1774 John Redcross to Samuel Williamson, both of the Town of Richmond, for 180 pounds, a wagon and harness, four horses, one mare, one colt, a bedstead and furniture, four rush bottom chairs, a large sealskin trunk and household items.
Wit: Micajah Brown, William Allen
Signed: John (his  X  mark) Redcross                   Recorded 7 March 1774

p.523  6 November 1773 Edward Whitlow to John James Woodfin, both of Henrico County, for 40 pounds, 50 acres on Four Mile Creek and on the Deep Run; adj. John Goode; said tract was purchased of John Goode by Edward Whitlow.
Wit: Peter McGill, Thomas Bates, Richd. Broadie, Jesse Roper, James Valentine
Signed: Edward Whitlow                                 Recorded 7 March 1774

p.525  6 December 1773 William Miller, Executor of the will of James Browning, deceased, to Nathaniel Wilkinson, both of Henrico County, for 28 pounds and 10 shillings, 100 acres whereon the said James Browning, deceased, did live, and which he directed to be sold for the payment of his just debts; adj. said William Miller, Augustine Smith, Dabney Pettus, John Williamson, Thomas Williamson and Charles Snead; but reserving unto Anne Browning, widow of the said James Browning, her life right to said 100 acres.
Wit: none                                              Signed: Wm. Miller
Recorded March Court 1774

p.526  7 March 1774 Hugh Moody and Ruth, his wife, of Chesterfield County, to Daniel Warriner of Henrico County, for 25 pounds, 50 acres adj. Benjamin East, Humphrey Smith and the other lands of said Daniel Warriner.
Wit: none                    Signed: Hugh Moody, Ruth (her ✚ mark) Moody
Recorded March Court 1774

p.527  7 March 1774 Davis Clark of Amherst County to John Tinsley of Henrico County, for 50 pounds, 100 acres adj. William Staples, William Morris, John Tinsley, Richard Cottrel and Peterfield Trent.
Wit: Nathaniel Clark, John Norvell, William Gasberry
Signed: Davis Clark, Sarah (her X mark) Clark
Recorded April Court 1774

p.528  4 April 1774 Joseph Gathright and Mary, his wife, of St. Paul's Parish, Hanover County, to John Carter of Henrico County, for 211 pounds and 5 shillings, 422 ½ acres on Boar Swamp; adj. Mr. White's Mill, Spears, Benjamin Gathright, William Mays, Sharp, Matthews, Ragland, Bethel and Abraham Freeman; being the land left Joseph Gathright by his father William Gathright by his last will and testament and the land said Joseph escheated that was called Mays' land.
Wit: George Adams, William Carter, Miles Gathright, Jr.
Signed: Joseph Gathright, Mary Gathright
Recorded April Court 1774

p.531  22 October 1773 James Powel Cocke to Ryland Randolph of Henrico County, for 20 pounds, 7 acres on the Great Road leading from Williamsburg to Richmond (metes and bounds description).
Wit: John Eldridge, John Browning, Joseph Jenkins
Signed: James P. Cocke                    Recorded April Court 1774

p.532  4 April 1774 Charles Lewis and Susanna, his wife, and Edward Curd and Mary, his wife, to John Edwards, all of Henrico County, for 22 pounds, 14 and 3/4 acres on the road leading from the said Curd's to Richmond; being part of the tract the said Lewis and Curd live on (metes and bounds description).
Wit: Daniel Price, John Harwood, Jr., David White
Signed: Charles Lewis, Edward Curd
(no signatures nor relinquishments of dower indicated for wives)
Recorded 1st Mon. in April 1774

p.533  4 April 1774 Thomas Bottom, Sr., of Henrico County to Thomas Bottom, Jr., of Chesterfield County, for 35 pounds, 100 acres adj. Michael Harefield, Ephraim Gathright, William Bethel, Abram Freeman and William Bottom, Sr.

Wit: George Adams  Signed: Thomas (his T mark) Bottom, Sr.
Recorded 4 April 1774

p.535  6 January 1774 John Frayser to William Frayser, both of Henrico County, for 60 pounds, 100 acres on the Main Road; adj. Jackson Frayser and Jonathan Williams.
Wit: Charles Hughes, Joseph Goode, John Perkins
Signed: John Frayser  Recorded April Court 1774

p.536  4 April 1774 Nicholas Scherer of Manchester Parish, Chesterfield County, to Samuel Scherer, son of George Scherer, of Richmond Town, for natural love and affection and five shillings, 3 ½ acres after mine and George Scherer's death, being part of the land which I bought of the Hon. William Byrd, Esq.; being the Meadow Green near Richmond and near to the place bounded by Maj. Richard Adams land on Shockoe Creek (metes and bounds description).
Wit: Obadiah Puryear, Elizabeth Hutcheson
Signed: Nicholas Scherer  Recorded April Court 1774

p.537  4 April 1774 Nicholas Scherer of Manchester Parish, Chesterfield County, to George Hutcheson of Richmond Town, after the death of his mother, Elizabeth Hutcheson, for natural love and affection and five shillings, ½ of Lot 20, joining Lot No.6; if said George should die before he has lawful issue, then houses and the ½ lot to be divided between Patty, Jane, Dorothy and Elizabeth Hutcheson.
Wit: Obadiah Puryear, Samuel Scherer
Signed: Nicholas Scherer  Recorded April Court 1774

p.538  11 December 1773 Power of Attorney from Daniel Willson the Elder, surviving administrator of the Estate of William Anderson, deceased, and Charles Anderson, heir-at-law to the said William Anderson, to Nathaniel Wilkinson of Henrico County, to demand and receive from Col. Augustine Claiborne, Executor of the last will and testament of John Herbert, late of Chesterfield County, deceased, all such sums of money he as Executor is due the Estate of the said William Anderson.
Wit: Daniel Willson, Junr., Willson Wilkerson
Signed: Daniel Willson, Chas. Anderson  Recorded March Court 1774

p.539  18 October 1773 John Martin to William Gathright, both of Henrico County, for 75 pounds, 39 acres; bounded by the Western Run on the southwest, Thomas Jolly, said John Martin and said Gathright.
Wit: Jonathan Pleasants, Thomas Bates, John Dollard, William Carter
Signed: John (his M mark) Martin

Recorded April Court 1774

p.540 Notation: The several deeds herein recorded in this book beginning on the next page and continued to page 550 were done by mistake and will be found recorded in another book beginning May 1774.
William White for Thomas Adams.

p.541  3 October 1774 John Cornet to Hebron Owen, both of Henrico County, for 31 pounds, 31 acres adj. said Owen, Thomas Prosser and Turner's Run (metes and bounds description).
Wit: none                               Signed: John (his ✚ mark) Cornet
Recorded 3 October 1774

p.541 [542]  6 June 1774 Joseph Goode to Edward Goode, both of Henrico County, for 20 pounds, 50 acres adj. Gathright on Clay Branch.
Wit: John Turpin, Thomas Williams, John Roper
Signed: Joseph Goode
Partly proved on 5 September 1774 and recorded 3 October 1774

p.544  1 October 1774 Charles Cottrell and Eleanor, his wife, of Buckingham County, to Richard Cottrell of Henrico County, for 60 pounds, 200 acres; 100 acres of which was bought of William Buxton and the other 100 acres bought of John Jack[son?]; adj. said Charles Cottrell, Christopher John Thomas, John Lucy, Pettis Jones and a branch of The Brook.
Wit: John Lankester, John Lucy, George (his ✚ mark) Rice
Signed: Charles Cottrell, Ellenner Cottrell
Recorded October Court 1774

p. 546  25 April 1774 William Clopton to Lusby Turpin, for a consideration not given, 125 acres; adj. Nicholas Giles, Lusby Turpin, Peter Randolph's estate and Thomas Harris; except six square feet of land reserved to said William Clopton for a burying place.
Wit: George Markham, Matt. Branch, Jesse Roper
Signed: William Clopton                     Recorded 3 October 1774

p.548  3 October 1774 Thomas Griffin and Rachel, his wife, to John Pettus, all of Henrico County, for 45 pounds, 96 acres on Hungry Branch whereon the said Griffin now lives; adj. Pearce Griffin, John Staples and formerly John Gill.
Wit: R. Richard Allen, Dick Holland, Benjamin Sheppard
Signed: Thomas Griffin, Rachel Griffin
Recorded 3 October 1774

p.550  5 September 1774 Thomas Booth of Henrico County to Patrick Coutts of Richmond Town, for 150 pounds, a lot containing 100 acres bought of the Hon. William Byrd by a deed recorded in the General Court.
Wit: none  Signed: Thos. Booth
Recorded October Court 1774


\*\* Note:
It should be kept in mind that the Julian calendar, according to which 25 March was reckoned as the first day of the New Year, was in use together with the Gregorian calendar until 1752 when it was abandoned and the 11 days difference between the two calendars was dropped out of the year. The occurrence of an event between 1 January, the first day of the New Year according to the Gregorian calendar and 25 March, the New Year's day of the Julian calendar, may be indicated by a diagonal line. If the is not so indicated, one must think in terms of the date in which the Gregorian calendar was adopted. VLHD

Acknowledgments:
It is with appreciation to and admiration for Gary Murdock Williams for his meticulous transcription and abstraction of these works.  VLHD
And with the upmost admiration of the Publishing Consultant for the superb condition of the material submitted by Mr. Williams.  J. Thomas Wadkins III


*References:*  *Tidewater Virginia Families:*
*A Magazine of History and Genealogy*


*Volume  8, No. 3, pages 159-169; No. 4, 235-243.*
*Volume  9, No. 1, 30-45; No. 2, 103-117; No. 3, 173-187; No. 4, 242-256.*
*Volume 10, No. 1, 35-51; No. 2, 104-123; No. 3, 172-191; No. 4, 238-258.*
*Volume 11, No. 1, 29-54; No. 2, 100-121; No. 3, 172-190; No. 4, 247-257.*
*Volume 12, No. 1, 48-58; No. 2, 118-124; No. 3, 175-180.*


## *Conclusion*

# INDEX

NFN No first name given; NLN No last name given

Abbot
  Edward 177
Abner
  Melicent 165
Abney
  Denitt 181
  Dennitt 181
  Melisent 173
  Millicent 183, 197, 198
Acrill
  William 46, 101
Adair
  William 35, 92, 116
Adams
  Elizabeth 151, 201
  George 15, 19, 22, 37, 44, 45, 76, 88, 102, 106, 113, 123, 134, 136, 140, 144, 145, 160, 162, 180, 189, 197, 234, 235, 240, 246, 247
  Lucy 113, 140
  Maj. 77, 93
  NFN 150, 162, 199
  Richard 46, 103, 109, 121, 133, 135, 138, 140, 141, 143, 148, 149, 151, 158, 172, 175, 191, 192, 200, 201, 204, 207, 217, 227, 247
  Thomas 35, 46, 60, 73, 77, 81, 92, 97, 100, 101, 104, 110, 112, 119, 156, 164, 166, 201, 208, 216, 230, 244, 248
Adderby
  George 35
Adkins
  Ann 179
  Joseph 19, 95
  Robert 82, 110
Adkinson
  David 20
  Joseph 42
  William 140
Adkisson
  Susanna 159, 160
  William 159, 160
Agee
  Bernard 113

Akins
  Joseph 160
Alberto
  Thomas 220
Alday
  Anna 104
  James 70
  John 17, 19, 70, 80, 86, 94, 95, 104, 116, 219
  Josiah 70, 94, 95, 103, 104
  Mary 104
  NFN 80
  Richard 94
Aldway
  John 134
Allday
  John 20, 167, 241
Alldays
  John 66
Allen
  Agnes 14, 103
  Charles 191, 196, 234, 240
  Christian 138, 156, 160, 161, 170, 205
  Daniel 231, 242
  David 95, 106, 110, 120, 121, 123, 131, 138, 151, 168, 183, 184, 189, 202, 211, 222
  Drury 231, 242
  Edmond 110
  Elizabeth 5, 60, 102, 127, 128, 186
  Frances 238
  George 190
  Henry 59
  Isham 9, 12, 16, 18, 58, 67, 71, 102, 103, 113, 156, 171, 234, 235, 240
  James 9, 17, 19, 102, 111, 117, 125, 226, 243
  Joseph 61, 183
  Julian 196
  Julius 1-4, 12, 14, 17, 20, 22, 25, 32, 67, 72, 83, 90, 96, 97, 102, 116, 138, 141, 149, 150, 156, 163, 170, 173, 174, 180, 189, 190, 199, 205, 212, 221, 234, 240, 241
  Littleberry 12, 102

Allen
  Mary 117, 120, 121, 184, 241
  Richard 55, 58, 62, 128, 147, 183, 184, 202, 210, 238, 248
  Robert 55, 61, 62
  Royal 168, 179
  Royall 95, 231, 238
  Sam 19
  Samuel 16, 31, 107, 127, 128, 181, 186, 211
  Sarah 242
  Susanna 58
  Will 55
  William 5, 14, 16, 21, 24, 161, 169, 245
Alley
  David 58, 102, 134, 164, 167, 168, 182, 185, 206, 221, 222, 224, 238
  Edmond 14, 88, 102, 243
  Edmund 58, 85, 91, 134, 146, 148, 164, 166-168, 184, 192
  Elizabeth 134, 224
  James 65, 72, 102, 119, 141, 145, 161, 164, 167, 168
  John 17
  NFN 57
  Samuel 58, 145, 148, 161, 167, 168, 221
  Thomas 4, 17, 19, 21, 45, 58, 59, 72, 82, 85, 95, 99, 100, 102, 119, 124, 125, 134, 145, 146, 161, 164, 167, 168, 182, 206, 210, 222
  William 147, 168, 182, 184, 186, 187, 214, 222, 224, 231
Allin
  Agness 52
  David 145
  Edmund 72
  James 40, 43, 45, 72
  Julius 34, 42, 56, 88, 94
  Littleberry 34, 43, 45
  Mary 40, 67
  Robert 52
  Samuel 33, 34

250

Allin
  William 33, 48, 52
Amos
  Charles 18, 21
  John 237
  Nicholas 67, 84, 145, 155, 168, 179
  William 67
Amoss
  John 229
Anderson
  Andrew 11
  Charles 247
  Elkanah 42
  Henry 132
  James 177, 181
  Jonathan 245
  Pouncey 52, 53, 127, 163, 184, 185, 222
  Richard 204
  Robert 32, 50, 117, 132
  Thomas 194
  William 247
Archer
  Archer 240
  Henry 240
  John 240
Armour
  John 86
Arnold
  Samuel 215
Aselby
  Thomas 198
Ashurst
  Jacob 31
Atcheson
  Thomas 19, 33, 204
Atchison
  Thomas 9, 16, 33, 49, 155
Atkins
  David 56, 57
  Joseph 17, 83
  Magdelin 57
  Robert 63
  Shadrick 137
  William 56, 57
Atkinson
  David 16
  James 29
  Roger 29, 169
  Thomas 3, 61, 217
Atkison
  Thomas 11
Atkisson
  David 159

Attkings
  Stephen 117
Attkinson
  Solomon 117
Austin
  James 17, 19, 140, 152, 159, 208, 234
  Mary 159
Bacon
  Harwood 123, 128, 213
  Izard 128, 169, 192, 193, 199, 218
  John 65, 105, 181, 199, 218
  Langston 12, 15, 19, 39, 53, 65, 182
  Lydall 72
  Lyddal 53, 203
  Mary 23, 199, 213
  Nathaniel 2, 16, 19, 23, 42, 65, 81, 84-86, 101, 116, 156, 169, 193
  NFN 228
  Sarah 65
  Susannah 65
  Thomas 126, 218
  William 17, 19, 23, 30, 68, 115, 199, 228
Bailey
  Abraham 9, 10, 51, 79, 80, 86, 94, 95, 109, 116, 122, 124, 171, 202, 209, 212, 214, 215, 237, 241, 242
  Alexander 201
  Anselm 28
  David 212
  Davis 212
  Frances 219
  Henry 80, 94, 169, 170, 241
  Jean 212
  Johnston 212
  Joseph 9, 17, 20, 40, 104, 167, 169, 242
  NFN 86
  Peter 80, 94, 116, 134, 212, 219, 241, 242
  Roger 122, 236, 242
Bailie
  Francis 227
Bain
  Robert 197
Baine
  Alexander 138, 195, 204, 205, 217-220, 223, 225, 232
  Robert 182, 213, 234

Baird
  George 65
Baker
  Elizabeth 51, 170
  George 16, 18
  Jerman 205
  John 229
  Theodorick 151
  Thomas 170
Baldwin
  Elizabeth 220
  Richard 220
Baley
  NFN 70
Balfour
  Andrew 225
  James 225
  Margaret 225
Ball
  James 87, 89, 103, 110, 128, 149, 185
  Lewis 145, 243
  Susanna 119
  Susannah 110
  Valentine 16, 21, 69, 103, 119
Ballard
  John 178
Ballow
  Charles 7, 9, 35
  Temperance 35
Banks
  Alexander 194, 195
Barbour
  Robert 214
Barclay
  George 74
Bard
  John 3
Barker
  George 36
  Rebecca 36
  William 16, 20, 67, 85
Barnes
  Anderson 239
  John 58, 69, 87, 90, 93, 108, 115, 126, 127
  Mary 93
  Sarah 90
  William 58, 77, 93, 96, 107, 151, 239
Barnett
  Edward 157, 209
  John 120
Barnhill
  James 37

Barrett
  Charles 117, 220
  William 233
Barrow
  John 57
Bass
  Joseph 212, 213
Bassett
  William 148
Bates
  Abner 55
  Annis 67
  Elizabeth 25
  Fleming 152
  James 26
  John 25
  NFN 208, 237
  Thomas 18, 21, 25, 28, 37, 51, 65, 67, 85, 103, 109, 110, 120, 133-135, 149, 155, 157, 158, 165, 166, 172, 174, 180, 195, 202, 204, 208, 209, 224, 245, 247
Batte
  James 7
Battersby
  Elisabeth 214
  Jane 214
  Sophia 214
  W. 38
  William 72, 76, 78, 182
Baugh
  Isaac 178
  Richard 150
Baughan
  Thomas 87
Baughn
  Thomas 4
Bayley
  Abram 9
  Joseph 36
Bayly
  Abraham 82
Baze
  Ann 8
Beale
  NFN 129
Beckley
  John 228
Bell
  David 2
  George 91
  Jemima 56
  John 47, 60
  Mary 91

Bell
  Nathan 181
  Samuel 91
Bellamy
  Samuel 42
Bengsugh
  Henry 178
Bennet
  Richard 214
Bennett
  Richard 199, 226
Berns
  William 86
Bethall
  Thomas 148, 150
  William 148
Bethel
  Rebeckah 228
  William 228, 246
Bethell
  Thomas 187
Bethill
  Thomas 17, 19
Betts
  Thomas 187
Binford
  James 92, 101, 120, 178, 200, 201
  John 61, 178
  Thomas 16, 19, 139, 154, 172, 178, 200, 203
  William 29, 178, 200, 203
Binns
  Christopher 57, 69, 90, 120, 130, 235, 236
  Colder 224
  Daniel 120
  David 8, 18, 21, 53, 57, 58, 69, 79, 87, 91, 126, 130, 147, 235
  Demetrious 130
  Dioneshus 79
  Dionishous 57
  Joseph 57, 79, 130, 224, 235
  Judith 130
  Martha 235
  Mildred 235
  Milret 130
  Obedience 235
  Peter 57, 58, 79, 130
Black
  Rowlin 168
Blackborn
  Rowland 16
Blackbourn
  Rouland 21

Blackburn
  Andrew 219
  John 6, 85, 98, 102, 168, 196, 227, 238
  NFN 95
  Randolph 145
  Roland 84, 145, 155, 183
  Rowland 34, 55
Blackwell
  John 72
Blair
  John 130, 135
Bland
  Richard 5, 12
Blause
  Robert 7
Blaws
  Richard 155
  Robert 7
Blaydes
  George 184
Blunt
  William 208
Boatwright
  Benoni 22
Bogle
  John 3
  Matthew 3
  Patrick 3
  William 11
Boles
  David 129
  Elizabeth 129
  John 228
  Thomas 50
  William 129
Boling
  Boling 194
Bolland
  Thomas 154
Bolling
  Anne 216
  John 11, 16, 19, 48, 82, 181, 182
  Junior 223
  NFN 96
  Robert 216, 223, 228
  Susanna 216
  Susannah 216
Bond
  Charles 27
Booker
  John 148, 164, 166
  Richard 49
Booth
  Thomas 214, 227, 249

Borum
  Edmond 50
  Edmund 30
  John 25
Boselt
  William 83
Boswell
  Pangran 241, 243
  Parrobe 212
Bottom
  John 17, 20, 61
  NFN 12
  Rebecca 61, 148
  Thomas 17, 19, 61, 63, 88, 105, 147, 148, 171, 246, 247
  William 17, 19, 63, 64, 152, 153, 246
Boulders
  Ben 63
Boull
  William 79
Bow
  John 232
Bowe
  John 84
Bowler
  Thomas 224
Bowles
  Benjamin 60, 111, 118, 128, 137, 140, 141, 147, 151, 171
  David 80, 146, 164, 183, 185, 188, 189, 209
  Elijah 188
  John 128, 141, 151
  Thomas 47, 50, 97, 158, 159
  William 90, 111, 141, 235
Bowls
  Thomas 16, 20
Bowman
  Francis 208
Bowyer
  James 174
Boyd
  Alexander 50, 220
  Edward 124
  John 124
  Robert 225
  Thomas 124
Brackell
  John 19
Bracket
  John 76, 136
Brackett
  Elizabeth 203

Brackett
  John 17, 38, 83, 91, 109, 159, 203
Braezeal
  Drury 174
Bragg
  William 3
Branch
  Archd. 240
  Archer 240
  Benjamin 240
  Brazieh 10
  Christopher 147, 148, 166, 208, 221, 240, 245
  Henry 240
  John 224
  Martha 148
  Matthew 30, 94, 248
  Olive 55
  Thomas 18, 20
Branfford
  John 127
Bransford
  James 191
  John 15, 18, 22, 191, 204, 217
  Judith 191
  Sarah 191
Braxton
  Carter 11, 172, 244
Brazeab
  Henry 45
Brazeal
  Drury 66, 92, 171, 240
  Henry 78, 92
Brazeil
  Drury 79, 181
  Henry 79
Brazell
  Henry 68
Breazeal
  Drury 142, 185, 211
Breeden
  David 78, 98
Breeding
  Charles 114, 142
  David 17, 19, 63, 133, 142, 157, 179, 184, 202
  Isaac 1, 46, 54, 78, 111
  NFN 54
  Rachell 63
Brett
  William 180, 227
Brewer
  Edmund 40
  James 40

Brewer
  Martha 117
  Sackvill 100, 117
Brice
  Archibald 238
Brickhil
  John 151
Bridgeigian
  Matthew 19
Bridgeman
  Matthew 18, 40
  William 40
Bridgewater
  Elenora 236
  Jonathan 59
  Moses 234, 236
  Nathaniel 15, 21
  William 17, 21
Bridgman
  Hezekiah 57, 105
  Mary 105, 146
  Matthew 57, 145, 146, 220
Bridgmater
  Moses 215
Bridgwater
  Agness 78
  Eleanor 214, 215
  Elizabeth 31
  Johnnathan 46
  Jonathan 77, 113, 116, 128, 170, 173, 186, 206, 217, 222, 225
  Moses 180, 214, 215
  Nathaniel 31, 46, 47, 78, 90, 123, 151, 170, 173, 176, 186
  Samuel 90
  William 31, 46, 50, 116, 142, 170, 214, 215, 217, 222
Briggs
  James 188
  Joseph 188
Brigman
  Hezekiah 105
Britain
  James 20, 206
  Ludwell 206
Briton
  James 16
  William 17, 21
Brittain
  James 78
  Royal 114
  Samuel 87
  William 128

Brittan
  William 84, 224
Britton
  Elizabeth 48
  James 58, 60, 87, 88, 162, 175
  John 53, 77
  Ludwell 175
  Lya 232
  Lyddall 162
  Samuel 60
  Sarah 162
  William 48, 61
Broadie
  Richard 245
Broadway
  William 109
Brodne
  David 38
Brook
  Dudly 42
Brooke
  Dudley 46
  John 200, 244
  Samuel 172
Brookes
  Samuel 192
Brooks
  Samuel 186
Brown
  Alexander 111, 112, 208
  Benjamin 148, 175, 180
  John 1, 39, 65
  Joseph 88, 124, 148, 161, 164, 167, 168, 175, 182, 196, 206, 211, 214, 215, 227, 238
  Margaret 143
  Micajah 245
  Peter 46
  R. 229
  Richard 170
  Richmond 236
  Robert 92, 130, 144, 170, 181, 182, 192, 227
  Shilldrake 229
Brownen
  James 13
Browning
  Anne 213, 214, 222, 245
  James 109, 128, 170, 181, 213, 214, 222, 245
  John 246
Brownley
  John 243, 244

Bryan
  Archer 223
  Benjamin 125, 147, 149, 159, 161, 211
  Hannah 211
  John 58, 79, 84, 88, 97, 101, 103, 117, 154, 204, 217
  Judy 223
  Mary 159, 211
  Nancy 223
  Obedience 58, 117
  William 159
Bryant
  John 16, 18, 89
Bryce
  Archibald 218, 229
Buchanan
  Alexander 211, 238
  James 138, 140, 156, 166, 171, 187, 191, 196, 206, 207, 210, 215, 216, 233, 238
  John 230
  Robert 182
Bugg
  Anselm 25
  Jacob 9, 17, 20, 52, 55, 56, 63
  Margaret 56
  Sam 17, 19
  Samuel 12, 25
  Sarah 12, 25
Bullington
  Benjamin 94, 96, 115, 116
  Elizabeth 79, 116
  John 18, 20
  Josiah 82, 96, 115, 129, 143, 156, 173, 192, 207, 208, 241, 242
  Mary 79
  NFN 198, 243
  Robert 17, 19, 93, 143, 156
  Sarah 192, 241, 242
  Syer 245
  William 79, 209
Bunn
  William 4
Burdet
  Gerret 15, 20
Burdett
  Gervas 8, 47
  Jervas 69
  Sarah 100
Burdit
  NFN 80

Burditt
  Gervis 101
  NFN 89
Burges
  Daniel 178
Burk
  Samuel 27
Burley
  Harding 27, 45
Burnley
  Hard. 41
  Harding 45, 126
Burrus
  Henry 60
Burton
  Anne 24
  Ben 16, 18, 19
  Benj. 39
  Benjamin 9, 13, 24, 25, 29, 53, 55, 59, 65, 66, 68, 76, 79, 91, 135, 136, 142, 147, 161, 221
  Charles 98, 211
  David 9, 15, 20, 38, 76, 143
  Elizabeth 142
  Hutchens 160, 182, 227
  Hutchings 15, 18, 20, 21, 211
  Hutchins 32, 95
  Jacob 16, 18, 25, 51, 59, 62, 82, 135
  Jesse 112, 135, 180, 221
  Jessee 128, 129, 142
  John 113, 128, 176, 180, 187, 208, 213, 221, 243, 245
  Julius 95, 106, 121, 171, 182, 211, 227
  Martin 16, 21, 42, 66, 131-133, 162, 181, 190, 192, 201, 217, 231, 241, 243
  Mary 104, 129, 135, 143, 216
  NFN 96, 120, 121, 147, 212, 236
  Noel 59
  Norvel 182
  Norvell 182
  Nowell 48
  Peter 28, 65
  Richard 95, 102, 209
  Robert 29, 39, 48, 59, 135, 162
  Susanna 209
  Susannah 160

Burton
  William 15, 18, 160, 169, 181, 211, 226, 228, 236, 238, 239, 241, 243
Burwell
  Lewis 2, 12, 109
Butcher
  James 37
Buxton
  Ann 5
  Jane 48
  Joyce 118, 131, 196
  NFN 99
  William 5, 15, 20, 41, 42, 44, 45, 48, 50, 66, 100, 101, 103, 104, 117-119, 122-124, 131, 196, 248
Byrd
  Col. 151
  Colonel 176
  H. 37
  Mary 194, 195, 201
  Mr. 32
  William 15, 18, 31, 39, 41, 46, 47, 50, 51, 55, 57, 59, 60, 63, 64, 66, 70, 73-75, 77, 90, 92, 97, 98, 103, 113, 114, 148, 155, 161, 176, 183, 187, 194-196, 198-201, 204, 210, 218, 223, 227-230, 232, 234, 240, 241, 244, 247, 249
Cabell
  W. 119
  William 27, 61, 119
Calder
  Thomas 127, 133, 160, 204, 217, 236
Caldwell
  David 138
Campbell
  Charles 210
  Neil 192, 206, 207, 215, 216, 222, 233, 245
  Neill 227
Cannon
  Benjamin 71
  Jeremiah 71
  John 27, 40, 219
  Mildred 49, 50
  NFN 32
  Susannah 71
  William 40, 41, 49, 216
Car
  John 91

Cardwell
  Thomas 17, 19, 143, 174
Carey
  John 123
Carr
  Dabney 174
Carrington
  George 177, 232
Carson
  William 204
Carter
  Charles 37, 40, 140, 148, 183, 187, 194-196, 201, 207, 229, 230, 232, 240, 241, 244
  Edward 187
  Giles 222, 230
  Jacob 244
  John 22, 37, 44, 45, 76, 140, 151, 197, 231, 246
  Merry 53, 145
  Povall 10, 55
  Theodorick 15, 18, 22
  William 246, 247
Carver
  Daniel 74
Cary
  Archibald 15, 18, 37, 41, 77, 119, 178, 187, 212
  NFN 34
  Robert 224
Casants
  John 241
Cash
  Howard 12
Casson
  Margaret 199
  Thomas 150, 199
Castle
  Andrew 154
Castlen
  Andrew 72, 143
Castlin
  Andrew 30, 39
Cation
  David 176, 191, 233
Caudle
  Ann 29
  John 29
  Mary 24
  Richard 24
Cauthorn
  John 192
  Margaret 192
  William 142

Cawthorn
  James 146, 147
  John 147, 164
Chalmer
  Andrew 241
Chalmers
  Ch. 33
  Charles 49
Chamberlane
  Mary 233
  Richard 233
Chamberlayne
  Edward 27
  Mary 233
  Richard 233
Chambers
  Elizabeth 6, 7
  George 2, 6, 8, 85, 107, 118
  NFN 241
Chappel
  John 241
  NFN 171
Chappell
  Abram 140
  Agnes 188
  Robert 137, 188
Charles
  Walter 3
Cheadle
  John 26
  Thomas 7
Cheatham
  Christopher 212
  Thomas 212, 213
Chedle
  Thomas 7
Cheek
  James 39
Childers
  Abra 205
  Abraham 48, 59, 73, 75, 80, 82, 133, 134
  Ann 75
  Ben 66
  Benjamin 16, 18, 83, 135, 158
  Elijah 122
  Elizabeth 22
  Frederick 75, 134, 173
  Henry 75, 133, 134, 148
  James 172, 207
  Joel 215
  John 16, 18, 122, 124, 145, 177
  Joseph 1, 15, 19, 20, 22, 32, 56, 75, 173, 180, 205

Childers
  Judith 244
  NFN 98
  Nicholas 65, 121
  Philemon 65, 85, 100, 110, 172
  Robert 16, 21, 50, 99
  Samuel 75, 103, 149, 173
  Stephen 68
  Susanna 160
  Thomas 112, 122
  William 160, 173, 199, 205
Childres
  Benjamin 157, 158
  Joseph 3
  Robert 3
  Samuel 156
  William 160
Childress
  Ann 212
  Joel 229
  John 95
  Joseph 4, 212
  Samuel 138
  Thomas 221
  William 78, 212
Childrey
  Thomas 80, 112, 175, 183, 184
Chiles
  Micajah 214
Chilo
  Micajah 214
Chiswell
  John 11
Christian
  Andrew 27
  James 27
Christie
  Robert 2
Claiborne
  Augustine 247
Clark
  Benjamin 31, 98, 99, 113, 121
  David 211
  Davis 246
  Edward 242
  Frederick 148, 208
  Fredrick 234
  George 148, 208
  Jesse 164
  John 100, 124, 142, 164, 171, 238
  Joseph 100
  Josiah 148, 174

Clark
  Margaret 225
  Mark 86, 126
  Nathaniel 152, 239, 246
  Peter 99, 119, 124
  Sarah 246
  Turner 100
  William 48, 148, 225, 231
Clarke
  Ann 81
  Ben 21, 31
  Benjamin 17, 48, 69, 70, 76, 88, 103, 109, 116, 128, 222
  Charles 157, 220
  David 116, 128, 170
  Edward 32
  Edwarde 229
  Frederick 102, 146, 197, 200, 221
  George 87, 102, 145, 197, 221
  Henry 186
  James 39
  John 16, 21, 32, 69, 81, 82, 84, 99, 109, 186, 187, 190, 210
  Joseph 116, 186, 187, 210, 211, 222
  Margaret 242
  Mark 22, 25, 51, 82, 83, 90, 95
  Mary 116
  Nathaniel 152-154, 186, 216, 228
  Peter 81, 91, 109, 131, 164, 169, 170, 192, 196, 210
  Robert 43, 45
  Samuel 4
  Sarah 82, 84
  Susanna 197
  Susannah 32
  William 18, 21, 67, 79, 169, 200, 213, 242
Clarkson
  Charles 215
  David 219
  John 214, 215, 220, 234, 235
  Mary 219, 220
  Nancy 219
  Susanna 234
Clements
  John 35

Clopton
  George 83, 105, 107, 120, 148, 229, 239
  Jenny 148
  NFN 34
  Unity 105, 147
  Unity1 94
  Waldegrave 88, 105, 106, 147, 148, 171
  Waldugrove 94
  Walsey 61
  William 84, 158, 167, 180, 229, 239, 242, 248
Cobbs
  John 3
Cochran
  Andrew 233
Cock
  John 76
Cocke
  Benjamin 4
  Bowler 9, 18, 21, 22, 37, 40, 45, 110, 121, 150, 151, 185, 193, 194, 212
  Brazure 38
  Breazare 38
  Capt. 8
  Cocke 113
  Elizabeth 138, 213, 230
  James 7, 13, 41, 53, 57, 59, 62, 64, 70, 71, 84, 87, 91, 94, 97, 105, 113-115, 119, 121, 126, 138, 147, 163, 179, 191, 212, 213, 230, 246
  John 17, 19, 22, 36, 151
  Martha 62
  Mary 119, 165
  NFN 130, 134
  Pleasant 116
  Pleasants 187
  Richard 4, 165, 237
  Robert 17
  Sarah 13, 64
  Theodosia 104, 116, 137
  Thomas 9, 38, 41, 57, 91, 121
  William 38, 57, 87, 91, 104, 116, 121, 123, 126, 137, 138, 147
Cockes
  William 8
Cockran
  Andrew 50
Cocks
  James 1

Cocks
  Thomas 1
Cockson
  Andrew 82
Codam
  Hugh 29
Cogbill
  George 42
Coke
  John 29
  Samuel 29
Colder
  Thomas 188
Cole
  John 37, 78
  Matthew 22
  NFN 236
Colebrooke
  George 87
Coles
  Isaac 192, 206
  Jane 92
  John 92, 105, 143, 206
  Walter 105, 111, 112, 130, 142, 143, 208
Comron
  John 204
  Sarah 204
Conaway
  Ann 5
  Hannah 184
  James 5, 24, 52, 57, 141
  John 108, 137, 173, 190
  Nicholas 41, 50, 108, 183, 184, 190
  Thomas 8, 57, 66, 101, 108, 127, 128, 190, 222
Connaway
  Agnes 42
  Ann 42, 48
  James 41, 42, 48, 71, 78
  John 77
  Nicholas 42, 78
  Sarah 71
  Thomas 77, 78
Conner
  Thomas 39
Connoway
  Nicholas 166
Constantine
  NFN 208
Conway
  Ann 146
  Elizabeth 31, 170
  James 5, 146
  John 31, 78, 170

Conway
  Nicholas 146, 147
  Thomas 2, 54, 146
Cook
  Ann 10
  Anne 239
  Francis 163, 210
  Frank 160
  Robert 10, 111, 239, 240
Cooke
  Elizabeth 65
  Francis 132
  James 41
  John 65
  Robert 20, 63, 68, 72, 73, 97, 208, 222
  William 161
Cooper
  Edward 35, 36
Copeland
  William 4
Corbin
  Andrew 61
Cornell
  John 17
Cornet
  Francis 108
  Frank 141
  French 176
  John 47, 248
  William 176
Cornett
  Francis 21, 84, 216
  James 60
  John 21, 58, 128
  William 155, 170
Cornit
  Francis 239
  John 239
Cosby
  David 219
Cotteral
  Richard 50
Cotterall
  Charles 48
  Richard 48
Cotterell
  Richard 211
Cottrel
  Jacob 222
  Richard 210, 222
Cottrell
  Benjamin 196
  Charles 41, 42, 84, 196, 228, 248
  Eleanor 248

Cottrell
  Mary 170
  NFN 127
  Richard 5, 14, 17, 19, 44, 45, 71, 80, 82, 84, 91, 103, 110, 118, 125, 131, 146, 147, 163, 170, 190, 192, 225, 227, 228, 238, 246, 248
  Thomas 4, 27
  William 117
Count
  John 210
Coupland
  James 28, 149
Courin
  Sarah 218
Coutts
  Patrick 130, 171, 204, 218, 227, 229, 230, 244, 249
  Reuben 244
Coward
  Rachel 184
  Richard 37
Cowley
  Abraham 10, 13, 15, 18, 25, 33, 47, 60, 63, 70, 97, 98, 104, 110, 116, 121, 127, 139, 147, 157, 174, 220, 221, 230, 239
  Ann 127, 157
Cowman
  Daniel 109
Cox
  Alice 67
  Bolling 194
  George 82, 98, 147, 166, 193, 194, 220
  Henry 36, 80, 134, 219
  Hickason 86
  John 9, 36, 51, 67, 74, 98
  NFN 94, 122
  Richard 9, 36, 86, 109
  Thomas 194
  William 109
Crafford
  James 1
  NFN 84
Craig
  Robert 11
Crawford
  George 209
  James 39
Crawley
  William 148, 164, 166

Creighton
  Elizabeth 200
  William 200
Crenshaw
  Charles 192, 193
  Sarah 193
  Susanna 192
  Susannah 193
Crew
  John 25, 26, 120
  Walter 50
Crewes
  Walter 124
Crosse
  John 87
Crouch
  Richard 74, 143, 160, 189, 191, 198
Crump
  Daniel 233
  Jesse 235
  Richard 94, 233
  Susanna 233
Crumpler
  David 184
Cumming
  John 219
Cunningham
  William 244, 245
Curd
  Edward 31, 41, 45, 66, 94, 113, 119, 126, 135, 138, 155, 181, 185, 186, 199, 210, 217, 246
  Elizabeth 185
  John 185, 186
  Mary 94, 246
  Richard 185, 186
  Sarah 186
Cureton
  James 201
Currey
  Robert 109
Currie
  James 218, 223, 224
Curtis
  Benjamin 140
  Thomas 36
Cutberth
  William 245
Cuthbert
  Gilliam 227
  William 206, 207
Dabney
  Anne 5
  George 4, 5, 166

Dabney
  William 4, 5
Daley
  Ann 200
  Joseph 200
  Sarah 200
Dalton
  Elizabeth 234
  John 234
Dandridge
  Nathaniel 27
  William 189, 232
Daniel
  Samuel 25
Darby
  NFN 241
Dasey
  Dasey 41
Davenport
  Sam 154
Davers
  George 175
Davies
  John 220
Davis
  Bartlet 225, 231
  James 157
  John 120, 240
  Nicholas 241
  Robert 27
  William 67, 174
Dawson
  Thomas 29
Day
  William 145
de Botetourt
  Baron 193
  Norborne 193
Dean
  Richard 152
  Thomas 39
Deans
  James 91
Decree
  John 52
Dennis
  John 206, 211
  Nathaniel 72, 117, 119, 125, 134, 145, 148, 151, 161, 167, 168, 182, 206, 211, 238
  Rachel 119, 206
Dennistonne
  James 33
Dennistoune
  James 64, 65

Depriest
  Randall 155
  William 155
Dick
  Walter 164, 165
Dickerson
  Peter 154
  William 95
Dickinson
  James 220
Dickson
  Michael 161
Dillard
  James 201
Dinguid
  William 64, 69, 79, 88, 89, 143
Dinquid
  William 45
Dixon
  Thomas 3
Dollard
  John 159, 163, 170, 171, 179, 204, 221, 247
Dolton
  Elizabeth 116, 241
  John 241
  Mary 241
Donald
  Dorothea 204, 217
  George 72, 73, 77, 81, 86, 105, 113, 117, 135, 136, 180, 191, 204, 206, 207, 217, 219, 223, 230, 233, 234, 236
  James 2, 50, 61, 82, 242
  Robert 2, 41, 50, 82, 187, 233, 242
  William 129, 132, 137, 156, 189, 220
Dorton
  Elizabeth 67, 83
  John 83
Douglas
  John 34
Drake
  James 226
Dueguid
  William 143
Duglass
  Jonathan 180
Duguids
  William 56
Duiguid
  William 72

Dumbar
  Robert 132
Dunaway
  Nathan 80, 209
Dunlop
  James 37, 219
Dunn
  Barbara 191
  Barbary 191
  James 48
  Thomas 191, 209
Dupree
  John 16, 20
DuVal
  Benjamin 82, 88, 99, 101, 148, 172, 179, 180, 205
  Robert 143, 155, 204, 209, 217, 243
  Samuel 10, 51, 64, 77, 88, 89, 97, 100-102, 104, 118, 123, 124, 127, 130, 140, 141, 143, 154, 162, 168, 172, 182, 187, 188, 190, 210, 217, 222, 225
  William 204, 222, 238
Duvall
  Benjamin 132, 203
  Mr. 31
  Robert 217, 219
  Sam 18, 19
  Samuel 29, 41, 43, 45, 70, 137, 222, 231, 242
  William 217
Eaddy
  James 61
Eales
  Elizabeth 90, 91
  John 68, 80-82, 84, 85, 90, 91, 99, 118, 149
  NFN 99
  Richard 108
  Thomas 81, 82, 84, 90, 124, 149, 185
Eals
  John 18, 20
Earnest
  Adam 88
Easely
  Rhoderick 62
East
  Aggy 132
  Benjamin 178, 246
  Edward 18, 20, 134, 238
  Elizabeth 8, 51
  Isham 77

East
  Jesse 134, 144
  Navel 43, 45
  Richard 8, 17, 20, 50, 51, 77
  Samuel 61
  Thomas 43, 45, 127, 132, 151, 164, 220, 234
Eccleston
  W. 12
Echo
  Isaac 197, 200, 221
  Lucy 221
Edmonds
  Andrew 213
Edmondson
  Andrew 213
  John 213
Edmondstone
  John 192, 198
Edmundston
  John 170
Edwards
  Elizabeth 45
  John 169, 246
  William 17, 20, 45, 79, 80
Ege
  Bernard 9
  Jacob 47, 54, 59
  NFN 222
  Samuel 206, 229
Egge
  Jacob 70
Eggy
  Jacob 15, 18
Eippen
  John 131, 134
Elam
  Gervas 77
  John 154
  Joseph 77
Elan
  Robert 38
Eldridge
  Bolling 150
  John 212, 237, 246
  Mary 178
  Rolfe 150
  Thomas 91, 101, 150, 186, 212, 237
Elliott
  Robert 108, 150, 198
Ellis
  Charles 11, 14, 15, 18, 45, 46, 48-50
  Elizabeth 99

Ellis
  George 154, 165, 188, 194, 195, 200, 201
  Henry 15, 18, 26, 27, 32, 59, 82, 84, 98-100, 107, 111, 118
  Jane 200, 208
  Jesse 24, 155
  John 7, 9, 17, 19, 21-23, 26, 27, 46, 51-53, 84, 94, 98, 99, 107, 111, 118, 138, 139, 146, 151, 168, 172, 184, 190, 196
  Joseph 16, 19, 26, 27, 46, 95, 225, 234
  Mary 100
  NFN 99, 102, 115, 235
  Stephen 226
  Susanna 45, 46
  Thomas 13, 14, 67, 82, 99, 100, 111, 117, 145, 155, 180
  William 17, 19, 22, 26, 27, 41, 45, 46, 49, 58, 68, 72, 85, 99, 100, 102, 107, 111, 117, 118, 134, 151, 184, 186, 187, 190, 192, 195, 200, 208
Ellyson
  Gearrard 28, 36
  Gerrard 15, 18, 25, 51, 63, 64, 67, 123
  John 165, 184
  Joseph 120
  Robert 25, 26
  Sarah 64
Elmore
  Elizabeth 72
  Hannah 199
  John 71, 72, 102
  Peter 127, 170, 173, 181, 199, 232
  Rebeckah 72
  Thomas 12, 34, 43, 45, 72, 102, 115, 127, 130, 171, 235
Enroughty
  Anne 36
  Darby 179
  Derby 78
  Edward 16, 19, 36, 42, 60, 132
  Edy 60
  John 60, 68, 105, 122, 132, 142, 214, 224

Enroughty
  Martha 132
Epperson
  Littleberry 143
Eppes
  Francis 73, 208, 240
  J.W. 183
  Mary 92, 165, 174, 200
  NFN 96, 147
  Richard 73, 92, 129, 165, 174, 200
  William 73
Epps
  Richard 142
Esdale
  John 117, 166, 187
Est
  Benjamin 179
Estes
  Benjamin 123
Eubank
  James 28, 128, 224
Evan
  Thomas 172
Evans
  Rodorick 7
  Thomas 144, 146, 163, 183
Eventon
  Mardun 105
Everton
  M. 169
Fair
  Arthanabue 96
  Mary 96
Fairly
  Robert 210
Faris
  Jacob 34
  John 152, 203, 221
  Lucy 203
  Martha 153
  Robert 51, 197, 221
  William 123, 152, 153, 200, 221
Fariss
  John 243
Farquharson
  John 170
Farr
  Richard 149
Farrar
  John 211, 213, 214, 226
  Richard 170
  Susanna 213, 214, 226
  Sutton 170

Farrar
  Thomas 9, 80, 85
Farrell
  Joseph 35
Farris
  Robert 234
  William 4, 32
Farrow
  NFN 228
Fartane
  Mr. 188
Faudree
  Joseph 202
Fauquier
  Francis 97, 112, 123, 124, 128, 129
Favour
  Elizabeth 21, 22
  Theophil 6, 15, 21, 22
  Thomas 20
Fawcett
  James 152
Fear
  Arthanatius 103
  Mary 103
Fearis
  Robert 153
  Sherwood 153
  William 153
Fearon
  Benson 169
Feild
  Ann 6
Fenton
  Thomas 85, 226
Ferell
  Joseph 35
Ferguson
  Alexander 184
Ferrie
  Alexander 79
Ferris
  Esau 203
  Jacob 107, 199
  Robert 148, 174
  Ruth 107
  William 18-20
Field
  Thomas 193
Fields
  Tom 70, 94
Finncy
  William 55
Finney
  NFN 109

Finton
  Thomas 2, 6
Fisher
  John 240
  Joseph 29
  William 149
Fitchpatrick
  Daniel 1, 2
Fitzgerald
  Peter 213
Fitzpatrick
  Daniel 137
Fleming
  John 11, 125, 126
  Thomas 212
  William 232
Flowers
  Jesse 64
  William 155
Floyd
  Charles 17, 19, 28, 65, 96, 103
  Sarah 103
Foard
  NFN 45
Focitt
  William 37
Fontaine
  Joseph 135, 136, 180
  Peter 161
Ford
  David 58, 128, 176
  Eleanor 76
  John 15, 20, 21, 62, 76, 183
  NFN 99
  Rachel 173
  Sam 21
  Samuel 58
  William 50, 58-60, 84, 124, 125, 173, 176
Forsee
  John 213
Forsie
  John 13, 38, 39
Foster
  William 75
Fowler
  John 212, 213
Frankland
  Francis 20
Franklin
  Francis 17, 113, 236
  Mary 9
  NFN 71
  Thomas 63, 68, 92, 206, 240

Franklin
  Zebulon 181
Frankling
  Thomas 10
Fraser
  John 83
  William 19
Frayer
  Mary 42
Frayser
  Jackson 247
  John 63, 95, 127, 160, 213, 247
  Mary 63
  Philemon 9, 42, 63
  Simon 242
  Susanna 160
  William 34, 42, 63, 98, 114, 126, 160, 166, 172, 184, 213, 237, 247
Frazer
  John 17
Frazier
  John 73
  William 150, 179
Freeman
  Aaron 72, 99
  Abigail 14
  Abraham 246
  Abram 246
  Agnes 228
  Anna 228
  George 23, 59, 67, 70, 89, 110
  Gideon 224-226
  Jane 22, 23, 50, 82
  Jeane 23
  John 14, 70, 228
  Joseph 16, 22, 23, 50, 82, 148
  Rebeckah 228
  Richard 228
  Sarah 224-226
  Valentine 12, 34, 43, 45, 67, 72, 102
Freizur
  John 20
Freizure
  Philip 18, 20
  William 18
Friend
  Nathaniel 147
  Thomas 147
Frith
  George 62, 63

Frogmorton
  NFN 155
  Richard 105, 202, 237, 242
  Robert 68, 202
  William 68
Fry
  Joshua 11
Fussel
  John 77, 175, 177, 183
  Solomon 187
Fussell
  John 13, 37, 122, 133, 144, 145
  Mary 133
  NFN 122
  Solomon 144, 189
Fussill
  John 66
Fuzel
  John 162
  Soloman 162
Gabriel 174
Gadbury
  Thomas 81
Gaddy
  James 58
Gainings
  William 57
Gaithright
  Samuel 4
Galt
  Gabriel 174, 180, 229
  James 174
Garner
  James 108
Garret
  Elizabeth 93
  William 93
Garris
  William 59
Garthright
  Ann 15
  Anselm 140, 161
  Ephraim 14, 15, 17, 19, 43, 45, 63, 163
  Ephriam 140
  Jean 127
  John 17, 19
  Miles 4, 15, 20, 25, 32, 56, 111, 138
  Samuel 4, 13-15, 18, 19, 22, 32, 56, 59, 75, 88, 125, 126, 138, 160

Garthright
  William 1, 12, 14, 15, 25, 32, 34, 56, 83, 87, 127, 163
Garthwright
  Ann 25
  Ephraim 123
  Samuel 25, 28
Gasberry
  William 246
Gascoyne
  Crisp 52
Gathright
  Agnes 228, 244
  Anselm 159, 177, 189, 190, 234
  Benjamin 246
  Elizabeth 199
  Ephraim 113, 152, 153, 163, 174, 189, 190, 197, 200, 208, 228, 234, 246
  John 156, 163, 176, 205
  Joseph 163, 231, 234, 246
  Judah 156
  Mary 246
  Miles 4, 149, 156, 163, 171, 179, 180, 191, 199, 230, 238, 246
  Samuel 72, 152, 153, 159, 161, 177, 178, 187, 189, 205, 226, 244
  See Garthright 25
  W. 171
  William 73, 115, 152, 153, 156, 163, 176, 180, 189, 199, 205, 208, 212, 231, 234, 244, 246, 247
Gathwight
  Samuel 69
Gathwright
  John 69
  Miles 71
  Samuel 69, 71, 72, 95, 101
  William 94, 96
Gathwrite
  Samuel 69
Gawin
  David 146
  John 146
  Michael 146
Gay
  Charles 95, 98
  William 216
Geddy
  Elizabeth 81

Geddy
  James 81
Gehee
  Samuel 136
Genett
  Robert 7
  Thomas 7
Gennett
  Thomas 72
Gentry
  Moses 90
George
  James 220
  King 232
Gibbs
  John 55
Gibson
  Robert 53
Gicheffele
  Samuel 232
Gilchrist
  Robert 79
Giles
  Andrew 2
  Ann 34
  David 63
  John 9, 17, 21, 34, 164
  Nicholas 17, 21, 34, 75, 122, 158, 236, 248
  William 16, 20, 34
Gill
  David 37, 47, 73, 82, 83
  John 248
  Mary 83
Gilley
  NFN 40
Ginguid
  William 59
Gining
  George 22
Ginins
  David 137
  George 137
Ginnet
  Robert 134
  Ruth 187
  Thomas 187
Ginnett
  Ruth 166, 167
  Thomas 157, 164, 166, 167, 202
Ginnins
  William 22
Ginnitt
  Thomas 134, 166

Gist
  C. 161
Gladowe
  NFN 143
Gleadome
  Samuel 13
Gleadon
  Samuel 11, 35
Gleadone
  Samuel 13, 14
Gleadowe
  Sam 38
  Samuel 38, 47, 69, 89
Gleen
  John 141, 222
Glen
  John 146, 164, 166, 168, 224
Glenn
  John 182, 184, 190
Glover
  Samuel 27
Goff
  John 169
Goings
  David 203
  Michael 50
Gomer
  John 22
Goode
  Ben 19
  Benjamin 17, 66, 79, 139, 166, 172
  Edward 16, 19, 28, 37, 48, 66, 94, 115, 144, 166, 169, 177, 229, 242, 248
  Goode 172
  John 24, 32, 79, 139, 147, 148, 166, 229, 242, 245
  Joseph 13, 109, 114, 115, 144, 169, 221, 232, 247, 248
  Mary 166
  Robert 60, 66, 74, 76, 112, 144, 147, 166
  Sarah 242
  Thomas 18, 19, 144, 169, 221
  William 175, 202
Gooding
  Robert 41
Gordan
  Robert 17, 21
  Sam 17

Gorden
  Daniel 222
  Giles 227
Gordin
  Robert 4
Gording
  Giles 111
  John 109, 111, 125
  NFN 121
  Richard 14
  Robert 65, 85, 111
  Samuel 32, 111
  William 111
Gordon
  Ann 206
  Giles 103, 206
  John 206
  Kitty 206
  Robert 206
  Sam 21
  William 95, 202
Gottie
  Peter 88
  Sarah 88
Gowan
  Archibald 232
Gowin
  David 209
  Elizabeth 209
Gowing
  James 8
Graham
  Dun. 9
  Duncan 3, 9, 33
  James 61
Gravitt
  William 136
Gray
  James 11
Green
  Richard 42, 43
Gregory
  James 168
  Peter 175
  Silvanus 218
Griffin
  LeRoy 73
  NFN 238
  Pearce 137, 248
  Peirce 15, 21
  Pierce 22, 39, 57, 160, 225
  Rachel 248
  Samuel 133, 135, 140, 149, 163
  Thomas 21, 22, 248

Griffin
  William 172, 191, 204, 218
Griffing
  Pierce 5, 6
Griffith
  Gabriel 4
Grinstead
  John 2, 160, 224
Grinstone
  John 16, 20
Gromarrin
  Gillee 143
  Wiltshire 143
Gunn
  Capt. 239
  James 23, 38, 39, 56, 91, 149, 159, 161, 185, 196, 211, 240
  John 10, 16, 21, 56, 64, 68, 70
  Mary 159, 211
  Robert 199
Gunter
  Stephen 60
Gutry
  Garet 168
Guttry
  Agnes 116
  William 116
Gwin
  Rachel 61
Gwine
  David 200
Haden
  Anthony 107
  Thomas 107
Hailes
  John 196
Hales
  John 16, 19, 76, 101, 120, 163, 178, 203, 230
Halket
  Jasper 192, 206, 207
Hall
  Darkes 102
  David 85, 95, 102, 145, 148, 149, 161, 168, 175, 182
  Davis 182
  Dorcas 102
  Elizabeth 7, 72
  Story 7, 15, 20, 72
  William 54, 98, 102, 179
Hallaway
  Bremillon 221
  Majer 221

Halling
  John 25
Hallock
  James 132, 142, 213
Hambleton
  Joseph 90
  William 54
Hamblett
  Morris 83
Hammock
  William 220
Hampton
  Moses 207
Hanbury
  Capel 12
  John 12, 51, 52
Hancock
  Lewis 84, 155, 164
Hanly
  William 188
Happer
  Cary 9
Harbord
  John 86, 95, 96
  Matthew 86
  Thomas 198
  William 198
Harburt
  Matthew 70
  NFN 70
Harding
  Giles 225, 226
  Groves 88, 143, 157, 175, 211, 213
  Robert 68
  Sarah 68, 100, 102, 213, 225, 226
  Thomas 34, 44, 45, 67, 113
  William 6, 8, 14, 20, 23, 24, 29, 33, 34, 41, 44, 45, 52, 61, 67, 68, 82, 85, 88, 100, 102, 107, 118, 142, 148, 164, 188, 225, 234
Hardman
  James 221
Hardson
  Ellis 50
Hardwick
  NFN 8, 80, 89, 131
Hardyman
  William 92
Harefield
  Michael 246

Harfield
  Michael 88, 94, 105
Harford
  James 149
Hargess
  Sarah 49
  William 49
Harlow
  John 129, 209
  Thomas 203
  William 146, 200, 203
Harlowe
  John 80
  William 80
Harralson
  Burgis 182
Harrelson
  Alisheba 168
  Alistraba 168
  Burges 206
  Burgis 161, 168
  Ezekiel 168
  Lichaba 168
Harris
  Benjamin 11, 73, 91
  David 102, 243
  Henrietta 137
  John 137, 198, 234
  Joseph 243
  NFN 106
  Thomas 187, 248
  William 93, 127, 137, 163, 219
Harrison
  Benjamin 15, 18, 49, 96, 103, 178, 223
  W. 103
  William 68, 95, 174, 191, 218
Harrod
  NFN 119
Hartfield
  Michael 171
Harvie
  John 11
Harwick
  NFN 117
Harwood
  Daniel 126, 142, 235
  Elizabeth 92
  John 12, 16, 19, 45, 57, 72, 92, 105, 119, 121, 126, 143, 174, 180, 181, 246
  Lesha 235
  Lister 240

263

Harwood
  Samuel 174, 201, 241
  Thomas 241
  William 65
Hatcher
  James 8, 9, 13, 17, 19, 26, 139
  William 86, 92, 101, 120, 139, 150
Haw
  Peter 30
Heastie
  Robert 117
Heilhouse
  William 178
Helhous
  William 178
Henderson
  George 85
  William 245
Henley
  Evan 122
  Hezekiah 202
  Leonard 8, 45, 50, 60, 80, 85, 89, 101, 103, 104, 107, 109, 111, 117, 118, 121, 122, 125, 131, 137, 150, 151, 170, 183, 186, 187, 189, 196, 206, 209, 210
  Mary 122, 130, 164
  Molly 80
  NFN 89, 129
  Richardson 209, 243
  Turner 210
  William 60, 106, 118, 122, 129, 131, 150, 164, 188, 189, 202
Henly
  Leonard 65, 76
  William 88
Henroughty
  Edward 19
Henry 185
  John 4, 35, 176
Herbert
  John 247
  Mat 202
  Matthew 19, 21, 94, 95, 110, 124, 198, 226
  NFN 80, 134, 219
Herrids
  Michael 64, 65
Herries
  Michael 33

Hibdon
  James 69
  Lucy 132, 174
Hibton
  James 79
Hicks
  George 200
  Isabella 176
  John 176
Higginbothem
  Aaron 10
Higginbottom
  Moses 10
Hill
  John 220
Hilton
  Daniel 224
  James 130
Hines
  Mary 109
  Richard 109
Hinson
  John 27
Histole
  Francis 42
Hix
  Amos 16, 20, 23, 89
  Elizabeth 150
Hoars
  Ben 89
Hobbs
  Robert 56
Hobden
  William 175
Hobson
  Aggy 13
  Benjamin 22
  Henry 92, 172
  John 13, 184, 207, 208
  Joseph 13, 101, 138
  Lucy 183
  Mathew 152
  Matthew 1, 47, 87, 107, 159, 206, 231
  NFN 139
  Nicholas 13
  Samuel 13, 75, 172, 183
  William 13, 25, 101, 122, 133, 139, 144, 146, 163, 172, 173, 177, 183, 184, 189
Hodges
  John 182, 201, 206
Hogg
  Jesse 141

Hogg
  Richard 182, 230, 239, 241
  Thomas 233
Holdsworth
  Thomas 141
Holland
  Dick 180, 221, 248
  Henry 244
  Michael 23, 52, 55, 56, 62, 87, 127, 163, 185
  Mitchell 222
  NFN 77, 78, 88, 99, 104, 108
  Richard 14, 22, 23, 29, 41, 47, 50, 59, 61, 67, 82, 85, 93, 127, 244
  Sarah 23, 50, 82
Holliday
  John 3
Holloway
  Bermelion 228
  Breavs 100
  Bremillion 15, 20, 108
  Cremillion 120
  Lacy 31
  Mager 226
  Major 210, 228
  NFN 115
Holman
  Nathaniel 129
Holmes
  John 155, 207
  Martha 143
  Thomas 15
Holt
  David 9
  Mabel 9
Hombs
  Thomas 142
Homes
  John 146
Hon
  Peter 205
Hood
  John 11
  Nathaniel 202
Hooper
  George 216
  Richard 40, 127, 192, 220
Hopkins
  Arthur 157
  Elizabeth 197
  John 157, 196, 197
  Joseph 16, 18, 29, 30, 53, 182, 184, 197

264

Hopkins
  Mary 30
  William 35
Hopson
  Ben 15
  Benjamin 18
  John 16, 18, 208, 244, 245
  Joseph 17, 19
  Matthew 17, 19, 216, 226
  William 17, 20
Houlder
  John 54
How
  Peter 29, 30
Howard
  Allen 27
  John 142, 161
Howerton
  Gerzle 170
  Thomas 115, 128, 170
Howl
  Epaproditus 233
Howlett
  John 55
  Thomas 98
Hubbard
  Benjamin 81
  Mathew 237
Hudson
  David 50
  George 50
  Tur. 233
  William 75, 233
Hughes
  Ann 93
  Archelus 106
  Charles 202, 247
  John 103, 163
  NFN 210
  Robert 27, 85
  Stephen 27
  Susanna 201
  Thomas 234
  William 23, 47, 50, 93, 106, 132, 137, 190, 201
Hughs
  James 6
Humphrey
  Edmond 129
  Edmund 80
  Mary 129
Humphry
  Ralph 221
Hundley
  NFN 115

Hunnicutt
  Wyke 7
Hunt
  Memucan 171
  Percevall 74
  Ralph 60, 63, 74, 188
  Robert 141
Hunter
  John 12
Hutchens
  John 179
Hutchenson
  Elias 204
Hutcheson
  Dorothy 247
  Elizabeth 247
  George 247
  Jane 247
  Mathew 221
  Matthew 100
  Patty 247
Hutchings
  John 157
  Strangemen 150
Hutchins
  John 135
Hyldon
  John 204
Hylton
  Daniel 243
  Eliza 73
  Hylton 185
  John 73, 151
Hyndman
  John 2
Ingram
  James 73
Irby
  William 28, 83
Jack(son)
  John 248
Jackson
  Joseph 42
  NFN 186
  Ralph 42
  Thomas 95
James
  Francis 11
Jameson
  Andrew 124
Jefferson
  Peter 11
Jenell
  Thomas 18

Jenkins
  Ann 200
  Drusiller 200
  Joseph 246
  William 136
Jennett
  Thomas 7, 21
Jennings
  David 6, 16, 20, 140
  George 6, 108
  NFN 141
  William 58, 238
Jobson
  Philip 173
Johnson
  Alee 131, 132
  Andrew 11
  Benjamin 24, 47, 52, 60, 74, 80, 89, 122, 129, 131, 132, 150, 164, 170, 183, 188, 194
  David 26, 120, 194
  Elizabeth 80, 131
  Emanuel 87
  Isaac 41
  Jacob 167, 184, 190
  James 4
  Jeremiah 147
  John 164, 232
  Matthew 34, 67, 83, 116, 138, 234
  Michael 131, 132, 183, 188, 196
  Philip 95
  Robert 87
  Sarah 132
  Thomas 194
  William 61
Johnston
  Caleb 212
  Samuel 212
Joines
  Thomas 19
Jolley
  Elizabeth 178
  Thomas 17, 20, 189
Jolly
  Mary 77
  Thomas 76, 77, 208, 212, 247
Jones
  Ann 87
  Anna 64
  Anne 55

265

Jones
  Benjamin 14, 19, 21, 120, 121, 228
  James 17, 21, 175, 206
  John 14, 100, 227
  Micael 1, 16, 20
  Michael 54, 55, 57, 58, 64, 69, 87, 97, 141
  Michel 8, 42
  NFN 115
  Pettis 248
  Richard 164
  Robert 74
  Samuel 14, 18, 21, 106, 120, 121, 221, 228
  William 14, 76, 80, 87, 91, 105, 106, 121, 123, 130, 131, 138, 145, 146, 189
  Wood 43
Jordan
  Ben 213, 221
  Benjamin 26, 28, 37, 44, 45, 76, 92, 123, 140, 150, 174, 200, 208, 234
  Charles 98-100
  Elizabeth 158
  Henry 82, 243
  John 13, 16, 18, 48, 49, 66
  Josiah 28
  Lydia 234
  Martha 144
  Matthew 11
  NFN 174
  Noble 175
  Pleasants 109, 150
  Robert 234
  Samuel 27
  Thomas 16, 18, 82, 93, 96, 98, 143, 144, 156, 213, 224
Jordane
  Noble 202
Jordone
  John 204
  Noble 204
Jude
  George 121
  John 16, 19, 67, 71, 76, 85, 89, 101-103, 107, 109, 113, 117-119, 121, 122, 150, 226, 234
  Mary 89, 109, 117, 121, 122, 234
Jurdan
  Thomas 226

Keesee
  Charles 120
Keesse
  Charles 203
Kelley
  Daniel 173, 214, 222
  George 31, 186
  John 70, 113, 176, 186
  Martha 77
  William 16, 21, 31, 40, 46, 77, 113, 118, 128, 140, 170, 222
Kellie
  John 152
Kelly
  Agness 222
  George 217, 222
  John 222
  William 217, 222
Kemp
  Francis 198
Kendall
  John 104
Kennedy
  Mr. 188
  William 214, 223, 233, 236, 237
Kennon
  William 3, 67
Kenny
  John 41
Kenson
  Phillip 219
Ker
  John 86
Kersey
  John 13
Killey
  Francis 220
  William 31
King
  Benjamin 35
  Walter 11
  Zachariah 170
Kippen
  George 222, 227
  John 139
Knaile
  John 4
Knott
  William 62
Lacey
  John 21, 50, 118, 123
Lacy
  Elliott 214, 215

Lacy
  John 17, 84, 228
  NFN 99, 115
  Stephen 132
  Susannah 71
Ladd
  James 120, 149
Laffoon
  NFN 50
  William 24, 88
Lafoon
  William 29, 132
Laforce
  Rena 6
  Rene 6, 41
Lamby
  William 83
Lancaster
  John 5, 7, 17, 20, 104, 106, 138, 139, 145
  Nathaniel 103, 106
Lane
  John 34
Lankaster
  John 44, 45, 48, 52, 179
  Judah 213, 226
  Judith 226
  William 213
Lankestar
  John 29
Lankester
  Hope 131, 189
  John 41, 84, 111, 127, 131, 132, 138, 155, 163, 170, 189, 196, 210, 231, 243, 248
  Joseph 224
  Nathaniel 130, 131, 189, 196
  Nicholas 142
  William 131, 138, 142, 151, 189, 196, 218
Lankford
  John 30, 31, 109
Lankister
  Francis 80
  John 80
  Nathaniel 80
Larey
  John 54
Largeon
  Thomas 145
Law
  John 17, 21, 34, 47, 114
  Sarah 47, 114

Lawless
  Sarah 8, 107, 118
  William 2, 6, 8, 17, 21, 24,
    47, 69, 106, 107, 118,
    129, 164, 166, 183, 188,
    189
Lead
  James 26
Leason
  John 127
Leavons
  William 6
Lee
  Agnes 123
  Ambrose 119
  John 101
  Walter 123
Leeson
  John 1, 8
Leforce
  Rachel 100
  Renny 100
Leggy
  Sam 18
Leigh
  Walter 17, 37, 102
  Wat. 20
Leitch
  David 225
  John 225
LeMay
  Leo 216
Lester
  Obedience 207
  William 95
Letcher
  Giles 14, 47, 49, 67, 85, 182
  Hannah 14
  Silas 10
  Stephen 181
Lettuck
  Harruet 165
Levin
  Richard 52
Lewes
  Joseph 58
  William 60
Lewis
  Charles 52, 68, 127, 157,
    171, 173, 193, 213, 215,
    246
  Elizabeth 234
  John 109
  Joseph 1, 12, 16, 21, 31, 54,
    64, 68, 69, 77-79, 85,
    90, 91, 93, 97, 104, 105,

Lewis
  Joseph 111, 127, 129, 142,
    146, 156, 163, 179, 241
  Mary 52, 192
  NFN 54, 115, 126
  Susanna 193, 246
  Thomas 109, 111, 125, 128,
    187, 190, 206
  William 10, 13, 15, 20, 52,
    68, 85, 90, 91, 140, 157,
    192, 199, 201, 241
Liggan
  Elijah 129
Liggon
  John 160, 191, 198
  NFN 89
  Samuel 160, 180, 200, 214,
    215
  William 200
Liggy
  Sam 20
Lightfoot
  Henry 171, 200
Ligon
  James 119
  John 119
  Judith 119
  Sam 16, 21
  Samuel 72, 130, 131, 143
  Simon 24
Linch
  Mary 49
  William 49
Lindsay
  James 69, 77, 122-124, 126,
    144, 169
  NFN 239
Lindsey
  Campbell 230
  George 245
  James 64, 75, 80, 86, 125,
    135, 144, 146, 163, 173,
    183, 237
  John 173
  Landy 243
  Mary 230
Linsey
  James 25
Lipscomb
  John 50, 59, 90, 152, 206,
    209, 231
  Judith 50
Lipscombe
  John 17, 20
Lipshott
  James 37

Liptrol
  Amos 49
Liptrot
  Amos 17
Liptrott
  Amos 19
  Ursula 98
Littlepage
  James 5
Lively
  Joseph 202
Lloyd
  Daniel 70
  James 218
  Sarah 218
Lock
  Thomas 210
Lockhart
  James 214
Lomax
  Lunsford 11
Long
  Alexander 15, 18, 63, 93, 96
Lovell
  Richard 203
Loving
  Randal 209
  Richard 16, 20, 44, 45, 200
  William 157
Low
  William 70
Lowit
  Thomas 69
Lowitt
  Gording 69
Loyd
  James 204
  Sarah 204
Lucas
  Aaron 242
  George 80
Lucy
  John 248
Lyle
  James 33, 36, 39, 61, 64,
    134, 136, 144, 214, 227
Lyles
  David 7
  James 49
Lynch
  John 188
Lynn
  Peter 217
Lyon
  Robert 39

Lyons
  Peter 204
Mackie
  Alexander 91
  Charles 77
  David 94, 202
Macon
  William 163
Madderra
  Priscilla 98
Maddox
  Robert 16, 134, 144, 145, 162, 177, 178
Makie
  Alexander 2
Malor
  Peter 194
Maralester
  Archibald 242
Markham
  Bernard 127, 230, 232
  George 248
  John 100, 164, 195
Marr
  Gideon 27
Marrin
  Gilley 76
  Gilleygron 193
  Gilly 76
  Mary 76, 193
  NFN 236
  Susanna 193
  Wiltshire 111, 143, 193
Marriott
  NFN 147
Martain
  Elizabeth 159
  James 136
  John 130, 136
  Martain 43, 136
  William 144
Martin
  Barbara 161
  Barbary 43, 45
  Frances 74
  George 74
  Glais 74
  Henry 52, 53, 127, 163, 184, 185, 222
  Isham 182
  James 136, 159, 161
  Jane 158
  John 2, 3, 24, 45, 48, 60, 76, 86, 89, 108, 109, 113, 131, 136, 146, 149, 158, 159, 161, 208, 247

Martin
  Judith 74
  Lewis 95
  Martin 12, 34, 43, 45, 76, 102, 113, 136, 159-161
  Mary 74
  NFN 202
  Orson 76
  Owen 22
  Richard 229
  Samuel 2, 74
  Shadrack 22
  Thomas 231
Martins
  Martin 113
Mason
  John 148, 166
Massie
  Peter 110, 137
  William 219
Mathews
  Anne 189
  Anthony 113, 189, 190
  Susanna 190
  Thomas 83
Mathie
  Alexander 37
  Gabriel 37
Mathis
  Edward 68
  Gregory 9
Matthew
  Anthony 138
Matthews
  Anthony 1, 9, 12, 17, 19, 34, 43, 45, 63, 71, 102, 113, 149, 173, 180, 199, 212
  Charles 239
  Edward 47-49, 66, 68, 86, 102, 238
  Elizabeth 1
  Gregory 9
  Henry 48, 49
  James 209
  John 48, 49
  Joseph 29, 71
  Martha 49
  NFN 240, 246
  Samson 142
  Samuel 209
  Thomas 15, 18, 20, 49, 86, 135, 158
  William 15, 32, 71
Mattox
  Robert 18

Mayes
  William 34
Maynard
  Edward 62
Mayo
  Joseph 135, 180
  Maj. 101
  Major 66
  NFN 199, 214, 215
  Philip 8, 10-13, 46, 54, 60, 76, 78, 79, 95, 97, 104, 105, 111, 113, 116, 118, 119, 121, 124, 129, 138, 205, 237
Mays
  William 150, 246
Mayse
  NFN 198
McAlester
  Hector 141
McBride
  John 186
  Mary 186
McCaul
  Alexander 49, 61, 72, 97, 130, 131, 135, 138, 139, 162, 166, 170, 171, 182, 198
  NFN 245
McDaniel
  Thomas 11
McDonald
  George 210
McDowall
  Anguish 222
  James 223
  John 233
McDowell
  James 117, 207, 209, 218, 223, 224
McGhee
  John 194
McGill
  Peter 245
McKeand
  John 156, 196, 219, 220
McKenzey
  Alexander 4
  John 37
McKindley
  John 191, 238
McLean
  John 213
McNemara
  John 70

McPherson
  Charles 138
Meade
  David 4
  R.K. 150
  Richard 212
Mealer
  Ann 120
  Nicholas 17, 79, 96, 119, 120
  Peter 79, 95
  William 198
Mealor
  Nicholas 194, 198
  William 194, 198
Meggenson
  William 11
Melar
  Nicholas 20
Menzies
  Ninian 234, 235, 241
Meredith
  Elisha 23
  James 23, 47, 48, 50
Merrit
  Eleanor 87
  Joseph 242
  Thomas 87
Merritt
  Joseph 183
  Thomas 18, 20, 57
Micheaue
  Paul 11
Middleton
  John 17, 19, 38, 61, 96, 103, 109, 135
Miler
  Philip 194
Mill
  John 61
Millar
  Elisha 16, 18
Miller
  Anne 216, 223
  Dabney 200
  David 223
  Elisha 39, 81, 107, 131, 139-141
  Elizabeth 124, 213, 214
  James 238, 243
  John 27, 66, 101-103, 119, 131, 224, 227, 231
  Martha 216, 223
  NFN 99
  Priscilla 102
  Sarah 243

Miller
  Thomas 54, 123, 124
  Tom 118
  William 2, 34, 107, 108, 117, 120, 132, 170, 213, 214, 217, 222, 223, 231, 243, 245
Mills
  John 3
  Matthew 3
  Nicholas 220
  William 15, 19
Minzier
  Ninian 138
Minzies
  Mr. 222
Mitchell
  Henry 147, 148, 166
  Joseph 1, 17, 20, 28
  Mary 28
  Priscilla 148, 166
  Robert 210, 227, 233, 236
  Samuel 137, 138, 155, 180, 189, 191, 197-199, 201, 210
  William 207, 210, 220, 222, 236, 245
Monrow
  John 37
Mood
  Christopher 101
Moody
  Hugh 229, 237, 246
  Ruth 246
Moore
  Agness 51
  Daniel 110, 184
  John 102, 176
  Mark 211
  Pelham 28
  Richard 37, 51, 101, 102, 163
  Robert 101, 123, 140, 148, 163
  Susannah 163
  William 234
Morosini
  Hutonio 25
Morris
  Elizabeth 226
  Gennings 228
  Hughes 158
  Joshua 42
  NFN 141, 238
  Philip 27
  Robert 6, 17, 20, 23, 39, 88

Morris
  Samuel 42, 106, 181
  William 87, 137, 138, 140, 149, 156, 158, 160, 173, 222, 224, 246
Morriss
  Robert 56
  William 56, 179, 191
Morson
  Alexander 3
Mosby
  Benjamin 141, 206
  John 15, 20, 21, 33, 34, 84, 108, 116, 129, 146, 159, 176, 183, 242
  Lucy 84, 129
  NFN 171, 175
  Robert 81, 141, 206
Moseby
  John 54, 56, 58, 62
  Robert 48, 61
Moseley
  Thomas 34
Mosely
  John 55, 232
  Thomas 164
Mosley
  Hallary 122
  John 231
Moss
  Alexander 160, 180
Mouat
  William 4
Mouatt
  William 89, 143
Mouldon
  John 48
Mourat
  William 69
Moxley
  Elijah 123
Mulatto
  Aley 227
Muller
  C. 188
  Christian 188
Munford
  Robert 164
Munro
  Ebenezer 65
Murchie
  John 242
Murdock
  George 2
  John 2, 233

269

Murray
  James 178
  Robert 134, 136
Murrer
  John 236
Muter
  George 232, 233
Mutton
  George 61
Nance
  John 69, 90
  Mary 97
  NFN 136, 235
  William 54, 64, 90, 97, 111, 126, 130, 235
Necks
  Robert 151
Negro 227
  Aberdeen 206, 233
  Abigail 141
  Abraham 159
  Abram 167
  Agee 91
  Agg 131
  Aggy 167
  Agie 245
  Aley 227
  Alley 192
  Alse 214
  Amy 110
  Anaky 139
  Anna 211
  Anne 206
  Anthony 211
  Beck 211
  Ben 142, 152
  Beth 244
  Bett 131, 157, 174
  Betty 96, 174, 207, 211, 245
  Big Will 245
  Bob 60, 131, 223, 227
  Bobb 214
  Caesar 138, 207
  Carter 167
  Cesar 214
  Charles 189
  Chloe 60
  Cis 171
  Cloe 174, 206, 233
  Cuffie 223
  Cuffy 199
  Daniel 50, 67, 214, 227
  Davey 22
  David 174
  Davis 174
  Day 55

Negro
  Dick 24, 89, 96, 159, 242
  Dinah 67, 211, 214
  Dirk 1
  Doll 157
  Dooke 167
  Dublin 174
  Essex 222
  Esther 88, 90
  Eve 214
  Evy 227
  Fanny 1, 62, 63, 114, 153, 174, 189, 190
  Febey 211
  Frank 68, 88, 90, 141, 174, 206, 211, 233
  George 68
  Grace 67, 174
  Gwin 189
  Hampshire 138
  Hampton 171
  Hannah 41, 55, 96, 139, 223
  Harris 206
  Harry 50, 68, 136, 153, 189, 199, 214, 237
  Isaac 167, 199, 206, 214, 227, 233
  Isabell 55
  Isom 153
  Jack 22, 49, 60, 68, 210, 236
  Jacob 91, 124, 142
  Jame 90
  James 227
  Jamey 88
  Jane 60, 138, 189, 190, 228, 231
  Jean 136
  Jenny 41, 167, 174, 237
  Jesse 228
  Joan 211
  Joe 60, 162, 171, 205, 214, 224
  John 133
  Jone 211
  Judith 231
  Judy 1, 193, 214
  Kate 243, 245
  Kemp 233
  Leadenhall 174
  Leddis 41
  Lucretia 231
  Lucy 60, 138, 211, 223, 226, 227
  Martin 244
  Mary 110
  Mat 174

Negro
  Matilda 60
  Matt 67, 174
  Milley 160
  Mima 167
  Mingo 68
  Moll 60, 157, 189, 237
  Molly 174, 214
  Moses 167
  Nan 219
  Naomi 167
  Nead 41
  Ned 114, 136
  Nell 190, 222
  Newport 56
  Patience 223
  Patrick 210, 236
  Patt 60, 167, 170
  Peg 174
  Pegg 138, 189, 211
  Peter 89, 138, 160, 176, 189, 228
  Phebe 138, 152
  Philis 223
  Phill 139, 214
  Phillis 41, 62, 189
  Phoebe 211
  Phyllis 58
  Pompey 67, 244
  Prince 68, 136
  Rachel 138, 153, 189, 228
  Robin 50
  Rose 174, 211
  Sall 138
  Sam 60
  Sarah 1, 41, 60, 67, 114, 189
  Sesar 100
  Sheeba 223
  Silve 167
  Silvia 49
  Simon 141
  Smith 211
  Stephen 167, 244
  Stepney 141
  Sue 1, 49, 63, 100, 174, 199
  Sye 171
  Sylvia 211
  Tamar 244
  Tamer 174, 190
  Tark 62, 63
  Temp 55, 60
  Tempey 153
  Thom 227
  Toby 68
  Tom 1, 55, 110, 214, 245
  Toney 37, 67, 209

Negro
  Ursley 153
  Venus 211, 233
  Will 1, 55, 131, 212, 214, 227, 245
Neilson
  John 79
Nelson
  Thomas 35, 92, 116
  William 109, 215
Netherland
  Anne 241
  Claude 241
  Wade 241
Nevell
  James 119
New
  Benjamin 97
  John 63, 70, 97, 143, 180, 206, 223, 236
  William 97, 98, 223
Newsum
  Robert 169
Nicholas
  George 10, 169
  John 10
  Robert 182, 202, 227
Nixon
  Henry 95
  NFN 198
NLN
  Richard 174
Noble
  Ann 169
  William 168, 169
Nohnes
  William 62, 63
Nolms
  William 62, 63
North
  Abraham 46, 98, 138
  Anthony 52, 138, 145, 155, 179
  Dorothy 145
  John 41, 42, 80, 106, 121, 138
  Lucy 179
  Mary 41
  Sarah 106, 138
  Susannah 98
  Thomas 52, 138, 145, 155
  William 13, 17, 21, 41, 52, 98
Norton
  John 52

Norvell
  George 63, 74
  James 81
  John 158, 224, 246
  Mary 224
O'Bryan
  Mary 59
Oakley
  Elizabeth 46, 54
  Erasmus 22
  John 16, 18, 46, 54, 55, 78, 129, 136, 141, 235
  Martha 235
  Thomas 46, 54
Oakly
  John 42
Old
  John 139
Oliver
  Jon. 186
Orange
  John 15, 20, 34, 114, 239
  Judith 35, 239
Orr
  John 33, 69, 72, 92, 101, 113, 127, 144, 170
  William 63
Orrange
  John 180, 181
  Judith 181
Orring
  John 128
  Judah 128
Osborne
  Edward 15, 18, 82, 98, 147, 148, 166
  Elizabeth 98, 148
Oswald
  Alexander 3, 64, 65
  Richard 3, 49, 61, 64, 65
Overton
  Samuel 230
Owen
  Ambrose 93
  Anne 153
  Even 3
  Fontaine 153
  Hebron 248
  Hobden 152
  Hobson 152-154, 239
  Hopson 107, 173
  John 1, 17, 19, 42, 47, 107, 139, 181
  Judith 152
  Mary 152, 153
  Mildred 139

Owen
  Sarah 152-154, 213
  Thomas 1, 17, 19, 39, 70, 88, 107, 114, 152-154, 167, 188, 199, 205
  William 47, 107, 139, 152-154, 212, 213, 232
Owens
  John 114
Owing
  Francis 128
Owl
  William 34
Padason
  Alexander 4
Page
  John 183, 187, 194-196, 201, 229, 230, 232, 240, 244
Pankey
  John 183, 229, 230, 236
  Stephen 1, 84, 118
Parham
  Lewis 175
Parker
  Benjamin 207
  Edward 86, 93
  Francis 171, 209
  James 11, 95
  John 24, 142, 214, 224, 241
  Joseph 207
  Mary 171
  NFN 199
  Ruth 83
  Sarah 241
  William 17, 20, 43, 45, 66, 83, 93, 143, 171, 186, 207
Parks
  John 227
Parrlie
  James 225
Parson
  NFN 61, 139
Parsons
  Agnes 167
  Agness 202
  Elizabeth 167, 202
  Joseph 1, 56, 107, 114, 167, 198, 202
  Josiah 167, 198, 202
  Judith 167, 202
  Mary 56, 167, 202
  Samuel 152-154, 165, 166, 180, 186, 187, 221, 239
  Sarah 167, 202

Parsons
　Ursley 202
　Ursulah 167
　William 167, 202
　Woodson 167, 202
Paslay
　William 177
Pass
　Lucy 54
　Thomas 16, 21, 50, 54
Paterson
　Alexander 210
　Simon 245
Patison
　Andrew 137
Patman
　Agness 226
　Elizabeth 226
　Mary 226
　NFN 84
　Sarah 105, 108, 125, 128, 213, 224, 226
　Susanna 213, 226
　Watson 72, 108, 109, 159
　William 2, 57, 105, 125, 128, 214, 224, 226, 232
Patrick
　Edmund 1
　NFN 84, 214
　Peter 1
Patten
　Thomas 85
Patterson
　Alexander 15, 21, 72, 85, 102, 186, 230, 231, 238
　Andrew 129, 146, 147
　David 183, 194-196, 199, 201
　Elizabeth 147
　James 237
　Jonathan 123
　Sicily 230, 231
Patteson
　David 229, 230, 232, 241
　Gideon 243
Pattison
　John 42
Pattman
　William 116
Paulette
　Thomas 117, 118
Payne
　Archibald 175
　George 109
　John 11, 55

Pearce
　Francis 110
Peek
　Isaac 238
Peers
　Anderson 136
Peirce
　Francis 17, 19
　William 17, 20
Peluter
　Patrick 242
Pemble
　John 231, 236
　Thomas 145, 185, 236
Perkins
　Constant 117
　Elizabeth 220
　John 87, 247
　Joseph 117
　Mary 117
　NFN 147
　Philemon 67
　Thomas 17, 19, 73, 82, 93
　William 220
Perrin
　Henry 232
　Joseph 116, 232
Perrot
　William 62, 63
Peterson
　Alexander 98
　John 236
Pettipool
　Colwell 193
　Mary 193
Pettit
　J. 54
　John 46
Pettus
　Dabney 107, 128, 133, 181, 200, 205, 228, 245
　George 124
　John 248
　Mr. 228
Phelps
　John 64
Philbord
　Archibald 207
Phillips
　Thomas 187
Pierce
　John 74
Piers
　Anderson 192
Pike
　George 139, 154

Pike
　William 135, 139, 154, 203
Piles
　Godfrey 44, 45, 119, 124
　Godfry 4
　Godphra 182
Pimble
　John 45, 124, 225
　Thomas 196, 225
Pincham
　Jane 4
　Samuel 4
Pleasant
　Robert 208
Pleasants
　Archibald 165, 167
　Bailey 101
　Dorothy 152
　Elizabeth 26, 28, 114, 115, 118, 136, 138, 175, 238
　Exum 152
　J. 209
　Jacob 165, 175, 194, 195, 200, 218, 238, 241
　James 118
　Jane 25, 26
　Jesse 167, 175, 238
　John 7, 16, 18-20, 24-26, 28, 36-38, 41, 44-49, 55, 59, 60, 66, 71, 73, 75, 83, 85, 88, 90, 92, 95, 98, 101, 110, 114, 115, 118, 120, 126, 129, 133, 134, 138, 141, 152, 154, 155, 158, 162, 165, 167, 173, 175, 177, 186, 187, 195, 202, 205, 212, 213, 229, 237, 238, 243, 244
　John2 44
　Jonathan 241, 247
　Joseph 6, 28, 37, 47, 59, 66, 84, 109, 114, 115, 118, 135, 152, 155, 175, 177, 205, 218, 223, 237
　Josiah 115, 237, 238
　Mary 25, 26, 56, 167
　NFN 208, 237
　Peggy 176
　Richard 55
　Robert 5, 15, 18, 25, 26, 37, 48, 59, 73, 75, 83, 91, 92, 101-103, 109, 110, 120, 123, 133-135, 140, 141, 146, 148-150, 152-154, 158, 164, 165, 172, 174-179, 184,

272

Pleasants
  Robert 200-203, 205, 208, 211, 213, 229, 232, 237, 238
  Sally 160
  Samuel 83
  Sarah 26
  Susanna 7, 167, 174
  Tarleton 7
  Thomas 7, 24-26, 28, 37, 47, 48, 57, 66, 73, 83, 84, 115, 118, 120, 144, 152, 160, 172, 175-177, 183, 184, 186, 201, 211, 213, 218, 220, 221, 229, 243, 244
Poindexter
  Thomas 175
Poke
  George 16, 19
Pollard
  Ben 227
  Benjamin 206, 207, 227, 233, 236
Pool
  Colwel 143
Porce
  Daniel 7
Porter
  Ben 19
  Benjamin 16, 77
  Elizabeth 192
  Hannah 76
  NFN 92, 136
  Rebecca 205
  William 76, 134, 136, 159, 178, 205
Povall
  John 16, 19, 21, 62, 65
  Robert 146, 201, 203, 208, 215
  Robin 213
Powell
  William 160
Power
  Anne 22
  Foliott 22
Powers
  Catherine 191
  Foliott 15
  Folliot 19
  Jacob 54
Poynter
  Elizabeth 218
  Richard 218

Poythress
  Elizabeth 26
  Jane 26
Pretlow
  Thomas 29
Prewit
  John 220
Price
  Barrett 201
  Charles 234
  Daniel 1, 16, 17, 19, 20, 31, 54, 58, 60, 64, 78, 79, 91, 97, 113, 116, 119, 121, 123, 126, 132, 138, 147, 156, 157, 179, 188, 192, 193, 207, 221, 234, 246
  Hannah 123
  James 176, 222, 235
  John 14, 16, 20, 21, 31, 42, 59, 69, 70, 110, 123, 129, 138, 151, 157, 159, 176, 180, 188, 192, 201, 221, 231, 241
  Joseph 126, 235
  Mary 123, 192, 221
  Robert 91, 171, 215
  Samuel 121, 176, 205, 215, 221, 235, 244
  Susannah 103, 209
  William 1, 91, 99, 102, 103, 138, 157, 164, 166, 200
Pride
  John 87, 92, 147, 149, 198
Pringle
  Richard 53, 65
Prior
  Edward 8, 15, 21
Prosser
  NFN 213, 231
  Thomas 139, 159, 193-196, 201, 205, 206, 209, 210, 216, 223, 225, 231, 239, 240, 248
Pryar
  Edward 118
Pryer
  Edward 50, 82, 91, 123, 124
  Sarah 124
Pryor
  Christopher 165
  Edward 54, 81, 103, 124
  William 23, 24
Puller
  John 184

Pulliam
  Agness 81
  Benjamin 141
  John 81
Pure
  John 59
Puryear
  Hezekiah 146
  John 23, 127
  Obadiah 247
  Peter 146, 185
  Susannah 146
  William 185
Pyechamberlayne
  Edward 27
Rabon
  William 143
Raborne
  George 176, 177
Radford
  Andrew 126, 127
  John 112
Ragland
  Gideon 232
  John 94
  NFN 246
Raglin
  Benjamin 120
  John 171, 174
  Judith 171
Randolph
  Ann 98, 99, 212
  Anne 110
  Beverley 3, 29, 40, 197, 198
  Beverly 165
  Col. 3
  Edward 54
  Elizabeth 197, 198
  Jacob 158
  Jane 5
  John 51, 101, 139, 150, 203
  Mr. 211
  NFN 82, 83, 89, 155
  Peter 10, 12, 15, 18, 27, 36, 39, 66, 76, 77, 80, 85, 103, 104, 134, 138, 157, 161, 165, 166, 197, 198, 208, 212, 219, 248
  Peyton 40, 183, 187, 194-196, 201, 207, 229, 230, 232, 240, 241, 244
  Richard 5, 11-13, 25-27, 46, 51, 56, 57, 59, 66-69, 73, 75, 98-101, 110, 111, 115, 129, 138-140, 144, 149-151, 159, 161,

Randolph
  Richard 172, 178, 187, 211-213, 221, 230
  Ryland 68, 101, 110, 115, 125, 150, 187, 189, 211-213, 230, 246
  Thomas 93, 121, 125, 138, 143, 148, 150, 168, 175, 178, 180, 196, 207, 208, 227, 238
  William 9, 12-15, 26, 35, 37, 39-41, 53, 63-65, 74, 82, 86, 91, 95, 96, 98, 103, 107, 114, 121, 129, 142, 157, 178, 184, 212, 218, 221, 242
Rane
  John 192
Ratchford
  Thomas 197
Ratterly
  William 177
Ray
  Jonathan 43
Read
  Jeremiah 219
Reams
  Mary 102
  William 102
Reaves
  Edward 149, 185
Redcross
  John 245
Redford
  Anthony 164
  Francis 48, 66, 67, 73, 89, 167
  James 167
  John 16, 18, 48, 59, 64, 66, 67, 82, 84, 96, 103, 104, 109, 127, 132, 143, 173, 179, 192, 236
  Joseph 173, 221
  Josiah 109
  Mary 104, 164
  Milener 18
  Miliner 20
  Milner 45, 67, 75, 83, 84, 143, 179, 186, 229
  NFN 34
  Sarah 75, 84
  William 67, 80, 96, 104, 109, 156, 173, 179, 192, 207
  Wishier 59

Reins
  John 187
Ren
  Richard 9
Renard
  Richard 96, 107, 116, 151, 169, 187
Renyard
  Richard 15, 19
Rers
  Anderson 172
Rice
  George 248
  John 40
Richardson
  George 74, 94, 127
  Isham 27, 185
  John 185
  Mary 185
  Samuel 94, 232
  Turner 42
  William 236
Riddell
  George 175
Ridley
  Nathaniel 208
Ritchie
  Archibald 11
Rives
  Edward 84
Roane
  Lucy 69
  William 69, 105
Robards
  John 27
Robenson
  Thomas 16
Roberson
  Ann 43, 45
  Anne 53
  Jacob 76
  John 43, 45, 53
Robertson
  Alexander 40, 53, 56, 59, 78, 143, 192, 229
  Amey 1
  Arthur 79
  George 37, 87, 177
  Isaac 40
  Jacob 7, 52
  James 240
  John 1, 32, 33, 40, 79, 86, 121, 126, 239
  NFN 69, 78, 79
  Thomas 79
  William 79, 86, 87, 188

Robinson
  Alexander 17, 21, 33, 40, 42, 54, 72, 87, 160, 166, 188, 236
  George 9, 63, 94, 103, 113, 122, 135, 226
  Jacob 33
  Jane 94
  John 8, 32, 33, 40, 43, 45, 87, 103, 126, 166, 178, 188, 220, 223, 224, 242
  Margery 103
  Mary 9
  Robert 3
  Samuel 166, 235
  St. George 226
  Susannah 188
  Thomas 8, 9, 16, 18-20, 40, 57, 63, 86, 94, 122, 130, 188, 203, 223, 226
  William 122, 124, 133, 135, 144, 163, 166, 173, 175, 177, 183
Robson
  Alexander 1
  Joseph 149
Rochell
  Richard 13, 15, 18
  Ware 13
Rockett
  Baldwin 26, 81, 130
  John 25-27, 130, 204
  NFN 102, 107, 111
  Richard 25, 38, 80, 81, 130, 134, 147, 183, 187, 204
  Ware 81, 130
Rodgers
  Thomas 103
Rogers
  Thomas 14, 134, 178
Rootes
  Philip 35, 38, 39, 49, 198
Roper
  Jesse 245, 248
  John 226, 243, 248
  Lewis 143, 191, 202
Rorkett
  NFN 57
Rorriss
  Edward 68
Rose
  John 155
  Robert 155
  William 54, 58
Ross
  David 219, 224

Ross
  William 1, 17, 20
Rosser
  NFN 218
Roughty
  Darby 63
Rountree
  William 85
Rowe
  William 189
Rowen
  Henry 138
Rowland
  George 239
  John 94
  Zach. 239, 241
  Zachariah 210
Royall
  James 231
  NFN 88
Royster
  John 16, 19, 135, 137, 154,
    164, 177, 178, 203, 215
  Nathaniel 203
  Thomas 48
Rutherford
  William 220
Ryall
  James 151, 171, 175, 188
  John 188
  NFN 171
Ryalls
  John 137
Sadler
  Benjamin 186, 220
Salmons
  Ann 187
  John 187
Samuel
  Duval 204
Sanders
  John 114, 179, 180, 239
Scherer
  George 59, 63, 66, 88, 91,
    104, 155, 165, 206, 236,
    247
  Nicholas 54, 55, 59, 114,
    127, 148, 149, 155, 165,
    174, 206, 247
  Sally 165
  Samuel 247
Scherrer
  George 36, 108, 114, 143
  Nicholas 36, 47, 108
Scoearts
  John 129

Scott
  Ben 63
  Benjamin 114
  Betty 98
  Elizabeth 83
  Francis 133, 134
  James 28
  Jane 47
  John 79, 105, 157, 160, 172,
    184, 216
  Joseph 105
  Nicholas 133, 134
  Robert 3, 61, 73, 75, 83, 95,
    150
  Sarah 134, 140
  Thomas 133
  William 157, 160, 184
Scudmore
  Rowles 36
Seaton
  George 233
Sedgley
  Samuel 178
Segrief
  Henry 172
Selden
  Mary 221
Miles 89, 110, 116, 121,
    127, 130, 147, 157, 163,
    205, 220, 221, 235
Sellar
  William 64
Seller
  William 9
Sellor
  William 3
Sexton
  George 222
Sharp
  Francis 166
  Henry 24, 25, 36, 49, 68, 75,
    80
  Isaac 28, 74, 207
  James 173, 174, 196, 199,
    205, 207, 212, 215, 228
  John 75, 182
  Mary 49
  NFN 246
  Richard 132, 155, 238
  Robert 7, 30, 40, 68, 77, 90,
    93, 152-154, 192, 232
  Susanna 37, 40
  William 25, 28, 37, 40, 48,
    74, 75, 77, 90, 207
Sharpe
  Isaac 16, 19, 229

Sharpe
  Julius 181
  Richard 229, 237
  Robert 13, 16, 19, 20, 242
  William 17, 19
Sheilds
  William 109
Shelton
  James 27, 126
  John 95
Shepard
  Benjamin 176
  John 188
  Samuel 102, 175, 180, 196
Shephard
  Elizabeth 238
  Samuel 69, 238
Shepherd
  Benjamin 151, 158, 222,
    224
  Isabella 176
  John 88, 151, 176
  Joseph 151, 158, 222, 224
  NFN 141
  Robert 85, 155
  William 151
Sheppard
  Benjamin 111, 118, 137,
    248
  Elizabeth 238
  John 111, 118
  Joseph 118
  Samuel 125, 238
  William 111, 118, 123
Sherrer
  George 15, 18
  Nicholas 15, 18
Shewmaker
  Ann 45
  Evan 8, 52, 100
  John 44, 45, 66, 119, 141,
    151
  NFN 189
Shields
  William 18, 19, 38
Shiffely
  Sally 88
  Samuel 88
Shoemaker
  Evan 18, 21, 24, 47, 80, 101,
    122
  John 40, 44, 45, 57, 77, 101,
    108, 117, 124, 141
  Judith 80
Simcock
  John 68

Simcocks
  John 185
Simcoks
  John 149
Sims
  Susannah 90
  William 46, 50, 59, 90, 152
Sincock
  John 186
Sincocks
  John 84
Skelton
  John 199
Skinner
  Ann 39, 154, 189
  Thomas 49, 154
  William 154, 189
Slave
  Absalom 197
  Agg 121
  Aggy 38
  Agnes 197
  Alse 214
  Anakey 102
  Ary 198
  Beck 121
  Bess 26
  Bett 121
  Betty 5, 220
  Billey 26, 38
  Bob 223
  Bobb 214
  Boumshire 5
  Caesar 61, 121
  Cate 5
  Cesar 38, 214
  Charlotte 38
  Cuffie 223
  Cuffy 89
  Cupid 220
  Daniel 214
  David 121
  Dennis 233
  Dinah 214
  Essex 222
  Eve 214
  Fanney 102
  Farthing 121
  Frank 197
  Gabriel 197
  George 5, 233
  Gilly 233
  Grace 26
  Hannah 92, 121, 223, 233
  Hannibal 5
  Harry 38, 214, 220

Slave
  Iris 89
  Isaac 214
  Jacob 26, 69
  James 227
  Jamy 5
  Jane 26
  Jenney 5
  Jo 26
  Joan 5
  Joe 214, 224
  John 38
  Johnny 197
  Judith 26
  Judy 214
  Lucy 38, 223, 227, 233
  Malo 198
  Margaret 61
  Matilda 102
  Moll 26, 223
  Molly 214
  Nan 26
  Naneo 121
  Ned 121
  Nelly 5
  Nelsey 121
  Neptune 233
  Nimrod 38
  Patt 61, 102
  Peter 26
  Pharoah 38
  Phebe 38
  Philis 223
  Phill 214
  Phillis 5, 121
  Phyllis 89
  Pompey 233
  Primus 38
  Rachael 197
  Rachel 102
  Rhodah 5
  Robert 197
  Sally 197
  Sam 26, 197
  Samuel 38
  Sarah 38, 121, 223
  Sheeba 223
  Sue 121, 223
  Sukey 5, 197
  Terry 61
  Tom 38, 102, 214
  Ursley 121
  Venus 233
  Viney 220
  Will 214
  York 61

Slaves
  Anthony 185
  Betty 185
  Billy 185
  Bob 185
  Caesar 185
  Ciss 185
  Cuffy 185
  Davy 185
  Fanny 185
  Fib 69
  Frank 185
  Godfrey 185
  Hannah 69, 185
  Harry 185
  Isaac 69
  Jack 185
  Jacob 69
  Jenny 185
  Jude 69
  Judy 185
  Katey 185
  Langston 185
  Nancy 185
  Neby 185
  Suckey 185
  Tommy 185
  York 69
Smith
  Anne 32
  Augustine 170, 173, 181, 222, 245
  Capt. 93
  Elizabeth 55, 56, 191, 229
  Humphrey 64, 91, 139, 154, 203, 205, 229, 246
  Humphry 15, 19
  Jacob 15, 20, 32, 39, 41, 42, 51, 99, 108, 123, 129, 147, 155, 171, 210, 225, 226, 234
  Jesse 121, 124, 137, 170, 186, 189, 206, 210, 211, 227
  John 5, 6, 16, 21, 22, 51, 162, 192, 241
  Joseph 162
  Luke 52, 64
  Mary 5, 39, 51
  Obadiah 5, 40, 42, 162, 165, 190-192, 206, 215
  Obediah 99, 101, 175
  Parks 227
  Peyton 134
  Richard 140, 188
  Robert 118

Smith
  Susanna 192
  Thomas 218, 220
  William 31, 32, 39, 42, 46, 51, 55, 56, 95, 97, 100, 119, 121, 127, 131, 132, 135, 192, 201
Smth
  Charles 222
Snead
  Archbill 158
  Charles 81, 173, 213, 245
  Robert 214
  Thomas 174
  William 16, 20, 46, 90, 123, 146, 151
  Williamson 40
Sneed
  William 176
Snowton
  James 56
Southall
  Darcey 4
  Darey 20
  Darry 18
  Dasey 68, 70, 73, 78, 79, 97, 124, 128
  Turner 78, 97, 98, 124, 126-128, 136, 154, 163, 174, 194-197, 201, 206, 207, 210, 211, 230, 240, 244
Spain
  Alexander 211, 219
Spear
  John 24, 25
  Robert 24, 180
Spears
  James 34
  John 34
  NFN 246
  Robert 34, 72, 91, 115, 163
Spencer
  Elizabeth 184
  Samuel 11
  William 157, 172, 179, 184
Spragen
  Glora 8
  Martha 8
  William 8
Spraggings
  William 38
Spraggins
  Amey 1
  NFN 69, 157, 221
  William 1, 8, 91

Spraile
  Andrew 3
Spurlock
  Agness 183
  NFN 189
  Stephen 52, 183, 185
Stabler
  Edward 120
Staples
  Anne 57
  Christian 32, 50
  David 14, 16, 20, 32, 44, 45, 50, 59, 84, 85, 94, 95, 124, 125, 145, 168, 196, 227
  John 5, 16, 20, 22, 57, 105, 108, 118, 128, 129, 146, 170, 218, 238, 248
  Judith 128, 129
  NFN 102
  William 211, 218, 246
Stark
  James 37
  John 182
  Thomas 182
Starke
  Thomas 145, 159, 182
  Wyatt 241
Starks
  Thomas 201
Steagar
  Francis 21
Stegar
  Francis 17, 88, 92, 165, 232
  Hans 231, 232
  John 232
  NFN 46
  Thomas 231, 232
Steger
  Francis 10, 78, 236
  Hans 236
  John 229, 236
  Sarah 229
Stegge
  Thomas 88
Stego
  Francis 54
Stephenson
  Daniel 28, 29
  Thomas 169
Sterlin
  George 39
Sterling
  George 39
Stevens
  John 158

Stevenson
  John 64, 65
Stewart
  Alexander 117
  James 117
  John 16, 19, 53, 70, 71
Stewerton
  Thomas 128
Still
  Linder 164
  Thomas 164
Stith
  A. 86
  Anderson 54, 67
  William 10, 15, 18
Stoakes
  Henry 30, 42, 181, 214
Stobs
  Robert 35
Stokes
  Henry 16, 19, 33, 34, 131, 181, 206
  Mary 174
  Thomas 36
Stone
  Caleb 91, 241
  Daniel 132, 137, 152, 159, 161, 169, 178, 184, 187
  Giles 208, 209
  Lancelot 208
  Thomas 223, 235, 236
  William 53, 55, 57, 87, 203, 224, 235, 236, 243
Stoors
  Thomas 38
Stores
  Joshua 127
Storres
  NFN 235
Storrs
  Joshua 151, 154, 165, 187, 188, 194-196, 201, 205
  Thomas 48, 71, 73, 75, 83
Stovall
  George 201
Strachan
  Elizabeth 191
  Peter 232, 233
Strait
  William 206
Strange
  Sarah 142
Street
  Anthony 2
  Jane 40
  John 119, 145, 161

277

Street
  Joseph 40
  William 2, 6, 7, 22, 23, 26,
    27, 40, 46, 47, 55, 70,
    72, 84, 85, 95, 99, 117,
    121, 131, 145, 151, 155,
    161, 164, 167, 168, 170,
    180, 182
Strong
  John 146
Stuart
  Charles 4
  John 119
  Judith 119
  Mary 119
  Sarah 119
Sturdivant
  John 213
Sumpter
  Edmund 95, 124
Sutton
  F. 179
  J. 189
  John 204, 217, 231
  Susanna 211
Sweeny
  Edmund 171
Swepson
  James 171
Swinney
  Edmund 238
Sydnor
  Elizabeth 208
  Fortuanatus 207
  Fortunatus 116, 123, 128,
    135-138, 141, 149, 156,
    160, 161, 193, 194, 208,
    239, 244
Syme
  Andrew 219
Symes
  John 112
  Richard 112
Tabb
  Thomas 49, 50
Taggart
  Alexander 117
Tait
  Sarah 154
  Zachariah 151, 152, 154
  Zacharias 90
  Zephaniah 203
Talbot
  John 205
Tallock
  John 134

Talman
  Henry 185
Talmon
  Henry 151
Tanner
  Branch 147, 148, 166
  Mary 148
Tate
  Zachariah 113, 176
Tatum
  Josiah 147, 148, 166
  Sarah 148
Taylor
  Mark 42
  Matthew 42
  Miles 101, 110, 139, 140,
    142, 149, 181, 206, 213,
    221, 236, 237
  Richard 74
  William 13, 25, 83, 122,
    146, 158, 163, 172, 173,
    218
Teck
  John 114
  Susannah 114
Teek
  Susanna 167
Telfer
  Patrick 39
Templeton
  Robert 4
Terrell
  David 7
  Henry 7
Terril
  David 26
  Henry 26
Terry
  Samuel 49, 50
Tharp
  Agness 226
  Thomas 226
Thom
  John 177
Thomas
  Charles 29, 30, 71
  Christopher 5, 6, 24, 27, 41,
    42, 48, 52, 54, 61, 71,
    80, 82, 84, 90, 91, 99,
    102, 103, 111, 123, 124,
    131, 137, 138, 142, 163,
    170, 189, 210, 231, 248
  Dorothy 191
  James 201
  Mary 189, 231
  Olive 143

Thomas
  Thomas 227
Thomason
  John 185
  NFN 189
Thompson
  John 32, 50, 129, 146
Thomson
  Henry 14
Thornton
  Presley 187, 194-196, 229,
    230, 232
  Sterling 169
Thorp
  Thomas 72, 121, 167, 176,
    224
Thorpe
  Thomas 18, 21
Thurman
  John 241
  Richard 226, 229
Thwates
  Richard 74
Tillock
  John 136
Timberlake
  Ben 181
  Henry 33, 35, 38
  John 216, 228, 232
  Mary 165
  Richard 38, 132, 162, 165,
    200, 208
  William 162
Timberland
  Henry 35
Tinsley
  John 190, 246
Tirpin
  Lizbit 51
Toms
  John 44, 45, 114, 115
  Robert 114, 115
Topling
  Thomas 11
Totty
  William 9
Townley
  John 114, 115
Trent
  Alexander 209, 216, 240
  Elizabeth 216
  NFN 231
  Peter 187, 216, 240, 246
Trotter
  Ann 158

278

Trueman
  Abraham 150, 159, 171
  John 106, 159, 170, 171, 228
  NFN 163
  Richard 159, 170, 171
  Sarah 170
  Valentine 170
  William 170, 171
Truhart
  Aaron 42
Truman
  Abraham 93
  Elizabeth 94
  John 94, 171
  Joseph 20
  Richard 18, 19, 21, 34, 42, 88, 94, 153
Tucker
  Nathaniel 105
  Robert 80
  Valentine 150
Tudman
  William 51
Tulley
  Blacey 243
  Francis 243
Tulloh
  William 147
Turnbull
  Charles 2, 38, 187, 194-196, 201, 229, 230, 232, 240, 244
Turner
  Daniel 129
  Elizabeth 137
  James 156
  Nathan 108, 137, 147
  NFN 141
  Thomas 223
  William 5, 15, 20, 39, 108, 137, 147, 155
Turpin
  Edith 150
  John 239, 243, 248
  Lisbit 62, 221
  Lizbe 10
  Lizby 65, 66
  Lusby 15, 18, 248
  Luzby 82, 83, 91, 96, 103, 104, 107, 109, 151, 164, 167, 169, 179, 187, 202, 236
  Michael 151, 169, 243
  NFN 86
  Sarah 83

Turrell
  Henry 7
Turrill
  David 7
  Henry 7
Tyree
  David 30, 169
  Elizabeth 50
  George 93
  James 31, 169
  NFN 170, 211
  William 30, 31, 40, 50, 169, 190, 221, 228
Umphries
  Ralph 14
Underwood
  George 149, 150
Valentine
  Jacob 78, 111, 129, 229
  James 64, 76, 97, 111, 116, 129, 136, 141, 235, 245
  Nicholas 64, 76, 77, 141
Vallentine
  Jacob 54, 55
  Nicholas 54
Vanderwall
  Nathaniel 10, 41, 68
Vandevall
  Ann 181
Vandevall
  Ann 181
  Markes 210
  Nathaniel 51, 181, 210
Vandewall
  Ann 181
  Daniel 38
  Elizabeth 113
  Markes 239
  Nathaniel 6, 19, 30, 45, 113, 181
  Nt. 17
Vaughan
  David 55
  Edmund 199
  Elizabeth 174
  James 78, 114, 131, 139, 142, 149, 165, 172, 174, 177, 180, 185, 197, 218, 221, 233, 234, 236, 237, 245
  Matthew 142
  NFN 99
  Shad. 141, 143
  Shadrack 174
  Thomas 174
  Timothy 101
Waddill
  Charles 61

Waddy
  Samuel 117
Wade
  David 141
  Dudley 226
  Edward 221
  John 202
  NFN 129
  Rebekah 212
  Richard 212
  Robert 212
  William 89, 122, 188, 200, 202
Wadlow
  Sarah 150
  Susannah 150
Wager
  Frances 61
Wagstaff
  Francis 15, 19, 25, 36, 51
  NFN 67
Wales
  John 225, 226
Walker
  Alexander 64, 65
  Ann 168
  Emanuel 213
  Gerard 168, 169
  Henry 168, 169
  John 131
  Robert 212
  William 12
Wall
  James 227
Wallace
  William 131, 139
Waller
  Benjamin 26
Walley
  Richard 141
Wallis
  NFN 164
Walrond
  Benjamin 227
Walters
  John 5, 42, 48, 61, 71
Walthoe
  N. 162
Walton
  Elizabeth 231
  Frances 231
  John 180, 231, 239
  Mary 231
Warbourton
  William 58

Warburton
  William 31
Ward
  Leighton 41
  Leonard 109, 119, 147, 193, 194
  Sarah 119
  Seth 37, 147
Ware
  Henry 85
  Markham 121
  NFN 67, 192
  William 93
Warinner
  Benjamin 93, 189
  Daniel 189
  Joseph 93, 189
Warren
  Daniel 229
  Peter 152
Warriner
  Anna 228
  Benjamin 152
  Daniel 18, 93, 152, 154, 200, 203, 205, 246
  John 14, 93, 205, 208, 228
  Sarah 93
  Thomas 93, 200
  William 93, 150
Warrinner
  Daniel 20, 67
  John 16, 18, 42, 44, 45
  William 43, 45
Warrock
  Loudwick 91, 103, 130, 144, 186, 187
  Mary 144
Watkins
  Andrew 3
  Benjamin 37, 181, 183
  Edward 41, 42, 113, 114, 126
  F. 164
  Francis 51, 195
  Henry 28, 37, 42, 44, 45, 47, 49, 91, 203
  James 113
  John 34, 42, 114
  Joseph 232, 235
  NFN 119, 213
  T. 149
  Thomas 22, 25, 28, 37, 42, 51, 61, 63, 67, 71, 76, 91, 147, 179, 196, 199, 203, 229
  William 108, 113, 198

Watson
  Capt. 34
  Elizabeth 113, 216
  John 5, 31, 57, 67, 84, 95, 97, 101, 102, 105, 111, 115, 118, 127, 180, 216
  Joseph 72, 116
  Martha 216
  NFN 1, 55, 57, 64, 128, 176, 192, 214
  Phil 33, 35
  Phil. 75
  Philip 38, 39, 68, 73-75, 86, 92, 101, 103, 113, 121, 156, 198, 205
  Phillip 57-59
  Susanna 216
  Susannah 128, 216
  William 116, 117
Watt
  James 237, 244
Wayles
  J. 73
  John 2, 40, 46, 73, 85, 151
  Tabitha 73
Weatherby
  Robert 36
Weatherley
  Robert 16, 21
Weatherly
  Robert 165
Weaver
  John 87, 108, 126
Webb
  Charles 137
  Christian 137
  Edward 219
  George 46, 244
  Jacob 15
  James 122, 123
  John 123
  Leticia 158
  Robert 16, 21, 23, 29, 47, 50, 56, 87, 88, 111, 137, 158
  William 137, 158
Webber
  Philip 151
Webster
  Betsy 150
  James 224
  John 26, 38
Weir
  George 209
  Richard 9, 11, 16, 19, 35

Weisiger
  Benjamin i
  Daniel 242
Welden
  Samuel 62
Wennington
  James 169
West
  Elizabeth 108, 191
  Francis 13, 16, 20, 108, 191, 198
  Isham 86, 107, 108, 151, 187
  John 17, 20, 59, 86, 88-90, 96, 97, 107, 108, 120, 126, 129
  Mary 89, 90
  Richard 86
  Robert 187, 224, 239
  Sarah 90, 96, 108
  William 151, 185
Whealer
  John 6
Wheeler
  John 108, 129, 141, 155
  NFN 88, 147
  Roland 141
  Rowland 141
Wheler
  John 23
White
  Barrett 4, 39
  Charles 106
  David 105, 145, 161, 221, 224, 246
  Edward 135, 154, 237
  Elisha 138
  Hannah 160
  Henry 223, 224
  Isaac 51, 102, 106
  James 70
  John 4, 8, 16, 20, 21, 39, 42, 43, 50, 52, 63, 66, 88, 101, 104, 118, 181
  Joseph 23
  Mary 104
  Richard 135, 142
  Samuel 105
  Widow 163
  William 43, 243, 248
  Zachariah 42, 43
Whitehead
  William 188
Whiteman
  Joseph 18, 23, 148

Whitewan
  Joseph 21
Whitlaw
  John 83
Whitle
  John 78
  Richard 78
  William 78
Whitlock
  Ann 115
  David 23, 30, 31, 115, 169, 170, 228
  Hannah 120
  James 120, 150, 199, 230
  John 197
  Nathaniel 120, 221
  Richard 12, 25, 61, 147, 148
  Sarah 150
Whitloe
  Hays 16, 18
  Henry 16, 18
  James 16
  John 18, 20, 90, 107
  Mary 90
  Richard 16-18, 20, 89
  William 17, 21
Whitlow
  Cox 94, 95, 124, 237
  Darby 106, 157, 160, 171, 172, 179, 184, 242, 243
  Edith 142
  Edward 214, 224, 229, 242, 245
  Elizabeth 226
  Francis 106
  Hayes 73
  Hays 62, 83, 95, 98, 150, 208
  Henry 105, 106
  James 18, 24, 32, 95, 105, 106, 108, 129, 142, 171, 198, 214, 224, 226, 243
  John 14, 59, 62, 65, 86, 96, 151, 171, 214, 224, 226
  Joseph 208
  Lory 106, 129
  Mary 243
  Nathan 171, 179, 184, 243
  Nathaniel 157
  NFN 199, 241
  Richard 14, 151, 179, 187
  William 14, 62, 106, 142, 171, 172, 179, 224
Whitlowe
  Cox 70
  Derby 78

Whitlowe
  Francis 82
  Henry 63
  Iduzo 63
  James 82
  Nathan 78
  Richard 26
  Sarah 78
  William 78
Whitney
  Jeremiah 216
Wild
  Mary 116
  Thomas 46, 116
Wilkerson
  Willson 247
Wilkins
  James 70
Wilkinson
  Ford 62
  Francis 12, 25, 93
  George 62
  H. 45
  John 242
  Judith 242
  Maraget 231
  Margaret 93, 225, 231
  Nathaniel 9, 21, 22, 37, 45, 61, 65, 73-75, 81, 87, 123, 169, 176, 181, 190, 217, 225, 231, 233, 238, 242, 245, 247
  T. 23
  Thomas 53, 62, 74, 81, 93, 112, 123, 199, 213, 225, 231, 233, 242
  William 62
Williams
  Eleanor 113
  Ellinor 9
  Gary i
  Hannah 114, 157
  John 13, 18, 17, 19, 20, 42, 48, 49, 60, 65, 66, 76, 85-87, 103, 128, 134, 142, 144-146, 149, 158, 162, 172, 177-179, 200, 203, 207
  Jonathan 63, 78, 83, 95, 113, 114, 140, 157, 208, 209, 213, 226, 247
  Mary 65, 66, 104, 145, 162, 178
  Philemon 44, 45, 52, 65, 142, 183
  Richard 224

Williams
  Robert 8, 17, 21, 24, 66, 112
  Sarah 179, 208, 209
  Thomas 8, 45, 104, 105, 112, 113, 133, 134, 144, 178, 187, 189, 198, 205, 236, 239, 242, 248
Williamson
  Allen 108, 128, 133, 192, 213, 214
  Anne 213
  Cuthbert 107, 133, 171
  Cuthburt 60
  Elizabeth 213, 226
  George 60, 63, 132, 155, 237
  John 2, 7, 8, 10, 13, 14, 17, 19, 29-34, 53, 54, 58-60, 64, 65, 68, 76, 85, 107-110, 121, 125, 127, 128, 147, 164, 166, 182, 190, 213, 214, 218, 239, 240, 245
  Judah 213
  Judith 33, 34, 58, 226
  Lucy 213
  Mary 213, 226
  Richard 1, 12, 21, 32, 42, 69, 90, 116, 207, 241
  Robert 17, 31-34, 54, 68, 108, 109, 112, 121, 123, 128, 131, 133, 171, 179, 190, 192
  Sam 68
  Samuel 107, 123, 127, 128, 133, 185, 199, 213, 214, 218, 239, 240, 245
  Susanna 60, 171
  Thomas 123, 213, 214, 218, 245
Willis
  Agge 7
  Agnes 52
  Pleasant 200
  Price 52
  Susannah 70
  William 7, 14, 52, 70, 167, 170, 182, 238
Wills
  Melicent 165
  Melisent 173
  Millicent 183, 197, 198
  William 61, 112, 165, 173, 174, 177, 183, 197, 198, 232

Willson
  Daniel 247
Wilson
  Benjamin 108
  Elizabeth 148, 166
  James 159
  John 83
  Robert 189
  Thomas 147, 148, 166
  William 139
Winston
  Elizabeth 190, 191
  Geddes 33, 52, 62, 225, 231
  Isaac 18, 20, 38, 48, 53, 61, 137, 153, 181, 190, 191, 199, 233
  John 94, 114
  Mary 53
  NFN 171, 190
  Peter 153, 199, 215, 225, 231
  Philip 180
  William 94, 153, 175
Withearle
  Robert 36
Woddie
  Henry 20
Womack
  David 104
Wood
  Ann 38
  Drury 6, 18, 20, 25, 32, 40, 41, 49, 51, 72, 113, 144, 146, 155, 230, 235
  George 140, 204, 217
  Henry 240
  John 38, 62, 70, 91, 222, 230, 241
  Martha 47, 70
  Stephen 38, 41
  Susanna 51
  Thomas 17, 19, 47, 64, 70, 222
  Valentine 11
  William 70, 97
Woodcock
  John 96, 156
  Mark 96, 116, 143, 156, 179, 207, 229
Wooddie
  Henry 15
Wooddy
  Augustine 202
  Austin 130
  Henry 130
  Susannah 202

Woodey
  Henry 88
  NFN 89
Woodfin
  Darcus 135
  George 239, 242
  James 8, 15, 18, 31, 58, 83, 87, 135, 144, 146, 157, 158, 163, 239
  John 135, 157, 158, 239, 242, 245
  Moses 226, 239
Woodford
  T. 244
  Thomas 244
Woodroff
  Cliffin 182
Woodroof
  Benjamin 182
Woodrow
  Alexander 79
Woods
  Stephen 8
Woodson
  Agnes 56, 67
  Charles 1, 4, 7-9, 25, 28, 36, 62-64, 67, 72, 74, 77, 86, 89, 94, 102, 104, 105, 120, 122, 133, 134, 152
  Elizabeth 56, 140
  F. 237
  Francis 75
  George 186, 187, 237
  Jacob 7, 62, 63
  James 9, 173, 177
  John 10, 11, 24, 43, 45, 53, 54, 57, 61, 74, 110, 182, 232, 234, 236
  Joseph 8, 17, 20, 24, 28, 75, 134
  Judith 56
  Mary 7, 56
  Matthew 1, 52
  Pleasants 91
  Robert 43, 45, 138
  Stephen 56, 91-93, 96, 103, 192, 194, 202
  Tarleton 7, 56, 61-63, 139, 221, 224
  Tarlton 114, 115
  Tucker 11, 48, 219
Woodward
  John 99, 100
Woody
  Augustine 188

Woody
  Austin 131
  Henry 60, 122
  Samuel 105
  Webby 61
Wooldridge
  Thomas 123
Wootten
  John 31
Wootton
  Simon 186
Worrack
  Loudwick 30
Worrock
  Loudwick 47, 189, 191, 237
Worsham
  John 34
Wyche
  Benjamin 148, 166
Yarbrough
  William 78
Yaxley
  Robert 48, 64
Young
  Alexander 184
  James 4, 5, 8
  Judith 223
Younghusband
  Isaac 29, 52, 56, 76, 86, 130, 132, 135, 162, 193, 204
  Israel 28, 29
Yuille
  Thomas 2, 37

www.ingramcontent.com/pod-product-compliance
Lightning Source LLC
Chambersburg PA
CBHW052104230426
43671CB00011B/1926